LANGUAGE FROM A COGNITIVE PERSPECTIVE

Etching by Gabrielle Brill

Photographed by Susanne Riehemann
The editors and the publisher gratefully acknowledge
Judith Wasow's assistance for obtaining the cover art
that appears on the front cover of the paperback edition.

CSLI LECTURE NOTES NUMBER 201

LANGUAGE FROM A COGNITIVE PERSPECTIVE

Grammar, Usage, and Processing

STUDIES IN HONOR OF THOMAS WASOW

edited by

EMILY M. BENDER & JENNIFER E. ARNOLD

CSLI PUBLICATIONS
STANFORD

Copyright © 2011
CSLI Publications
Center for the Study of Language and Information
Leland Stanford Junior University
Printed in the United States
15 14 13 12 11   1 2 3 4 5

Library of Congress Cataloging-in-Publication Data

Language from a cognitive perspective : grammar, usage, and
processing / edited by Emily M. Bender and Jennifer E. Arnold.
    p. cm. – (CSLI lecture notes number 201)

"This book is a collection of papers on language processing, usage, and
grammar, written in honor of Thomas Wasow to commemorate his career
on the occasion of his 65th birthday."

Includes bibliographical references.
ISBN 978-1-57586-611-6 (alk. paper) –
ISBN 978-1-57586-610-9 (pbk. : alk. paper)
1. Cognitive grammar. 2. Grammar, Comparative and
general–Syntax. I. Bender, Emily M., 1973- II. Arnold, Jennifer E.
III. Wasow, Thomas.

P165.L38 2011
415—dc22
                                                              2011002689
                            CIP

∞ The acid-free paper used in this book meets the minimum requirements
of the American National Standard for Information Sciences—Permanence
of Paper for Printed Library Materials, ANSI Z39.48-1984.

CSLI was founded in 1983 by researchers from Stanford University, SRI
International, and Xerox PARC to further the research and development of
integrated theories of language, information, and computation. CSLI headquarters
and CSLI Publications are located on the campus of Stanford University.

CSLI Publications reports new developments in the study of language,
information, and computation. Please visit our web site at
http://cslipublications.stanford.edu/
for comments on this and other titles, as well as for changes
and corrections by the author and publisher.

Contents

1

Introduction

JENNIFER E. ARNOLD & EMILY M. BENDER

This book is a collection of papers on language processing, usage, and grammar, written in honor of Tom Wasow to commemorate his career on the occasion of his 65th birthday. Tom is a professor of linguistics and philosophy. But more accurately, he is a renaissance academic, having done work that connects with many different disciplines, including formal linguistics, sociolinguistics, historical linguistics, psycholinguistics, computational linguistics, and philosophy. Appropriately, this book reflects the diversity of Tom's research and interests, including topics from multiple branches of linguistics and human information processing. These papers are written with minimal background assumed, so they can be used as teaching materials for beginning scholars. As such, this volume is a tribute to what is perhaps Tom's most lasting contribution to the field—the mentorship and inspiration he provided to his students and collaborators, many of whom have contributed to this volume.

If you page through the dissertations that line the walls of the chair's office in the Stanford linguistics department, you find that Tom has been a consistent source of support and guidance to students for decades. The acknowledgments sections of his students' dissertations repeatedly make reference to Tom's patience, encouragement, and his solid intellectual support through thoughtful and constructive criticism. As Dan Flickinger writes, "I thank ... Thomas Wasow, whose patience, cheerful persistence, unstinting support, solid critique, creative ideas, and common sense made the writing of this thesis possible and enjoyable. Every student should have such an advisor." We represent all

Language from a Cognitive Perspective.
Emily M. Bender and Jennifer Arnold, Editors
Copyright © 2011, CSLI Publications.

of Tom's students in saying that we are grateful for his time and encouragement and that our enjoyment of graduate school was greater because of him.

Apart from Tom's work as a mentor, researcher, and teacher, he quietly provides an example of how one ought to live. He has been commuting to work by bicycle ever since joining the faculty at Stanford. He has served on the board of the Community Working Group, a local organization that addresses the needs of the homeless. He once mentioned that when he flies, he puts his carry-on bag under the seat in front of him, so as to leave the overhead space for people with longer legs. In essence, Tom is a generous guy who thinks about other people. He doesn't talk much about it either and probably will be embarrassed when he reads this.

In keeping with Tom's focus on teaching and mentorship during his career, we have designed this book as a tool for both teachers and researchers. These papers are written for an audience of upper level college students, or beginning graduate students, with the goal of providing the reader with an introduction to specific topics in linguistics, language processing, and cognitive science. The papers cover both theoretical and methodological issues, in keeping with Tom's focus on both in his career.

The first two papers in the book represent Tom's influence on grammar engineering. Bender, Flickinger, and Oepen describe the methodology of grammar engineering in "Grammar Engineering and Linguistic Hypothesis Testing: Computational Support for Complexity in Syntactic Analysis" and explore how it helps syntacticians cope with various kinds of complexity. In "Accuracy vs. Robustness in Grammar Engineering", Dan Flickinger considers methodological issues that arise in balancing the demands of robustness and accuracy as computational grammars are scaled-up to models that are able to handle real-world language use.

Several papers address specific issues in syntax or grammatical theory. Ash Asudeh's "Local Grammaticality in Syntactic Production" explores resumptive pronouns in English as a case study of mismatches between grammaticality judgments and production data. He argues that such mismatches motivate syntactic models that countenance a notion of local grammaticality as well as production models that incorporate incremental planning. In "Blocking and the Architecture of Grammar", Peter Sells considers derivational and declarative approaches to grammar and argues that blocking phenomena are more naturally accommodated in declarative approaches. Amy Perfors' paper, "Simplicity and Fit in Grammatical Theory", describes a Bayesian method of comparing linguistic theories and measuring their relative goodness of fit and simplicity.

The paper by Tom's first Ph.D. student, James Gee, "'Basic Information Structure' and 'Academic Language': An Approach to Discourse Analysis", looks at language from the perspective of discourse analysis. In this paper, Gee examines how discourse is structured in such a way as to allow the speaker to strategically include, or exclude, relevant information, and applies this approach to the understanding of academic language.

Not surprisingly, many of the papers focus on questions about variation in language usage, centered around two questions that Tom has focused on recently. One such question is why speakers sometimes do and do not produce relativizers, e.g., *The dog (that) I walked belongs to Tom*. In "Relativizer Omission in Anglophone Caribbean Creoles, Appalachian, and African American Vernacular English [AAVE] and Its Theoretical Implications", John Rickford writes about variable relativizer use by creole and vernacular English speakers, for the purpose of understanding both the historical origins of the different varieties, as well as the extent to which the same processing issues constrain this phenomenon in all varieties. Florian Jaeger writes about the related topic of optional reduction of subject relative clauses, in "Corpus-based Research on Language Production: Information Density and Reducible Subject Relatives", focusing on relationship between redundancy and syntactic reduction. Jaeger's paper provides seldom-found methodological details about corpus analysis and analysis with mixed logit regression.

Several papers pay tribute to Tom's significant contribution to research on the way that speakers order constituents, e.g., *Read all these papers before dinner*, or *Before dinner read all these papers*. Jennifer Arnold provides an overview of research on constituent ordering in "Ordering Choices in Production: For the Speaker or for the Listener?" and examines the extent to which it is sensitive to speaker-internal or addressee-oriented processes. In "Weight and Word Order in Historical English", Hal Tily describes a corpus analysis that tests whether weight and other constraints influenced speakers' word order choices in Old and Middle English, when basic word order was more flexible. Neal Snider's paper "Investigating Syntactic Persistence in Corpora" presents a review and example analysis of the phenomenon of persistence (the tendency for speakers to repeat recently used syntactic structures) and argues that persistence can provide a useful test of theories about representation and processing. In "Discontinuous Dependencies in Corpus Selections: Particle Verbs and Their Relevance for Current

Issues in Language Processing", Jack Hawkins examines variation between split and joined verb-particle constructions as support for the idea of a general efficiency constraint on ordering.

The final paper in the book, Susanne Riehemann's "Information in Virtual Spaces", extends linguistic analysis to information more broadly. Riehemann describes recent innovations in the representation of information and explores how visually-based information can effectively complement linguistically-represented information.

In sum, the papers in this book are for Tom. They also represent his legacy as a colleague, inspiration, and teacher: By getting us started, or enriching our research and ideas, Tom enabled the work represented by these papers. By collecting them into this volume, we hope to share with others part of what Tom has taught us: a sense of the possibilities that open up when we take a broad view of linguistics as situated in cognitive science, while integrating sound theoretical work with close attention to data.

2

Grammar Engineering and Linguistic Hypothesis Testing: Computational Support for Complexity in Syntactic Analysis

EMILY M. BENDER, DAN FLICKINGER &
STEPHAN OEPEN

Preface

The work described in this chapter is closely connected to the authors'
experience in the LinGO (Linguistic Grammars On-Line) project at
Stanford's Center for the Study of Language and Information (CSLI).
Since the early 1990s (and still today), LinGO brings together syntacticians and computational linguists around the development of broad-
coverage, precise, and implemented grammars, and of the software required to build and maintain such linguistic resources. Tom participates
in this group as a syntactician and more generally as a linguist-sage.
The group's project meetings feature lively debates about the structure and analysis of frequently out-of-the-way syntactic constructions.
In these debates, we can always rely on Tom to find additional constructions or example types that we should be considering. More generally,
the project meetings and the project as a whole have benefited from
Tom's view of the primacy of linguistic data and the strength of linguistic theories as deriving from their ability to account for actual natural
language data. To a large extent, the work presented here can be seen
as an implementation of that conviction. Specifically, this work builds

Language from a Cognitive Perspective.
Emily M. Bender and Jennifer Arnold, Editors
Copyright © 2011, CSLI Publications.

on the earlier Natural Language project at the Hewlett Packard Corporation (HP) in the 1980s, where Tom and other core LinGO staff had already collaborated on the development of a software system anchored in and, in fact, advancing contemporary linguistic theory. At the time, Tom contributed carefully selected and constructed data to the so-called HP test suite, a resource still in wide use today. Finally, we cannot end this preface without mentioning the sense of fun that Tom brings to the LinGO project and to his work more generally: working with Tom, we work for the pleasure of exploring language and grammar; theories are useful because they lead to more interesting data, rather than having data serve only to bolster or shoot down theories. Thanks in large part to this attitude, we remember the LinGO project meetings as enjoyable, even funny, in addition to being productive.

1 Introduction

Formal grammars are sets of rules meant to model linguistic systems (Harris, 1951; Bar-Hillel, 1953; Chomsky, 1965): we work with the hypothesis that speakers of a language have internalized a set of rules that allow them to relate surface forms of utterances (written or spoken) to their meanings, even for novel utterances that they haven't heard before. Working linguists usually focus on one component of grammar (pragmatics, semantics, syntax, morphology, phonology, phonetics) or the interface between two of them, and within that component, one or two phenomena at a time. Any single utterance, however, involves all of the levels of structure as well as at least several phenomena within each level, all interacting in order to produce a pairing of form and meaning at the utterance level.

The first step in validating our models of grammar, therefore, is to make sure that the various parts work together as intended. However, checking these interactions is tedious, difficult, and the kind of work that is best left to a computer. This chapter is intended as a brief introduction to the methodology of grammar engineering, or the practice of encoding linguistic hypotheses in machine readable form, so that they can be validated by computer. In this chapter, we will focus on syntax and its interfaces to semantics and morphology, though similar arguments can be made about other levels of linguistic structure. We argue that grammar engineering allows syntacticians to handle greater complexity, and that, though it does take additional effort beyond the original development of the analyses, that effort can be reduced and is furthermore well repaid.

The rest of the chapter is structured as follows: In § 2, we describe grammar engineering, its prerequisites and workflow, with a special emphasis on regression testing. In § 3, we review three ways in which grammar engineering facilitates the management of complexity, ranging from simple examples of the interaction of analyses, to collaborative work and work with unfamiliar languages. Finally, § 4 presents the LinGO Grammar Matrix, which is both another example of grammar engineering managing complexity (in this case, the complexity of crosslinguistic analysis) as well as a means of lowering the barriers to entry for grammar engineering projects.

2 What is Grammar Engineering?

As noted above, work in formal grammar involves the modeling of a complex domain using sets of rules. This combination of properties suggests that computers could be fruitfully used to support the investigation, and, in fact, computational implementations of formal grammar go back to at least the early 1960s (see Kay, 1963; Zwicky, Friedman, Hall, & Walker, 1965; Petrick, 1965; Friedman, Bredt, Doran, Pollack, & Martner, 1971). Since then, many syntactic frameworks have been developed or refined specifically with computational tractability in mind, e.g., Augmented Transition Networks (ATN, Woods, 1970), Tree-Adjoining Grammar (TAG, Joshi, Levy, & Takahashi, 1975), Lexical-Functional Grammar (LFG, Kaplan & Bresnan, 1982), Generalized Phrase Structure Grammar (GPSG, Gazdar, Klein, Pullum, & Sag, 1985), Head-driven Phrase Structure Grammar (HPSG, Pollard & Sag, 1987, Pollard & Sag, 1994), and Combinatory Categorial Grammar (CCG, Ades & Steedman, 1982, Steedman, 1996). In addition, many software platforms for grammar development and testing have been created (see § 2.1 below). Such software means that grammar engineers don't need to be programmers: We work in descriptive formalisms, rather than programming languages, and encode declarative knowledge rather than procedures. Nonetheless, we benefit from advances in parsing technology and computer hardware which have made it possible for a test suite of thousands of sentences to be processed in minutes on a single processor, and of course arbitrarily fast given unlimited numbers of processors.

The core idea of grammar engineering is thus that the formal rules we use to model linguistic knowledge can be made precise enough that a computer can work with them. Many grammar engineering projects do this for practical applications, encoding linguistic knowledge so that computers can deal with natural language text (or speech).[1] In this chapter, however, our focus is on using grammar engineering for linguistic research.

2.1 Requirements for Grammar Engineering

A grammar engineering project requires the following tools:

1. A well-defined and stable descriptive formalism
2. Parsing (and generation) algorithms
3. Interactive grammar visualization and debugging tools
4. Test suite management/regression testing software

A stable descriptive formalism is required because without one, it is prohibitively expensive to maintain parsing and generation algorithms. Thus while it is common practice in theoretical syntax to couch results in terms of formalism revisions, it is in fact more prudent to separate the formalism from the theory, as proposed by Chomsky (1965), who expressed the separation as one between "formal" and "substantive" universals.[2] In other words, the formalism should be flexible enough yet precise enough to allow the exploration and testing of various theoretical alternatives.

Parsing algorithms take a grammar and a string as input, and return the structure or structures assigned by the grammar to the string as output. Depending on the grammar, the output might be only syntactic representations, or it might include semantic representations. Generation algorithms go in the other direction, taking some underlying representation (e.g., semantics) and a grammar as input, and returning as output the surface string(s) that the grammar assigns to the underlying representation.

While it is possible to do grammar engineering by examining only input and output, it is much more efficient (and enjoyable) when one also has interactive grammar visualization and debugging tools. Such tools allow the grammar engineer, for example, to step through the derivation of a sentence that is not parsing and identify the point(s) of failure.

Finally, grammar engineering requires test data management and regression testing software. A *test suite* is a set of linguistic examples, hand-constructed by the grammar engineer or another linguist, in order to illustrate various grammatical phenomena. A *test corpus* is a sample of naturally occurring text drawn from some domain of interest. In

---

[1]See Butt, King, Niño, & Segond, 1999 and Bender, Clark, & King, to appear for more discussion.

[2]See also Pollard & Sag, 1994, p.6.

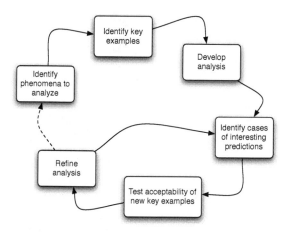

FIGURE 1 Workflow in syntactic research without computer assistance

both cases the strings can be optionally annotated with acceptability judgments, expected grammatical structures, and other information. Software tools for regression testing send all of the items in the test set to the parser (or generator) for processing, provide summary statistics of grammar behavior, and allow the grammar engineer to explore which items have different (or more or fewer) analyses in one test run (with one version of the grammar) as compared to another. This is described further in § 2.3 below.

Grammar development environments exist for a variety of frameworks. Some of the more widely used current platforms include the Linguistic Knowledge Builder (LKB, Copestake, 2002), TRALE (Meurers, Penn, & Richter, 2002), Visual CCG (Baldridge, Chatterjee, Palmer, & Wing, 2007), the Xerox Linguistic Environment (XLE, Crouch et al., 2001), XTAG (Paroubek, Schabes, & Joshi, 1992), and others. The so-called [incr tsdb()] environment (Oepen & Flickinger, 1998) is a test suite management, regression testing, and annotation tool compatible with several of the above systems.

2.2 Grammar Engineering Workflow

This section describes the workflow of syntactic research with and without computer assistance in the form of grammar engineering. Figure 1 schematizes the workflow of syntactic research as it is traditionally practiced. The process begins with identifying a phenomenon to analyze and isolating a manageable number of key examples to work with. With reference to those examples (and of course the previous litera-

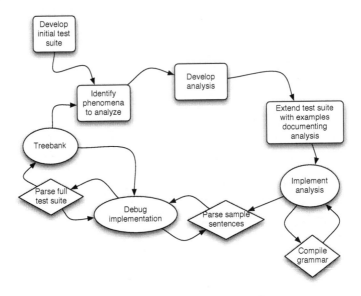

FIGURE 2 Workflow in syntactic research with computer assistance:
Rectangles represent off-line work, the ovals work done through interaction
with the computer, and the diamonds tasks carried out fully automatically.

ture) the syntactician then develops an analysis. The next step is to
validate the analysis by considering cases where it makes predictions
that are both interesting and typically different from previous analyses. These predictions are then tested by asking native speakers for
their judgments regarding the acceptability (or meaning, or degree of
ambiguity) of a new set of key examples. In some cases, this leads to
further refinements of the analysis, identification of further interesting
predictions etc. At some point, the linguist moves on to the next phenomenon to analyze. This is represented in the figure with a dashed
arrow to indicate that the next analysis is often treated as an independent project, and while subsequent work often builds on previous
work, it is not generally possible to keep track of all previous analyses
without the aid of a computer.

Figure 2 schematizes the workflow of a grammar engineering project.
Here, the first step is typically the selection of some initial set of development data. This might include hand-constructed examples or a
selection of data from some domain of interest to the project. The next
step is to pick some initial phenomena to analyze. When starting a new
grammar project, there are typically a few relatively core phenomena

which have to be addressed first, in order for the grammar to assign complete (if underspecified) analyses to any input items. These include things like basic word order facts and the combination of heads with arguments. On later iterations through the cycle, the phenomena to be analyzed may be chosen for a variety of reasons, including prominence in the development data (how many examples illustrate it) and/or the research interests of the grammar engineer.

Once the phenomena have been selected, the next step is to develop the initial analysis. This happens in the same way as it does in syntax without grammar engineering, making reference to the literature and exploring various possibilities. Typically, in the context of developing an analysis, the syntactician notes several key examples (as discussed above). In the context of a grammar engineering project, these examples can then be incorporated into the test suite.

Once the initial analysis is developed, the next step is to implement it in the grammar (or, on the first pass through this cycle, to create an initial grammar). This involves taking the ideas from the analysis and making them precise in terms of the descriptive formalism. Typically, the analysis gets somewhat refined in the process, especially as the grammar grows in complexity: When confronted with trying to integrate the new analysis into the existing grammar, the linguist is often reminded of details that were not apparent before.

The first step after an initial pass at implementing the grammar is to have the grammar development environment try to "compile" it. Some initial debugging usually takes place at this step as the software catches and flags errors in the implementation of the grammar rules and constraints. At this level, the errors that are caught aren't errors in content so much as errors in form: cases where the statement of the grammar rules doesn't conform to the syntax (format) of the computer language used to state them. There are, however, some errors in content which can be caught at this stage, such as inconsistent constraints in the grammar (e.g., saying that the same lexical type is both transitive and intransitive).

It often takes a few iterations to get to a grammar that compiles, but once it does, the grammar can be given a few sample items to process. These items are typically the key examples that the grammar engineer identified in the course of developing the analysis. By processing them with the grammar, the grammar engineer can verify that they have the intended analyses, including: whether they are analyzed at all; whether they are assigned appropriate representations; and whether they have the expected degree of ambiguity.

With interactive grammar debugging and visualization tools, the grammar engineer can also explore what has gone wrong in cases where the grammar does not have the expected behavior.[3] If the item is not given the expected analysis (either because the grammar fails to find any parse for it, or because the expected analysis is not among the parses), it is helpful to examine the parse chart. The parse chart is a record of the partial analyses that the parser found. The grammar engineer can examine these partial analyses to see where the (first) point of failure was, and then interactively ask the system to try to build the next expected step in the derivation for more information. Conversely, if the grammar is assigning too many analyses (spurious ambiguity), then tools which compare the analyses and enumerate the atomic differences between them (e.g., modifier attachments, different lexical choices, multiple possible orders of a set of lexical rules) can assist the grammar engineer in cutting back any spurious ambiguity.[4] Oftentimes, of course, unexpected ambiguity turns out not to be spurious; computers are much better than people at spotting logically possible (but pragmatically implausible) analyses of natural language strings (cf. Abney, 1996).

Again there is usually an iterative process of grammar refinement (implementation debugging) and parsing of individual examples. Once the grammar engineer is satisfied with the analyses the grammar assigns to these sample sentences, the next step is to parse the full test suite. On the first pass through this cycle with any given test suite, the first test run is used to establish a baseline for comparison as the grammar changes later. The validation of this baseline is discussed further below. On later iterations, the results of the full test suite run can be compared to previous runs (typically the most recent one) to see how the changes to the grammar have affected the analyses of the items in the test suite. Test suite management software (such as [incr tsdb()]; Oepen & Flickinger, 1998) allows the grammar engineer to get both summary statistics (how many examples parsed, the average degree of ambiguity, and many more) and detailed information, such as which items have more or fewer analyses in one run compared to another, or which items are assigned different (syntactic or semantic) structures.

---

[3]The exact nature of this exploration depends on both the descriptive formalism and the tools provided by the grammar development environment. The description here is based on HPSG and the LKB.

[4]These are called "discriminants", and are discussed briefly in § 2.3; see Carter (1997); Bouma, Noord, and Malouf (2001); Oepen, Toutanova, et al. (2002); Rosén, Meurer, and Smedt (2007) and Flickinger (this volume), inter alios.

As argued earlier, often, and increasingly as grammars grow in complexity, changes to the grammar have unexpected interactions with previously implemented analyses (Carroll, 1994; Oepen & Flickinger, 1998). Running the full test suite after each addition to the grammar makes it possible to identify these interactions (to the extent that they are illustrated by relevant examples in the test suite). Thus there is usually another iterative process of debugging to fix any "regressions" in grammar behavior. We note here that with modern computer hardware and parsing technology, even a test suite with thousands of examples can be processed with a relatively complex grammar in reasonable time. In fact, because the processing of any given item (or more generally, small groups of items, to accommodate phenomena like intersentential anaphora) is independent of the processing of all the others, the test suite run can be easily parallelized. This means that it can be done arbitrarily quickly in the context of a server cluster. Even on a single CPU, however, it is typical for a test suite run to take less than 10 minutes. This means that grammar engineers can engage in what Oepen, Bender, Callmeier, Flickinger, and Siegel (2002) describe as "a strongly empiricist style of grammar engineering" running the full test suite to explore the effects of a single isolated change to the grammar in the process of developing new analyses, i.e., at multiple different points in the cycle schematized in Figure 2.

Once this iterative process stabilizes (or after the initial run of a new test suite), the next step is "treebanking", or the validation of the analyses assigned by the grammar. Again, in the context of the LKB and [incr tsdb()] this process is supported by various software tools. In particular, the treebanking tool (Oepen, Toutanova, et al., 2002) allows the grammar engineer to efficiently select one or more of the analyses as correct/preferred in context, or to reject them all as incorrect.[5] This is done by selecting properties of the correct analysis from among those extracted by the software as distinguishing between analyses in the set ("discriminants", see footnote 4 on page 12 and § 2.3). Importantly, these decisions are stored, along with the result of which tree is selected, so that on future iterations, the treebanking can be done partially automatically, leaving only new ambiguity to be resolved by the grammar engineer.

Finally, we note that the arrow connecting the treebanking step to the beginning of the cycle ("identify phenomena to analyze") in Fig-

---

[5]When the test data comes from naturally occurring text, it is usually possible to select one analysis as matching the intended meaning in context. Even when the surrounding context is not given, the sentence itself usually carries enough information to dismiss many analyses as generally pragmatically implausible.

ure 2 is solid in this figure. This is meant to represent the notion of incremental development. As new phenomena are analyzed, they become part of the grammar which is then the context for further analyses. The regression testing described above allows the grammar engineer to ensure that previously implemented analyses are maintained (or refined as necessary), even when his or her attention has moved on to new phenomena. As argued by Bender (2008b), we believe that this is only possible with the aid of a computer: The domain that formal grammars are meant to model (natural languages and their structure) is complex, and so the models in turn must be complex if they are to capture the nuances of their targets. This complexity in fact outstrips what humans can keep in working memory and manipulate reliably. However, by using computers as modeling tools, we can continue to work on formal grammars, even as they grow in complexity and approach coverage of interesting fragments of particular languages.

2.3 Regression Testing

We observed earlier that grammar engineering often serves one of two purposes: linguistic hypothesis testing (computational linguistics in the sense of linguistic research using computers) and natural language processing (in the context of building a language-enabled software system). In general, the systematic use of test suites and test corpora appears more commonly in application-oriented initiatives, though it is also found in projects doing grammar engineering solely for linguistic research, as well as those that synthesize both goals.[6] This section provides an overview of the history and evolution of regression testing for grammar engineering.

By *regression testing* we mean a largely automated regime that helps monitor the evolution of a computational grammar, specifically aiming to uncover unwanted changes in grammar behavior as early as possible. Even for a medium-complexity grammar (say one covering a handful of different linguistic phenomena), it can be difficult for the grammar engineer to predict exactly how a change in one part of the grammar affects overall behavior. The interaction of lexical and constructional specifications—largely based on implicit properties of individual analyses and expectations on the 'flow of information' in larger structures—yield a conceptual complexity that can be impossible to track without

---

[6]This observation, one might think, is surprising in that linguistic research is so dependent on language data. However, a common work pattern for a theoretical syntactician, say, is to maintain a collection of linguistic examples while working out the analysis of a given phenomenon, but to then to switch to a different set of examples when moving on to another phenomenon.

specialized tools. For example, a seemingly minor repair in one lexical class, such numeral adjectives as in (1), inevitably has the potential of breaking the interaction of that class with other phenomena, such as the construction deriving named (numeric) entities from a numeral (as in (2)) or the partitive construction (as in (3)).

(1) *Three* books were ordered.

(2) *Three* is my favorite number.

(3) *Three* have arrived already.

To help track such unforeseen interactions, test suites play a central role in regression testing. A key project in the development of this paradigm was the construction of the so-called Hewlett-Packard (HP) test suite (Flickinger, Nerbonne, Sag, & Wasow, 1987). As part of their work on building a general-purpose parsing system for English, HP Laboratories had contracted linguistics faculty at Stanford University to hand-construct a systematic collection of utterances that exemplify a broad variety of core syntactic constructions in English. The HP test suite applies several principles that have since become commonplace in the field. These include the goals of (a) isolating phenomena as much as possible, using short and simple sentences; (b) avoiding unwanted ambiguity, both lexical and structural; (c) limiting lexical variation as much as is sensibly possible; and (d) including negative test cases, i.e., ungrammatical utterances that the grammar is expected to reject.

The early HP work was extended in a series of projects in Europe in the 1990s, notably through the German DiTo test suite (Nerbonne, Netter, Diagne, Dickmann, & Klein, 1993) and later the multilingual Test Suites for Natural Languages project (TSNLP, Lehmann et al., 1996). In early 1994, the TSNLP consortium compiled a survey of existing test suites and their use, based on a questionnaire and queries into topical mailing lists and UseNet groups.[7] The results of the TSNLP survey are summarized by Estival et al. (1994); parallel to a more general overview of NLP evaluation by Sparck Jones and Galliers (1995), the survey provides a comprehensive snapshot of the state of the field in the mid-1990s.

One important, if somewhat surprising, finding of Estival et al. (1994) is that, although much NLP literature makes reference to test suites, these are typically neither widely distributed nor easily available. According to the TSNLP findings, the apparent reluctance of researchers and developers to share their data was at least in part owed to under-estimating the value of these resources. The TSNLP project

---

[7] UseNet groups were a kind of on-line bulletin board popular at the time.

aimed to improve this situation for at least three languages: the consortium developed open-source test suites of between 4,000 and 5,000 items each for English, French, and German (Lehmann et al., 1996).[8] The TSNLP data has occasionally been criticized for being overly 'verbose' (there are vastly more ungrammatical than well-formed examples), but jointly with the original HP test suite these data sets are still among the most widely used linguistic test suites today.

Besides its test data construction, TSNLP also laid the foundations for later work on an improved methodology and tools for semi-automated regression testing. In analogy to software engineering, Oepen and Flickinger (1998) coin the term *competence and performance profiling*, and our discussion of the grammar engineering workflow in § 2.2 above mirrors this approach quite closely. In a nutshell, the profiling metaphor emphasizes a central need in regression testing to obtain and record very detailed measures of both 'competence' and 'performance' properties of a grammar, e.g., aspects of coverage, overgeneration, local and global ambiguity, as well as of processing times, memory consumption, and the like. This approach is implemented in the so-called [incr tsdb()] software environment (pronounced '*tee ess dee bee plus plus*'), which is widely used for computational HPSG work but is also applied to LFG grammar engineering.

Finally, in a broad sense also with roots dating back to TSNLP, it is becoming more and more common to include a process of *treebanking* in the regression testing cycle. Any grammar with non-trivial coverage will assign multiple candidate analyses to a given input, typically ranging from implausible to outright ridiculous (and yet grammatical) interpretations. Even with carefully constructed test suites, it is not always possible to avoid such ambiguity. But ambiguity, of course, can obscure testing: if the purpose of a test item was to be part of a pair exemplifying the dative shift—as in *Abrams showed the office to Browne.*, for example—there will inevitably also be analyses of the PP as a directional modifier (as in *the train to Berlin*, say). Treebanking in general is the manual process of pairing natural language utterances with their 'correct' (as in most plausible, in context) analyses. Assuming an existing computational grammar, Carter (1997) proposes a method of extracting minimal contrasts among competing analyses. These are called *discriminants* and in a sense are the individual sources of ambiguity. To navigate the space of analyses, a human annotator can

---

[8]The original TSNLP web site is no longer functional, but most of the results are mirrored at http://www.delph-in.net/tsnlp.

then decide which of these minimal properties should be present in the correct analysis, and which should be excluded.

Discriminant-based treebanking has been successfully applied by a number of grammar engineering initiatives for several languages (van der Beek, Bouma, Malouf, & van Noord, 2002; Bond et al., 2004; Rosén et al., 2007; inter alios). Oepen, Toutanova, et al. (2002) suggest that it can be both a cost-efficient way of producing a relatively high-quality treebank but also an important diagnostic tool for the grammar engineer. Once information about the intended analysis for each test case is available, regression testing can go beyond the mere confirmation of parsability. Instead, the grammar engineer can obtain fully-automated feedback on whether the correct structure for each input is indeed among the analyses derived by the grammar. More importantly, however, Oepen, Toutanova, et al. (2002) further discuss a process of semi-automated treebank maintenance, where for each new revision of the grammar, annotator decisions on individual discriminants (for the set of analyses produced by an earlier version) are propagated and updated where necessary. This process provides in-depth feedback on ambiguity that was eliminated from the grammar, newly introduced, or recast in some way, while also dramatically reducing the manual effort required to maintain the treebank as the grammar changes.

In summary, regression testing involves using curated test data to track changes in the behavior of a complex system over time. Here, the systems are the grammars, and the test data begin with constructed examples (test suites) or collections of naturally occurring text (test corpora). In addition, annotations on the test data provide a rich source of information for regression testing. These annotations include those automatically assigned by the grammar engineering system, as well as human-provided annotations from the process of treebanking. In the next section, we reflect on how grammar engineering, including best practices in regression testing, allows us to manage greater complexity in our modeling domain.

3 Managing Complexity

In this section, we provide three examples to illustrate how grammar engineering helps syntacticians work with increased complexity. The first involves the interaction of analyses; the second considers how grammar engineering supports collaboration, which in turn supports investigations of greater complexity; and the third looks at complexity in the context of working with an unfamiliar language.

3.1 Example 1: Japanese number names

In the course of developing the Jacy grammar (Siegel & Bender, 2002), one of us had occasion to add an analysis of Japanese number names, which are quite similar to English (and Chinese) number names, as illustrated in (4):

(4) ni sen   go hyaku san
     two thousand five hundred three

In developing this analysis, Bender used the analysis of English number names by Smith (1999) as a starting point. On Smith's analysis, number names like *hundred* function as heads which select complements (here *three*) and specifiers (here *five*). The number name heads specify both the possible magnitude of their complements and specifiers (to rule out e.g., **one hundred hundred*) and how they combine semantically.

This analysis translated beautifully to Japanese, and in fact seemed to work even better (since Japanese doesn't have the equivalent of *a* or *and* in number names). When Bender compiled the grammar and tried parsing an example, though, the grammar wasn't able to find any analyses. On closer inspection, it turned out that the analysis wasn't working because the grammar didn't have a rule for combining heads with following complements (as required for e.g., *hyaku san* in (4)). This, in turn, is because in the rest of the language (at least as it was modeled to date) we had found Japanese to be strictly head-final (for example, verbs follow their complements).

The solution was to add a head-initial head-complement rule, and then constrain it appropriately so that the number name heads appeared in the head-initial construction and all other heads in the head-final construction. Once we had the head-initial construction, it proved useful in the analyses of other phenomena (Siegel & Bender, 2004).

One might think that it could have been foreseen that this analysis wasn't going to work (without the additional head-complement rule) without the aid of a computer. The reason for including the example here, however, is that it illustrates how by formalizing our analyses and implementing them in machine readable form, we can test them systematically and more efficiently discover what we might have missed. In other words, if the analysis exists only in non-implemented form, we can never be sure that it actually interacts properly with the rest of the grammar. If, on the other hand, it is implemented, we can test whether it works, for an interesting sample of sentences.

3.2 Example 2: Collaborative Grammar Development

A second way in which grammar engineering combined with regression testing assists us in dealing with complexity is by supporting collaborative research, even across great distances. As described by Oepen, Bender, et al. (2002), the Jacy grammar underwent a period of intensive development by two grammar engineers on two different continents. They would begin each day by downloading the changes made at the other site (conveniently separated by nine time zones), and running a test suite instance to take a snapshot of the grammar performance. The two grammar engineers were typically working on different aspects of the grammar, but as noted above, there are always interactions among analyses. By documenting the progress they made through the grammar's behavior on the test suite (in addition to prose reports of what they had worked on each day), they were able to work on the grammar at the same time, creating mutually consistent analyses, without extensive face-to-face collaboration.

The Jacy grammar was being developed for practical applications, but the same methodology could be applied in the context of language documentation or linguistic research. By making the analyses (models, theories) concrete, and by documenting them through regression testing, the methodology of grammar engineering makes it possible for working linguists to pool their efforts and more quickly create rich linguistic resources.

3.3 Example 3: Unfamiliar languages

The third example of complexity we would like to address is the added complexity of working with an unfamiliar language. Most grammar engineering projects, like most syntactic research, are undertaken by people with some internalized, deep knowledge of the language (though not necessarily native speaker knowledge). This knowledge provides the basis for intuitions of which kinds of analyses to try out, as well as which kinds of data might present relevant test cases. However, even without any internalized knowledge of the language in question, it is possible to do some syntactic analysis (provided sufficient translated data). In this case, grammar engineering can significantly speed up the process, by allowing the grammar engineer to automatically test candidate analyses against the translated data.

A case study of this is reported by Bender (2008a), describing the development of an implemented grammar for Wambaya (a non-Pama-Nguyen language of the West Barkly family from the Northern Territory in Australia). In this case, the development test suite was constructed from all 804 example sentences in the descriptive grammar of Wambaya by Nordlinger (1998). Working from the analyses in Nordlinger (1998), the morpheme-by-morpheme translations of the data she provided, and the LinGO Grammar Matrix (see Bender, Flickinger, & Oepen, 2002 and § 4) Bender was able to create, in the equivalent of 5.5 person weeks, an implemented grammar that assigned a correct analysis to 91% of the development data, and 76% of a held-out test set. (This test set came from one of the narrative texts included in Nordlinger, 1998.)

The graph in Figure 3 gives a sense of the progress of grammar development. The solid line indicates raw coverage (percentage of test examples assigned at least one parse).[9] The dashed line represents average ambiguity (number of analyses per item, for items assigned at least one parse). The x axis is in hours of development time, which total 210, though they were spread out over several months. The most striking thing about this graph is how linear the increase in coverage was. The flat part in the upper right hand corner represents time spent treebanking, which was done at the end of this project, and which was interleaved with some effort towards reducing ambiguity, as evidenced by the dashed line.

It is important to note that, in going from no analysis of Wambaya to an implemented grammar fragment for Wambaya, >95% of the work was in the original fieldwork and subsequent analytical work by Nordlinger. Nonetheless, the implemented grammar adds value beyond encoding the analyses in the descriptive grammar, including the ability to map from surface strings to semantic representations. The implementation work went quickly for two primary reasons: First, the LinGO Grammar Matrix (see § 4 below) provided a solid starting point, including a lot of general infrastructure for semantic compositionality and other important aspects of grammar. Second, the ability to rapidly test out analyses (in some cases directly following Nordlinger, in others exploring other options), and see which sentences they caused the grammar to analyze and how, made it possible to incrementally develop a model covering many intersecting grammatical phenomena without having to mentally master all the diverse facts of the language.

In this case study, the primary fieldwork (and subsequent descriptive analysis) was completed before the grammar engineering work began. However, the results suggest that it might be fruitful to have grammar

---

[9]See Flickinger (this volume) on raw coverage (his 'observed coverage') and 'verified coverage'. The raw coverage numbers shown in Figure 3 exceed the verified coverage, which was 91% at the end of the development period, since some sentences received (only) analyses that did not correspond to the translation given by Nordlinger (1998).

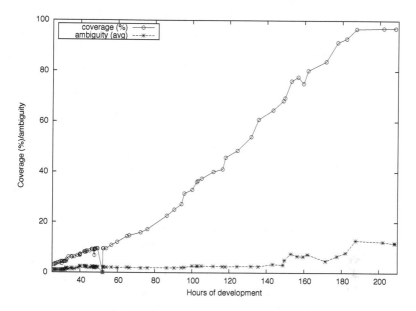

FIGURE 3 Wambaya grammar development

engineers working in collaboration with linguists currently engaged in primary fieldwork, to test out hypotheses generated in the field and suggest kinds of examples to check with native speakers.

3.4 Summary

In this section, we have argued that grammar engineering allows syntacticians to model systems of greater complexity than can be managed by hand. Computer implementation allows linguists to continually verify the interaction of analyses, to work together to build larger, more complex grammars, and to work with less familiar languages.

4 The LinGO Grammar Matrix

Given the benefits described in the previous section, one might ask why grammar engineering isn't more wide-spread than it is. Part of the answer surely has to do with the overhead costs of engaging in grammar engineering. First, one has to learn to use the software, as well as learning more general debugging skills, i.e., how to systematically determine what has gone wrong when the grammar won't compile or when it doesn't have the correct behavior. Second, implemented grammars acquire a certain inertia that is unfamiliar in pen-and-paper syntax.

Once an analysis is implemented, it takes effort to change it, and so old analyses end up constraining the form that new analyses take. While this may seem like a drawback, we argue (with Bender, 2008b) that it is in fact an advantage of grammar engineering: by having a computer keep track of all of the interacting analyses, we can do syntactic analysis in a fashion that leads to the incremental accumulation of results (cf. Wasow, 1985). Third, there is the issue that grammar development platforms aren't available for all syntactic frameworks. Finally, even when the supporting software is available, there is a per-language overhead in creating a grammar that covers the basics (e.g., word order, the linking of syntactic and semantic arguments) so that simple sentences can be processed. Only then is there a foundation on which to build analyses of additional phenomena.

This last cost is one of the principal motivations for the LinGO Grammar Matrix (Bender et al., 2002, forthcoming). We observe that the work of getting the basic core grammar running is less interesting because it is relatively well-understood, both from a pen-and-paper syntax point of view and from a grammar engineering point of view. Furthermore, natural languages are not arbitrarily different from each other, but share many commonalities, and, where they differ, tend to vary within some finite range.[10] This means that work done in large-scale grammar development from one language ought to be able to inform work done on other languages, and therefore ought to be able to provide a rich starting point for subsequent grammar development.

The original LinGO Grammar Matrix (Bender et al., 2002) consisted of a "core grammar" extracted from the LinGO English Resource Grammar (Flickinger, 2000, this volume), with reference to the Jacy Japanese grammar (Siegel & Bender, 2002). The core grammar provides such fundamental building blocks as the basic feature geometry, general means for combining heads and dependents (abstracting away from word order), general types for lexical entries (including dimensions of valence properties and part of speech), and an implementation of semantic compositionality (Flickinger & Bender, 2003), or the way that the semantic representations for phrases are calculated on the basis of the semantic representations of their constituents. In principle,

---

[10]This is, of course, not a new observation. It is similar in many respects to the basic idea behind the Principles and Parameters framework (Chomsky, 1980). There are several other multilingual grammar engineering projects which take advantage of crosslinguistic similarities, including the Parallel Grammar project (Butt, Dyvik, King, Masuichi, & Rohrer, 2002), work on multilingual XTAG metagrammars (Kinyon, Rambow, Scheffler, Yoon, & Joshi, 2006), and the GF Resource Grammar Library (Ranta, 2009).

this core grammar only contains types and constraints that are truly useful in all languages.

However, just because something isn't shared across all languages doesn't mean that it isn't shared by some. For example, SVO word order is not universal, but we hypothesize that the same analysis of SVO word order should work for all SVO languages. More recent work on the Grammar Matrix (Bender & Flickinger, 2005; Drellishak & Bender, 2005; Drellishak, 2009; O'Hara, 2008; Bender et al., forthcoming) has developed a methodology for creating reusable analyses of grammar properties (e.g., SVO word order, ergative-absolutive case marking, etc.) and making them available to grammar engineers through a web-based interface. This interface, called the "customization system", elicits a specification for a grammar through a typological questionnaire and then outputs a small, working starter grammar according to the specification. These starter grammars parse and generate only a relatively small fragment of the language they are designed for, but are ready to support sustained development of larger, more interesting grammar fragments. The result is that the overhead costs of creating an initial grammar in which to explore analyses of additional phenomena are much reduced.

Another way to look at the Grammar Matrix is as a means of taking grammar engineering *qua* hypothesis testing to the crosslinguistic level. Here, again, the assistance of a computer is what allows us to manage much greater complexity than would be possible by hand, as we strive for both typological breadth and syntactic and semantic depth in the analyses we implement when adding phenomena to the customization system. The Grammar Matrix produces HPSG grammars, though there is nothing framework-specific about the idea of grammar customization. We believe that other frameworks could similarly benefit from the cross-linguistic hypothesis testing enabled by this approach. To our knowledge, the only other grammar customization system currently under development is PAWS (Black & Black, 2009), which produces unification-based phrase structure grammars. As more grammar customization systems are developed, interesting opportunities for cross-framework comparison should emerge.

5 Conclusion

This chapter has focused on the methodology of grammar engineering, with the goal of explaining this approach to linguistic analysis to those who haven't yet tried it. We hope that by describing the work flow in some detail, including both the process of building a grammar as well as the process of building a test suite and testing the grammar against it, we have been able to make concrete the issues of complexity in linguistic analysis that grammar engineering is well placed to address. We have further tried to make the case through three examples of the kinds of complexity that can be handled. Finally, readers might be left wondering whether the benefits of grammar engineering out-weigh the costs. In this light, we briefly summarized the LinGO Grammar Matrix, which is designed to lower those costs.

References

Abney, S. (1996). Statistical methods and linguistics. In J. Klavans & P. Resnik (Eds.), *The balancing act: Combining symbolic and statistical approaches to language* (pp. 1–26). Cambridge MA: The MIT Press.

Ades, A. E., & Steedman, M. J. (1982). On the Order of Words. *Linguistics and Philosophy*, *4*, 517–558.

Baldridge, J., Chatterjee, S., Palmer, A., & Wing, B. (2007). DotCCG and VisCCG: Wiki and programming paradigms for improved grammar engineering with OpenCCG. In T. H. King & E. M. Bender (Eds.), *Proceedings of the GEAF 2007 Workshp* (pp. 5–25). Stanford CA: CSLI.

Bar-Hillel, Y. (1953). A quasi-arithmetical notation for syntactic description. *Language*, *29*(1), 47–58.

van der Beek, L., Bouma, G., Malouf, R., & van Noord, G. (2002). The Alpino Dependency Treebank. In M. Theune, A. Nijholt, & H. Hondorp (Eds.), *Computational linguistics in the Netherlands 2001: Selected papers from the twelfth CLIN meeting* (pp. 8–22). Amsterdam, The Netherlands: Rodopi.

Bender, E. M. (2008a). Evaluating a crosslinguistic grammar resource: A case study of Wambaya. In *Proceedings of the 46th meeting of the Association for Computational Linguistics: Human Language Technologies* (pp. 977–985). Columbus OH.

Bender, E. M. (2008b). Grammar engineering for linguistic hypothesis testing. In N. Gaylord, A. Palmer, & E. Ponvert (Eds.), *Proceedings of the Texas Linguistics Society X conference: Computational linguistics for less-studied languages* (pp. 16–36). Stanford CA: CSLI Publications ONLINE.

Bender, E. M., Clark, S., & King, T. H. (to appear). Computational syntax. In T. Kiss & A. Alexiadou (Eds.), *Syntax—an international handbook of contemporary research*. Berlin: Walter de Gruyter Publishers.

Bender, E. M., Drellishak, S., Poulson, L., O'Hara, K., Fokkens, A., & Saleem, S. (forthcoming). *Grammar customization.*

Bender, E. M., & Flickinger, D. (2005). Rapid prototyping of scalable grammars: Towards modularity in extensions to a language-independent core. In *Proceedings of the 2nd international joint conference on natural language processing IJCNLP-05 (posters/demos)* (pp. 203–208). Jeju Island, Korea.

Bender, E. M., Flickinger, D., & Oepen, S. (2002). The grammar matrix: An open-source starter-kit for the rapid development of cross-linguistically consistent broad-coverage precision grammars. In J. Carroll, N. Oostdijk, & R. Sutcliffe (Eds.), *Proceedings of the workshop on grammar engineering and evaluation at the 19th international conference on computational linguistics* (pp. 8–14). Taipei, Taiwan.

Black, C. A., & Black, H. A. (2009). PAWS: Parser and writer for syntax: Drafting syntactic grammars in the third wave. In *SIL forum for language fieldwork* (Vol. 2). Dallas, Texas.

Bond, F., Fujita, S., Hashimoto, C., Kasahara, K., Nariyama, S., Nichols, E., et al. (2004). The Hinoki treebank: A treebank for text understanding. In *Proceedings of the first international joint conference on natural language processing* (pp. 554–559). Hainan Island, China.

Bouma, G., Noord, G. van, & Malouf, R. (2001). Alpino: Wide-coverage computational analysis of Dutch. In W. Daelemans, K. Sima'an, J. Veenstra, & J. Zavrel (Eds.), *Computational linguistics in the Netherlands* (pp. 45–59). Amsterdam, The Netherlands: Rodopi.

Butt, M., Dyvik, H., King, T. H., Masuichi, H., & Rohrer, C. (2002). The Parallel Grammar project. In *Proceedings of the COLING workshop on grammar engineering and evaluation* (pp. 1–7). Taipei, Taiwan.

Butt, M., King, T. H., Niño, M.-E., & Segond, F. (1999). *A grammar writer's cookbook.* Stanford CA: CSLI Publications.

Carroll, J. (1994). Relating complexity to practical performance in parsing with wide-coverage unification grammars. In *Proceedings of the 32nd meeting of the Association for Computational Linguistics* (pp. 287–294). Las Cruces NM.

Carter, D. (1997). The TreeBanker: A tool for supervised training of parsed corpora. In *Proceedings of the workshop on computational environments for grammar development and linguistic engineering* (pp. 9–15). Madrid, Spain.

Chomsky, N. (1965). *Aspects of the theory of syntax.* Cambridge MA: MIT Press.

Chomsky, N. (1980). *Lectures on government and binding.* Dorrecht Holland: Foris Publications.

Copestake, A. (2002). *Implementing typed feature structure grammars.* Stanford CA: CSLI Publications.

Crouch, D., Dalrymple, M., Kaplan, R., King, T., Maxwell, J., & Newman, P. (2001). *XLE documentation.* (On-line documentation, Palo Alto Research Center (PARC))

Drellishak, S. (2009). *Widespread but not universal: Improving the typological coverage of the Grammar Matrix.* Unpublished doctoral dissertation, University of Washington.

Drellishak, S., & Bender, E. M. (2005). A coordination module for a crosslinguistic grammar resource. In S. Müller (Ed.), *Proceedings of the 12th international conference on Head-Driven Phrase Structure Grammar* (pp. 108–128). Stanford CA: CSLI Publications.

Estival, D., Falkedal, K., Balkan, L., Meijer, S., Regnier-Prost, S., Netter, K., et al. (1994). *Survey of existing test suites* (TSNLP Deliverable No. D-WP1). Colchester, UK: University of Essex.

Flickinger, D. (2000). On building a more efficient grammar by exploiting types. *Natural Language Engineering (Special Issue on Efficient Processing with HPSG), 6*(1), 15–28.

Flickinger, D. (this volume). Accuracy vs. robustness in grammar engineering. In E. M. Bender & J. E. Arnold (Eds.), *Language from a cognitive perspective: Grammar, usage, and processing.* Stanford: CSLI.

Flickinger, D., & Bender, E. M. (2003). Compositional semantics in a multilingual grammar resource. In E. M. Bender, D. Flickinger, F. Fouvry, & M. Siegel (Eds.), *Proceedings of the workshop on ideas and strategies for multilingual grammar development, ESSLLI 2003* (pp. 33–42). Vienna, Austria.

Flickinger, D., Nerbonne, J., Sag, I. A., & Wasow, T. (1987). *Toward evaluation of NLP systems* (Technical Report). Stanford CA: Hewlett-Packard Laboratories. (Distributed at the 24th Annual Meeting of the Association for Computational Linguistics)

Friedman, J., Bredt, T. H., Doran, R. W., Pollack, B. W., & Martner, T. S. (1971). *A computer model of transformational grammar.* New York: Elsevier.

Gazdar, G., Klein, E., Pullum, G., & Sag, I. (1985). *Generalized phrase structure grammar.* Cambridge MA: Harvard University Press.

Harris, Z. (1951). *Methods in structural linguistics.* Chicago: University of Chicago Press.

Joshi, A., Levy, L. S., & Takahashi, M. (1975). Tree adjunct grammars. *Journal of Computer Systems Science, 10*(1), 136–163.

Kaplan, R. M., & Bresnan, J. (1982). Lexical-functional grammar: A formal system for grammatical representation. In J. Bresnan (Ed.), *The mental representation of grammatical relations* (pp. 173–281). Cambridge MA: The MIT Press.

Kay, M. (1963). Rules of interpretation. An approach to the problem of computation in the semantics of natural language. In C. M. Popplewell (Ed.), *Proceedings of IFIP Congress 62* (pp. 318–21). Amsterdam, The Netherlands: North-Holland Publishing Company.

Kinyon, A., Rambow, O., Scheffler, T., Yoon, S., & Joshi, A. K. (2006). The metagrammar goes multilingual: A cross-linguistic look at the V2-phenomenon. In *Proceedings of the Eighth International Workshop on Tree Adjoining Grammar and Related Formalisms (TAG+8)* (pp. 17–24). Sydney, Australia.

Lehmann, S., Oepen, S., Regnier-Prost, S., Netter, K., Lux, V., Klein, J., et al. (1996). TSNLP — Test Suites for Natural Language Processing. In *Proceedings of the 16th international conference on computational linguistics* (pp. 711–716). Copenhagen, Denmark.

Meurers, W. D., Penn, G., & Richter, F. (2002). A web-based instructional platform for constraint-based grammar formalisms and parsing. In *Proceedings of the ACL 2002 workshop on effective tools and methodologies for teaching NLP and CL* (pp. 18–25). New Brunswick NJ.

Nerbonne, J., Netter, K., Diagne, K., Dickmann, L., & Klein, J. (1993). A diagnostic tool for German syntax. *Machine Translation, 8*, 85–107.

Nordlinger, R. (1998). *A grammar of Wambaya, Northern Australia*. Canberra: Pacific Linguistics.

Oepen, S., Bender, E. M., Callmeier, U., Flickinger, D., & Siegel, M. (2002). Parallel distributed grammar engineering for practical applications. In *Proceedings of the workshop on grammar engineering and evaluation at the 19th international conference on computational linguistics* (pp. 15–21). Taipei, Taiwan.

Oepen, S., & Flickinger, D. P. (1998). Towards systematic grammar profiling. Test suite technology ten years after. *Journal of Computer Speech and Language (Special Issue on Evaluation), 12*(4), 411–436.

Oepen, S., Toutanova, K., Shieber, S., Manning, C., Flickinger, D., & Brants, T. (2002). The LinGO Redwoods treebank: Motivation and preliminary applications. In *Proceedings of the 19th interna-*

tional conference on computational linguistics. Taipei, Taiwan.

O'Hara, K. (2008). *A morphosyntactic infrastructure for a grammar customization system.* Unpublished master's thesis, University of Washington.

Paroubek, P., Schabes, Y., & Joshi, A. K. (1992). XTAG – a graphical workbence for developing tree-adjoining grammars. In *Proceedings of the 3rd conference on applied natural language processing* (pp. 216–223). Trento.

Petrick, S. R. (1965). *A recognition procedure for transformational grammars.* Unpublished doctoral dissertation, MIT.

Pollard, C., & Sag, I. A. (1987). *Information-based syntax and semantics. Volume 1: Fundamentals.* Chicago, IL and Stanford, CA: Center for the Study of Language and Information. (Distributed by The University of Chicago Press)

Pollard, C., & Sag, I. A. (1994). *Head-driven phrase structure grammar.* Chicago IL and Stanford CA: The University of Chicago Press and CSLI Publications.

Ranta, A. (2009). The GF resource grammar library. *Linguistic Issues in Language Technology, 2*, 1–62.

Rosén, V., Meurer, P., & Smedt, K. D. (2007). Designing and implementing discriminants for LFG grammars. In *Proceedings of LFG07* (pp. 397–417). CSLI On-line Publications.

Siegel, M., & Bender, E. M. (2002). Efficient deep processing of Japanese. In *Proceedings of the 3rd workshop on Asian language resources and international standardization at the 19th international conference on computational linguistics.* Taipei, Taiwan.

Siegel, M., & Bender, E. M. (2004). Head-initial constructions in Japanese. In S. Müller (Ed.), *Proceedings of the 11th international conference on Head-Driven Phrase Structure Grammar* (pp. 244–260). Stanford CA: CSLI Publications.

Smith, J. D. (1999). English number names in HPSG. In G. Webelhuth, J.-P. Koenig, & A. Kathol (Eds.), *Lexical and constructional aspects of linguistic explanation* (pp. 145–160). Stanford CA: CSLI.

Sparck Jones, K., & Galliers, J. R. (1995). *Evaluating natural language processing systems. An analysis and review* (Vol. 1083). Berlin, Germany: Springer.

Steedman, M. (1996). *Surface structure and interpretation.* Cambridge MA: The MIT Press.

Wasow, T. (1985). The wizards of ling. *Natural Language and Linguistic Theory, 3*, 485–491.

Woods, W. (1970). Transition network grammars for natural language analysis. *Communications of the ACM, 13*, 591–596.

Zwicky, A., Friedman, J., Hall, B. C., & Walker, D. E. (1965). The MITRE syntactic analysis procedure for transformational grammars. In *Proceedings of the fall joint computer conference* (pp. 317–326). Las Vegas NV.

3

Accuracy vs. Robustness in Grammar Engineering
DAN FLICKINGER

Preface

The conceptual origins of the English Resource Grammar go back to the days of GPSG grammar development in the Natural Language Project at Hewlett-Packard Laboratories beginning in the early 1980s, with Tom Wasow serving as one of the initiators and guiding forces of that research group, which this author joined starting as a summer intern in 1983. It was at HP Labs that we developed the methodology of building and using test suites exhibiting core linguistic phenomena, for regression testing and measurement of progress as we extended grammar coverage while maintaining a high level of linguistic accuracy.

1 Introduction

The implementation of a computational grammar for a natural language is an extended exercise in the art of compromise, since the emerging grammar will strive to excel on several measures which are in competition for primacy. The ideal grammar would produce a completely accurate result for every input presented to it, with a mimimum of computational effort. But short of that ideal, any existing grammar will necessarily either emphasize robustness at the expense of accuracy, or favor accuracy while conceding some limitation in robustness. Many modern broad-coverage grammars maximize robustness, often for good practical reasons, but the inevitable corresponding sacrifices in accuracy can be difficult to quantify, since public standards for testing

Language from a Cognitive Perspective.
Emily M. Bender and Jennifer Arnold, Editors
Copyright © 2011, CSLI Publications.

and comparing grammars are either inadequate or lacking altogether. Hence the relative benefits and costs of using a more robust grammar vs. a more accurate one are often judged instead by task-based success rates within applications. Such 'black-box' measures are not helpful in predicting the success of a grammar in a new application, nor do they afford direct illumination of the linguistic shortcomings of the grammar, insights which could guide its further development.

Robustness and efficiency are relatively easy to measure, but for some applications accuracy is of equal importance, and better methods and annotated corpora will be necessary to enable its effective evaluation. This paper examines some of the engineering trade-offs that have been made in the development of one broad-coverage grammar over the course of its fifteen-year development, with the aim of contributing to the design of more effective grammar evaluation standards. Greater clarity about the nature of the compromises embodied in a grammar should help in designing annotation schemes for test data which reveal the consequences of these choices for accuracy, and thus enable better evaluation of suitability for a given task, and more fine-grained comparison across grammars.

2 English Resource Grammar

The English Resource Grammar (ERG: Flickinger, 2000, Flickinger, Copestake, & Sag, 2000, Copestake & Flickinger, 2000) is a broad-coverage grammar which was started in 1994,[1] and which has been under continuous development since then within the Linguistic Grammars Online (LinGO) laboratory at CSLI (Center for the Study of Language and Information, Stanford University).

As an implementation within the theoretical framework of Head-driven Phrase Structure Grammar (HPSG: Pollard & Sag, 1994), the ERG has since its inception encoded both morphosyntactic and semantic properties of English, in a declarative representation that enables

---

[1] The first version of the English Resource Grammar was designed and implemented at CSLI by Rob Malouf; several other Stanford graduate students also contributed to early implementation work, most notably Emily Bender. The grammar has also benefited significantly over the years from the suggestions, critique, and wealth of syntactic expertise that Tom brought to our weekly meetings, matched by LinGO director Ivan Sag (also a co-founder of the HP Labs NLP effort), and assisted by a steady stream of visiting scholars to the LinGO lab at CSLI. Ann Copestake and Stephan Oepen each authored software platforms central to the ERG's implementation (LKB: Copestake, 2002, [incr tsdb()]: Oepen & Carroll, 2000) and both continue as vital contributors to its development. Broader support now comes from the international research network DELPH-IN (cf. http://www.delph-in.net). An online interface is available at http://www.delph-in.net/erg.

both parsing and generation. While development has always taken place in the context of one or more applications at a time, primary emphasis in the ERG has consistently been on the linguistic accuracy of the resulting analyses, at some expense to robustness. Its initial use was for generation within the German-English machine translation prototype developed in the Verbmobil project (Wahlster, 2000), so constraining the grammar to avoid overgeneration was a necessary design requirement that fit well with the broader aims of its developers.

The ERG consists of a rich hierarchy of types encoding regularities both in the lexicon and in the syntactic constructions of English. As of 2010, the lexicon contains 35,000 manually constructed lexeme entries, each assigned to one of 980 lexical types at the leaves of this hierarchy, where the types encode idiosyncracies of subcategorization, modification targets, exceptional behavior with respect to lexical rules, etc. The grammar also includes 70 derivational and inflectional rules which apply to these lexemes (or to each other's outputs) to produce the words as they appear in text. The grammar provides 200 syntactic rules which admit either unary or binary phrases; these include a relatively small number of highly schematic rules which license ordinary combinations of heads with their arguments and modifiers, and a larger number of construction-specific rules both for frequently occurring phrase types such as coordinate structures or appositives, as in (1):

(1) Kim, my colleague, has arrived.

and for phrase types that occur much less frequently in most corpora, such as vocatives, as in (2):

(2) Kim, can you wait for me?

Statistical models trained on some of the treebanks discussed below are used both in parsing (Toutanova, Manning, Shieber, Flickinger, & Oepen, 2002) and in generation (Velldal, 2008) to rank the relative likelihoods of the outputs, to address the issue of disambiguation which is central to the use of any broad-coverage grammar for almost any task.

3   Accuracy Measures via Treebanking

While the measure of *coverage* of a grammar over a corpus is often simply the percentage of items in the corpus for which the grammar assigns at least one analysis, this is a relatively uninformative measurement taken alone, revealing little about either the linguistic adequacy of the analyses or their utility in a given application. For almost any use of an implemented grammar, the accuracy of these analyses is crucially important, whether measured in terms of the phrasal structures or the semantic dependencies that are assigned to each sentence.

The notion of accuracy for ERG analyses has been determined on the basis of sentence-by-sentence human judgments, with local experts in syntax and semantics meeting weekly for most of the past fifteen years to assist in designing and judging analyses of linguistic phenomena as they appear in application-specific corpora, or in hand-built collections of test sentences (cf. Bender, Flickinger, & Oepen, this volume). The central aims in the design of the grammar are that it will assign one fully correct syntactic structure relating a sentence and its meaning representation, and that all other analyses that the grammar licenses should be linguistically defensible even if pragmatically dispreferred. Correctness of syntactic structures and their corresponding meaning representations is of course theory-dependent, variable in granularity, and subject to lively debate for all but the most basic phenomena, but over time a steadily growing collection of sentences and their preferred ERG analyses has been manually validated, and has been further tested by the use of these analyses in a variety of applications. These annotations of test suites and naturally occurring corpora are recorded in *dynamic treebanks* using the methodology described in Oepen, Flickinger, Toutanova, & Manning, 2004. Of course, there is a more ambitious notion of accuracy in parsing, where the correct analysis is not only produced, but identified as the most likely one out of all the competing analyses licensed by the grammar. These issues of disambiguation and parse ranking are taken up below.

Given the primary emphasis on accuracy, where every word in a sentence (and even every punctuation mark) must be explicitly licensed by some rule of the grammar, some sentences in any naturally occurring corpus of reasonable size will exhibit linguistic phenomena which fall outside the capabilities of the current grammar. These shortcomings of the grammar can be for several reasons: (1) no theoretically sound analysis of the phenomenon in sufficient detail is known; (2) implementation of an existing analysis has so far proved unworkable, due to limitations either of the formalisms employed, or of the ingenuity of the grammarian; (3) adding an available analysis to the grammar would lead to an unacceptable overall increase in ambiguity or in processing costs. It is clear that continued efforts can overcome these shortcomings for many phenomena over time, but Zipf's law (Zipf, 1949) governing the distribution of word frequencies may hold as well for syntactic phenomena in a corpus of sufficient size (cf. Culy, 1998). Since there are many phenomena that occur with relatively low frequency even in very large corpora, any grammar which insists on a high degree of linguistic accuracy will inevitably encounter obstacles to full robustness.

Fifteen years of development of the ERG have led to a grammar which now consistently assigns fully correct syntactic and semantic analyses to more than 75% of the sentences in previously unseen English texts of many types. There are of course specialized genres which can prove more challenging, such as online newsgroup discussions, chemistry research articles, or technical manuals authored by non-native writers. But recent experiments using the ERG to parse such corpora still consistently give accurate coverage rates above 65%, indicating that the flip side of Zipf's law works here in favor of the grammar: providing analyses of enough of the relatively frequent phenomena will enable relatively robust coverage even for specialized genres. Note that the *observed* coverage numbers for the ERG on any corpus will inevitably be higher, since the grammar can sometimes assign semantically or pragmatically flawed analyses to sentences whose correct analysis would require treatment of phenomena which the grammar does not yet include. For example, the intended meaning of the sentence

(3)   Abrams didn't write as many essays as you did poems.

compares the number of essays to the number of poems, but the current ERG, lacking an analysis of comparative sub-deletion (Bresnan, 1973), only assigns the logically possible but unwanted analysis where "as you did poems" is interpreted as "while you wrote poems". Such a sentence in a corpus would count as being parsed by the ERG in the *observed* coverage number, but would be excluded from the *verified* coverage total, after manual annotation of the corpus to construct the treebank.

To date, ERG treebanks identify exactly one analysis (or none) as 'correct' for each sentence, even though for some sentences, the grammar may assign multiple analyses which can be judged correct, even in context. It can be that two syntactically distinct analyses correspond to the same underspecified semantic representation assigned by the ERG, which uses Minimal Recursion Semantics (MRS: Copestake, Flickinger, Pollard, & Sag, 2005) as its formalism. For example, the sentence

(4)   They took a nap while he spoke.

might have the subordinate clause "while he spoke" attach either to the verb phrase "took a nap", or to the whole main clause "they took a nap", but the MRS representation will be the same on both attachment decisions. Alternatively, two syntactic analyses may correspond to distinct semantic representations which are pragmatically difficult to resolve, as in some noun-noun-noun compounds such as "airline reservation counter", where it generally doesn't matter whether reference is to a counter for airline reservations, or a reservation counter for an airline. Such 'spurious' ambiguity can in principle be reduced in a grammar, either by increasing the expressivity of the semantic formalism to allow more underspecification, or by more fine-grained syntactic constraints on the interactions among phenomena. But in practice any broad-coverage grammar implementing a linguistic theory will give rise to instances of spurious ambiguity in any sizeable corpus. At present, this kind of ambiguity is resolved in ERG treebanks via a set of a few dozen heuristics (such as "Attach subordinate clauses as high as possible") which the annotators have negotiated and apply at attachment choice points when treebanking in order to arrive consistently at a single best parse. An alternative approach, not yet investigated for the ERG, would be to leave spurious ambiguity unresolved in the treebank, so some sentences would have multiple analyses all annotated as correct.

Table 1 summarizes the success rates of the current ERG in parsing a variety of collections of English text which have formed the development corpora for NLP projects over the lifespan of the grammar to date. Each of these data sets was parsed and then fully treebanked manually as described above.

TABLE 1 ERG Treebanks

Corpus type	Number of items	Av. item length	Observed coverage	Verified coverage
Meeting scheduling	11660	7.5	96.8%	93.8%
E-commerce	5392	8.0	96.1%	93.0%
Norwegian tourism	10834	15.0	94.2%	90.1%
SemCor (partial)	2501	18.0	91.8%	82.0%
Wikipedia (CmpLng)	11558	19.5	87.4%	80.0%
Online user forum	578	12.5	85.5%	77.5%
Dictionary defs.	10000	6.0	81.2%	75.5%
Essay	769	21.6	83.2%	69.4%
Chemistry papers	637	27.0	87.8%	65.3%
Technical manuals	4000	12.5	86.8%	61.9%

Each row of the table records

- the total number of individual sentences in a corpus
- the average number of tokens per item in the corpus
- the *observed* coverage: the number of items for which the parser assigned at least one syntactic analysis

- the *verified* coverage, where a correct analysis was identified from among these candidates.

For the first three treebanks, the manually constructed lexicon was extended to ensure that all words used in the corpus have corresponding lexical entries in the ERG. For the remainder, default lexical entries were added automatically for unknown words while parsing, guided by part-of-speech tags assigned by the TnT tagger (Brants, 2000). Brief descriptions of each of these treebanks can be found in the appendix to this chapter.

The parser used in constructing these treebanks was the PET parser (Callmeier, 2000), a bottom-up exhaustive chart parser with packing which employs a statistical model to compute the relative likelihood of each candidate analysis, and selective unpacking to present these analyses in ranked order. Since a few difficult sentences could consume a disproportionate share of the total time and memory required to parse a given corpus, resource limits were imposed on the parser when constructing these treebanks (up to 60 CPU seconds per sentence, or 100K chart edges, or one gigabyte of memory). Some longer sentences in a corpus hit one of these resource limits during parsing, halting before any analyses were found, even though the grammar might well be capable of analyzing such sentences given more time or memory. The negative practical effect of these limitations is most noticeable in the chemistry corpus, where up to 10% of the sentences failed to parse within the resource limits imposed. These limits illustrate one rather obvious but significant compromise between the aim of robustness (treebanking as many sentences as possible in a corpus), and the need for efficiency (constructing the parsed corpus on available hardware in the available time).

Unsurprisingly, the 'survival' rate of treebanked items in a corpus parsed by the ERG is largely correlated with the average sentence length in a corpus, in part simply because longer sentences carry with them a greater likelihood of encountering an occurrence of a linguistic phenomenon outside the scope of the grammar. One other factor bringing down this survival rate is a consequence of the method of preparing these treebanks, involving the strategy employed to contend with highly ambiguous sentences when treebanking.

The Redwoods (Oepen et al., 2004) platform used for treebanking presents the 'forest' of candidate parse trees to the annotator in the form of binary *discriminants* (Carter, 1997), each of which divides the parse forest into one set of trees which have a given property and the complement set which do not. While this approach enables efficient and consistent annotation, its practical use requires that some upper bound be imposed on the number of candidate analyses (the size of the parse forest) recorded for any one sentence. Depending on how well the statistical model used in parse ranking matches the linguistic phenomena observed in a given corpus, the intended analysis for some sentence may be within the scope of the grammar, yet be unhappily ranked beyond the limit imposed on the number of analyses the annotator considers when treebanking.

This second factor is partly responsible for the more marked contrasts between 'observed' coverage and 'verified' coverage in the treebank of chemistry articles, and the one for the essay "The Cathedral and the Bazaar". The statistical model used when parsing these smaller corpora had been trained on annotations of the Norwegian tourism corpus, which did not provide enough training instances of some linguistic phenomena observed more frequently in these additional corpora. Training new corpus-specific statistical models will very likely lead to a reduction in the damage caused by this mismatch between training data and parsed corpus, enabling more success when treebanking, but this dependence on customized parse-ranking models presents a minor but appreciable obstacle when treebanking a previously unseen corpus. Here the relevant compromise is between the desire on the one hand for both coverage and accuracy, and on the other for minimizing the manual customization costs when treebanking a new text corpus.

4 Expanding Grammar Coverage

Throughout its development, the ERG has both benefited and suffered from the fundamental design decision to make primary the accuracy of its linguistic analyses. One significant benefit is the relative ease of applying the grammar to the task of generating well-formed and natural-sounding sentences of English from input meaning representations (MRSs), enabling its use as a generator in the machine-translation systems of Verbmobil (German/English) and LOGON (Norwegian/English: Lønning et al., 2004). Indeed, the ability to generate has proven to be valuable in grammar development itself, since the generator is quick to reveal syntactic structures erroneously licensed by the grammar. Observing and diagnosing such overgeneration often leads to quick and rewarding improvements in the implementation, with the additional benefit of reducing unwanted ambiguity when parsing.

A second important benefit has been the ability to sustain discussions with linguists, through years of grammar development, consulting on the detailed design and evaluation of syntactic and semantic analyses of phenomena implemented in the ERG. By ensuring that the structures licensed by the grammar correspond well to the expectations of the theoretician, the grammar engineer can continue to co-design computationally tractable treatments of new phenomena with (fellow) theoreticians, even as the grammar's complexity inexorably increases.

However, one ongoing consequence of this emphasis on linguistic accuracy is the lack of analyses for some portion of the sentences in any naturally occurring corpus of English text. While this percentage of unanalyzed sentences steadily shrinks as development of the ERG continues, the remaining shortcomings in robustness are nontrivial, and practical applications using the grammar may require hybrid processing strategies which include an additional and more robust if less accurate analysis engine, in an architecture of the kind studied in Schäfer, 2007. An alternative strategy already used by other linguistically rich broad-coverage grammars such as the PARC LFG English grammar (Butt, Dyvik, King, Masuichi, & Rohrer, 2002) produces a partial analysis when no full analysis is available; an investigation of this approach using the ERG is reported in Zhang & Kordoni, 2008.

As already noted, some kind of hybrid strategy will always be necessary when using linguistically rich grammars if every sentence in a corpus must get some analysis. But the grammarian's aim in development is to continuously reduce the work load for such robustness safety nets. While much of the development of a broad-coverage grammar comes in quite small increments, the ERG has seen several more noteworthy steps in its steady quest for more robust coverage.

One important step was a careful diagnosis of the classes of errors made by the ERG in parsing a nontrivial set of sentences extracted from the British National Corpus (BNC). This study (Baldwin et al., 2005) provided a baseline of coverage and accuracy for the ERG on data from a large corpus, and highlighted the need for a more effective treatment of open-class vocabulary, and in particular multi-word expressions.

A second step in the development of the ERG which significantly improved its robustness focused on an intensive expansion of the manually constructed lexicon, driven by the observation that predicting suitable lexical entries for unknown nouns and adjectives is typically easier than for verbs, which exhibit more variation in the kinds of complements they select. Manually constructed lexical entries were added to the ERG's lexicon for all words which occurred as verbs more than 100 times in the 100-million word BNC. The working hypothesis is that infrequently occurring verbs are more likely to be either simple intransitive or transitive verbs, so the creation of on-the-fly lexical entries for remaining unknown verbs encountered in a text should be straightforward. With this addition of some 2000 verb entries, plus another 3000 entries for other high-frequency words identified by Zhang, 2007's application of van Noord, 2004's error-mining technique, the 'observed' coverage for the ERG on one subset of the BNC roughly doubled from less than 20% to above 40% when coupled with a simple unknown word predictor based on part-of-speech tags again using the TnT tagger. Evaluation of the accuracy of these analyses has not been carried out for the BNC corpus, but a smaller-scale evaluation of the efficacy of this method (among others) was conducted by Zhang & Kordoni, 2006 using the manually-annotated 2005 Redwoods corpus.

A third and more recent advance in robustness for the ERG has come in the form of a preprocessing component which enables declarative statements of grammar-specific tokenization and normalization rules (Adolphs et al., 2008). These rules cope with phenomena such as time and date expressions, telephone numbers, measure phrases, integers, ratios, and web addresses, while also defining the triggering conditions for introducing on-the-fly lexical entries for proper names and for open-class words which lack the necessary lexical entries in the manually constructed ERG lexicon. While the ERG has employed a preprocessing component for several years already, including accommodation for unknown words, this more recent chart-based approach enables greater consistency and more fine-grained interactions between token-level properties such as mixed case (capitalization) and morphosyntactic or semantic properties defined in the ERG lexicon. One example of improved robustness using this approach is the ability to posit a generic proper name entry for a capitalized word which is already included in the ERG lexicon as some other part of speech, even though in general native lexical entries block the addition of on-the-fly entries to avoid massive spurious ambiguity. Thus in sentence (5), a proper name entry is now created for "Grumpy" even though an adjective entry already exists in the ERG lexicon, so this sentence parses correctly.

(5)   We saw Grumpy at Disneyland.

Such re-assignment of words for use as proper names is particularly prevalent in scientific texts that we have analyzed, including the Sci-Borg chemistry articles and the Wikipedia articles on computational linguistics.

These three improvements to the ERG not only increased the overall robustness of the grammar, but interestingly also improved its accuracy. A richer lexical inventory of frequently occurring verbs avoids shortcomings in part-of-speech tag-based unknown word prediction, leading to an increase in the number of sentences that receive correct analyses, since the lack of a correct lexical entry for even one token in a sentence will prevent the grammar from assigning the right analysis to that sentence. Likewise, better integration of preprocessing with the constraints of the core grammar enables a closer match in tokenization to the expectations of the grammar, and more accurate on-the-fly lexical entries for unknown words. The result has been a modest but visible improvement of some 5% in the 'survival' rate in the treebanks where not all of the vocabulary is included in the manually constructed lexicon, since a correct parse is now more often available for sentences that previously only got spurious analyses due to erroneous unknown word guesses or incorrect tokenization.

5 Limitations to Accuracy

As already noted, giving a precise characterization of accuracy in linguistic analyses has proven to be an elusive goal. Reaching consensus on the correct syntactic structures for sentences of a corpus is difficult even within a single project, and simply not possible across linguistic frameworks, since the phrasal structures assigned are too theory-dependent. Agreement on the semantic dependencies expressed within a sentence may be more achievable across frameworks, and there have been some constructive moves in this direction such as the COLING parser evaluation shared task and workshop (Bos et al., 2008).

Even with the emphasis on linguistic accuracy in the analyses licensed by the ERG, including semantic representations for each sentence, many desirable elements of a 'full' analysis are notably lacking. While the assertions included in the MRS representation assigned by the ERG as the correct analysis of a sentence should all be true, they are far from complete. For one, the ERG currently draws few distinctions in lexical semantics, instead assigning almost every lexical entry its own semantic predicate, and thus failing to express semantic commonality for regularities such as the non-productive nominalization of "arrive" as "arrival", or for synonyms like "buy" and "purchase". Some productive category-changing regularities are expressed in the grammar, such as nominalization with *-ing* ("walk/walking") and the *-ly* adverbial suffix ("quick/quickly"), as well as some productive derivational prefixes like *re-* as in "re-hire".

Idioms are accommodated to some extent in the grammar, adapting the approaches of Nunberg, Wasow, & Sag, 1994 and Riehemann, 2001, but they are only sparsely included as illustrative examples of the formal mechanisms designed to represent them, since they only appear with any significant frequency in one of the corpora treebanked to date, namely SemCor, which includes works of fiction that employ many idioms. Thus the grammar, if it lacked a particular entry in the idiom lexicon, would assign a plausible-looking but incorrect analysis to a sentence like the following, where in context it is the idiomatic reading that is intended:

(6)   They kept tabs on him.

More generally, the ERG expresses few constraints on interpretation that are imposed on a sentence by its linguistic context, instead treating each sentence as an isolated expression. Thus the grammar currently makes no attempt to bind ordinary pronouns to their antecedents, not even when the antecedent is present in the same sentence. Likewise, no attempt is made to constrain the interpretation of elided verb phrases like the "should" used in the sentence in (7).

(7)   They didn't even try to win, but we should.

These shortcomings in annotation detail do not sharply distinguish the ERG from other broad-coverage grammars, many of which provided comparable dependency representations for a small set of sentences for the COLING 2008 shared task workshop. Yet the lack of such detail will inevitably limit the utility of these grammars for some tasks and for some linguistic investigations that might otherwise benefit from the analyses the grammars provide.

In the case of the ERG, some of this lack of annotation in its semantic representations is due to quite practical considerations. For example, after observing the productive regularity employing the notion of a "Universal Grinder" (Pelletier, 1975) which, for example, relates words for animals to morphologically identical words which denote the "meat" sense of those animals, the grammarian might be expected to add a derivational rule which captures this regularity, enabling a successful parse of the sentence in (8).

(8)   They had dog for lunch.

However, such a rule would effectively double the number of lexical entries introduced into the parse chart for every count noun in a given sentence, leading to an additional computational cost that is rarely repaid, since instances of such "grinding" are very rare in many corpora, including the ones discussed above. This awkward tension is compounded by a corresponding rule for the "Universal Sorter" (Bunt, 1985) which relates mass nouns to derived ones with a countable sense, as in (9).

(9)   This is an excellent wine.

Adding a further derivational rule for this regularity would mean that in fact every noun, whether originally count or mass, would now introduce two entries into the parse chart, compounding the computational costs for every sentence, and again providing only rare benefits in increased robustness and accuracy. The current ERG once again compromises, simply listing in the lexicon a small number of the most frequent nouns which exhibit these two alternations, like "chicken" and "wine", sacrificing some small degree of robustness and accuracy in favor of a substantial gain in processing efficiency.

6 Conclusion

Since every broad-coverage grammar implementation will make distinct design choices in the face of the inevitable tensions among the goals of accuracy, robustness, and efficiency, any effective evaluation of the resulting analyses must be fine-grained enough to reveal the consequences of these compromises. As noted, measurements for robustness and for efficiency are relatively straightforward and widely reported as parsing results. But it is ultimately the accuracy of these resulting analyses which determines the effectiveness of a grammar for a given task, and thus better methods and annotated corpora for measuring linguistic accuracy would be welcome. The profile presented here of one grammar's compromises in balancing a desire for high accuracy with a steady push toward more robustness will perhaps contribute to the design and production of these improved measures of linguistic analyses.

Appendix: ERG Treebanks

Meeting/hotel scheduling: VerbMobil

The VerbMobil project (Wahlster, 2000) developed, among its many results, a collection of transcriptions of spoken dialogues each of which reflected a negotiation either to schedule a meeting, or to plan a hotel stay. One dialogue usually consists of 20–30 turns, with most of the utterances relatively short, including greetings and closings, and not surprisingly with a high frequency of time and date expressions as well as questions and sentence fragments. A typical example from this corpus (where commas are often used by the transcribers to indicate short pauses in the recorded dialogue):

> *Looks like we, need to schedule another meeting, in the next couple of weeks*

Discussion of this treebank, along with reports on the development and evaluation of statistical models trained on it, can be found in Oepen et al., 2002, Toutanova et al., 2002, and Toutanova & Manning, 2002.

E-commerce: YY Software

While the ERG was being used in a commercial software product developed by the YY Software Corporation for automated response to customer emails, a corpus of training and test data was constructed and made freely available, consisting of email messages composed by people pretending to be customers of a fictional consumer products online store. The messages in the corpus fall into four roughly equal-sized categories: Product Availability, Order Status, Order Cancellation, and Product Return. A typical example from the corpus:

Don't ship the order and send me a refund immediately.

Like the Verbmobil corpus, this data consists of relatively short utterances, including a high frequency of sentence fragments, and some questions, but also a much more frequent use of commands.

Norwegian tourism: LOGON

The Norwegian/English machine translation research project LOGON (Lønning et al., 2004) acquired for its development and evaluation corpus a set of tourism brochures originally written in Norwegian and then professionally translated into English. The project paid for additional professional English translations of these brochures to enable better evaluation studies, producing a sentence-aligned pair of freely available data sets, with the English corpus consisting of 9000 sentences. These are augmented with another 1300 English sentences taken from public-domain Norwegian tourism web sites. The corpus, not surprisingly, consists almost entirely of declarative sentences and many sentence fragments, where the average number of tokens per item is higher than in the Verbmobil and e-commerce data. A typical example:

If you would rather go fishing, there are opportunities in both Øvre Sjodalsvatn and Bessvatn.

More information on the LOGON project can be found at the web site http://www.emmtee.net.

SemCor

The freely available SemCor corpus (Miller, Leacock, Tengi, & Bunker, 1993) consists of 230,000 words of text extracted primarily from the one-million-word Brown corpus (Kucera & Francis, 1967), and tagged with WordNet senses. Work is now underway in collaboration with researchers at the University of Melbourne to construct a treebank for the subset of SemCor which is fully sense-tagged. At present 2500 sentences are included in this emerging treebank, whose average sentence length is greater than in the LOGON texts. A typical example:

Anyone's identification with an international struggle, whether warlike or peaceful, requires absurd oversimplification and intense emotional involvement.

Wikipedia: Computational Linguistics

In collaboration with researchers at Oslo University, we have constructed a treebank for 100 Wikipedia articles on Computational Linguistics and closely related topics, for use in studies including information extraction and parse selection (Ytrestøl, Flickinger, & Oepen, 2009). The treebank of 11558 sentences comprises 13 of the 16 sets of articles, with the remaining three sets held out for testing. The corpus contains mostly declarative, relatively long sentences, along with some fragments. The original wiki markup is preserved in the treebank, accommodated in the ERG by a small number of wiki-specific preprocessing rules. A typical example:

'"Computational linguistics"' is an [[interdisciplinary]] field dealing with the [[Statistics—statistical]] and/or rule-based modeling of [[natural language]] from a computational perspective.

Online user forum: ILIAD

Again in collaboration with the University of Melbourne, construction is underway on a treebank of data extracted from Linux user web forums, as part of the ILIAD (Improved Linux Information Access by Data Mining) project. Only a few hundred sentences have been treebanked so far, and the mix of non-native English and highly informal usage presents an engaging challenge for a high-precision grammar like the ERG. A typical example from the corpus:

Not sure if you ever got Linux installed dbessell, but this brings up a good point.

Dictionary definitions: GCIDE

In a study with researchers at NTT on the feasibility of extracting ontology relationships from dictionary definitions (Nichols, Bond, & Flickinger, 2005) using the ERG, a treebank was constructed with 10,000 English definition sentences from the GNU Contemporary International Dictionary of English (GCIDE). The data includes a very high frequency of relatively short fragments, but also a perhaps surprising wealth of linguistic phenomena. A typical example:

Form: to shape, mold, or fashion into a certain state or condition;

Essay: "The Cathedral and the Bazaar"

The ERG is just one of many grammars under development within a common implementation framework provided by researchers working in the international collaboration called DELPH-IN (http://www.delph-in.net). To further the study of cross-linguistic comparisons among these grammars, and in particular the semantic representations they compose, the consortium resolved to construct treebanks for each grammar of translations of the essay "The Cathedral and the Bazaar" by Eric Raymond. The average length and the linguistic complexity of these sentences is markedly higher than the other treebanked corpora. A typical example:

> One key to understanding is to realize exactly why it is that the kind of bug report non-source-aware users normally turn in tends not to be very useful.

Chemistry papers: SciBorg

In the context of a joint project with researchers at University of Cambridge on an eScience project called SciBorg (Rupp et al., 2008), focused on knowledge extraction from a large collection of chemistry research papers, we collaborated with a domain expert to construct a treebank of papers from this collection. The average length of the sentences in this corpus is considerably greater than in the other treebanked corpora, and consists almost entirely of full declarative sentences. The text is preprocessed with a set of chemistry-specific rules to deal with chemistry compound names, formulae, etc. A typical example after this preprocessing:

> By taking advantage of the growth steering properties of the OSCAR-COMPOUND film we were able to prepare nearly perfectly ordered hexagonal arrays of OSCARCOMPOUND clusters with a uniform distance of 4.5 nm between the particles.

Technical manuals: CheckPoint

The German Artificial Intelligence Research Center (DFKI) conducted an investigation into the use of deep grammars like the ERG and its German counterpart in a hybrid system for grammar-checking for technical manuals (Crysmann, Bartomeu, Adolphs, Flickinger, & Klüwer, 2008). Using anonymized real-world data provided by the Berlin-based software company Acrolinx GmbH, we built a treebank of 4000 sentences (many containing errors), to train a genre-specific statistical model. For this task, the ERG was extended with a small set of robustness rules to explicitly license some mild but frequent instances of mismatches with the standard register defined in the ERG, such as omitted determiners or the null objects also found in recipes (Culy, 1996). The relative noisiness of this data is reflected in the lower survival rate of the resulting treebank. A typical example:

> *Park tractor on flat level surface, shut engine off and place transmission in park.*

References

Adolphs, P., Oepen, S., Callmeier, U., Crysmann, B., Flickinger, D., & Kiefer, B. (2008). Some fine points of hybrid natural language parsing. In *Proceedings of the 6th international conference on language resources and evaluation* (pp. 1380–1387). Marrakech, Morocco.

Baldwin, T., Beavers, J., Bender, E. M., Flickinger, D., Kim, A., & Oepen, S. (2005). Beauty and the beast: What running a broad-coverage precision grammar over the BNC taught us about the grammar — and the corpus. In S. Kepser & M. Reis (Eds.), *Linguistic evidence: Empirical, theoretical, and computational perspectives* (pp. 49–70). Berlin: Mouton de Gruyter.

Bender, E. M., Flickinger, D., & Oepen, S. (this volume). Grammar engineering and linguistic hypothesis testing: Computational support for complexity in syntactic analysis. In E. M. Bender & J. E. Arnold (Eds.), *Language from a cognitive perspective: Grammar, usage, and processing*. Stanford: CSLI.

Bos, J., et al. (Eds.). (2008). *COLING 2008: Proceedings of the workshop on cross-framework and cross-domain parser evaluation*. Manchester, UK: Coling 2008 Organizing Committee.

Brants, T. (2000). TnT - A statistical part-of-speech tagger. In *Proceedings of the 6th ACL conference on applied natural language processing* (pp. 224–231). Seattle, WA.

Bresnan, J. (1973). Syntax of the comparative clause construction in English. *Linguistic Inquiry, 4*, 275–343.

Bunt, H. C. (1985). *Mass terms and model theoretic semantics*. Cambridge University Press.

Butt, M., Dyvik, H., King, T. H., Masuichi, H., & Rohrer, C. (2002). The parallel grammar project. In *Proceedings of COLING-2002 workshop on grammar engineering and evaluation* (pp. 1–7).

Callmeier, U. (2000). PET — A platform for experimentation with efficient HPSG processing techniques. *Natural Language Engineering (Special Issue on Efficient Processing with HPSG), 6*(1), 99–108.

Carter, D. (1997). The TreeBanker. A tool for supervised training of parsed corpora. In *Proceedings of the workshop on computational environments for grammar development and linguistic engineering* (pp. 9–15). Madrid, Spain.

Copestake, A. (2002). *Implementing typed feature structure grammars.* Stanford, CA: CSLI Publications.

Copestake, A., & Flickinger, D. (2000). An open-source grammar development environment and broad-coverage English grammar using HPSG. In *Proceedings of the second linguistic resources and evaluation conference* (pp. 591–600). Athens, Greece.

Copestake, A., Flickinger, D., Pollard, C., & Sag, I. A. (2005). Minimal recursion semantics: An introduction. *Journal of Research on Language and Computation, 3*(4), 281–332.

Crysmann, B., Bartomeu, N., Adolphs, P., Flickinger, D., & Klüwer, T. (2008). Hybrid processing for grammar and style checking. In *Proceedings of the 22nd international conference on computational linguistics* (pp. 153–160). Manchester, England.

Culy, C. (1996). Null objects in English recipes. *Language Variation and Change, 8*, 91–124.

Culy, C. (1998). Statistical distribution and the grammatical/ungrammatical distinction. *Grammars, 1*(1), 1–13.

Flickinger, D. (2000). On building a more efficient grammar by exploiting types. *Natural Language Engineering (Special Issue on Efficient Processing with HPSG), 6*(1), 15–28.

Flickinger, D., Copestake, A., & Sag, I. A. (2000). HPSG analysis of English. In W. Wahlster (Ed.), *Verbmobil: Foundations of speech-to-speech translation* (pp. 321–330). Berlin, Germany: Springer.

Kucera, H., & Francis, W. N. (1967). *Computational analysis of present-day American English.* Brown University Press.

Lønning, J. T., Oepen, S., Beermann, D., Hellan, L., Carroll, J., Dyvik, H., et al. (2004). LOGON. A Norwegian MT effort. In *Proceedings of the workshop in recent advances in Scandinavian machine translation* (pp. 1–6). Uppsala, Sweden.

Miller, G. A., Leacock, C., Tengi, R., & Bunker, R. T. (1993). A semantic concordance. In *Proceedings of the 3rd DARPA Workshop on Human Language Technology* (pp. 303–308). Plainsboro, NJ.

Nichols, E., Bond, F., & Flickinger, D. (2005). Robust ontology acquisition from machine-readable dictionaries. In *Proceedings of the 19th international joint conference on artificial intelligence* (pp. 1111–1116). Edinburgh.

van Noord, G. (2004). Error mining for wide-coverage grammar engineering. In *Proceedings of the 42nd meeting of the Association for Computational Linguistics* (pp. 446–453). Barcelona, Spain.

Nunberg, G., Wasow, T., & Sag, I. A. (1994). Idioms. *Language, 70*, 491–538.

Oepen, S., & Carroll, J. (2000). Performance profiling for parser engineering. *Natural Language Engineering (Special Issue on Efficient Processing with HPSG), 6*(1), 81–97.

Oepen, S., Flickinger, D., Toutanova, K., & Manning, C. D. (2004). LinGO Redwoods. A rich and dynamic treebank for HPSG. *Journal of Research on Language and Computation, 2*(4), 575–596.

Oepen, S., Toutanova, K., Shieber, S., Manning, C., Flickinger, D., & Brants, T. (2002). The LinGO Redwoods treebank: Motivation and preliminary applications. In *Proceedings of the 19th international conference on computational linguistics* (pp. 1–5). Taipei, Taiwan.

Pelletier, F. J. (1975). Non-singular reference: Some preliminaries. *Philosophia, 5*, 451–465.

Pollard, C., & Sag, I. A. (1994). *Head-driven phrase structure grammar.* Chicago, IL, and Stanford, CA: The University of Chicago Press and CSLI Publications.

Riehemann, S. (2001). *A constructional approach to idioms and word formation.* Unpublished doctoral dissertation, Stanford University, Department of Linguistics.

Rupp, C., Copestake, A., Corbett, P., Murray-Rust, P., Siddharthan, A., Teufel, S., et al. (2008). Language resources and chemical informatics. In *Proceedings of the 6th international conference on language resources and evaluation* (pp. 2196–2200). Marrakech, Morocco.

Schäfer, U. (2007). *Integrating deep and shallow natural language processing components - representations and hybrid architectures.* Doctoral dissertation, Saarland University, Saarbrücken, Germany.

Toutanova, K., & Manning, C. D. (2002). Feature selection for a rich HPSG grammar using decision trees. In *Proceedings of the 6th conference on natural language learning* (pp. 1–7). Taipei, Taiwan.

Toutanova, K., Manning, C. D., Shieber, S. M., Flickinger, D., & Oepen, S. (2002). Parse disambiguation for a rich HPSG grammar. In *Proceedings of the 1st workshop on treebanks and linguistic theories* (pp. 253–263). Sozopol, Bulgaria.

Velldal, E. (2008). *Empirical realization ranking.* Unpublished doctoral dissertation, University of Oslo, Department of Informatics.

Wahlster, W. (Ed.). (2000). *Verbmobil. Foundations of speech-to-speech translation.* Berlin, Germany: Springer.

Ytrestøl, G., Flickinger, D., & Oepen, S. (2009). Extracting and annotating wikipedia sub-domains: Towards a new escience community resource. In *Proceedings of the seventh international workshop on treebanks and linguistic theory* (pp. 185–197). Groningen.

Zhang, Y. (2007). *Robust deep linguistic processing.* Doctoral dissertation, Saarland University, Saarbrücken, Germany.

Zhang, Y., & Kordoni, V. (2006). Automated deep lexical acquisition for robust open texts processing. In *Proceedings of the 5th international conference on language resources and evaluation* (pp. 275–280). Genoa, Italy.

Zhang, Y., & Kordoni, V. (2008). Robust parsing with a large HPSG grammar. In *Proceedings of the 6th international conference on language resources and evaluation* (pp. 1888–1893). Marrakech, Morocco.

Zipf, G. (1949). *Human behavior and the principle of least-effort.* Addison-Wesley.

4

Local Grammaticality in Syntactic Production

Ash Asudeh

Preface

I first met Tom in 1996 when he picked me up after dark on El Camino Real near the Stanford Shopping Center. I was a prospective student in Stanford's doctoral program in linguistics. Tom and his wife Judith had kindly offered to put me up, along with fellow prospie and Canuck, David McKercher.[†] The Wasows' hospitality was peerless and I remember being impressed at how balanced and grounded their family life seemed. Now that I have a family of my own, I realize what a striking feat that is and I often think of the Wasows as role models in this respect.

Tom is someone who I very much look up to in the fields of cognitive science and linguistics. An important aspect of his research program is the search for deep connections between linguistic theory, psycholinguistics, and computational linguistics. This includes a careful consideration of the two-way relationship between knowledge of language and its use in other cognitive systems, particularly parsing and production. I was lucky enough to serve as a research assistant on a project that Jennifer Arnold and Tom were initiating when I started my doctoral work at Stanford. The project concerned language production and that is also the topic of this paper. The paper is adapted from part of a

---

[†] I'm reasonably confident that this Canadian quarantine was just a coincidence. If not, all the more kudos to the Wasows for undertaking this potentially thankless and dangerous task.

Language from a Cognitive Perspective.
Emily M. Bender and Jennifer Arnold, Editors
Copyright © 2011, CSLI Publications.

chapter of my Stanford doctoral thesis (Asudeh, 2004). The body of the paper is quite similar to the antecedent material, but I have attempted to better contextualize the ideas in broader questions concerning the relationship between grammar and processing. In doing so, I hope to have found some closer connections to Tom's own work and ideas. I'm sure that Tom will find much to disagree with here, but I hope that he recognizes that this work is very much under the influence of and, hopefully, in the spirit of his own work, even though it concerns different research questions and empirical phenomena.

1 Introduction

Let us consider the following question:

(1) How and why do speakers systematically produce (i.e., utter) sentences that they consider ungrammatical?

Speech errors are set aside, because only systematic productions are under consideration.

There are three possible sorts of answer to this question:

1. **There are different grammars for production and parsing**. The production grammar generates the sentence, but the parsing grammar does not.

2. **The sentence is underlyingly *grammatical***. The production is licensed by the grammar, but some kind of parsing difficulty results in unacceptability.

3. **The sentence is underlyingly *ungrammatical***. The production is not licensed by the grammar, but the language processing system nevertheless yields such productions.

I reject the first answer for two reasons. First, the postulation of dual grammars for production and parsing is unparsimonious, since there will be massive redundancies between the two grammars. Second, the standard view in cognitive science is that grammars are systems of knowledge (Chomsky, 1965, 1986) and, as such, are non-directional. This is embodied most strongly in declarative linguistic theories, such as Head-Driven Phrase Structure Grammar (Pollard & Sag, 1994), the related theory of Sag, Wasow, and Bender (2003), and Lexical-Functional Grammar (Kaplan & Bresnan, 1982; Bresnan, 2001).

The main goal here is to consider the second and third answers in light of data on so-called resumptive pronouns in English. A resumptive pronoun is a normal pronoun that occurs at the base of an unbounded dependency and is interpreted as bound by an operator at the top of the dependency (McCloskey, 1979; Chao & Sells, 1983; Sells, 1984).

The pattern of grammaticality that has been reported in the theoretical literature, based on native speaker intuitions, is shown in (2) and (3).

(2)　a.*Who does Maggie like him?

　　b. Who does Maggie like __?

(3)　a.*The man who Maggie likes him is here.

　　b. The man who Maggie likes __ is here.

The version of each sentence with the resumptive has been reported as ungrammatical, in contrast to the grammatical version with a gap in place of the resumptive (Chao & Sells, 1983; Sells, 1984). This contrasts with various other languages, e.g. Hebrew and Irish, in which the version with the resumptive is perfectly grammatical (McCloskey, 1990, 2006). In such languages, the version with the gap is typically also grammatical, although the pattern varies depending on the grammatical function. Further evidence for the distinct status of English resumptives stems from their interpretation, which is distinct from the 'bound variable interpretation' (using this term pretheoretically) that grammaticized resumptives receive (Chao & Sells, 1983). For a recent overview of resumption, see McCloskey (2006).

These theoretical claims have been corroborated experimentally. A series of psycholinguistic studies, using various methodologies, have found that English native speakers reject examples like (2a) and (3a) as significantly worse than their gap alternants (McDaniel & Cowart, 1999; Alexopoulou & Keller, 2002, 2007; Swets & Ferreira, 2003; Ferreira & Swets, 2005).

These studies show that participants did not even prefer resumptives in island conditions in which the corresponding gaps were also degraded,[1] as in the following pair from Alexopoulou and Keller (2007, 117):

(4)　a. Who does Jane think that Mary meets the people that will fire __?

　　b. Who does Jane think that Mary meets the people that will fire him?

---

[1]Philip Hofmeister (p.c.) suggests that there may be a ceiling effect in some of these results. However, the Alexopoulou and Keller (2007) findings show significant preference for gaps over resumptives in English in almost every experimental condition and never any preference for resumptives. This indicates that, even if the gap acceptability is hitting some kind of ceiling, the resumptives are still less grammatical, since they fall significantly short of the acceptability ceiling.

Alexopoulou and Keller (2002, 2007) studied resumptive pronouns in islands using Magnitude Estimation (Stevens, 1956, 1975; Bard, Robertson, & Sorace, 1996), which allows subjects to construct their own scale instead of imposing a forced scale. They found that islands have a significant effect on grammaticality of filler-gap extraction, as expected (Alexopoulou & Keller, 2007, 118–119). They also found that, no matter the level of embedding (single or double), resumptives do not improve the grammaticality of extraction from an island, whether the island is a weak island or is a strong island, as in the examples above. That is, sentences like (4b) were not judged as significantly more grammatical than sentences like (4a). These results have recently been replicated for complex noun phrase islands and relative clause islands by Heestand, Xiang, and Polinsky (to appear). McDaniel and Cowart (1999) also studied resumptive pronouns in islands using Magnitude Estimation and similarly found no significant improvement of grammaticality of resumptive pronouns over gaps, although they did find an improvement of pronoun over gap in Comp-trace configurations (e.g., *That's the girl that I wonder when *__/?she met you*).

Ferreira and Swets (2005) ran two grammaticality judgment experiments, one of which presented stimuli visually and the other auditorily. Participants were asked to rate sentences like the island resumptive (5) and its corresponding control item (6) on a forced scale of 1 (perfect) to 5 (awful) for acceptability in English.

(5) This is a donkey that I don't know where it lives

(6) This is a donkey that doesn't know where it lives.

In the visual presentation, resumptive sentences like (5) received average ratings of 3.3, while control sentences received average ratings of 1.9. The difference was confirmed by the auditory presentation, where the average ratings were 3.0 (resumptive) and 1.7 (control). Both pairs of means were significantly different. These results are all the more noteworthy, because the participants who rate the resumptive island sentences as degraded in comprehension are from a population that reliably produces them, as we will see in section 3 below.

The second answer to (1)—that utterances like (2a) and (3a) are grammatical but induce parsing difficulties that render them unacceptable—is not compelling in light of these theoretical and experimental findings. It raises more questions than it answers. First, the utterances in (2) and (3) are grammatically very simple: the only difference between the ungrammatical resumptive version and the grammatical gap version is the very presence of the resumptive. What a priori reason is there to assume that the pronoun is difficult enough to parse that it renders such sentences ungrammatical? It is not an option to claim that computing the identity of the pronoun's binder is to blame, because this same computation must take place with respect to the binding involved in the gap alternant. Furthermore, why would we not assume that an overt pronoun is in fact easier to identify than a covert gap? We might expect the parser to find it easier to identify the presence of something than an absence.

At this point, it is important to address a possible misconception with respect to answer two. On the face of it, the claim seems to be the very standard one that not all grammatical sentences will be acceptable, as evidenced by the famous case of center embeddings (Chomsky & Miller, 1963), such as (7).

(7)   The rat the cat the dog chased bit died.

The standard claim about center embeddings is that they are generated by the grammar, but are so difficult to process that they are not produced and are perceived as ungrammatical. In contrast, answer two claims that English resumptive sentences are not just generated by the grammar, but are also produced (i.e., uttered), yet constitute a problem for parsing.

Another problem with answer two is that it commits us to the claim that other languages, e.g. Hebrew or Irish, likewise have grammars that generate the equivalents of the degraded English examples, but that the parsers of Hebrew and Irish speakers somehow deal with these utterances better (since their Hebrew and Irish equivalents are not judged as ungrammatical). However, parsers are typically thought of as capacities of speakers, not of grammars. Therefore, it would be an unusual claim that parsers are parametrized to grammars. It is certainly possible, but in the absence of an explicit theory of how this would work, this remains a problematic implication for answer two.

Answer two is thus not a promising answer to question (1). This leaves answer three, which states that things are essentially as they seem: English resumptives are judged as ungrammatical, because they in fact are ungrammatical. The remaining concern is whether we can make sense of how such utterances can nevertheless be produced by the processing system. In what follows, I present a theory of production that offers an explanation. The key assumption of the production model is that incremental production concentrates on local well-formedness over global well-formedness. The linguistic theory that I assume is Lexical-Functional Grammar (LFG; Kaplan & Bresnan, 1982, Bresnan, 2001, Dalrymple, 2001), but the aspects of LFG that are of central importance are shared by other constraint-based theories, such as HPSG (Pollard

& Sag, 1994; Sag et al., 2003). It should therefore be possible to adapt the proposed production model to work with other constraint-based architectures.

2   The Production Model

The 'Correspondence Architecture' of LFG assumes that distinct linguistic representations are present in parallel and related to each other by correspondence functions that map elements of one representation to elements of another (Kaplan, 1987, 1989; Halvorsen & Kaplan, 1988; Asudeh, 2004, 2006; Asudeh & Toivonen, 2009). The key syntactic representations in this architecture are constituent structure (c-structure) and functional structure (f-structure). C-structure represents word order, dominance and constituency, as modelled by a standard (non-tangled) tree; see the left side of (8). F-structure represents more abstract aspects of syntax, such as predication and grammatical functions, null pronominals, and local and unbounded dependencies. F-structure is modelled as a feature structure; see the right side of (8). The ϕ correspondence function maps elements of c-structure to elements of f-structure, as exemplified in (8).

(8)

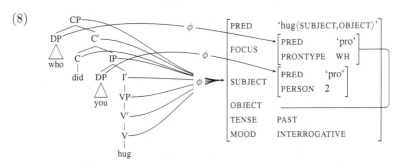

I assume that production is incremental (Levelt, 1989; Kempen & Hoenkamp, 1987). The simplified production model that I propose, based on Levelt (1989), is shown in Figure 1.

The incrementality of the model is based on the ability of LFG grammars to handle fragments—what Bresnan (2001, 79–81) refers to as the "fragmentability of language". The need to deal with fragments has been recognized in LFG since the theory's foundation (Kaplan & Bresnan, 1982) and is also implemented in the major computational treatment of LFG, the Xerox Linguistic Environment (Crouch et al., 2009). Bresnan points out that LFG grammars can characterize the internal structural relations of sentence fragments and differentiate between informative fragments and others. She contrasts the fragment

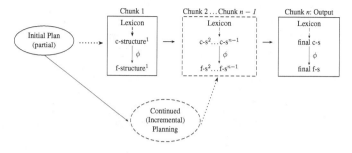

FIGURE 1 The production model

... *seems to* ..., as in (9a), with the fragment ... *to by for* ..., as in (10).

(9) a. [Speaker A:] And he agrees?
     [Speaker B:] — seems to.

(10) The one he should be spoken to by, for God's sake, is his mother.

Bresnan shows that the fragment *seems to* constructs an informative partial c-structure and f-structure, which form subparts of the c-structure and f-structure for a full sentence like *He seems to agree*, whereas the fragment *to by for* constructs only three unrelated structures. Bresnan (2001, 81) notes that the ability to construct informative fragments stems from the fact that the main predicator or head of a c-structure/f-structure (e.g., *seems* in this case) contains a lot of information about the larger structures in which it can be embedded.

3 The Problem of English Resumptives

Creswell (2002) investigates the problems raised by the production of English sentences containing resumptive pronouns in islands, from the perspective of Tree-Adjoining Grammar (Joshi, Levy, & Takahashi, 1975; Kroch & Joshi, 1985; Frank, 2002). She considers a proposal by Kroch (1981) that assumes an incremental model of speech production that generates a filler, such as a *wh*-phrase, before planning of the sentence has been completed. As production proceeds, the speaker finds that the intended base position of the filler-gap dependency is in an island or would violate the *that*-trace filter/Empty Category Principle (ECP). An NP is inserted to avoid the violation. Kroch (1981) notes that insertion of an epithet is also possible, as in (11), and therefore does not claim that the inserted element is necessarily a resumptive pronoun.

(11)   There was one prisoner that we didn't understand why <u>the guy</u>
       was even in jail.
       (Kroch, 1981, 129, (13a))

Kroch's proposal is essentially that some NP, typically a pronoun, is inserted to avoid a grammatical violation that is caused by poor planning.
Creswell (2002) does not adopt Kroch's proposal, in light of theoretical tensions it would have with developments in TAG theory. I will
return to Creswell's own proposal, but I first want to introduce some
psycholinguistic evidence which is relevant to construction of the production model. The data also calls into question Kroch's planning-based
proposal.

Ferreira and Swets tested the production of resumptive pronouns
in *wh*-islands by native speakers of English (Swets & Ferreira, 2003;
Ferreira & Swets, 2005). They used a self-paced experimental design
in which subjects were required to complete (in full sentences) partial descriptions that were presented with a picture array. The target
sentences were sentences such as:

(12)   This is a donkey that I don't know where <u>it</u> lives.

Two control targets were also elicited. The first kind controlled for
surface length:

(13)   This is a donkey that doesn't know where it lives.

The second kind controlled for length of the *wh*-dependency without
an island violation:

(14)   This is a donkey that I didn't say lives in Brazil.

They also ran a preliminary grammaticality judgement experiment
(both auditory and visual presentation), which I discussed in section 1.
To sum up that discussion, the grammaticality judgement task showed
that subjects rated the resumptive sentences as worse than the structural length controls and this comports with independent experimental
findings (McDaniel & Cowart, 1999; Alexopoulou & Keller, 2002, 2007).

Ferreira and Swets conducted two versions of the production experiment. In the first experiment, subjects were under no pressure to begin
speaking quickly. In the second, subjects were under pressure to begin
speaking quickly due to a deadline procedure (Ferreira & Swets, 2002).
If the resumptive pronouns in *wh*-islands were a result of lack of planning, as in Kroch's theory, then, given enough time, speakers should
plan the utterance to avoid both the island violation and the resumptive
pronoun. For example, a subject could construct the following sentence
instead of (12):

(15)   This is a donkey and I don't know where it lives.

Subjects instead overwhelmingly produced island violations like (12) in both experiments. In the no-deadline experiment, where subjects could take as much time as they needed to plan their utterance before speaking and typically took over 2 seconds to begin, 47.3% of the targets produced for the *wh*-island condition consisted of an island containing a resumptive, as in (12). Subjects did not use the extra time in the no-deadline experiment to plan an utterance that avoids a resumptive pronoun. In fact, the proportion of island-resumptive sentences decreased to 39.4% in the deadline experiment. The biggest increase in the deadline experiment was in well-formed sentences that were not targets, like *I don't know where this donkey lives.* Swets and Ferreira (2003) conclude that despite rating the island-resumptive sentences as ungrammatical, speakers plan to produce them. They sketch a TAG solution for generating the island-resumptive sentences and speculate that the reason that the structures are rejected, despite being produced, is that "the production and comprehension systems may set different parameters for accepting these structures" (Swets & Ferreira, 2003). The crux of the proposal is that the elementary trees required for producing the island-resumptives are part of the grammar and that the grammar therefore treats island-resumptive sentences as well-formed (in terms of production). They must countenance the fact that certain grammatical forms are for some reason rejected in comprehension, but this is known to be true in any case (e.g., center embedding). Their proposal contains elements of both answers one and two: they posit different grammars for production and parsing and they claim that island-resumptives are underlyingly grammatical for the production grammar.

Creswell (2002) also arrives at the conclusion that the grammar produces the island-resumptive structures, but for theoretical reasons. She observes that the TAG theory of Frank (2002) does not permit generation of the trees necessary for island violations and notes that TAG-based models of incremental production (Ferreira, 2000; Frank & Badecker, 2001) do not permit Kroch's solution for the island-resumptive structures:

> In this model of production where we assume that a speaker only has grammatical resources with which to work, we cannot use Kroch's explanation of the appearance of resumptive pronouns in island-violation contexts. The resources needed to produce the island-violating structures are not available in the grammar that licenses the set of tree building blocks. On the face of it then, it seems that the existence of resumptive pronouns in island violating contexts would prove devastating for this model of sentence production. Based on the assumptions

that 1) the processing system has only grammatically-licensed trees with which to create larger structures and 2) the structures needed to extract from island-violation contexts are not grammatically-licensed, speakers could not be remedying violations that should not even be created given their underlying grammars. (Creswell, 2002, 103)

Creswell (2002) argues that in fact the grammars of English speakers must independently have the resources required to form island-resumptive structures.

The basis of Creswell's argument is the observation that resumptive pronouns in English can be found in relative clauses even in non-island structures (Prince, 1990):

(16) You get a rack that the bike will sit on it.
      (Prince, 1990, (15d))

(17) I have a friend who she does all the platters.
      (Prince, 1990, (4c))

These and other examples that Prince (1990) presents are attested examples produced by native speakers. Prince (1990) analyzes this kind of resumptive as a discourse pronoun (in opposition to a bound variable, such as a gap or bound pronoun). This is essentially the solution of Sells (1984) for English resumptive pronouns (which he dubs *intrusive pronouns*). Erteschik-Shir (1992) develops a very similar theory for certain Hebrew resumptives. Further evidence for the discourse pronoun status of the resumptives in (16) and (17) comes from the fact that they can be replaced by non-coreferential pronouns or even full NPs that serve similar discourse functions (Prince, 1990, (34a–d)):

(18) I had a handout and notes from her talk that that was lost too.

(19) He's got this lifelong friend who he takes money from the parish to give to this lifelong friend.

(20) I have a manager, Joe Scandolo, who we've been together over twenty years.

(21) You assigned me to a paper which I don't know anything about the subject.

In the first example, we have a singular deictic pronoun that does not even properly agree in number with its plural discourse antecedent. In the second example, the discourse antecedent is repeated in its entirety. In the third, the resumptive takes as its discourse antecedent the generally available speaker discourse marker (in construction with the marker for *Joe Scandolo* to form the plural antecedent). In the last example, the form that is used is a relational noun that takes as its implicit argument the antecedent *a paper*. As a native speaker of English, I find all of the examples in (16) to (21), especially these last four, quite ungrammatical. But I have produced similar examples and have heard other native speakers do so, too.

4 English Resumptives as the Result of Prioritized Local Well-Formedness

The solution I propose incorporates elements of the proposals of Kroch (1981), Creswell (2002), Swets and Ferreira (2003), and Ferreira and Swets (2005) into the production model in Figure 1, but it is ultimately significantly different from these previous proposals. I will first present the proposal and show how it explains the production of ungrammatical forms. Afterwards I will relate the proposal to the other production proposals of Creswell and Ferreira and Swets discussed above, identifying the similarities and differences. The major distinction to bear in mind is that my proposal does *not* treat the resumptive pronoun outputs of production in either the island examples or the discourse examples as grammatical.

Based on a consideration of various experimental results, Levelt (1989, 258) notes that

> Taken together, these findings are supportive of the notion that the rhythm of grammatical encoding follows the semantic joints of a message—its function/argument structure—rather than syntactic joints. It is the partitioning of the message to be expressed that a speaker is attending to, and this (co-)determines the rhythm of grammatical encoding.

The function/argument structure that Levelt refers to, which encodes planning units at the *message* level, is a rough thematic structure similar to the Conceptual Semantics of Jackendoff (1990, 1997, among others). The outline of my proposal, which is compatible with (a simplified version of) Levelt's theory, is as follows. When a speaker begins initial planning s/he puts together a message that identifies the event or state, its basic function, the function's arguments and their rough thematic relation to each other and then identifies what sort of utterance s/he wants to make with respect to these elements. S/he may declare something, ask something, etc. This rough thematic structure unfolds through the incremental construction of fragments of grammatical structure that are added to the grammatical structure that initiates implementation of the speaker's message plan. Incremental production is based on the subcategorization requirements of heads, which is lexically encoded and will in general bear a close relationship to the function/argument structure of the planning unit. Incrementality of production is thus based on producing successive chunks that are integrated into what has already been produced. Each successive chunk of grammatical representation must be *locally* grammatical in order to be generated by the grammar. This results in incremental generation of a grammatical structure that satisfies local grammaticality requirements at each incremental step but whose end result does not necessarily satisfy global grammaticality requirements. The key idea is that satisfaction of local well-formedness takes precedence over satisfaction of global well-formedness in processing. My proposal concerns production, but this prioritization of local over global well-formedness has been previously demonstrated in parsing (Tabor, Galantucci, & Richardson, 2004).

The interaction of the incremental production model with the theory of unbounded dependencies provides another important part of the explanation of English resumptives. I assume the LFG theory of unbounded dependencies initially developed by Kaplan and Zaenen (1989). The most relevant aspect of this theory is that the unbounded dependency is launched at the top of the dependency and searches 'downwards/inwards' for a gap (or resumptive pronoun in syntactically-licensed binder-resumptive dependencies). This is captured in terms of an *outside-in* functional uncertainty of the form ($\uparrow$ ... GF), where $\uparrow$ represents the top of the dependency and GF represents the gap at f-structure. The ellipsis represents possible path continuations. Island constraints and other constraints on extraction are stated by modifying the path or by stating off-path constraints on the path (e.g., $\neg$ ($\rightarrow$ SUBJ) could be used to indicate that the path cannot pass through an f-structure that contains a SUBJECT). LFG is a declarative, monostratal theory of grammar. In terms of statements of grammatical well-formedness there is no real directionality in the theory, just declarative constraints. As such, there is no sense in which *in the grammar* there is a downward search for a gap. However, production and parsing are irreducibly directional and each must start with the material that is to be produced or parsed first. It is uncontroversial that production and parsing must go in the direction of the speech stream, not in the opposite direction. In other words, although LFG as a declarative theory does not have a notion of procedural grammatical generation, it is clear that production and parsing, if they are to be incremental, are procedural and involve notions of timing. Indeed, the procedurality of production and parsing and the question of timing of grammatical operations are central to psycholinguistics (for overviews from different perspectives, see Frazier & Clifton, 1996; Frazier, 1999; MacDonald & Seidenberg, 2006; Gompel & Pickering, 2007).

Given these facts of production and parsing and given the top-down theory of unbounded dependencies, there is an important consequence for the construction of locally well-formed grammatical representations. As the chunk that contains the unbounded dependency enters construction for production, the top of the unbounded dependency contributes the outside-in equation that initiates a search for an empty grammatical function (GF). This GF will be functionally equated with the filler, thus integrating filler and gap. But notice that what we pretheoretically call a gap does not leave a marker that actually identifies the presence of a gap in any of the local structures. There in fact is no gap. There is nothing: just an absence of structure at c-structure and an absence of a grammatical function at f-structure. This has a crucial implication for incremental construction of fragments. The outside-in function contributed by the filler is unbounded and defines a path through f-structure material that might continue to be incrementally constructed. If the grammar cannot integrate the filler into the local f-structure being constructed because all grammatical functions are locally filled, it should not automatically fail, because the integration site could be in the next chunk of f-structure that is yet to be constructed or in the chunk after that. The one case where this is not true is when there is an island, because then the functional uncertainty terminates unsuccessfully; I will return to this shortly. The fundamental point is this: the unbounded nature of the functional uncertainty equation, the fact that it is initiated at the top of the unbounded dependency, and the fact that the gap is not marked in the local f-structure together mean that it is reasonable to assume, in a model of incremental production and parsing, that integration of the filler by the grammar takes place after the local structure under construction has been built.

In constructing a local structure, the production system can do one of two things with each GF. First, it can leave the GF empty, to be licensed by integration of a filler. A filler must be functionally equated with this GF before moving on to the next chunk, or else the local structure would not be well-formed. Recall that the processing model assumes that incremental production and parsing construct locally well-formed structures. The second thing the production system can do is to posit lexical material, such as a pronoun or NP, that will add its information to the GF and which is consistent with the other specifications of the local structure. For example, in English, if the GF in question is an OBJ, if a pronoun is inserted, it must have accusative case. Whatever lexical material is chosen to fulfill the local requirements for the GF must also be consistent with the current plan. If this option is chosen, the filler is not integrated but the local structure is well-formed. The filler continues along its path looking for a gap.

The two possibilities are shown in (22a) and (22b). I use UDF (for 'unbounded dependency function') to generalize over the standard LFG grammatical functions for unbounded dependencies (FOCUS and TOPIC).

(22)

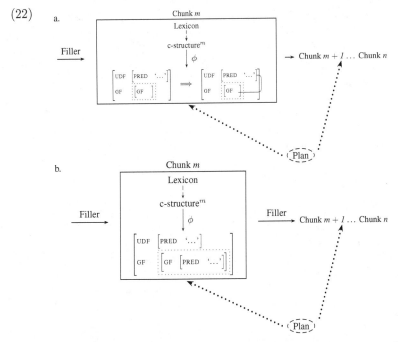

Diagram (22a) shows what happens when the filler is locally integrated. Diagram (22b) shows what happens if the filler is passed through the local structure, rather than being integrated, and some contentful lexical material is inserted instead. The second pattern is the relevant one for explaining how ungrammatical resumptives/epithets/deictics are generated instead of a gap.

The Prince (1990) example in (16) is particularly appropriate for demonstrating the theory, because it is syntactically quite simple. Its lack of structural complexity underscores the fact that my account of production does not depend on complexity to explain the Prince and Kroch examples. The issue of complexity (with respect to resumptive pronouns) is discussed in Asudeh (2004, 317–344). Example (16) is repeated here:

(23)   You get a rack that the bike will sit on <u>it</u>.

The production begins as in (24). The local structure under construction is indicated by the dashed box. I have represented the planned message rather informally. I do not claim that entire utterances are planned in advance—that would no longer be a Levelt-style model. However, the findings of Ferreira and Swets (2005) indicate that the production system plans at least far enough in advance to include a message of this length and complexity in the initial plan, because subjects produced syntactically more complex utterances than this in the experiment with the deadline condition.

(24)

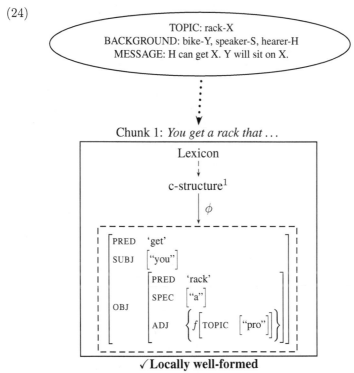

✓ **Locally well-formed**

The first fragment that is constructed consists of the head *get* and its arguments. I have assumed that construction of the relative clause also begins at this stage. This seems reasonable given that the relative pronoun may be prosodically grouped with the relative head (unlike in a non-restrictive relative). This chunk is locally well-formed, since all of *get*'s arguments are locally filled.

At this point an unbounded dependency has been launched due to the relative pronoun. This is represented by the TOPIC 'pro' in the innermost f-structure f in (24). The unbounded dependency functional uncertainty that is initiated by the relative pronoun is carried over to construction of the next chunk. The details of the functional uncertainty equation need not concern us here yet, but will be taken up on p. 70 when we look at islands.[2] All that needs to be represented at this point is how much of the path has been encountered. In this case, we are still in the functional-structure where the dependency was launched, (arbitrarily) labelled f. The up arrow meta-variable in the outside-in functional uncertainty is set to f and the path encountered so far is therefore $(f \ldots)$, where I again use the ellipsis to indicate material yet to be discovered.

During construction of the next chunk, the production system can choose either of the options outlined in (22a) and (22b). If the first option is taken, the filler is integrated into the local structure being constructed and the relative clause is constructed with a gap:

(25)   You get a rack that the bike will sit on.

The construction of the local structure is shown here:

(26)

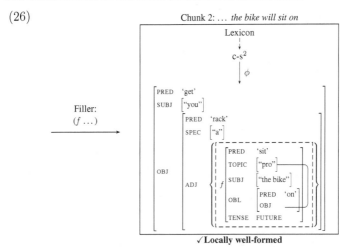

✓ Locally well-formed

The filler is integrated into the local structure, the path $(f \ldots)$ being resolved as $(f \text{ OBL OBJ})$. This satisfies both the demands of the filler and the local demand that the OBJ must be integrated into the f-structure. The overall construction of the sentence is illustrated here:

(27)

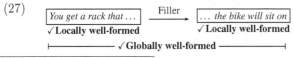

---

[2]See also Dalrymple, 2001, p. 404

Each of the local structures here is well-formed and consistent with the plan and the overall result is also globally well-formed.

If in constructing the local material in Chunk 2 the production system exercises the option, sketched in (22b), of inserting lexical material that is consistent with the plan, rather than leaving the GF empty for integration with the filler, then the Prince example (23) is produced instead. The local structure under construction is again shown in the dashed box. Notice that the pronoun *it* has been inserted as the prepositional object.

(28)

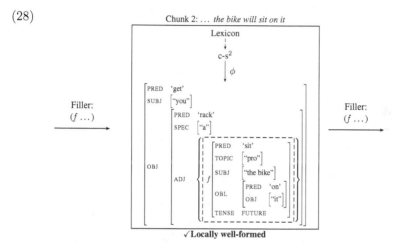

After construction of the local structure in the dashed box, the production system passes the filler on and attempts to continue. Having passed up the opportunity to integrate the filler, there is no longer anywhere to put it. There is no remaining structure to be built and insertion of the filler in the structure built so far is impossible. The situation is shown here:

(29)

The grammar ultimately fails to sanction the structure that has been attempted. Crucially though, due to incremental production, the ungrammatical sentence has been *uttered*. At each stage of producing (23), incremental production results in local grammaticality. The result of production is however globally ungrammatical and is perceived as such by native speakers. The perception of ungrammaticality does not arise through production, but rather through parsing. What the parser does with the result of productions like (23) is considered in Asudeh (2004, 317–344).

The account of production that I have been giving here requires the grammar to incrementally deliver locally well-formed structures. The incremental construction of grammatical structure starts from an initial plan and then continues in lockstep with incremental planning. One might wonder whether the construction of locally well-formed grammatical structures of the kind allowed by (22b)—which is what leads to the construction of sentences like *You get a rack that the bike will sit on it*—is constrained at all. In a sense the question is whether examples like this sentence and the others above are speech errors. I argue here that they should not be regarded as speech errors. First, they are constrained at the level of local grammatical structure by the kinds of local structure that can be well-formed. For example, in constructing the sentence *You get a rack that the bike will sit on it*, insertion of a pronoun as the object of *on* is locally licensed by the rule that constructs PPs, the lexical requirements of *on* which require an OBJ, the fact that the OBJ of *on* must be realized by an NP, etc. If local grammatical well-formedness is a criterion, then speakers could not instead produce things like *You get a rack that the bike will sit it*. To the extent that this kind of form is produced at all, it really is a speech error. But that must be distinguished from locally well-formed structures that arise from purely incremental production. Second, the kinds of things that can be inserted are constrained by the plan itself. If the speaker wants to say something about a rack, then s/he will select a lexical item that is consistent with that plan. In English, the kinds of lexical items that are consistent with the plan are pronouns (*it*), deictics (*that*), names and definite descriptions that refer to the requisite element (*the rack*), and epithets (*the damn thing*). This is part of what prevents the production system from producing examples like the following, which Creswell (2002, 106, (11–12)) worries about:

(30)   the police officer who John prefers spinach

(31)   the smell that my mom is baking bread

Firstly, bare nouns like *spinach* do not have the correct semantic properties to be used referentially. A plan to say something about a police officer would not lead to insertion of *spinach*. Creswell (2002, 106) also notes that phrases like the second one are grammatical in Japanese and Korean (see, e.g., Matsumoto, 1997). I agree with her position that the pragmatic discourse conditions that determine the discourse relation between the relative head and the material in the relative clause must be subject to some cross-linguistic variation. That is a fact about *grammars* though, not the production system.

The case remaining to be dealt with is island violations like the Ferreira and Swets (2005) donkey example, repeated here, or the attested example in (33).

(32)   This is a donkey that I don't know where <u>it</u> lives.

(33)   You have the top 20% that are just doing incredible service, and then you have the group in the middle that a high percentage of <u>those</u> are giving you a good day's work ...
(Creswell, 2002, 102, (4d); `http://www.ssa.gov/history/WEIKEL.html`[3])

The explanation of these cases basically reduces to the cases that we have already looked at plus the fact that the island prevents integration of the filler.

I will illustrate the analysis of the island cases with the simpler donkey example. Production starts as follows:

---

[3] The original URL is no longer functional, but see `http://web.archive.org/web/20041217051431/http://www.ssa.gov/history/WEIKEL.html`; retrieved 23/9/2009.

(34)

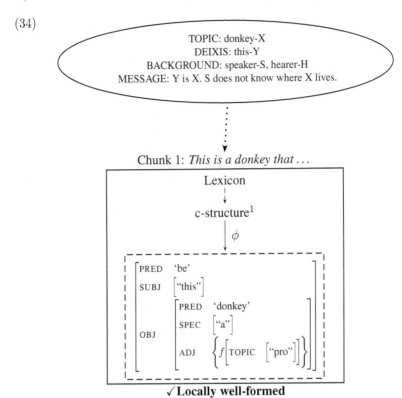

Chunk 1: *This is a donkey that ...*

√ **Locally well-formed**

An unbounded dependency is once again launched by the relative pronoun. Island constraints in versions of LFG that use outside-in functional uncertainty for filler-gap dependencies are stated through limitations on paths—either by limiting the grammatical functions in the path itself or by limiting the environments of these grammatical functions through off-path constraints (for further details on this kind of functional uncertainty, see Dalrymple, 2001, 389ff.). Let us assume that the *wh*-island constraint is stated as an off-path equation to the effect that the functional uncertainty cannot pass through a COMP that contains a UDF, where UDF ≡ FOCUS ∨ TOPIC. A simplified version of the functional uncertainty that the TOPIC initiates is shown here:

(35) $(\uparrow \text{TOPIC}) = (\uparrow \quad \text{COMP}^* \quad \text{GF})$
$$\neg (\rightarrow \text{UDF})$$

The equation states that the grammatical function to be equated with the TOPIC can be found by going through zero or more COMP f-structures, but none of the COMP f-structures may have an unbounded dependency function of their own. This is an oversimplification, but it captures the case at hand. After construction of the first chunk, the TOPIC has not been integrated and the beginning of the path has already been instantiated to one COMP.

I assume for simplicity that the next chunk is the remainder of the sentence. Nothing hinges on this. In producing the next chunk, the production system constructs the following partial local structure (indicated by the dotted box):

(36)

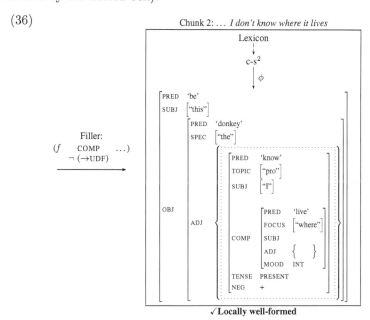

√ Locally well-formed

At this point, the production system still has an unintegrated unbounded dependency and now it has encountered a new one. The option of positing a gap for the most deeply embedded SUBJ, as in (22a) is not possible. The presence of the embedded FOCUS (a UDF) means that there is no way to locally satisfy the TOPIC's functional uncertainty equation. In fact there is no way to satisfy the equation, period: as soon as a COMP containing a UDF is encountered, satisfaction is impossible. The result is that the only way to construct a locally well-formed f-structure is to exercise the option in (22b) of inserting some lexical material that is consistent with the plan (i.e., that refers to the donkey). The filler does not pass through the chunk, though, because there is no way for it to do so and satisfy its equation. The new unbounded dependency also needs to be integrated and this can done using option (22a).

The final local structure is shown here in the dashed box:

(37)

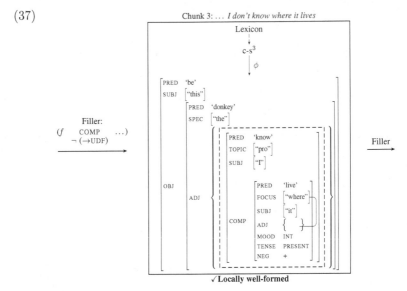

Since the local structure is an island, there is no way for the filler to be integrated. The situation is sketched here:

(38)

Once again, the grammar ultimately fails to sanction the structure that has been attempted. However, the sentence is uttered due to incremental production.

5   Conclusion

I have shown how a production model that is based on incremental planning and production can account for the production of both resumptives in non-islands, as in (39), and resumptives in islands, as in (40).

(39)   You get a rack that the bike will sit on it.

(40)   This is a donkey that I don't know where it lives.

A number of features of LFG were used in the production model. The ability of the theory to construct locally well-formed fragments (Bresnan, 2001) was the basis for incremental construction of structure. This ability of the grammatical theory to construct fragments is also fundamental to the Tree-Adjoining Grammar analyses of Creswell (2002) and Swets and Ferreira (2003). The filler-driven theory of unbounded-dependencies provided the basis for the assumption about the timing of production, according to which local structures are constructed before filler-integration is attempted.

We can now attempt to answer the main question posed at the beginning of the paper, based on the theory developed for English resumptives. The question is repeated here:

(41) How and why do speakers systematically produce (i.e., utter) sentences that they consider ungrammatical?

The answer to the 'how' part of the question is that globally ill-formed utterances can be produced through incremental construction of locally well-formed structures. The answer to the 'why' part is that such utterances are produced because speakers attempt to locally well-formed structures that are consistent with the message plan. The productions are nevertheless rejected as ungrammatical, because although they result from incremental production of locally well-formed structures, they are globally ill-formed according to the grammar (for further details, see Asudeh, 2004, p. 317–344).

The resulting account is broadly similar to that of Kroch (1981), in the sense that it denies a formal grammatical treatment of the phenomenon and instead localizes in the production system the phenomenon of producing resumptive pronouns that are not grammatically sanctioned by the language. A key difference between this account and Kroch's is that his account depended on lack of planning while this account does not. The findings of Ferreira and Swets (2005) indicate that these resumptives cannot simply be due to poor planning, because they occur even in the no-deadline condition. The theory that I have presented respects this subsequent finding and explains how the resumptives could be produced in accordance with a plan, even though they are grammatically ill-formed.

This sets the theory apart from those of Creswell (2002) and Swets and Ferreira (2003). They capture these data by letting them be grammatically well-formed. This fails to explain native speakers' judgements that the resulting forms are not actually grammatical. While it is true that there are grammatical forms that are nevertheless perceived to be ungrammatical, such as center embeddings, the sort of explanation that is offered for those cases cannot be readily extended to the resumptive cases. The basic explanation for the perceived ungrammaticality of center embedding is that the perception arises because they are hard to parse (see Gibson, 1998, for an overview). There is no metric of complexity that would account for the perceived ungrammaticality of a simple Prince example like (39). A proponent of the view that such examples are grammatical might be tempted to claim that they are perceived as ungrammatical precisely because the corresponding gap sentence is grammatical. This would constitute a transderivational explanation of a sort that has been proposed for syntactic resumptives (Shlonsky, 1992; Aoun, Choueiri, & Hornstein, 2001). There are two problems with this view. The first is that if resumptive pronouns in English are grammatically generated and if they are avoided due to corresponding sentences with gaps, then there is no explanation for the fact that languages with demonstrably grammaticized resumptive pronouns allow their resumptives to occur where gaps occur (in some but not all environments) without loss of perceived grammaticality. Second, the island examples without the resumptive pronoun are not perceived as grammatical and neither are the sentences with the resumptive pronoun, according to the findings of Ferreira and Swets (Swets & Ferreira, 2003; Ferreira & Swets, 2005) and other findings (McDaniel & Cowart, 1999; Alexopoulou & Keller, 2002, 2003, 2007).

Creswell (2002) notes that the view that English resumptives are generated grammatically rather than through production is a result of the current understanding of islands in Tree-Adjoining Grammar (Frank, 2002). Naturally, the theory will undergo revisions that might remove this problem. In the meantime, though, it is useful to localize the point of divergence between LFG and TAG (and other relevantly similar theories) that allows the account developed here to avoid the problem. The key difference between the model of TAG that Creswell (2002) has in mind and the model of LFG that I have been assuming is how the theories handle islands. In the TAG theory, islands are defined *internally* to the island (Frank, 2002, 199ff.), as in the phase approach in the Minimalist Program (Chomsky, 2000, 2001) and the subjacency approach of Principles and Parameters Theory (Chomsky, 1986). There is something about the local structure that constitutes the island that is wrong. This can mean either that the relevant sort of structure cannot be constructed in the first place, as in TAG, or that the relevant sort of structure is constructed but there is no way for the filler to exit it, due to a phase boundary (MP) or a bounding node (P&P). In the theory I have presented, following Kaplan and Zaenen (1989) and Dalrymple (2001), islands are defined *externally* to the island, through constraints on outside-in functional uncertainty. This means that the local structure that in fact constitutes the island is not necessarily ill-formed locally. The difference in how islands are constructed and defined is deeply related to whether the grammar treats filler-gap dependencies as gap-driven or filler-driven. The ideas in this paper could therefore likely be extended to other theories that have a filler-driven approach to filler-gap dependencies, such as Categorial Grammar (Steedman, 1987; Morrill, 1994), or to approaches that have a mixed system, such as Head-Driven Phrase Structure Grammar (Pollard & Sag, 1994; Bouma, Malouf, & Sag, 2001; Sag et al., 2003).

The proposal developed here is programmatic in many respects. The claims about the production system in particular need to be tested experimentally. Two particularly important issues in this regard have been suggested to me by Peter Sells and Neal Snider (p.c.). Neal Snider points out that the answer to the 'why' part of question (1) also depends on a precise theory of the production mechanisms for producing underlyingly ungrammatical resumptive pronominals (and other intrusive nominals), especially since the Ferreira and Swets results show that planning pressures are not the cause. Peter Sells raises an important question that has import for both linguistic theory and psycholinguistics: what is the size of the chunks to which the requirement of local grammaticality applies? On the theoretical side, question (1) leads to the further question of how to properly factor out adjuncts in capturing local grammaticality. On the psycholinguistic side, the answer to this question likely dovetails with results concerning local grammaticality in parsing (e.g., Tabor et al., 2004) and with answers to the much broader question of how the linguistic system interfaces with other cognitive systems, such as memory and attention.

Acknowledgements

I would like to thank the following people for helpful comments and suggestions on this paper: Jennifer Arnold, Emily Bender, Joan Bresnan, Philip Hofmeister, Florian Jaeger, Peter Sells, Neal Snider, Mike Tanenhaus, and audiences at Carleton University, the Linguistics Association of Great Britain, the University of Canterbury and the University of Rochester. Peter and Neal provided particularly incisive comments on some of the paper's fundamental questions and claims. A special thanks to Tom Wasow, for providing feedback on the chapter from my Ph.D. thesis on which this paper is based. Any remaining errors are my own.

References

Alexopoulou, T., & Keller, F. (2002). Resumption and locality: A crosslinguistic experimental study. In M. Andronis, E. Debenport, A. Pycha, & K. Yoshimura (Eds.), *CLS 38: The main session* (Vol. 1, pp. 1–14). Chicago, IL: Chicago Linguistic Society.

Alexopoulou, T., & Keller, F. (2003). Linguistic complexity, locality and resumption. In *Proceedings of WCCFL 22* (pp. 15–28). Somerville, MA: Cascadilla Press.

Alexopoulou, T., & Keller, F. (2007). Locality, cyclicity, and resumption: At the interface between the grammar and the human sentence processor. *Language, 83*(1), 110–160.

Aoun, J., Choueiri, L., & Hornstein, N. (2001). Resumption, movement, and derivational economy. *Linguistic Inquiry, 32*(3), 371–403.

Asudeh, A. (2004). *Resumption as resource management.* Unpublished doctoral dissertation, Stanford University.

Asudeh, A. (2006). Direct compositionality and the architecture of LFG. In M. Butt, M. Dalrymple, & T. H. King (Eds.), *Intelligent linguistic architectures: Variations on themes by Ronald M. Kaplan* (pp. 363–387). Stanford, CA: CSLI Publications.

Asudeh, A., & Toivonen, I. (2009). Lexical-functional grammar. In B. Heine & H. Narrog (Eds.), *The Oxford handbook of linguistic analysis* (pp. 425–458). Oxford: Oxford University Press.

Bard, E. G., Robertson, D., & Sorace, A. (1996). Magnitude estimation of linguistic acceptability. *Language, 72*(1), 32–68.

Bouma, G., Malouf, R., & Sag, I. A. (2001). Satisfying constraints on extraction and adjunction. *Natural Language and Linguistic Theory, 19*, 1–65.

Bresnan, J. (2001). *Lexical-Functional Syntax.* Oxford: Blackwell.

Chao, W., & Sells, P. (1983). On the interpretation of resumptive pronouns. In P. Sells & C. Jones (Eds.), *The proceedings of NELS 13* (pp. 47–61). Amherst, MA: GLSA.

Chomsky, N. (1965). *Aspects of the theory of syntax.* Cambridge, MA: MIT Press.

Chomsky, N. (1986). *Knowledge of language: Its nature, origin, and use.* New York, NY: Praeger.

Chomsky, N. (2000). Minimalist inquiries: The framework. In R. Martin, D. Michaels, & J. Uriagereka (Eds.), *Step by step: Essays on minimalist syntax in honor of Howard Lasnik* (pp. 89–155). Cambridge, MA: MIT Press.

Chomsky, N. (2001). Derivation by phase. In M. Kenstowicz (Ed.), *Ken Hale: A life in language* (pp. 1–50). Cambridge, MA: MIT Press.

Chomsky, N., & Miller, G. (1963). Introduction to the formal analysis of natural languages. In R. D. Luce, R. R. Bush, & E. Galanter (Eds.), *The handbook of mathematical psychology* (Vol. 2, pp. 269–321). New York: Wiley.

Creswell, C. (2002). Resumptive pronouns, wh-island violations, and sentence production. In *Proceedings of the sixth international workshop on tree adjoining grammar and related frameworks (TAG+ 6)* (pp. 101–109). Universitá di Venezia.

Crouch, R., Dalrymple, M., Kaplan, R., King, T., Maxwell, J., & Newman, P. (2009). XLE documentation [Computer software manual]. Palo Alto, CA.

Dalrymple, M. (2001). *Lexical functional grammar.* San Diego, CA: Academic Press.

Erteschik-Shir, N. (1992). Resumptive pronouns in islands. In H. Goodluck & M. Rochemont (Eds.), *Island constraints: Theory, acquisition and processing* (pp. 89–108). Dordrecht: Kluwer.

Ferreira, F. (2000). Syntax in language production: An approach using tree-adjoining grammars. In L. Wheeldon (Ed.), *Aspects of language production.* Philadelphia, PA: Psychology Press.

Ferreira, F., & Swets, B. (2002). How incremental is language production? Evidence from the production of utterances requiring the computation of arithmetic sums. *Journal of Memory and Language, 46*, 57–84.

Ferreira, F., & Swets, B. (2005). The production and comprehension of resumptive pronouns in relative clause "island" contexts. In A. Cutler (Ed.), *Twenty-first century psycholinguistics: Four cornerstones* (pp. 263–278). Mahway, NJ: Lawrence Erlbaum Associates.

Frank, R. (2002). *Phrase structure composition and syntactic dependencies.* Cambridge, MA: MIT Press.

Frank, R., & Badecker, W. (2001). *Modeling syntactic encoding with incremental tree-adjoining grammar.* (Presented at the 14th Annual CUNY Conference on Human Sentence Processing)

Frazier, L. (1999). *On sentence interpretation.* Dordrecht: Kluwer.

Frazier, L., & Clifton, C., Jr. (1996). *Construal.* Cambridge, MA: MIT Press.

Gibson, E. (1998). Linguistic complexity: Locality and syntactic dependencies. *Cognition, 68*, 1-76.

Gompel, R. P. G. van, & Pickering, M. J. (2007). Syntactic parsing. In G. Gaskell (Ed.), *Oxford handbook of psycholinguistics* (pp. 289–307). Oxford: Oxford University Press.

Halvorsen, P.-K., & Kaplan, R. M. (1988). Projections and semantic description in lexical-functional grammar. In *Proceedings of the International Conference on Fifth Generation Computer Systems* (pp. 1116 1122). Tokyo.

Heestand, D., Xiang, M., & Polinsky, M. (to appear). Resumption still does not rescue islands. *Linguistic Inquiry*.

Jackendoff, R. (1990). *Semantic structures*. Cambridge, MA: MIT Press.

Jackendoff, R. (1997). *The architecture of the language faculty*. Cambridge, MA: MIT Press.

Joshi, A. K., Levy, L. S., & Takahashi, M. (1975). Tree adjunct grammars. *Journal of Computer and System Sciences, 10*(1), 136–163.

Kaplan, R. M. (1987). Three seductions of computational psycholinguistics. In P. Whitelock, M. M. Wood, H. L. Somers, R. Johnson, & P. Bennett (Eds.), *Linguistic theory and computer applications* (pp. 149–181). London: Academic Press.

Kaplan, R. M. (1989). The formal architecture of lexical-functional grammar. In C.-R. Huang & K.-J. Chen (Eds.), *Proceedings of ROCLING II* (pp. 3–18).

Kaplan, R. M., & Bresnan, J. (1982). Lexical-functional grammar: A formal system for grammatical representation. In J. Bresnan (Ed.), *The mental representation of grammatical relations* (pp. 173–281). Cambridge, MA: MIT Press.

Kaplan, R. M., & Zaenen, A. (1989). Long-distance dependencies, constituent structure, and functional uncertainty. In M. Baltin & A. Kroch (Eds.), *Alternative conceptions of phrase structure* (pp. 17–42). Chicago, IL: University of Chicago Press.

Kempen, G., & Hoenkamp, E. (1987). An incremental procedural grammar for sentence formulation. *Cognitive Science, 11*(3), 201–258.

Kroch, A. S. (1981). On the role of resumptive pronouns in amnestying island constraint violations. In *Papers from the 17th regional meeting of the Chicago Linguistic Society* (pp. 125–135). Chicago, IL: Chicago Linguistic Society.

Kroch, A. S., & Joshi, A. K. (1985). *The linguistic relevance of tree adjoining grammar* (Tech. Rep. No. MS-CIS-85-16). Department of Computer and Information Sciences, University of Pennsylvania.

Levelt, W. J. M. (1989). *Speaking: From intention to articulation*. Cambridge, MA: MIT Press.

MacDonald, M. C., & Seidenberg, M. S. (2006). Constraint satisfaction accounts of lexical and sentence comprehension. In M. J. Traxler & M. A. Gernsbacher (Eds.), *Handbook of psycholinguistics* (2nd ed., pp. 581–611). Amsterdam: Elsevier.

Matsumoto, Y. (1997). *Noun-modifying constructions in Japanese: A frame semantic approach*. Amsterdam: John Benjamins.

McCloskey, J. (1979). *Transformational syntax and model theoretic semantics: A case-study in Modern Irish.* Dordrecht: Reidel.

McCloskey, J. (1990). Resumptive pronouns, Ā-binding and levels of representation in Irish. In R. Hendrick (Ed.), *Syntax of the Modern Celtic languages* (Vol. 23, pp. 199–248). San Diego, CA: Academic Press.

McCloskey, J. (2006). Resumption. In M. Everaert & H. van Riemsdijk (Eds.), *The Blackwell companion to syntax* (pp. 94–117). Oxford: Blackwell.

McDaniel, D., & Cowart, W. (1999). Experimental evidence for a minimalist account of English resumptive pronouns. *Cognition, 70*, B15–B24.

Morrill, G. (1994). *Type logical grammar.* Dordrecht: Kluwer.

Pollard, C., & Sag, I. A. (1994). *Head-driven phrase structure grammar.* Chicago, IL and Stanford, CA: The University of Chicago Press and CSLI Publications.

Prince, E. (1990). Syntax and discourse: A look at resumptive pronouns. In K. Hall, J.-P. Koenig, M. Meacham, S. Reinman, & L. Sutton (Eds.), *Proceedings of the sixteenth annual meeting of the Berkeley Linguistics Society* (pp. 482–497). Berkeley, CA: Berkeley Linguistics Society.

Sag, I. A., Wasow, T., & Bender, E. M. (2003). *Syntactic theory: A formal introduction* (2nd. ed.). Stanford, CA: CSLI Publications.

Sells, P. (1984). *Syntax and semantics of resumptive pronouns.* Unpublished doctoral dissertation, University of Massachusetts, Amherst.

Shlonsky, U. (1992). Resumptive pronouns as a last resort. *Linguistic Inquiry, 23*, 443–468.

Steedman, M. (1987). Combinatory grammars and parasitic gaps. *Natural Language and Linguistic Theory, 5*, 403–440.

Stevens, S. S. (1956). The direct estimation of sensory magnitudes — loudness. *American Journal of Psychology, 69*, 1–25.

Stevens, S. S. (1975). *Psychophysics: Introduction to its perceptual, neural, and social prospects.* New York: John Wiley.

Swets, B., & Ferreira, F. (2003). *The effect of time pressure on the production of resumptive pronoun relative clauses.* (Poster presented at the Sixteenth Annual CUNY Conference on Human Sentence Processing)

Tabor, W., Galantucci, B., & Richardson, D. (2004). Effects of merely local syntactic coherence on sentence processing. *Journal of Memory and Language, 50*(4), 355–370.

5

Blocking and the Architecture of Grammar

Peter Sells

Preface

It is my great pleasure to present this contribution as part of a celebration of Tom's achievements. Ever since I met him in the 1980s, Tom provided an inspiration for research which was concerned with the proper articulation of syntax by considering its place in the larger architecture of the system(s) of language.

1 Blocking and Competition

This paper concerns the analysis of a certain class of "Blocking Effects" and the consequences of this for the organization of grammar. "Blocking" is the name often given to a well-known phenomenon where one linguistic form appears to pre-empt the use of another. In English, *bigger* is often used in preference to *more big*, even though both intuitively mean the same. We say that the synthetic form *bigger* **blocks** the analytic form *more big* in certain contexts. In contrast, the conditions on -*er* suffixation mean that a putative word like **intelligenter* is a highly dispreferred form, and hence *more intelligent* would be used in (almost) all grammatical contexts.

Hence, blocking of this kind is about the relation between two different surface forms, when both forms intuitively express the same content. Recently, there has been some focus on this in the theoretical linguistic literature—what the conditions are which allow a blocking relationship, what the nature of the blocking relationship is, and what

Language from a Cognitive Perspective.
Emily M. Bender and Jennifer Arnold, Editors
Copyright © 2011, CSLI Publications.

grammar must be like, to have those properties. I discuss some conclusions that can be drawn about the nature of the system of grammar, in terms of what architecture it has and what kinds of mechanisms it has within that architecture. I will restrict myself here to cases like those described above, which are known in the literature as "Poser blocking", following the important discussion in Poser, 1992.

Consider English "*do*-support", with the familiar pattern in (1). The verb *do* cannot be used unless it has some semantic or syntactic function—and hence is not acceptable unstressed, as in (1b). In the terms of relevance here, (1a) blocks (1b).

(1)   a. Sam ran.

        b. *Sam dĭd run.   (*did* unstressed)

        c. Sam did not run.

        d. Sam DÍD run.   (*did* stressed)

However, if it is used for a syntactic reason, as in (1c), or a semantic one, as in (1d), the supporting verb is acceptable.

Poser has the following to say about the kinds of structures that are involved in blocking:

> Suppose that we say that a morphological category is a category *potentially* instantiated by a word-formation rule. [...] One question that arises is what kinds of phrasal constructs may instantiate morphological categories, and hence be blocked by lexical forms. [...] I conjecture that it is only what I call *small categories* that can instantiate morphological categories. By a *small category* I mean a category that dominates only zero-level projections. (Poser, 1992, p. 126)

In other words, for the structures in (2), both are small categories, and if both express the same information, (2a) blocks (2b).

(2)   a.

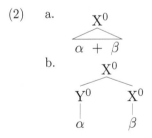

1.1 A Derivational Approach to Blocking

Embick and Marantz (2008; EM08) devote part of their paper "Architecture and Blocking" to the claims in (3). Presented within a derivational approach in which rules apply to phrase structures to create different phrase structures, they take the view that—as a theoretical concept—blocking has no status in the grammar, claiming instead that:

(3) a. There is no such thing as blocking (as a linguistic property of grammars), because there are no coexisting forms.

  b. If some form γ preempts a larger structure $\alpha + \beta$, this is because $\alpha + \beta$ is **derived into** γ (e.g., *more big* becomes *bigger*).

  c. All grammars have rules which apply (**when their structural description is met**) and in the case of 'blocking', there is nothing extra in the grammar: simply, RULES APPLY.

In their view (1a) does not block (1b), but rather (1b) is derived into (1a).

Returning to the English comparative, for EM08 the comparative is necessarily a structure, specifically, one with Deg(ree) modification of an adjective position as shown in (4a).

They hypothesize an operation of **Local Dislocation** which applies between adjacent nodes. This is one of several syntactic and post-syntactic rules which take an initial structure and successively manipulate it. The two nodes are collapsed and then the structure "spells out" with the correct inflected word:

(4) a.

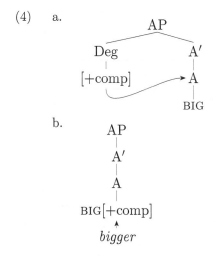

  b.

Hence, (4) is an illustration of RULES APPLY. In contrast, (5) is an illustration of "rules don't apply when their structural description is not met":

(5) a.

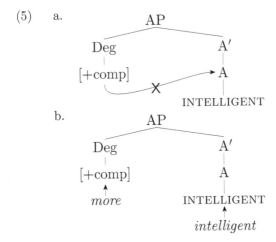

b.

If the rule of Local Dislocation can be sensitive to properties of the host/target, then the rule can be formulated so as not to apply in (5a). The rule does not apply to "phonologically heavier adjectives" (Embick & Marantz, 2008, p. 46). In that case, two nodes in the syntax must be subsequently lexicalized, so the output form is the analytic structure shown in (5b).

The approach in EM08 to the syntax-morphology interface is that known as Distributed Morphology, developed by Halle and Marantz (1993, 1994). The basic ideas are given in (5)—the phrase structure syntax is abstract, and is built up derivationally; there are local adjustment rules, which have universal properties (such as Local Dislocation) but language-specific details; and nodes are given morphological substance by Vocabulary Insertion, which finds a form to best express the featural content of each node:

(6) Distributed Morphology

  a. The syntax manipulates abstract nodes and elements
     (all languages are essentially identical).

  b. The 'morphology' further manipulates terminal elements
     (e.g., Local Dislocation).

     The resulting terminals are fleshed out with phonological substance by Vocabulary Insertion, inserting the most specific form to use up as many abstract features as possible.

  c. There is no 'lexicon', in the sense of a repository of words and sub-words which have form and meaning and which exist independently of syntactic structures.

As noted by Kiparsky (2005), the concept of blocking is not eliminated in this approach, in favor of deriving smaller forms from larger structures. Vocabulary Insertion itself involves blocking, as the guiding principle is to insert the most specific form to use up as many abstract features as possible.

At a very broad level of conception, the transformational/derivational approach assumes that "structure is information", and in fact this assumption has guided all work in transformational syntax since its inception.[1] In other words, if the overall structure conveys a certain piece of grammatical information, there must be a part of that structure whose dedicated function is to convey that information. In the narrowest understanding of the universality of language, it would be assumed that that part of the structure with a dedicated function occupies the same structural position in all languages. This is summarized and exemplified in (7):

(7) a. Each piece of grammatical information is structurally represented (in exactly one way);

b. so, Structure = Information; for example:

c. "comparative" = a node Deg with a feature [+comp]

d. "definite" = a node D with a feature [+def].

Consider the last example here—definiteness is assumed to be expressed on a D head, in a structure where NP is the complement of that D and the projected category is DP. This would be the structure of the abstract syntax **regardless of the surface expression** of definiteness in a given language.

RULES APPLY crucially assumes that Structure = Information, and that different surface expressions of the same information are due to different RULES APPLY events with respect to the same structures.

1.2 Information-Based Syntax

A constrasting approach to syntax is embodied in all "lexicalist" approaches, which are necessarily information-based, rather than structure-based. The fundamental organization in the grammar is that words carry information; and syntax combines that information. This is true in different particular approaches, such as:

---

[1] As a side remark, I note here that Embick and Marantz make the very common error of equating "derivational" and "generative" in terms of models of syntax, and contrast their "generative" approach with the "lexicalist" approach outlined here. In fact, every approach mentioned in this paper is generative, in the original sense developed by Chomsky (1957) of characterizing all and only the well-formed strings in a language, but differ in terms of whether they are derivational or declarative.

(8) a. Head-Driven Phrase Structure Grammar: Pollard & Sag, 1994, Sag, Wasow, & Bender, 2003

b. Lexical Decomposition Grammar: Kiparsky, 2001, 2005

c. Lexical-Functional Grammar: Kaplan & Bresnan, 1982, Bresnan, 2001b

d. Combinatory Categorial Grammar: Steedman, 2000

e. see also lexicalist approaches in Sells, 1995, 1998, Zwicky, 1992, *inter alia*

LEXICALIST theories take the positions that the **lexicon** and **syntax** are formed according to different structural principles; one representation is not derived into the other, but rather they both (can) express the same kinds of information:

(9) a. Words carry information which the syntax combines; the words and the syntax together put constraints on how the information is combined;

b. A lexical form or a syntactic form can in principle carry exactly the same kinds of grammatical information. Hence, different forms can compete as expressions of the same information.

OPTIMALITY THEORY is a way of further specifying an information-based theory (though it is not a necessary part of information-based approaches). Prince & Smolensky, 2004 is the classic overview of the theory; various applications to syntax can be found in Legendre, Grimshaw, & Vikner, 2001 and Sells, 2001a.

(10) Principles in Optimality Theory:

a. EXPRESSIVENESS: express grammatical information

b. ECONOMY: avoid unnecessary expression

As a brief illustration, if we have the structures in (11), both associated with the same information I, then both structures are equal on EXPRESSIVENESS, but (11a) is preferred due to ECONOMY.

(11) a. X^0 (associated with information I)

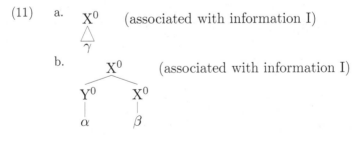

b. X^0 (associated with information I)

2 Theoretical Differences

2.1 Blocking: Expressing Definiteness

Hankamer and Mikkelsen (2005) discuss Danish definites. The expression of definiteness is analytic if there is an adjective, as in (12a), but synthetic if there is no adjective (as in (12b,c)):

(12) Danish

    a. den gamle hest
       the old   house

    b. *den hest
       the horse

    c. hest-en
       horse-the

Swedish shows a similar pattern, except both the determiner and noun express definiteness when an adjective is present (compare (13a) with (12a)):

(13) Swedish

    a. den gamla mus-en
       the old   mouse-the

    b. *den mus
       the mouse

    c. mus-en
       mouse-the

And let us consider these further Swedish facts:

(14) Swedish

    a. *den mus(-en)
       the mouse(-the)

    b. dén mus-en
       THE mouse-the

    c. *gamla mus-en
       old   mouse-the

    d. *mus-en   gamla
       mouse-the old

With no adjective present, only the synthetic form in (13c) is acceptable—no version with the determiner *den* is possible, unless *den* is itself focussed, as in (14b). When an adjective is present, a definite-marked determiner **and** the definite-marked noun must be used, as in (13a).

In all of these examples, the information to be expressed is that schematized in (15):

(15)
$$\begin{bmatrix} \text{DEF} & + \\ \text{PRED} & \text{'HORSE/MOUSE'} \\ \text{MOD} & \text{'OLD'} \end{bmatrix}$$

It is intuitively clear what principles govern the expression of this information. In Danish, the first element of NP must express definiteness; and an adjective must precede the noun. Swedish has these two constraints as well, plus one more: the head noun is always marked for definiteness. In other words, structures must satisfy the following requirements, regardless of how they are formally embodied in the grammar:

(16)   a. Definite-Left: the leftmost element marks definite.

        b. A ≺ N

        c. Head-Marking: the head (noun) marks definite.

The Swedish structure in (17) satisfies these constraints, as indicated in (18a). Other expressions are not fully satisfactory, as indicated in (18b,c).

(17)

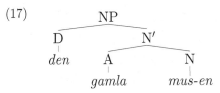

(18)   a. den gamla mus-en
          the old   mouse-the
          DEF-L: √ H-M: √ A ≺ N: √

        b. *gamla mus-en
          old   mouse-the
          DEF-L: * H-M: √ A ≺ N: √
          (*gamla* does not mark definiteness)

        c. *mus-en   gamla
          mouse-the old
          DEF-L: √ H-M: √ A ≺ N: *

Hence (18a) is the best expression of the required grammatical information, in Swedish.

The alert reader will have realised that in fact (18a) respects the constraint DEF-L with respect to the first word *den* but violates it with respect to the last word *musen*. This is where the analytical power of Optimality Theory becomes relevant—the theory provides a ranking of constraints, and violation of a given constraint is allowed if a higher-ranking constraint is satisfied. I leave it as an exercise for the reader to construct a detailed account of Swedish and Danish. As they are different languages, their grammars will have different constraint rankings. For determining those rankings, the key observations about the data above are these: (i) H-M is most important in Swedish, as (13a) does not violate it, but (12a) does; and (ii) DEF-L is most important in Danish, as (12a) does not violate it, but (13a) does (with respect to *musen*).

2.2 The RULES APPLY Approach

How is this data analyzed under the RULES APPLY approach? Let us consider the Swedish form *mus-en*:[2]

(19)

This is accounted for by Local Dislocation: Move [+def] to N. Note however, that this operation must be blocked for (14b) *dén mus-en*; if we assume a specification [+emph] for the emphatic expression of definiteness, it follows that [+def] can undergo Local Dislocation but [+emph] cannot.

Now, when an adjective is present, another rule would have to be invoked, which I will call 'Copying'. Such a rule would be necessary as the definiteness feature must originate on D, and in fact surfaces there, but it also surfaces on N.

---

[2]EM08 discuss Danish definiteness marking, but not Swedish. I hypothesize the rule of Copying below as a way of extending the RULES APPLY account of Danish to Swedish. Heck, Müller, and Trommer (2008) propose such a copying mechanism, based on feature movement, in their derivational account of the Scandinavian facts.

(20)

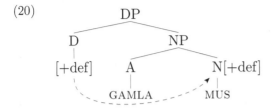

The rule of Copying (showed by the dashed line) must apply in Swedish, and may not apply in Danish. And unlike Local Dislocation, it may apply between non-adjacent nodes.[3]

It is well-known from the history of the development of transformational grammar that different derivational steps often have to have an extrinsic order of operation imposed on them. This is also true in this case. If Copying preceded Local Dislocation, for example in (19), this would derive *den mus-en, as the definite feature would be on both nodes in the structure. Hence, Local Dislocation is the first operation; if it fails, and therefore if D remains in situ with its features, then Copying may apply.

The outputs of the two operations are as shown:

(21)   a.   DP
            |
            NP
            |
            N[+def]
       b.   DP
                ⌒⌒⌒⌒
            D   NP
            | |
            [+def]   N[+def]

In summary, in Swedish, if the feature cannot move, it is copied. Either way, N is ALWAYS marked definite even though [+def] is NEVER an intrinsic feature of N. Not only is it that 'RULES APPLY', but something has to guarantee that *some* rule does apply.

2.3   The Declarative Approach

One putative argument against competition-based blocking approaches that EM08 present is that, if there were only ECONOMY, then only the

---

[3] As a reviewer pointed out, once an operation such as Copying is part of the grammar, applying between non-adjacent nodes, the basic idea that blocking is a phenomenon only holding with respect to adjacent nodes (at the relevant point in the derivation) seems to be potentially compromised.

structurally simplest examples would ever emerge. In fact, this consideration carries no force, as it is set against a background of incorrect assumptions about the nature of the syntactic representations. Consider again the expression of past tense in English. Relative to the information in (22), (23a) is the most economical expression of TENSE and PRED:

(22)
$$\begin{bmatrix} \text{TENSE} & \text{PAST} \\ \text{PRED} & \text{`EAT'} \\ \text{SUBJ} & \text{``SAM''} \end{bmatrix}$$

(23) a. Sam ate.

  b. *Sam did eat.

If we add negation into the grammatical representation, the overt expression of this in English is (arguably) as in (25):

(24)
$$\begin{bmatrix} \text{TENSE} & \text{PAST} \\ \text{PRED} & \text{`EAT'} \\ \text{NEG} & + \\ \text{SUBJ} & \text{``SAM''} \end{bmatrix}$$

(25)

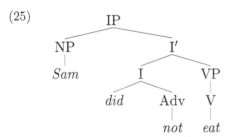

If ECONOMY were the only guiding principle, one of (26a,b) should be preferred over the actual form, (26c), whose structure is shown in (25). However, (26a,b) are both ill-formed: *not* has nothing to adjoin to in (26a), for there is no silent position I where tense is located if there is no overt auxiliary, on a lexicalist approach; and for (26b), a main verb cannot be in the I position of (25) in English.

(26) a. *Sam not ate.

  b. *Sam ate not.

  c. Sam did not eat.

If the examples in (26) were derived from a well-formed structure like (25) (exactly that structure, but without the overt form *did*), the examples in (26a,b) might be generated. However, there is no such structure in a non-derivational theory; only (26c) is, therefore it is the grammatical output.

2.4 'Popping Out'

EM08 further argue that the optimality-based approach has a problem with what they term 'popping out'. This concerns cases where the grammar should generate no output (there is a missing element in a paradigm or pattern), but the optimality-based account will always classify some form as having the best profile relative to the constraint ranking, and this form will therefore 'pop out' as the output.

EM08 argue that there appears to be no regular form of the past tense of the verb *forgo*:

(27)   What is the past tense of *forgo*?

    a.   *forwent

    b.   *forgoed

As these forms apparently do not exist, it would appear that the optimality-based approach predicts that the next best option will be grammatical, namely *did forgo*. EM08 claim that this form is also ungrammatical, and that the RULES APPLY approach can predict no output for the verb *forgo* (by positing no suitable vocabulary item).

But what are the actual facts in this case? First, it is by now well established that the great mass of grammatical expression contains variation, which is itself (partially) structured and systematic—here are just a few references: Anttila, 1997, 2007; Bresnan, 2001a; Bresnan, Cueni, Nikitina, & Baayen, 2007; Bresnan, Deo, & Sharma, 2007; Clark, 2004.

We know that alternate forms do exist in grammars. Sometimes the variation is 50-50, sometimes it is 99-1, and it differs between and among individuals. A grammar is a set of resources that speakers use in a variety of ways. And we can see that speakers of English have access to the relevant forms in this example:

(28)   a.   For our Christmas day feast we **forwent** (**forwent**? I didn't even know that was a word until I asked Nina what the past tense of **forgo** was) the standard Christmas fare and instead had frozen pizza, then reverted back to our standard pattern of watching bad Christmas TV and generally pigging-out. (`http://screen21.com/archie/`, April 2007)

b. I just measured over from the kerf, front and back—perfectly square. Not having access to a router (yet), I **did forgo** the sliding track for the miter gauge, but otherwise, this add-on has increased the performace and capability of the saw dramatically. (http://snbcreative.wordpress.com/tag/workshop/, April 2007)

Hence these forms exist, even if only marginally, and therefore must be admitted as candidate words by the grammar. Whatever governs their actual appearance in speakers' productions involves more than just abstract grammar.

2.5 Lexically-Based Blocking

Embick and Marantz offer another argument against Poser Blocking, observing that "blocking" appears to be governed by string adjacency—in their terms, Local Dislocation applies not between any two nodes, but only between adjacent nodes, as in (29):

(29)

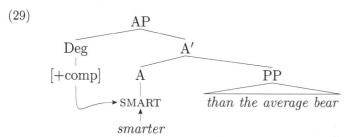

Let us assume that this characterization in terms of adjacency is correct. In fact, it follows from the lexicalist approach, precisely for an architectural reason.

On the RULES APPLY derivational approach, structures are built respecting the selecting properties of their heads, but then are possibly destructively modified by later operations. This has also been true of all generations of transformational approaches. However, in the information-based view, precisely because Lexicon ≠ Syntax, putting two random words into a structure may mean that their selection properties are not met, even if in principle the combination expresses the relevant information. Syntactic constraints and all well-formedness conditions have to be satisfied in every structure.

Consider once again the Swedish examples (14c,d):

(14)   c. *gamla mus-en
            old   mouse-the

    d. *mus-en   gamla
       mouse-the old

(14d) especially is very 'economical', but both examples are simply bad because they violate some constraint of Swedish—the first element in NP must express definiteness, and the adjective must precede the noun. As we have seen above, surface forms such as these would only ever be considered in a theory with an architecture where a well-formed representation at one point could be destructively modified into a non-well-formed representation at a later point. But no declarative theory has this property.

Exactly the same reasoning applies to the examples in (26):

(26)   a. *Sam not ate.

       b. *Sam ate not.

       c. Sam did not eat.

The question is—why can tense and the verb in (26c) not "combine" to give one of the outputs a–b? The answer is that the first two examples are simply ungenerable by the rules of English syntax. *not* may not left-adjoin to a finite VP (only to a non-finite VP—as in (26c), and *not* may not follow a finite main verb (only a finite auxiliary—as in (26c)).

The correct consequences follow in a declarative theory precisely because $\alpha + \beta$ (i.e., γ) in (11) is **not** derived from a well-formed $\alpha \ldots \beta$ structure. In other words, the information that structures carry is (partly) independent from the structures themselves.

3 Conclusion

In brief summary, I have argued for the points in (31), based on the architectural observations in (30):

(30)   a. Information-based (and constraint-based) theories provide words, which express information, and phrases, which combine the information from words.

       b. The differences between grammatical approaches is not a matter of being "generative" or not, but rather, whether the grammatical system is derivational or declarative.

(31)   a. Poser Blocking is about competing expressions of the same information.

       b. Poser Blocking interacts with—more precisely, is constrained by—well-formedness constraints on syntax.

c. The correct interactions are accounted for if all constraints are evaluated simultaneously, not derivationally.

In contrast to the declarative approach, the RULES APPLY approach has to posit extrinsic conditions on rules (e.g., the adjacency constraint on Dislocation), and on rule ordering (see section 2.2). These are necessary to prevent the grammar from generating structures which are otherwise unattested in the language in question. A declarative architecture avoids these complexities.[4]

Acknowledgements

A version of this material was presented at the Symbolic Systems Forum at Stanford, on April 12, 2007. The comments of two reviewers led to significant improvements in the final version of this paper; my thanks to them.

References

Anttila, A. (1997). Deriving variation from grammar: A study of Finnish genitives. In F. Hinskens, R. van Hout, & L. Wetzels (Eds.), *Variation, change and phonological theory* (pp. 35–68). Amsterdam: John Benjamins.

Anttila, A. (2007). Variation and optionality. In P. de Lacy (Ed.), *The Cambridge handbook of phonology* (pp. 519–536). Cambridge: Cambridge University Press.

Bresnan, J. (2001a). Explaining morphosyntactic competition. In M. Baltin & C. Collins (Eds.), *Handbook of contemporary syntactic theory* (pp. 11–44). Oxford: Blackwell.

Bresnan, J. (2001b). *Lexical-functional syntax*. Oxford: Blackwell.

Bresnan, J., Cueni, A., Nikitina, T., & Baayen, H. (2007). Predicting the dative alternation. In G. Bouma, I. Krämer, & J. Zwarts (Eds.), *Cognitive foundations of interpretation* (pp. 69–94). Amsterdam: Royal Netherlands Academy of Science.

Bresnan, J., Deo, A., & Sharma, D. (2007). Typology in variation: A probabilistic approach to *be* and *n't* in the survey of English dialects. *English Language and Linguistics*, *11*(02), 301–346.

Chomsky, N. (1957). *Syntactic structures*. The Hague: Mouton & Co.

Clark, B. Z. (2004). *A stochastic optimality theory approach to syntactic change*. Unpublished doctoral dissertation, Department of Linguistics, Stanford University.

---

[4] A parallel argument in favor of a derivational architecture is presented in Sells, 2001b, with respect to constraints on constituent order in Swedish.

Embick, D., & Marantz, A. (2008). Architecture and blocking. *Linguistic Inquiry*, *39*(1), 1–53.

Halle, M., & Marantz, A. (1993). Distributed morphology and the pieces of inflection. In K. Hale & S. J. Keyser (Eds.), *The view from Building 20* (pp. 111–176). Cambridge: MIT Press.

Halle, M., & Marantz, A. (1994). Some key features of distributed morphology. *MIT Working Papers in Linguistics*, *21*, 275–288.

Hankamer, J., & Mikkelsen, L. (2005). When movement must be blocked: A reply to Embick and Noyer. *Linguistic Inquiry*, *36*(1), 85–125.

Heck, F., Müller, G., & Trommer, J. (2008). A phase-based approach to Scandinavian definiteness marking. In C. B. Chang & H. J. Haynie (Eds.), *Proceedings the 26th West Coast conference on formal linguistics* (pp. 226–233). Somerville, MA: Cascadilla Proceedings Project.

Kaplan, R. M., & Bresnan, J. (1982). *The mental representation of grammatical relations*. Cambridge: MIT Press.

Kiparsky, P. (2001). Structural case in Finnish. *Lingua*, *111*(4-7), 315–376.

Kiparsky, P. (2005). Blocking and periphrasis in inflectional paradigms. In G. E. Booij & J. van Marle (Eds.), *Yearbook of morphology 2004* (pp. 113–135). Dordrecht: Springer.

Legendre, G., Grimshaw, J. B., & Vikner, S. (2001). *Optimality-theoretic syntax*. Cambridge: MIT Press.

Pollard, C. J., & Sag, I. A. (1994). *Head-driven phrase structure grammar*. Chigago, IL: University of Chicago Press.

Poser, W. J. (1992). Blocking of phrasal constructions by lexical items. In I. Sag & A. Szabolsci (Eds.), *Lexical matters* (pp. 111–130). Stanford, CA: CSLI Publications.

Prince, A., & Smolensky, P. (2004). *Optimality theory: Constraint interaction in generative grammar*. New York: Blackwell.

Sag, I. A., Wasow, T., & Bender, E. M. (2003). *Syntactic theory: A formal introduction* (Second ed.). Stanford, CA: CSLI Publications.

Sells, P. (1995). Korean and Japanese morphology from a lexical perspective. *Linguistic Inquiry*, *26*(2), 277–325.

Sells, P. (1998). Optimality and economy of expression in Japanese and Korean. *Japanese/Korean Linguistics*, *7*, 499–514.

Sells, P. (Ed.). (2001a). *Formal and empirical issues in optimality theoretic syntax*. Stanford, CA: CSLI Publications.

Sells, P. (2001b). *Structure, alignment and optimality in Swedish*. Stanford, CA: CSLI Publications.

Steedman, M. (2000). *The syntactic process.* Cambridge: MIT Press.

Zwicky, A. M. (1992). Some choices in the theory of morphology. In R. Levine (Ed.), *Formal grammar: Theory and implementation* (pp. 327–371). Oxford: Oxford University Press.

6

Simplicity and Fit in Grammatical Theory

Amy Perfors

Preface

This paper reflects two, somewhat independent, ways that Tom Wasow has influenced my work. The first concerns the motivating question: how should we evaluate different grammatical theories or formalisms? Which best account for human language, and how do we decide? This issue was emphasized beginning with the first syntax course I ever took (taught, of course, by Tom), and was an undercurrent in many of the discussions I had with him henceforth. The second way that Tom influenced my thinking was in his interest in using computational techniques to study aspects of language. In work with him, David Beaver, and several others, we used a genetic programming framework to explore a question in language evolution. Although the approach and question were different than the one discussed here, the general insight that computational methods can be a useful tool for investigating aspects of language dates back to my time spent working with Tom.

1 Overview

Much current research in linguistics and cognitive science is focused on the question of innateness: whether the cognitive capacities that enable humans to learn language are language-specific, or whether our linguistic skill is the result of more domain-general abilities and biases. Interest in this topic grew especially strong after Chomsky's (1965) claim that language learning is only explicable on the basis of an innate

Language from a Cognitive Perspective.
Emily M. Bender and Jennifer Arnold, Editors
Copyright © 2011, CSLI Publications.

language faculty, or Universal Grammar. Since then, much inquiry has focused on the dual questions of (a) to what extent this claim is true; and (b) to the extent that it is, what is the nature of this Universal Grammar, or UG?

Addressing these questions requires both the ability to accurately describe the data that need to be explained, as well as the capacity to evaluate the different theories that aim to explain that data. In this paper I describe a paradigm that meets both of these requirements. The paradigm is based on Bayesian computational modeling of grammars and complements existing linguistic methodologies.

The structure of the paper is as follows: In the first section, the utility of such an approach is motivated. Subsequent sections describe its basic underlying principles, and briefly consider two case studies that illustrate how it might provide additional insight. The paper concludes with a discussion of some of the issues and limitations associated with the paradigm.

2 A Motivation of the Bayesian Approach

Advances in understanding the bases of language learning in the brain require, among other things, an accurate characterization of the data (i.e., the language) being learned, as well as a means to evaluate theories explaining that data. In this section I discuss some of the issues that surround these two requirements. This motivates the ways in which the Bayesian paradigm fills some existing gaps.

2.1 Characterizing the Data as a Whole

As a field, linguistics relies on several different kinds of methodologies in order to properly characterize the data that need to be explained. One common approach, at least in the subfield of generative syntax (which we will be focusing on in this article), is a reliance on grammatical intuitions—introspective judgments as to an expressions' grammaticality or well-formedness. Though these intuitions can be a useful tool in guiding the formation of theories, Wasow and Arnold (2005) argue that using them as the primary or only source of empirical support for a theory can sometimes be problematic, since individual speakers may often disagree, and intuitions may be rather marginal even for a single speaker. Other sources of empirical evidence, emerging from subfields such as psycholinguistics, experimental psychology, and cognitive science, include reaction-time experiments (e.g., Spivey & Tanenhaus, 1998), eye-tracking paradigms (e.g., Just & Carpenter, 1980; Tanenhaus, Spivey-Knowlton, Eberhard, & Sedivy, 1995; Altmann & Kamide, 1999), corpus analyses (e.g., Nunberg, Sag, & Wasow,

1994; Lohse, Hawkins, & Wasow, 2004; Levy, 2008), and survey data (e.g., Langendoen, Kalish-Landon, & Dore, 1973; Wasow & Arnold, 2005), all of which result in a statistically valid and nuanced picture of grammatical acceptability.

However, all of these methods often yield data only regarding the particular constructions or phenomena in question. Though this may be interesting in its own right, because syntacticians are often focused on the question of which grammatical formalism or theory best describes an entire language, it is, of necessity, limited in scope: every theory includes some phenomena that it can explain easily and some that are only accounted for via more *ad hoc* measures. What may often be desirable is some method or mechanism that can objectively decide between entire theories on the basis of how well they account for observed natural language usage. But how is this achievable even in theory, much less in practice?

2.2 Evaluating Theories in a Principled Way

Intuitively, there are two main criteria that are essential when deciding between different linguistic theories. One is the issue of goodness-of-fit: what is the coverage of the theory to the observed linguistic data? Does it account for the important phenomena in a wide variety of languages, while not predicting phenomena that are unobserved or unattested? It is this criterion that empirical data are relevant to, and the evaluation of theories with respect to this criterion underlies the importance of acquiring accurate data. Another, equally important, criterion is that of *simplicity*: any theory can achieve complete coverage simply by exhaustively listing all of the phenomena in question, but we would quite clearly like to rule out those theories. Philosophers of science have long emphasized the importance of simplicity (e.g., Wrinch & Jeffreys, 1921; Good, 1968; Jaynes, 2003). Within linguistics, many people (including Chomsky) have called attention to the critical role that simplicity plays in the evaluation of a linguistic theory (e.g., Chomsky, 1956, 1957, 1965; Wolff, 1982; Chater & Vitányi, 2007, among others).

Despite the fact that almost everyone accepts the importance of simplicity in evaluating theories, there are few widely agreed-upon criteria for measuring it. One might argue that simpler formalisms or theories are those that are less expressive—those that license the fewest phenomena.[1] An important branch of research has focused on the expressive-

---

[1] This is a view of simplicity that overlaps somewhat with the traditional view of coverage or goodness-of-fit; one reason that more expressive theories are dispreferred is that they are so powerful they license grammars or phenomena that do not fall within the purview of natural language.

ness of different syntactic theories, including GB, HPSG, minimalism, and others: for instance, every recursively enumerable set of strings is a transformational language (Peters & Ritchie Jr., 1973), suggesting that transformational grammars are more powerful than necessary to account for natural language. (See also, e.g., Kornai & Pullum, 1990 and Rogers, 1998 for other formal analyses of the expressive power of different linguistic theories, and Immerman, 1999 for a mathematical overview).

However, equally important is the question of simplicity of explanation *within* a theory. Are the central linguistic phenomena accounted for easily by the theory, or must it contain a multitude of *ad hoc* exceptions, or increasingly complicated rules, in order to account for it? This sort of simplicity argument is the basis for Chomsky's famous conclusion that regular grammars (i.e., Markov models, also known as word-chain grammars) are inadequate to capture natural language (1956): because any actual corpus or set of data is finite, regular grammars are in principle capable of capturing them completely, but the presence of long-distance dependencies means that these grammars will be, in his words, "so complex as to be of little use or interest." (p. 115) Under this notion, then, the expressiveness of a linguistic theory or grammar is a good thing, because more expressive grammars will (as a general rule) find it easier to capture any given linguistic phenomenon in a parsimonious way.

Another measure of the simplicity of a formalism or theory focuses on the number of primitives or basic operations defined within that theory. By this measure, minimalism is very simple, since it focuses on the importance of economy of derivation and economy of representation when defining linguistic theories, and explains phrase structure in terms of only two operations, Merge and Move (Chomsky, 1995). In fact, minimalism is often justified on the basis of simplicity, or based on the related notion of "perfection" in a theory. However, it has also been criticized on the grounds that these notions of simplicity and perfection are too vague to be useful (e.g., Lappin, Levine, & Johnson, 2000).

It is possible to view much of the debate in formal syntax about different theories as actually a debate between different views of simplicity, and how it should be balanced with goodness-of-fit—both areas in which there is no substantial agreement. This is partly because, as already discussed, there is not agreement about what aspects of simplicity matter or how it should be measured; but it is also because it is unclear how to properly implement the tradeoff between the two. Is a theory with few primitives and operations, like minimalism, "better" than a theory that builds more in but produces more precise explanations? And how should one evaluate theories that explicitly shovel part of the explanation into another component of the language faculty—a component that is not fully fleshed out within the theory itself? For instance, it may be accurate to assume that lexical semantics and syntax are so intertwined that any good syntactic theory should displace much of the explanation onto word-specific knowledge, as does HPSG—but that still leaves us with the problem of how to balance HPSG's simplicity with its explanatory coverage. On some measures it appears quite parsimonious, but how much of that is because it has succeeded in offloading most of the explanation onto the lexical semantics of each word?

The tradeoff between simplicity and goodness-of-fit is a perennial issue in all of the sciences, and a central topic in philosophy of science as well. A common heuristic is that of Occam's Razor—*entia non sunt multiplicanda praeter necessitatem*—that an explanatory hypothesis or theory should not make assumptions (or "postulate entities") unless absolutely necessary. Although this heuristic is generally regarded as little more than a rule of thumb, it has deep connections with Bayesian probability theory and information theory (e.g., Jeffreys, 1931, 1939; de Finetti, 1974; Vitànyi & Li, 2000; Jaynes, 2003; MacKay, 2003). In the next sections, I will illuminate those connections, and demonstrate how the Bayesian framework may be used to compare and evaluate grammatical rules and grammatical theories in linguistics. In so doing, it can provide a means to address some of the difficulties that current linguistic approaches wrestle with.

3 Principles behind Bayesian Grammar Induction

In Bayesian probability, one's degree of belief in some hypothesis or theory is represented by a real number between 0 and 1. The mathematics of probability theory provides rules for "proper reasoning"—for how to validly combine different premises and beliefs in such a way as to be sure that you have arrived at the correct conclusion (e.g., Jaynes, 2003). In essence, it is an extension of deductive logic to the case where propositions, or hypotheses, have degrees of truth or falsity (and is identical to deductive logic if we know all of the hypotheses with 100% certainty). Thus, just as formal logic describes a deductively correct way of thinking, Bayesian probability theory describes an inductively correct way of thinking. As Laplace said, "probability theory is nothing but common sense reduced to calculation."

What does this mean? If we were to try to come up with a set of desiderata that a system of proper reasoning should meet, they might include things like consistency and qualitative correspondence with common sense—if you see some data supporting a new theory A, you should conclude that A is more plausible than it was, rather than less; the more you think A is true, the less you should think it false; if a conclusion can be reasoned in multiple ways, its probability should be the same regardless of how you got there; etc. The basic axioms and theorems of probability theory, including Bayes' Rule, emerge when these desiderata are formalized mathematically (Cox, 1946, 1961), and correspond to common-sense reasoning and the scientific method (Jeffreys, 1931, 1939; de Finetti, 1974; Jaynes, 2003).

This means that optimal inductive inference—of the sort we hope to achieve in scientific reasoning—should follow the Bayes' Rule, in which the probability of a hypothesis given some data $p(H|D)$ is proportional to the probability of the data given that hypothesis $p(D|H)$, or likelihood, times the prior probability of that hypothesis $p(H)$:

$$p(H|D) \propto p(D|H)p(H) \tag{6.1}$$

Hypotheses (and data) are defined within the Bayesian framework as the outgrowth of a generative process: for instance, data (such as spoken sentences) may be generated from some sort of underlying grammar, and grammars themselves are generated from a hypothesis space of candidate grammars. The job of the learner is to choose among different hypotheses—grammars—on the basis of which ones best account for the observed data. This choosing is done according to the laws of Bayesian probability theory, including Bayes' Rule.

Simplicity is naturally accounted for via the prior probability $p(H)$. The definition of simplicity and the corresponding calculation of $p(H)$ are not generally the result of some externally-imposed *ad hoc* mechanism; rather, they emerge naturally from the assumption that hypotheses (grammars) themselves are generated from a space of candidate hypotheses. For instance, the hypotheses in Figure 1 correspond to different sets of rectangular regions within a two-dimensional space. Simpler hypotheses require fewer "choice points" during the generation process: Hypothesis A can be fully captured by making only four choices, two for the coordinates of the lower-left-hand corner of the rectangle (x and y), one for its length (l), and one for its width (w). By contrast, hypothesis C contains thirty distinct rectangular regions, and therefore requires 120 separate choices to specify, four for each region. This notion of calculating complexity as a function of the number of choice points is a reflection of the idea that the more complicated something is, the more likely it becomes that it will be messed up at some point in the generation process. The more choices a hypothesis resulted from, the more likely it is that those choices could have been made in a different way, resulting in a different hypothesis.

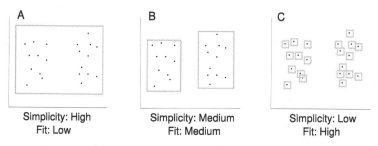

FIGURE 1 Hypothesis A is too simple, C is too complex, and B is "just right." Hypothesis A is quite simple, but fits the observed data poorly: C fits closely but is highly complicated. The best description of the data should optimize a tradeoff between complexity and fit, as in B.

The precise prior probability of a hypothesis is therefore not arbitrarily assigned, but rather falls out in a principled way from how the hypotheses are generated. The generative model for the hypotheses in Figure 1 is one that can result in any possible combination of rectangular regions within the space. A different generative model would result in a different—but no less principled—assignment of prior probabilities. For instance, if we assumed that the regions could be circles rather than rectangles, then each region would require three choice points rather than four (the x and y coordinates of the center of the circle, plus its radius). The logic favoring simple hypotheses would be the same: multiple regions will still be *a priori* less likely than a few. The precise generative model therefore matters for determining exactly what the relative probability of a hypothesis would be, but most reasonable models would give qualitatively similar relative probabilities to qualitatively similar hypotheses.

The Bayesian framework, then, offers a natural way to both calculate the simplicity of different hypotheses or theories, and also evaluate those theories on the basis of how well they account for the observed data.[2] Bayes' Rule offers a principled way to evaluate the tradeoff between simplicity (prior probability) and goodness-of-fit (likelihood).

---

[2]A quite similar insight is offered by a minimum description length (MDL) approach, which suggests that coding length (a measure of simplicity) can be an important tool for choosing between different linguistic analyses (e.g., Chater & Vitányi, 2007; Goldsmith, 2007). Indeed, such an approach has been used effec-

Thus, as in Figure 1, it will naturally tend to prefer hypotheses (like Hypothesis B) that—like Goldilocks in the famous story—are neither too weak nor too strong, but are "just right." Hypothesis C, for instance, clearly has a high degree of goodness-of-fit (likelihood): if the hypothesis is true—that is, if the data is truly generated by thirty distinct underlying processes corresponding to the thirty rectangles of C—the datapoints could hardly be anywhere else. In other words, it fits (or predicts) the data well. By contrast, hypothesis A has relatively low likelihood: it does not explain why the datapoints are where they are, rather than elsewhere within the rectangle. However, hypothesis A is simple, while C is quite complex. The best description of the data would be a hypothesis that optimizes the tradeoff between complexity and fit, as in hypothesis B.

This framework is applicable to hypotheses of much greater complexity than rectangles in a two-dimensional space. It is possible to define generative models for grammars in which specific grammars, G, are generated from a larger class of grammar types T (see Horning, 1969; and Feldman, Gips, Horning, & Reder, 1969 for other examples of this idea). Consider, for instance, context-free grammars, which naturally capture hierarchical phrase structure by being able to generate sentences in which clauses can be located inside other clauses. Context-free grammars, or CFGs, have productions of the form $X \to y$; X is a single non-terminal production (meaning that it can appear on the left-hand side of a production) and y is a string of non-terminals or terminals (terminals are constrained to appear on the right-hand-side, and consist of the output symbols of the grammar). Within the class of context-free grammars, one could generate a specific grammar by going through the following steps: (a) to choose the number of non-terminals n; (b) for each non-terminal k to generate P_k productions; (c) for each P_k^{th} production i, to generate N_i right-hand-side items (either one or two, if we constrain the grammars to be in Chomsky normal form), each of which are drawn from the grammars vocabulary V (the set of all non-terminals and terminals). If one wanted the grammars to be probabilistic, one would also have to assign a vector of production-probability parameters θ_k for each non-terminal k. This process imposes

---

tively for the acquisition of morphology (Goldsmith, 2001), word segmentation (de Marcken, 1995), and other aspects of grammar (e.g., Dowman, 1998; Grünwald, 1996). One of the main differences between the MDL and the Bayesian frameworks lies in how simplicity is measured: in the MDL approach, simplicity is captured by short encoding lengths, while in the Bayesian approach, it is captured by higher prior probability. However, there are deep similarities between the two approaches (see, e.g., Vitànyi & Li, 2000, for a discussion).

a prior probability, as in Equation 6.2, in which simpler grammars—those with fewer non-terminals, productions, and items—have higher prior probability (see Perfors, Tenenbaum, and Regier (under review) for a more thorough explanation of this process). This is captured by the equation below:

$$p(G|T) = p(n) \prod_{k=1}^{n} p(P_k)p(\theta_k) \prod_{i=1}^{p_k} p(N_i) \prod_{j=1}^{N_i} \frac{1}{V} \qquad (6.2)$$

Not only does this process naturally impose a prior probability metric in which shorter grammars with fewer non-terminals are simpler, the generative framework also naturally operates so that more expressive—i.e., more complex—grammar *types* will be effectively penalized. For instance, the generative model for regular grammars would be analogous to that of the process for context-free grammars, except that the form of the right-hand side of productions would be more constrained. Permissible productions for a (right-branching) regular grammar include only those of the form A → a B or A → a (where capital letters indicate non-terminals and lower-case letters indicate terminals), whereas context-free grammars may additionally include productions of the form A → B C, A → B, or A → B a. As a result of this, regular grammars are a subset of context-free grammars, and if a particular grammar could be generated as an example of more than one grammar type, it would receive higher prior probability when generated from the less expressive type. All other things being equal, one would have to make fewer "choices" in order to generate a specific regular grammar from the class containing only regular grammars than from the class of context-free grammars.

In essence, then, prior probability can be defined over grammars in such a way as to naturally capture our intuitive notion of simplicity, in such a way that simpler grammars *within* a theory will be favored, and simpler (less expressive) theories will also be favored, all else being equal. The Bayesian framework also provides a way to compare different grammars in terms of how well they fit the observed linguistic data in the world. Consider, for instance, data consisting of a corpus of sentences spoken by native English speakers. A grammar's degree of fit to that data—its likelihood—reflects the probability that the data would be generated by that grammar. Assuming that each sentence is generated independently from the grammar, this would be given by the product of the likelihoods of each sentences S_i in the corpus; with M unique sentences in the corpus, this would be:

$$p(D|G) = \prod_{l=1}^{M} p(S_l|G) \qquad (6.3)$$

Likelihood reflects the goodness-of-fit of a corpus of data to an underlying grammar in the same way that it reflects the goodness-of-fit of the dataset of dot points to an underlying rectangular "theory" in Figure 1. In that example, it seems intuitively that hypothesis B fits the data more closely than hypothesis A, but why? If A were the correct model, it would be quite a coincidence that all of the datapoints fall only in the regions covered by B. Similarly, if we were comparing two grammars X and Y, and X could generate all and only the sentences observed in the corpus but Y generated many others that were never observed, then X has better fit: if Y were the correct grammar, it would be an amazing coincidence that all of the sentences just happened to be the ones that X could generate. Likelihood is thus dependent on the quantity of data observed: while it would not be much of a surprise to see just one or a few sentences consistent with X if Y were in fact the correct grammar, seeing 1000 sentences—and none that could *not* be generated by X—would be very surprising indeed, if Y were correct.

The effective set of sentences that a probabilistic grammar can produce depends on several factors. All other things being equal, a grammar with more productions will produce more distinct sentence types. But the number of distinct sentences generated also depends on how those productions relate to each other: how many of the same left-hand side terms there are (and thus how much flexibility there is in expanding any one non-terminal), whether the productions can be combined recursively, and other factors. A penalty for overly expressive or flexible grammars exists here, too, because likelihood is assigned by considering all possible ways of generating a sentence under a given grammar and assigning probabilities to each derivation. The total probability that a grammar assigns over all possible sentences must sum to one, and thus the more flexible or expressive the grammar, the lower probability it will tend to assign to any one sentence.

So far I have demonstrated how the Bayesian framework can be used in theory to compare entire grammars in terms of their simplicity and their goodness-of-fit to actual corpora of real, naturalistic data. This approach is consistent with Chomsky's formulation of the problem of language learning, which presumes both a hypothesis space of grammars and the existence of an evaluation metric based on simplicity

(Chomsky, 1965). Prior probability produces an objective measure of a grammar's simplicity, while likelihood captures the degree of fit of a grammar to the data, and penalizes grammars or grammar types that are too expressive—that overgeneralize too much beyond the data.

Bayes' Rule and the mathematics of probability theory provides a principled way to combine these two factors in such a way to guarantee optimal inductive reasoning ability. Indeed, it has been formally proven that an ideal learner incorporating a simplicity metric will be able to predict the sentences of the language with an error that approaches zero as the size of the corpus goes to infinity (Solomonoff, 1978; Chater & Vitányi, 2007). It is therefore reasonable to think that the Bayesian approach may be well-suited to providing an objective way to compare different grammatical theories and formalisms within linguistics—and is thus another method for addressing many of the questions that have occupied linguists for years. In the next section, I will give some examples of how this method has been applied, and I will end with a discussion of the limitations and complexities inherent in applying it further.

4 Bayesian Grammar Comparison in Practice

4.1 Learning Abstract Syntactic Information

One issue that has been the focus of much work in linguistics for years is the question of abstract syntactic structure, and to what extent human learners are born with innate language-specific knowledge about that structure. It is widely accepted that natural language incorporates hierarchical phrase structure: that is, that the rules of syntax are defined over linguistic elements corresponding to phrases that can be represented hierarchically with respect to one another (Chomsky, 1965, 1980). By contrast, in a language without hierarchical phrase structure the rules of syntax might make reference only to the individual elements of the sentence as they appear in a linear sequence.

Why do linguists believe that language has hierarchical phrase structure? We have already discussed one of the main arguments, originally proposed by Chomsky in (1956). His conclusion that regular languages are inadequate to capture natural language centered around their inability to capture hierarchical phrase structure (and therefore long-distance dependencies based on that structure). The reasoning is, at its essence, a simplicity-based argument: because regular languages have so much less expressivity than language classes that incorporate hierarchical phrase structure, a regular grammar sufficient to capture natural language would have to be unrealistically complex. This argument, though intuitively compelling and reasonable, is still based on intuition; would an objective learner capable of trading off the complexity of regular grammars and how well they explained natural language data arrive at the same conclusion as Chomsky? And what implication might that have for the question of whether children learning language might also be able to arrive at the same conclusion?

To explore these questions, Perfors et al. (under review) presented a Bayesian learner capable of representing both regular and context-free grammars with a corpus of naturalistic child-directed speech. The learner was unbiased with respect to grammar type, meaning that it initially favored neither regular nor context-free grammars as being *a priori* more or less likely. Its prior probability and likelihood were defined as in Equations (6.2) and (6.3), so that it favored grammars that balance simplicity (containing fewer productions and terminals) with fit (overgeneralizing less). The data consisted of the sentences spoken by adults in the Adam corpus (Brown, 1973) of the CHILDES database (MacWhinney, 2000); in order to focus on grammar learning rather than lexical acquisition, individual words were replaced by their syntactic categories.[3] Furthermore, each grammar was evaluated based on the probabilities it assigned to the set of sentence types occurring in the corpus, independent of the frequencies with which those types occurred (i.e., the sentence token frequencies). This choice was based on the adaptor grammar framework of grammar induction introduced by Goldwater, Griffiths, and Johnson (2006). This parallels—and gives a principled justification for—the standard linguistic practice of assessing grammars based on the forms they produce rather than the precise frequencies of those forms.

A range of grammars was evaluated on this corpus, based on how well they optimized the tradeoff between simplicity and goodness-of-fit. Multiple context-free and regular grammars were identified and compared. Because the computational problem of searching the "grammar space" to identify the optimal one is intractable given current technology, we cannot be certain that the grammars considered represent the "best" of each type. However, every available method for searching the space as thoroughly as possible was implemented: some grammars were designed by hand; others were found via local search of the space using

---

[3] Although learning a grammar and learning a lexicon are probably tightly linked, this may be a fair assumption for several reasons: first, because grammars are defined over these categories, and second, because there is some evidence that aspects of syntactic-category knowledge may be in place even in young children (e.g. Louann, Rachel, & William, 2005).

the hand-designed grammars as a starting point; and other grammars were generated via an automatic search of the space.

Results indicated that the Bayesian learner preferred grammars that incorporated hierarchical phrase structure over grammars that did not: the model attributed the highest overall (posterior) probability to context-free grammars, and less to regular grammars or a simple list of memorized sentences. Interestingly, this remained true even if the data consisted of a tiny subset of the corpus, equivalent to just over an hour's worth of conversation at age 2;3. The reason for this is that although the regular grammars for the most part achieved a closer "fit" to the corpus by overgeneralizing less (i.e., producing fewer unobserved sentences) they accomplished this by sacrificing simplicity: just as Chomsky hypothesized, these grammars were unwieldy and long, containing many extra productions and non-terminals relative to the simpler context-free grammars. Regular grammars constructed to be as simple as the context-free grammars, on the other hand, lacked the expressivity to closely capture the sentences of natural language, and had a lower likelihood than equivalently simple context-free grammars. In essence, the grammars without hierarchical phrase structure were like hypotheses A and C in Figure 1, whereas the grammars with it were more like hypothesis B.

In addition to evaluating entire grammars, this framework can also be used to explore particular phenomena in linguistics. We will see an example of this in the next subsection.

4.2 Exploring Recursion

One of the most notable features of human language is its capacity to generate a potentially infinite number of possible sentences. Because such a capacity must result from an underlying generative mechanism (a grammar) that is recursive in some way, many linguists have concluded that recursion must be a fundamental, possibly innate, part of the language faculty (Chomsky, 1957). Some have gone further and claimed that the core mechanism underlying recursion is the only part of language that is specific to humans (Hauser, Chomsky, & Fitch, 2002). While the latter, stronger claim is contested (Pinker & Jackendoff, 2005), the former has been largely accepted for decades. However, recent work on Pirahã, a language spoken in the Amazon basin, suggests that there may be a language that does not contain any recursion in its phrase structure whatsoever (Everett, 2005).

The empirical claim about Pirahã is the subject of much debate (Nevins, Pesetsky, & Rodrigues, 2007; Everett, 2007), and an essential key to resolving the debate is to be able to objectively determine whether Pirahã is better described by a grammar with recursive elements or by one without. Lacking an objective and principled mechanism for comparing grammars with respect to linguistic corpora, it can be difficult to ascertain whether one grammar constitutes a "better description" than another. However, as before, the Bayesian framework provides a way of resolving this difficulty.

Here again we see the roles that simplicity and goodness-of-fit play. The standard reason for thinking that grammar is recursive is because of its property of discrete infinity: it is composed of discrete basic elements (words) which can be combined to produce apparently infinitely many sentences. An infinite set can be generated from a finite grammar only if the grammar contains some form of recursion; but is it true that natural language is infinite? After all, there are no infinitely long sentences, and only a finite number of sentences have been uttered. It is therefore possible to believe that the true grammar is one without any recursive rules. However, most linguists reject this possibility, on the grounds of simplicity: a non-recursive grammar capable of generating natural language would be very large, since it would require additional sets of rules for each additional depth of recursive expansion.

This simplicity-based argument is reasonable, but is not airtight, and is based on our intuitions about how much more complex a grammar with non-recursive instead of recursive rules would be. The complexity of a grammar would increase with each additional rule, and how many non-recursive rules would necessarily depend on the precise sentences being explained. Unfortunately, recursive productions hurt the fit of a grammar on any finite dataset, since they will always predict sentences that are not observed. The fewer sentences there are in the dataset that result from multiple expansions of recursive rules, the more a grammar with recursive rules is favored relative to one without.

Thus, recursion involves an inherent tradeoff between simplicity and goodness-of-fit, and we cannot conclude on *a priori* grounds that any grammar for natural language must contain recursion. At the very least, it may not be true in all cases, whether for a specific language (e.g., Pirahã), or for a specific rule or set of rules (e.g., center-embedded relative clauses in English). Perfors, Tenenbaum, Gibson, and Regier (2010) addressed this issue by comparing grammars (using the definitions of prior and likelihood given in Equations (6.2) and (6.3) based on how well they accounted for corpora of natural language data. Instead of comparing grammars of different types—those with hierarchical phrase structure and those without—they compared grammars with different levels of recursion.

All grammars were context-free, since CFGs are often adopted as a first approximation to the structure of natural language (Chomsky, 1959) and are standard tools in computational linguistics (e.g., Jurafsky & Martin, 2000; Manning & Schütze, 1999). Three main grammars were evaluated that differed from one another only in whether certain rules were recursive or not. The fully recursive grammar contained fully recursive noun phrases (e.g., NP → NP CP); another grammar contained no recursive noun phrases at all, but rather multiple-embedded non-recursive productions involving an additional new non-terminal, N2, which permitted parses of up to a depth of two. There was also a "middle ground" grammar containing both recursive and non-recursive "shadow" rules (which decrease the weight assigned to the recursive rules by accounting for the many non-recursive instances of noun phrases).

The grammar with both recursive and non-recursive rules was favored by the Bayesian learner, largely because it achieved an expressiveness similar to the fully-recursive grammar, but without an equivalent loss in goodness-of-fit. This suggests that syntax, while fundamentally recursive, might usefully employ non-recursive rules to parse simpler sentences that recursive rules could parse in principle. This would not change the expressive capability of the grammar, but might dramatically decrease the cost of recursion. This may also suggest how a learner could infer that language is recursive, despite never having heard sentences that go beyond only a few levels of embedding in the input: as long as the recursive rules have low enough weight, the penalty for "overgeneralizing" beyond a few levels of embedding would be minimal.

5 Further Issues and Concerns

The analysis discussed in this paper is potentially relevant to both of the two issues raised in section 2. It demonstrates how the Bayesian framework can provide a useful means for evaluating which specific grammars and grammar types best capture or explain natural language, going beyond qualitative, intuitive arguments to provide an objective criterion for grammar comparison. The analysis does incorporate certain assumptions—e.g., that sentence types rather than sentence tokens are the relevant data, or that grammars with fewer productions and non-terminals were simpler in the relevant sense—but the Bayesian framework forces those assumptions to be made explicit and provides a means to evaluate the extent to which the conclusions depended on them. Furthermore, this work may have implications for questions of innateness: if it is possible for an unbiased Bayesian learner to realize that language has hierarchical phrase structure on the basis of a limited amount of child-directed speech, what does this imply about whether such knowledge is (or need be) innate to children? By their nature, demonstrations of effective learning by Bayesian models cannot *necessarily* imply anything positive about the learning abilities of children, but they do serve as a proof-of-concept that something is learnable, given the assumptions built into the model. As such, they provide another path toward understanding the learning abilities children actually have.

Other examples of Bayesian methods—or, more generally, computational methods that combine structured representations with statistical inference machinery—abound in the computational linguistics and cognitive science literature. Some may have implications for human learning even if that was not the primary original purpose of the research. One example of work like this would include the adaptor grammar framework we briefly discussed earlier (Goldwater et al., 2006; Johnson, 2008). It was originally developed in order to create an adequate model for the unsupervised learning of morphology, but the general framework—including the notion of a two-part generative process for language, which separates the generation of allowable types from the process that explains their frequencies—may have much broader implications.

Bayesian methods are also increasingly common as a means to characterize the nature of the learning problem confronting the child, including a way to solve it. To list just a few examples, word segmentation may be accomplished by a learner sensitive to the transition probabilities between words, as well as further contextual dependencies among words (Goldwater, Griffiths, & Johnson, 2007); the problem of identifying the referents of nouns may be addressed by a learner who attends to the statistics of word use across multiple situations, and is attentive to social cues (Frank, Goodman, & Tenenbaum, 2009); and the acquisition of verb argument constructions, even without negative evidence, may be achieved by a learner sensitive to the statistics of what does not appear in the input (Alishahi & Stevenson, 2008; Perfors, Tenenbaum, & Wonnacott, 2010). This sort of research differs from the examples considered in this paper in that it does not involve the explicit comparison of specific grammars or grammar rules with the goal of identifying which theories best describe natural language, but the questions are similar.

One of my goals with this paper was to convince readers of the utility of applying the Bayesian framework for grammar comparison as a means of addressing two of the most important issues to linguists today: addressing the question of innateness, and deciding which formalisms or theories best capture natural language. The examples given here illustrate both how this framework can be useful for addressing these issues, but they also illustrate some of the potential limitations. Two of those are especially salient for our purposes here.

First, the utility of this method is limited by the extent to which it is possible to define and generate all of the grammars or grammatical rules in question, as a part of a coherent framework. Both of the examples given analyzed context-free and regular grammars, but none with greater sophistication: e.g., dependency grammars, grammars with explicit transformational rules, or minimalist grammars. In part this was because the simpler grammars were all that was necessary to address the questions under consideration—but in part it was because the simpler grammars were significantly easier to define within a generative framework, and to successfully calculate the likelihood for. Likelihood calculations require accurate and quick parsing of all sentences in the corpus, and the ability to assign a probability to each of those sentences. The technology for accomplishing this for context-free and regular grammars exists (Jurafsky & Martin, 2000; Manning & Schütze, 1999) but is less well-established for other types of grammars. This does not mean that the Bayesian framework for grammar comparison is not *in principle* extendible to higher-complexity grammars—but it does mean that such an implementation would need to co-occur, or build on, technical advances in these areas.

Second, the extent that one can draw strong conclusions from the performance of a Bayesian learner on a corpus of natural language data to the abilities of actual human learners may be somewhat limited. Something similar could probably be said for any single method, of course, but this is nevertheless good to keep in mind. Exploring what sort of grammars or theories a Bayesian learner favors, given some input, can shed light on (a) abstract learnability issues of what it may be *possible* to acquire, given certain assumptions about the learner and the data; (b) what different assumptions about the learner, the data, or the representation buys you in terms of how it changes the abstract learnability; and (c) in some objective sense, which theories better describe the observed data. But in order to draw stronger conclusions about the *actual* nature of human learners, the predictions of theoretical models (including Bayesian ones) crucially need to be compared against empirical evidence about language learning and language use.

In sum, then, this paper has described a computational framework for comparing grammars and grammatical rules, and given several examples intended to illustrate how it can be of utility when addressing two of the major questions of concern to linguists. The framework is not intended to supplant other methods in cognitive science or linguistics, but I suggest that it is a useful tool in the toolbox as we move toward constructing a full and accurate picture of the human mind.

Acknowledgements

The work discussed in this paper was done jointly with Josh Tenenbaum, Terry Regier, and Ted Gibson. Special thanks to David Beaver and James Gee for helpful comments on this manuscript.

References

Alishahi, A., & Stevenson, S. (2008). A computational model of early argument structure acquisition. *Cognitive Science*, *32*(5), 789–834.

Altmann, G. T. M., & Kamide, Y. (1999). Incremental interpretation at verbs: Restricting the domain of subsequent reference. *Cognition*, *73*(3), 247–264.

Brown, R. (1973). *A first language: The early stages.* Harvard University Press.

Chater, N., & Vitányi, P. (2007). 'Ideal learning' of natural language: Positive results about learning from positive evidence. *Journal of Mathematical Psychology*, *51*(3), 135–163.

Chomsky, N. (1956). Three models for the description of language. *IRE Transactions on Information Theory*, *2*(3), 113–124.

Chomsky, N. (1957). *Syntactic structures.* The Hague: Mouton.

Chomsky, N. (1959). On certain formal properties of grammars. *Information and Control*, *2*, 137–167.

Chomsky, N. (1965). *Aspects of the theory of syntax.* Cambridge, MA: MIT press.

Chomsky, N. (1980). *On cognitive structures and their development: A reply to Piaget* (M. Piattelli-Palmarini, Ed.). Cambridge, MA: Routledge & Kegan Paul.

Chomsky, N. (1995). *The minimalist program.* Cambridge, MA: MIT press.

Cox, R. T. (1946). Probability, frequency and reasonable expectation. *American Journal of Physics*, *14*(1), 1–13.

Cox, R. T. (1961). *The algebra of productive inference.* Baltimore, MD: Johns Hopkins University Press.

de Finetti, B. (1974). *Theory of probability.* New York: J. Wiley & Sons.

de Marcken, C. (1995). *Unsupervised language acquisition.* Unpublished doctoral dissertation, Massachusetts Institute of Technology, Cambridge, MA.

Dowman, M. (1998). *A cross-linguistic computational investigation of the learnability of syntactic, morphosyntactic, and phonological structure* (Tech. Rep. No. EUCCS-RP-1998-6). Edinburgh, UK: Edinburgh University, Centre for Cognitive Science.

Everett, D. L. (2005). Cultural constraints on grammar and cognition in Pirahã: Another look at the design features of human language. *Current Anthropology, 46*(4), 621–646.

Everett, D. L. (2007). *Cultural constraints on grammar in Pirahã: A reply to Nevins, Pesetsky, and Rodrigues (2007).* Available from http://ling.auf.net/lingBuzz/000427

Feldman, J. A., Gips, J., Horning, J. J., & Reder, S. (1969). *Grammatical complexity and inference* (Tech. Rep. No. CS-TR-69-125). Stanford, CA: Stanford University.

Frank, M. C., Goodman, N. D., & Tenenbaum, J. B. (2009). Using speakers' referential intentions to model early cross-situational word learning. *Psychological Science, 20*(5), 578–585.

Goldsmith, J. (2001). Unsupervised learning of the morphology of a natural language. *Computational Linguistics, 27*(2), 153–198.

Goldsmith, J. (2007). Morphological analogy: Only a beginning. In J. P. Blevins & J. Blevins (Eds.), *Analogy in grammar: Form and acquisition.* Oxford: Oxford University Press.

Goldwater, S., Griffiths, T. L., & Johnson, M. (2006). Interpolating between types and tokens by estimating power law generators. In *Advances in Neural Information Processing Systems* (Vol. 18). Vancouver, BC, Canada.

Goldwater, S., Griffiths, T. L., & Johnson, M. (2007). A Bayesian framework for word segmentation: Exploring the effects of context. *Cognition, 112*, 21-54.

Good, I. J. (1968). Corroboration, explanation, evolving probability, simplicity and a sharpened razor. *The British Journal for the Philosophy of Science, 19*(2), 123–143.

Grünwald, P. (1996). A minimum description length approach to grammar inference. *Symbolic, Connectionist, Statistical Approaches to Learning for Natural Language Processing. Lecture Notes in Computer Science, 1040*, 203–216.

Hauser, M. D., Chomsky, N., & Fitch, W. T. (2002). The faculty of language: What is it, who has it, and how did it evolve? *Science, 298*(5598), 1569–1579.

Horning, J. J. (1969). *A study of grammatical inference* (Tech. Rep. No. 139). Stanford, CA: Stanford University.

Immerman, N. (1999). *Descriptive complexity*. Springer Verlag.

Jaynes, T. J. (2003). *Probability theory: The logic of science*. Cambridge: Cambridge University Press.

Jeffreys, H. (1931). *Scientific inference*. Cambridge: Cambridge University Press.

Jeffreys, H. (1939). *Theory of probability*. Oxford: Clarendon Press.

Johnson, M. (2008). Using adaptor grammars to identify synergies in the unsupervised acquisition of linguistic structure. In *46th annual meeting of the Association for Computational Linguistics* (pp. 398–406). Columbus, OH.

Jurafsky, D., & Martin, J. H. (2000). *Speech and language processing: An introduction to natural language processing, computational linguistics and speech recognition*. New York: Prentice Hall.

Just, M. A., & Carpenter, P. A. (1980). A theory of reading: From eye fixations to comprehension. *Psychological Review, 87*(4), 329–354.

Kornai, A., & Pullum, G. K. (1990). The X-bar theory of phrase structure. *Language, 66*(1), 24–50.

Langendoen, D. T., Kalish-Landon, N., & Dore, J. (1973). Dative questions: A study in the relation of acceptability to grammaticality of an English sentence type. *Cognition, 2*, 451–477.

Lappin, S., Levine, R. D., & Johnson, D. E. (2000). The structure of unscientific revolutions. *Natural Language and Linguistic Theory, 18*, 665–671.

Levy, R. (2008). Expectation-based syntactic comprehension. *Cognition, 106*(3), 1126–1177.

Lohse, B., Hawkins, J., & Wasow, T. (2004). Processing domains in English verb-particle constructions. *Language, 80*(2), 238–261.

Louann, G., Rachel, W., & William, L. (2005). Infants can use distributional cues to form syntactic categories. *Journal of Child Language, 32*(02), 249–268.

MacKay, D. J. C. (2003). *Information theory, inference, and learning algorithms*. Cambridge: Cambridge University Press.

MacWhinney, B. (2000). *The CHILDES project: Tools for analyzing talk*. Lawrence Erlbaum Associates.

Manning, C. D., & Schütze, H. (1999). *Foundations of statistical natural language processing*. Cambridge, MA: MIT Press.

Nevins, A., Pesetsky, D., & Rodrigues, C. (2007). *Pirahã exceptionality: A reassessment*. Available from http://ling.auf.net/lingBuzz/000411

Nunberg, G., Sag, I. A., & Wasow, T. (1994). Idioms. *Language, 70*(3), 491–538.

Perfors, A., Tenenbaum, J., Gibson, E., & Regier, T. (2010). How recursive is language? A Bayesian exploration. *The Linguistic Review.*

Perfors, A., Tenenbaum, J., & Regier, T. (under review). The learnability of abstract syntactic principles. *Cognition.*

Perfors, A., Tenenbaum, J., & Wonnacott, E. (2010). Variability, negative evidence, and the acquisition of verb argument constructions. *Journal of Child Language, 37*, 607-642.

Peters, P. S., & Ritchie Jr., R. W. (1973). On the generative power of transformational grammars. *Information Sciences, 6*, 49–83.

Pinker, S., & Jackendoff, R. (2005). The faculty of language: What's special about it? *Cognition, 95*(2), 201–236.

Rogers, J. (1998). *A descriptive approach to language-theoretic complexity.* Stanford, CA: CSLI Publications.

Solomonoff, R. (1978). Complexity-based induction systems: Comparisons and convergence theorems. *IEEE transactions on Information Theory, 24*(4), 422–432.

Spivey, M. J., & Tanenhaus, M. K. (1998). Syntactic ambiguity resolution in discourse: Modeling the effects of referential context and lexical frequency. *Journal of Experimental Psychology: Learning Memory and Cognition, 24*, 1521–1543.

Tanenhaus, M., Spivey-Knowlton, M., Eberhard, K., & Sedivy, J. (1995). Integration of visual and linguistic information in spoken language comprehension. *Science, 268*(5217), 1632–1634.

Vitànyi, P., & Li, M. (2000). Minimum description length induction, Bayesianism, and Kolmogorov complexity. *IEEE transactions on Information Theory, IT-46*, 446–464.

Wasow, T., & Arnold, J. E. (2005). Intuitions in linguistic argumentation. *Lingua, 115*(11), 1481–1496.

Wolff, J. G. (1982). Language acquisition, data compression and generalization. *Language and Communication, 2*(1), 57–89.

Wrinch, D., & Jeffreys, H. (1921). On certain fundamental principles of scientific inquiry. *Philosophical Magazine, 42*(249), 369–390.

7

"Basic Information Structure" and "Academic Language": An Approach to Discourse Analysis

JAMES PAUL GEE

Preface

This paper was written for Tom Wasow's festschrift. I was at Stanford when what was a program in linguistics was turning into a department of linguistics. Tom was my last advisor, the one with whom I did my doctoral thesis (on the syntax and semantics of naked infinitives).

Elizabeth Closs Traugott was my first advisor. Since I was then one of the few if only students working on syntactic theory, when Joan Bresnan arrived, she became my second. When Joan left for a job at MIT (before coming back to Stanford after I left), Tom was hired to replace her.

However, Tom could not come for a semester and so the department, in an event that would no longer happen in today's academics, told me I could request anyone in the world to come to Stanford for a semester so I could study with him or her while I waited for Tom. I chose Richie Kayne then from the University of Paris.

By the time Tom arrived, I was tired of impressing new advisors. He gave me the great gift of not just being a wonderfully smart and supportive thesis advisor, but of both friendship and colleagueship. He finally made me feel as if I was on the way from no longer being a student to being an academic.

Language from a Cognitive Perspective.
Emily M. Bender and Jennifer Arnold, Editors
Copyright © 2011, CSLI Publications.

I have been an academic now for 35 years and have strayed far from theoretical linguistics—something that would have shocked me had anyone told me it would happen when I worked with Tom. I have worked on lots of topics in lots of academic areas and at lots of universities, always in my own mind, if not that of others, as a linguist.

I was blessed at Stanford by the best faculty I have ever since encountered (not just my advisors, but people like Joe Greenberg, Charles Ferguson, Will Leben, Dick Oehrle, and Eve Clark). But Tom was the one that in many ways "caused" my trajectory. My first job was at Hampshire College in Amherst, Massachusetts where I replaced Tom taking the position he had left to come Stanford. Tom was instrumental in getting me that job. Hampshire was a "special" place, especially in those days, and started my odd trajectory.

1 Introduction

This paper has two purposes. One purpose is to introduce a tool for analyzing some aspects of discourse. This tool is based on what I will call "Basic Information Structure" ("BIS" for short).[1] The second purpose is to apply this tool to a specific example so that I can speak to an issue I wish to address: "academic language".

"Academic language" (Gee, 2004; Schleppegrell, 2004) is a general name for many different varieties of language associated with academic disciplines or with academic content in schools, for example, the styles of language and other symbol systems associated with chemistry or social science.

Academic language is technical or specialist language. Of course, there are non-academic varieties of technical or specialist language. Domains such as video games, carpentry, or auto mechanics have their own specialist styles of language, as do professions like law, medicine, engineering, handicapping horse races, or fashion design, and so forth (some such professions, broadly speaking, could be counted as "academic", but not all).

The issue germane to academic language I want to address is this: some people have argued that academic varieties of language are func-

---

[1] I am a linguist who now usually writes for non-linguists. This paper is based on such work. Since the current paper is for Tom Wasow's festschrift, here is a note for linguists: First, what I call "BIS" has nothing to do with derivational structure of any sort in any theory of grammar. Whatever psychological reality BIS has would be discovered through processing studies in psycholinguistics (and there are studies that support the approach, though I do not discuss them here). Second, for those old enough to remember Generative Semantics, BIS bears some similarities to it, which just goes to show that GS was, to that extent, a theory of information structure imported into syntactic theory.

tional in the sense that they have evolved in history to do certain intellectual and interactional tasks necessary for an academic domain to make progress (M. A. K. Halliday & Martin, 1993). They cannot simply be replaced with less specialized versions of language, any more than a tool purpose-built for a specific job can simply be replaced, without loss, by a more generalized tool.

Others have argued that such academic varieties of language are forms of "jargon" and complexity invented to exclude, confuse, and frustrate outsiders (non-academics and people outside a given field) and to hide or evade political, cultural, institutional, and social issues in the name of "reason" or "logic" (see Wiley, 1996 for discussion). In this sense, such forms of language are "ideological" (in one sense of the word).

This issue—whether academic varieties of language are functional or ideological—has played a role in education. Some educators argue that children need to be introduced in school (for example, in science classrooms) to academic varieties of language early on, because mastery of these representational systems is crucial for true understanding and real participation in areas of science, for instance (M. A. K. Halliday & Martin, 1993). Others have argued that academic varieties of language simply serve to make the "rich" kids look smarter than the "poor" ones because they have had more home-based preparation for such varieties (Lee, 2002). Such academic varieties of language are barriers to understanding and participation, on this view, and need to be replaced with more democratic forms of language, interaction, and participation.

The paper will proceed in three parts. First I will introduce "Basic Information Structure" as a tool for analysis. Second, I will discuss the issue of academic and other specialized forms of language. Third, I will use BIS to analyze a specific case in order to illuminate the issue of academic language being "functional" and/or "ideological" (we will see, in fact, that it can be both at the same time).

Before I start, let me say that I do not separate "critical discourse analysis" from "discourse analysis" proper. All language use is political in the sense of expressing (tacitly or overtly) messages about things like status and solidarity and other "social goods" in society (Milroy, 1980). Thus, any form of discourse analysis must pay attention to such issues. I have discussed this issue elsewhere (Gee, 2003, 2005). It will be apparent by the end of this paper that the example I discuss is one where "giving information" and "expressing political, ethical, value-laden messages" go hand-in-hand.

2 The Design of Discourse and "Basic Information Structure"

This section contains the basic grammatical information necessary to understand what I will call "Basic Information Structure" (BIS). Clauses (subject-predicate structures) are the fundamental units of communication and information structure (Chafe, 1994; M. A. K. Halliday, 1994; Gee, 2005). Any clause is composed grammatically of required elements and optional ones. For example, a transitive verb requires a subject and object, but optionally allows prepositional phrases to follow the object and it also optionally allows various sorts of modifiers (e.g., "adverbs").

Within a clause, phrases also have required elements and optional ones. An NP can be just a noun or article + noun but can optionally be modified by adjectives and prepositional phrases. Let us call any clause made up of only required elements (thus required arguments whose own structure contains only required elements) a "basic clause" (we could also call it a "bare clause"). Thus, "Mary loved the boy" is a basic clause, but "Mary loved the boy from New York", "Mary loved the boy with all her heart", "Yesterday, Mary loved the boy" are not.

Why would we want to make this sort of distinction between basic clauses and non-basic ones? For this reason: When we want to talk about information, communication, and different styles of language used for different activities, the options people choose to include or not can be telling in terms of what they want to communicate and what they want to withhold. If I have to admit that I hurt Mary, the minimum I have to say is "I hurt Mary", but I have the option to say or withhold something like "on purpose" or "accidently": "I hurt Mary on purpose", "I hurt Mary accidently". If I want to tell you I am healthy, the minimum I have to say is something like "I am healthy", but I have the option to say or withhold something like "for someone who has cancer": "I am healthy for someone who has cancer". What people choose to say or withhold is, of course, crucial to discourse analysis.

Basic clauses, augmented or not by optional arguments or elements, can be combined or integrated in four ways. First is a "loose" way, when two or more clauses are combined by coordination and both clauses are main clauses (e.g., "Mary is healthy and she is quite old").

Second, clauses can be combined in a somewhat less loose way, when one or more clauses is juxtaposed, as a subordinate clause, to a main clause (e.g., "While John was not looking, Mary touched him on the head").

Third, two clauses can be tightly integrated by having one clause embedded inside another one (e.g., "John felt Mary touch him on the arm", "John believed that Mary was right", "Mary planned to kiss John"):

Fourth, in the tightest form of integration, a clause (really a clause's worth of information) can be turned into a phrase, losing its status as a clause (M. Halliday & Matthiessen, 1999). This can be done by changing a verb into noun, as when we change "destroy" into "destruction" (e.g., "Someone destroyed the city" → "The city's destruction"). It can also be done by changing a verb into an adjective, as when we change "abuse" into "abused" (e.g., "Someone abuses children" → "abused children"). It can also be done by turning an adjective into a noun, as when we change "happy" into "happiness" ("Mary is happy" → "Mary's happiness").

When we turn clauses (really a clause's worth of information) into phrases, we can lose information and gain options. Thus the verb "destroy" requires I name a destroyer, but the noun "destruction" does not ("The city's destruction", "The city's destruction by the allies", "the city's destruction at the hands of the allies"). And, again, when we have options, we get information that is either said or withheld (and we will want to know why when we engage in discourse analysis).

So far, in all the cases above, we have been moving from phrases and clauses to more complex combinations of clauses. But in discourse analysis we usually must go the other way round. We have to start with sentences that are composed of two or more (sometimes many more) clauses (combined or integrated in the ways we have just discussed above and others) and unravel these sentences into their basic clauses and whatever optional arguments or other elements those clauses contain. That is, we have to ask what basic clauses (and optional arguments and elements) the sentences are composed of or, to put it yet another way, what basic clauses (and optional arguments and elements) the sentences combine or integrate. So, to give one example, consider the case below:

(1) The present study sought to clarify previous work.

    a. The present study = someone (= researchers) study something (= topic) in the present

    b. sought = (1a) seek (1c–1d)

    c. to clarify = someone (= researchers) clarify (1d)

    d. previous work = someone (= the field) works on something (= topic) previously

(1) is a sentence that starts a published research article that I will discuss below (Pollak, Vardi, Putzer Bechner, & Curtin, 2005: I have shortened the sentence). The phrase "the present study" contributes the clause "someone study something in the present". In the phrase "the present study", "study" is a noun related to the verb "to study" (of course, since it is noun, it has no tense—no time marking—and thus we cannot know what tense it would have had had it been used as a verb). When this verb is changed to a noun, the subject of the verb does not have to be mentioned, but we can infer that this subject is the researchers who are publishing the paper (thus, "researchers" is place in parentheses to mark that it is an inference). What the researchers are studying need not be mentioned either, but, again, we can infer that the object of the verb "to study" is the topic of the paper, that is, the topic the researchers did their research on and are reporting on in the paper (thus, "topic" is in parentheses)—we could, of course, fill in more fully what the topic actually is.

"Sought" is the main verb (predicate) of the sentence. Its subject is the information contributed to the sentence by the phrase "the present study". The information this phrase contains is represented in line (1a)—so I place (1a) in the subject slot of "seek". "Sought" is the sort of verb that allows an infinitive to be embedded inside or below it—in this case the infinitive "to clarify". "To clarify", then, is the predicate of a clause embedded inside (or "underneath") "sought": "researchers clarify something". The "something" that is clarified is expressed in line (1d) (thus, (1d) is in the object slot of "clarify"). The object of "seek"—what is sought—is the information in lines (1c) and (1d) (and, thus, (1c–1d) is in the object slot of "seek").

The phrase "previous work" has a noun ("work") in it related to the verb "to work" and so this phrase contributes the clause: "the field works on topic previously". Here, again, we have to infer that something like "the field" is the subject of "works" (or "researchers who have done previous work in the field"). We can infer, as well, that the object of "works" is once again the topic of the paper, a topic that has heretofore been worked on by others in the field. When the verb "to work" is made into the noun "work", the adverb "previously" (which modifies a verb) becomes the adjective "previous" (which modifies a noun).

Thus, the short sentence "The present study sought to clarify previous work" combines, in various ways, four clauses—or, we can say, it combines four clauses' worth of information. Once we know what clauses a sentence combines, we can see that there were many other ways these same clauses could have been filled out and combined. Thus, there are many other ways in which the sentence "The present study sought to clarify previous work" could have been said or written (could have been "designed"). A few examples are given below. These sentences either fill out optional arguments and elements in a different way, spell out inferences that were left unspecified, or combine or integrate the same clauses in a different way. Some of these forms below, while grammatical, would hardly ever or never be used for stylistic or pragmatic reasons (but, of course, from a discourse analytic point of view, we want to know why). Let's assume for now that the topic of the study is "physically abused children":

(2)   a. We studied physically abused children because we sought to clarify previous work in the field.

   b. The present study sought to clarify work that others had done previously.

   c. The present study studies physically abused children. We seek to clarify previous work.

   d. This study we have done in the present seeks to clarify work done previously.

   e. The present study of physically abused children seeks to clarify previous work.

   f. This study was done in the present. It sought something. It sought to clarify something. What it sought to clarify was work others had done previously.

   g. What the present study sought was to clarify was previous work.

   h. The present study of physically abused children sought to clarify previous work.

When we generate a list of alternative ways clauses could have been filled out and combined, we also generate the key question: Why were the clauses combined and filled out as they were and not some other way? There can be lots of different answers to this question. For instance, some alternatives are ruled out by the type or style of language required by the communicative task or the genre, here a professional publication. Thus, most or all of the alternatives in (2) are not the "right" style for a professional academic publication. The sentence in (2h)—which just spells out something that is left to be inferred in "The present study sought to clarify previous work"—might be avoided either because the authors do not want to name their topic directly or they feel it is obvious from other things in the paper (e.g., the title or abstract) or they feel the topic needs to be named or discussed in a more nuanced way than is possible by placing it as a phrase in this sentence.

A representation like that in (3) shows what I will call the "basic information structure" (hereafter BIS) in an oral or written text. The BIS in the sentence "The present study sought to clarify previous work" is the four clauses below. Here I leave out the information in (2) that shows how the clauses are fit together and which information is left to be specified by inference:

(3) a. Someone study something in the present

b. Someone seek something

c. Someone clarify something

d. Someone work on something previously

Such basic information is "packaged"—put together into sentences— by: a) combining and integrating the clauses that the information expresses; b) adding optional arguments and elements to the clauses or the sentence as a whole; c) allowing for inferences to be made to specify information that is left out. Each such "move" (a-c) is a choice and one style of discourse analysis is to ask, for each such choice, why it might have been made and what communicative function it might be serving. We can ask, as well, why other alternative choices were not made (often the answer to this question illuminates the question about why a given choice was made and what it communicates).

When clauses are combined and integrated into sentences, other options arise. So if I combine "We studied what children do" and "Children are confronted with anger", I can say: "We studied what children do when they/children are confronted with anger" or "We studied what children did when confronted by anger". So we have the option to overtly mention "children" as the subject of "confront" or not. This is a case where even a required element can be left out because it is "recoverable" from context.

3 Social Languages and the Question of Specialist Language

This section takes up the issue of academic language (and, more generally, specialist or technical varieties of language). Any language comes in many different varieties or styles used for different purposes (Gee, 2004, 2005). There are different varieties of language used for different social identities and activities—for example, different varieties used by lawyers, doctors, gang members, biologists, carpenters, or video gamers for their characteristic activities. Such varieties are sometimes called "registers". I will refer to them as different "social languages". Social languages are differentiated from each by the use of different words (vocabulary) and sometimes by particular ways of using the morphological, syntactic, and/or discourse resources of the language.

One major distinction we can make (Gee, 2004, 2005) in regard to social languages is between "vernacular social languages" (vernacular styles of language) and "specialist social languages" (specialist styles of language). Vernacular styles are used by people when they are communicating as "everyday" non-specialist people. Vernacular styles differ across different social and cultural groups. Specialist styles are used by people when they are communicating as a specialist of some sort, whether this be a doctor, minister, academic, or gamer. Specialist styles, of course, draw on vernacular resources, but supplement them in a variety of ways through the use of distinctive words, distinctive uses of morphology, and/or distinctive uses of syntactic or discourse resources. For example, the sentence in (4) below is in the vernacular style and the sentence in (5) is in a specialist style associated with an academic discipline (in this case, some form of biology). In each case, I list the basic information that each sentence packages into a single sentence.

(4)   Hornworms sure vary a lot in how well they grow

    a. Hornworms vary a lot in (4b)

    b. Hornworms grow how well

(5)   Hornworm growth displays significant variation

    a. Hornworms grow

    b. (5a) displays (5c–5d)

    c. (5a) varies (5d)

    d. (5c) is significant

The vernacular differs from the specialist version in several ways. First the basic predicates (in the BIS) used are different in part: "vary" and "grow" in the vernacular and "grow", "display", "vary", and "is significant" in the specialist version. "Display" and "significant" are Latinate words that are typical of more specialist styles. Second, the two predicates that the two versions share—"vary" and "grow"—are in the specialist version turned into nouns ("growth" and "variation") and made arguments of other predicates ("growth" is the subject of "display" and "variation" is the object of "display").

(4a) says pretty much the same thing as (5c) and (4b) says pretty much the same thing as (5a)—so these pieces of information are shared

by the two varieties. The information in the specialist variety in (5d)—
"something is significant"—is conveyed in the vernacular by the adverb
"a lot" modifying "vary" and the affective marker "sure" which modifies
the whole sentence "Hornworms vary a lot in how well they grow". Of
course, "sure ... a lot" is not only less formal, it expresses the opinion
of the speaker, while "significant" in "significant variation" is both
more formal and expresses, not just the opinion of the speaker, but a
standard held by a social group (a profession, in this case biologists or
statisticians).

Note how in the specialist version the entity hornworms and the processes of varying and growing disappear. They are replaced by abstract
things: hornworm growth and variation. This is typical of the distinction between vernacular styles and specialist styles of the sort in (5)
above (academic styles of language).

In addition to asking why and how a given sentence packages its basic
information as it does, we can, thus, too, ask an additional question:
Why and how does a given sentence deviate from a vernacular style of
language? Thus, we could ask: Why would anyone use a sentence like
(5) rather than (4)?

4 An Example: Academic Language

Now I turn to use BIS to analyze a specific piece of academic language.
My goal here is to speak to the issue of whether and how such academic
language is either functional or ideological. The paper I will deal with
is "Physically Abused Children's Regulation of Attention in Response
to Hostility" by Pollak et al., a paper which appeared in the journal
Child Development (2005).

Before I turn to a small part of this paper, I need to tell you about
the paper in general. Already this raises an interesting issue, since part
of what I want to study here is how and why things are said (written) in
a certain way and whether they can be said (written) in other ways—
and why these other ways may have been avoided. So, I give a summary
of the paper, well aware that to say it differently is not really to say
the same thing.

The paper begins by asserting that the link between children expe-
riencing physical abuse and thereafter demonstrating behavioral problems (e.g., withdrawal and aggression, attributing hostility to others,
and displaying inappropriate affect and behavior) has already been well
established in the research literature. However, the authors claim that
the "precise mechanism" linking the two is not well understood. So, the
paper seeks, not to argue for a link between abuse and behavioral prob-

lems (which is already known), but to get at the causal "mechanism" linking the two.

The authors propose that "attentional effects" may be the link between abuse and behavior problems. The idea is this: all young children have limited processing capacity and so can pay attention to only a limited number of stimuli at a time. This limited capacity causes the child to privilege and focus on some (salient) aspects of the environment over others. For physically abused children these salient features are things like threat and anger. Physically abused children may learn to overly attend to threatening cues, perhaps at the expense of other contextually relevant information, and may, in turn, have less resources available to regulate their emotional reposes to events that seem threatening to them, but, in reality, would not seem so threatening to children who had not been physically abused.

The sample of children studied consisted of 11 four and five-year-old children who had been physically abused by their parents and 22 non-abused children (as a control group). Parents gave informed consent after receiving information about the study (the notion of "informed consent" for children from parents who have admitted to abusing their children is, it seems to me, problematic).

The researchers are experimental physiological psychologists, people who want to precisely measure physical reactions (things like heart rate and skin conductance). For them, emotions (e.g., fear) are signaled by such physical reactions and it is these reactions they measure directly, not the emotions. But, of course, they need to get people to react to stimuli in order to measure their reactions. In this study, they had the children engage with a task on a computer (which the children thought was the task they were there to engage in), while in the background the children heard what they thought was an angry argument between two adults. The researchers wanted to know how the children—abused and non-abused—would react to (pay attention to) this background anger.

The researchers recorded a seven minute scripted conversation by two professional actors. The conversation started with the actors pretending to be two co-workers meeting and engaging in casual conversation. Then the two characters intensely argue. After that, there is a period of "silent unresolved anger during which one character abruptly leaves the room". Finally, there is a resolution in which the two characters apologize to each other. The conversation was presented by means of a compact disc player placed in a room adjacent to where the child was located. An opening in the wall connected the two rooms, so that the children could hear the argument, but not see that it was a recording. The children were, thus, meant to believe the argument was real, not recorded.

The task the children did on the computer involved pictures of different objects appearing at the center of a computer screen. The child was instructed to press the space bar in response to every picture except for a soccer ball. This task was meant to be a measure of attention, which might be disrupted to various degrees when the argument occurred.

Various physiological measurements where taken of the children's responses to the anger. For example, the children's emotional arousal was measured by electrodes on their skin that indexed their "skin conductance level". Skin conductance level reflects arousal through changes in the relative activity of the "eccrine sweat glands" (eccrine glands occur in, among other places, the palms of the hands). Increases in skin conductance level indicate increases in emotional arousal. In order to get such measurements, a space heater was placed in the experiment room to facilitate the adequate release of sweat.

5   An Analysis: Part 1: BIS

Below I reprint the part of the paper on which I will base my analysis:

> The present study sought to clarify and extend previous work suggesting that physically abused children develop perceptual sensitivity to anger. First, we sought to further examine the ways in which physically abused children can regulate attentional processes when confronted with anger or threat. Second, because prior research suggested that physically abused children would be especially sensitive to anger, the anger-related stimuli presented to the children occurred in the background and were irrelevant to the child's purported task and not personally meaningful. This created a relatively conservative test of children's attentional regulation. The present data suggest that once anger was introduced, abused children maintained a state of anticipatory monitoring of the environment. In contrast, non-abused children were initially more aroused by the introduction of anger, but showed better recovery to baseline states once anger was resolved.

I will here just consider two sentences from this paragraph. Below I show the BIS for each. First, consider (6) below. Here I give the BIS only for part of the sentence, the part I have placed in brackets: "physically abused children can regulate attentional processes when confronted with anger or threat":

(6) First, we sought to further examine the ways in which [physically abused children can regulate attentional processes when confronted with anger or threat].

    a. physically abused children = someone (?) abuse children physically

    b. can regulate = (6a) can regulate (6c–6g):

    c. attentional = (6a) attend to (6e–6g)

    d. processes = (6a) process (6c)

    e. when confronted = someone (?) confront (6a) with (6f/6g)

    f. with anger = someone (?) get angry at someone (?)

    g. or threat = someone (?) threaten someone (?)

"Physically abused children" is a phrase that encapsulates the information in the clause in (6a): "someone abuse their children physically". Who is this someone? This sentence and the passage from which it is taken is systematically ambiguous in a way typical of this type of scientific writing. When the authors say they want to "examine the ways in which physically abused children can ..." are they talking about any and all physically abused children or the specific children studied in this research, children who were abused by their parents? Of course, they want to make a claim about any and all abused children based on these specific children and the ambiguity is, thus, functional.

"Can regulate" introduces another predicate "regulate". Its subject is the information in line (6a) (which becomes the phrase "physically abused children" in the text); thus, I write (6a) in its subject slot to yield "(6a) can regulate (6c–6g)".

The object of "regulate" (what is being regulated) is all the information in lines (6c) through (6g), thus I write (6c–6g) in its object slot: "(6a) can regulate (6c–6g)". What is being regulated (by the children)—the information given in (6c) through (6g)—is quite complicated, indeed: The children are regulating how they mentally process (6d) when they attend to (6c) in situations where they have been confronted (6e) with someone getting angry at someone or threatening someone (6f) and (6g). This is certainly a form of technical writing with a vengeance.

The verb "confronted" in the text is missing both its subject and object. The object must be inferred to be "physically abused children", the information in (6a). However, what we should infer the subject to be is less clear. Who confronted the children with anger or threat? We could be talking about what the researchers did in exposing the children to the taped (but thought to be real) anger. Or we could be talking in general terms about any time anyone confronts abused children (these specific children? all abused children?) with anger or threat. Equally, in (6f) and (6g), it is not clear who is getting angry at whom or who is doing the threatening of whom: Is it the actors that made the tape or anyone who might display anger in front of an abused child? Again, the authors want to draw a general conclusion based on what they did to the specific children in the study and so the ambiguity is, in this respect, functional.

Next, consider the sentence is (7) below:

(7) The present data suggest that once anger was introduced abused children maintained a state of anticipatory monitoring of the environment

    a. The present data suggest = the present data suggest (7b–7g)

    b. that once anger = someone (= actor) gets angry at someone (= actor)

    c. was introduced = someone (= researchers) introduce (7b) to someone (= abused children)

    d. abused children = someone (= parents) abuse children

    e. maintained a state = someone (= abused children) maintain a state of (7f–7g)

    f. of anticipatory = someone (= abused children) anticipate something (= threat/harm)

    g. monitoring of the environment = someone (= abused children) monitor environment by (7f)

So here "suggest" has as its object (what is being suggested) all the information in lines (7b–7g). The noun "anger" is related to the predicate "get angry at" and introduces the information in (7b). Since the authors used the noun and not the predicate, they did not have to overtly mention the subject (who is getting angry) or object (who or what the anger is directed at). However, the reader can infer that the subject and object of "get angry at" are the actors who role-played anger at each other for the tape and who the children thought were real people. I note this inference by placing "actor" in parentheses.

Similarly, we can infer that it was the researchers (the authors of the paper) who introduced the situation of someone getting angry at someone else (7b) to the abused children. Likewise in (7d) we can infer—from what the paper has told us—that the people who abused the children were their parents.

In (7e–7g), the state that the abused children are said to have maintained (see (7e)) is very complicated and technical. The state is this: the abused children monitor the environment (7g) by (engaging in the process of) anticipating something (7f). What are they anticipating? This is, for me, the crucial question. Nothing in the text explicitly tells us what they are anticipating. The inference most readers will make, I believe—if they read deep enough into this technical prose—is that the children feel threatened and are anticipating harm or abuse. Of course, that is the hypothesis of the paper—that abused children will look for and anticipate threat where there is none in reality. But, while in reality there was none in this environment, there is no way the abused children could have known this, since they were not aware that the argument was just on tape and not in the real world.

6 An Analysis: Part 2: Claims Based on the BIS

We have seen several ways in which this specialist prose is functional. And at a general level it is functional in the sense that as physiological psychologists these authors want to study and write about outward bodily behavioral effects (sweating, heart rate), rather than inner feelings or emotions. Their prose and their practices are well suited to do just that.

At the same time, this specialist prose allows and encourages the authors to evade any direct statement about *who did what to whom*. However, at the level of BIS and the inferences readers can make, it is apparent that the authors are evading (being allowed not to have to say directly) the information that *they threatened five year old children who they admit are particularly sensitive to and vulnerable to threats or anger*.

At the same time, this specialist language allows and encourages the authors, as well, to evade any direct statement about what the researchers did to the children *meant to the children*. The children's emotions, feelings, fears are obscured and ignored in the authors' prose (and in their practices—academic prose and practices go hand in hand—that is what is meant by "functional"). Their prose and practices foreground outer bodily behaviorial effects at the expense of a focus on feelings and emotions. But at the level of BIS the reader can infer that *the children feel fear*.

Finally, in the authors' practice and prose, emotion is effaced as a causal mechanism to be replaced by "attentional effects" displayed or signaled by bodily behavioral effects (like sweating and heart rate). This is really a double displacement of emotion: an emotion like fear is seen first in terms of cognitive processing mechanism ("attentional effects") and then these are signaled by or discovered through bodily mechanisms like sweating, which is what the researches pay attention to and write about. However, at the level of BIS these attentional effects amount to *young children anticipating harm and, thus, feeling fear.*

The evasion of what the researchers did to the children—something no one would approve of had it been said directly and in the vernacular as in "We threatened vulnerable five-year-olds"—is ideological (in this case, an attempt to evade a value-laden ethical issue). In this piece of academic writing, the functional and the ideological are "married at the hip". The function of the language is to allow researchers to distance themselves from the inner world so as to do a science based on the outer world of the body's reactions. In this particular case that also allowed the researchers not to have to directly state what they had done in terms of what it meant to the children. What things mean is the domain of another academic area, namely discourse analysis. In that sense, discourse analysis stands in a "critical" relation to other forms of language. This does not mean, of course, that it is not itself open to critique (by discourse analysis applied to itself).

Nothing I have said in my analysis implies the researchers themselves believe they did anything unethical or immoral. My only claim is that when we move from BIS (which is closer to the vernacular, though not itself vernacular, thanks to technical vocabulary) something is added (namely, the functional ability of these academics to practice their specialist discipline) and something is lost (namely, a direct focus on what makes the research ethically problematic to some others, some of whom are not specialists in the researchers' discipline and, perhaps, some of whom are).

The authors of the paper I have discussed can, of course, say that I am an "outsider", thus, not competent to comment on their practices or prose. But, in my view, that response is ideological. It is my belief that, morally, all of us academics must account for any situations where we have used our technical prose to evade what, said in the vernacular, is clearly a violation of the "lifeworld" (that is, a violation of what we as everyday people take to be moral). I do not say the authors I have studied have no such account, only that they owe even those outside their field one.

Can I give empirical evidence for this principle that we academics (and others) must, at a moral level, acknowledge our responsibility to give an account for any situations where we have used our technical prose to evade what said in the vernacular is clearly a violation of the "lifeworld"? As I have pointed out in earlier work (Gee, 1990, 1996), no I cannot. With such a principle—one that I have argued in earlier work is a basic moral principle of both discourse analysis and human linguistic interaction (Gee, 1990, 1996)—we reach the limits of our shared "form of life" (Wittgenstein, 1958). Outside the principle—that is, denying it—"we don't know what to say" (Austin, 1961) and must leave words and resort to actions in our own defense.

References

Austin, J. L. (1961). Other minds. *Philosophical Papers*, 44–84.

Chafe, W. L. (1994). *Discourse, consciousness, and time: The flow and displacement of conscious experience in speaking and writing.* Chicago, IL: University of Chicago Press.

Gee, J. P. (1990). *Social linguistics and literacies: Ideology in discourses.* London: Falmer.

Gee, J. P. (1996). *Social linguistics and literacies: Ideology in discourses* (Second Edition ed.). London: Taylor and Francis.

Gee, J. P. (2003). Discourse analysis: What makes it critical? In R. Rogers (Ed.), *An introduction to critical discourse analysis in education* (pp. 19–50). Mahwah, NJ: Lawrence Erlbaum.

Gee, J. P. (2004). *Situated language and learning: A critique of traditional schooling.* London: Routledge.

Gee, J. P. (2005). *An introduction to discourse analysis: Theory and method.* London: Routledge.

Halliday, M., & Matthiessen, C. M. I. M. (1999). *Construing experience through meaning: A language-based approach to cognition.* New York: Continuum.

Halliday, M. A. K. (1994). *An introduction to functional grammar.* London: Edward Arnold.

Halliday, M. A. K., & Martin, J. R. (1993). *Writing science: Literacy and discursive power.* Pittsburgh, PA: Univ of Pittsburgh Press.

Lee, O. (2002). Science inquiry for elementary students from diverse backgrounds. In W. G. Secada (Ed.), *Review of research in education* (pp. 23–69). Washington, DC: American Educational Research Association.

Milroy, L. (1980). *Language and social networks.* Oxford: Basil Blackwell.

Pollak, S. D., Vardi, S., Putzer Bechner, A. M., & Curtin, J. J. (2005). Physically abused children's regulation of attention in response to hostility. *Child Development*, *76*(5), 968–977.

Schleppegrell, M. J. (2004). *The language of schooling: A functional linguistics perspective.* Mahwah, NJ: Lawrence Erlbaum.

Wiley, T. G. (1996). *Literacy and language diversity in the United States.* Washington, DC: Center for Applied Linguistics and Delta Systems.

Wittgenstein, L. (1958). *Philosophical investigations.* Oxford: Basil Blackwell.

8

Relativizer Omission in Anglophone Caribbean Creoles, Appalachian, and African American Vernacular English [AAVE], and Its Theoretical Implications

JOHN R. RICKFORD

Preface

It is a pleasure, first of all, to contribute this paper to a volume honoring my friend and colleague Tom Wasow. Tom and I have been faculty colleagues in the Linguistics Department at Stanford since 1980, and neighbors in Barron Park, Palo Alto (our fences touch at one corner) since 1982. More than that, I have collaborated with him on several different morphosyntactic variables, resulting in four publications so far (Rickford, Wasow, Mendoza-Denton, & Espinoza, 1995; Sells, Rickford, & Wasow, 1996; Rickford, Wasow, Zwicky, & Buchstaller, 2007; Buchstaller, Rickford, Traugott, Wasow, & Zwicky, to appear), and in every case I have found his contributions to be richly illuminating. Indeed, Tom and I practice what some might call socio-syntax, and at the summer meeting of the Linguistic Society of America at Ohio State University in 2008, we presented a paper on the value of this kind of collaboration across Linguistics subfields.[1]

---

[1] "Collaborations: *As far as* different subfields, we're *all*, "*Aint* no reason ∅ we shouldn't work together." Invited plenary talk, July 2008.

Language from a Cognitive Perspective.
Emily M. Bender and Jennifer Arnold, Editors
Copyright © 2011, CSLI Publications.

Tom has also been an invaluable consultant on my three-year National Science Foundation project on Grammatical Variation and Change, and it is out of this research that the present paper grows. I am delighted that one of its first published results should appear in a volume dedicated to him.

1 Introduction

The primary focus of this paper is the empirical question of how (how **often**, and with what linguistic **conditioning**) creole and vernacular English speakers in Guyana, Jamaica, Appalachia and African America omit *that, who, what* (i.e. have zero instead of an overt relative pronoun or relativizer) in relative clauses like:

(1) I saw the boy that/*who(m)*/*what*/Ø you like.

From quantitative studies of the past twenty years (e.g. Kikai, Schleppegrell, & Tagliamonte, 1987; Adamson, 1992; Guy & Bayley, 1995; Tottie & Rey, 1997; Wasow, Jaeger, & Orr, 2004; Tagliamonte, Smith, & Lawrence, 2005), we know a **lot** about this in British and American varieties, but **nothing** about this in Caribbean Creole English, Appalachian or modern African American Vernacular English [AAVE].

In attempting to answer this first question, I'll consider a second: Can the patterns of relativizer omission in these vernacular/creole varieties contribute any new insights to the old debate about the creole vs English origins of AAVE? If 'Black' AAVE patterns like Caribbean Creole Englishes (speakers of which were well-represented in the founding populations of Black English speakers in the American colonies; see Rickford, 1997), while 'White' Appalachian behaves more like English in Ulster and other 'Northern' British areas from which the ancestors of today's Appalachians came (see Montgomery, 2001), we might conclude that the creolists are right and that this case confirms Labov's more general claim (1980:xvii) that "quantitative patterns can apparently preserve linguistic history over several centuries and several continents."

A third, related question arises as well: Are the variable patterns for relativizer omission specific enough to particular dialects or regions that they can be used reliably to reconstruct historical relations from cross-variety comparisons, or do they reflect broad processing constraints that might be found in all Englishes, if not universally (Wasow et al., 2004; Jaeger & Wasow, 2007)?

To answer these questions, I'll look at data on relativizer omission in Guyanese and Jamaican Creole English, Appalachian English, and

AAVE, but I should note that the research reported on in this paper is part of a larger project including Barbadian English, and two other variables, plural marking and question formation. The goals of the project are to increase understanding of quantitative linguistic variation in these varieties, provide better data for the AAVE creole origins debate, and contribute to the question of whether variable constraint patterns can be reliably used for dialect-specific historical reconstruction, as previously assumed (e.g. Poplack, 2000).[2]

One question that some readers may already have is how relativizer omission is relevant to the debate over the creole origins of AAVE. The answer is that relativizer omission has, over the past decade (Tottie & Rey, 1997; Tottie & Harvie, 2000), been added to the evidence of copula absence and other variables in the debate over the creole origins of AAVE. In particular, Tottie and Harvie (2000), considering relativizer omission data from "Early African American English" [EAAE] including recordings of US ex-slaves, and descendants of African Americans who went to Nova Scotia (Canada), and Samaná (Dominican Republic) in the early 19th century, conclude (p. 225) that these varieties descend from English rather than creole stock, since they seem to have constraints similar to those of English dialects.

But although Tottie and Harvie (2000) was a welcome, pioneering study, it was limited in three major respects:

a. The **absence of quantitative studies** of relativizer omission in Anglophone (or any other) creoles to which the "Early" AAE findings could be compared. This absence was not their fault, but without quantitative creole data on this variable, one could not reliably conclude that relativizer omission in EAAE patterned more like English than Creole.

b. The corpora that Tottie and Harvie used for EAAE (e.g. the Ex-Slave Recordings) yielded **very few tokens** of restrictive relative clauses. Again, this was not the authors' fault, but the resulting quantitative distributions were weak, with only five of their eighteen tables achieving statistical significance. (See Rickford, 2006 for further discussion.)

c. As a result of (b), the authors **did not have enough tokens for Variable Rule (Varbrul)** multivariate analysis, which simultaneously controls for the effect of different factors, long considered the gold standard in variationist studies.

---

[2] The three variables chosen for this larger project (funded by NSF grant #BCS-0545424) were among the nine examined by contributors to Poplack, 2000. See Rickford, 2006 for a review article on this book.

Hence the need for this study.

2 Relativizers: Some Preliminaries

English restrictive relative clauses [enclosed in square brackets below], "restrict the denotation" (Huddleston, Pullum, & Bauer, 2002) of an antecedent NP (underlined below), and may be introduced in one of three ways:

- By a [+/- human] *wh* pronoun (*who(m)*, *which*), as in:
  (1a) I saw the boy [*who(m)* you like]
  (1b) I saw the ball [*which* you like]
- By *that,* in:
  (1c) I saw the boy/ball [*that* you like]
- By *zero,* as in:
  (1d) I saw the boy/ball [Ø you like]

Excluded from this variation are non-restrictive relative clauses, where the antecedent is already uniquely denoted. These often have "comma pronunciation" and can be introduced only by *wh* pronouns:

(2)   I saw Mary, *who(m)/ *that/ *Ø* you like.

Following Schachter (1985) and many recent works on this variable, we'll refer to *who/which, that, Ø* as *relativizers* and include in this category too the Creole and English dialect variant *what∼wa∼wi,* which occurs with both human and non-human antecedents.

At least since the 1960s (Bailey, 1966, 110ff) and 1970s (Quirk & Greenbaum, 1973, 380ff), descriptive and generative linguists have noted the variation between these relativizers and made informal observations about the factors that seem to favor the zero variant. An early generalization is that Standard or Mainstream English allows relativizer omission (the zero variant) with OBJECT relatives (the object of the verb in the relative clause) as in (1) above, but not with SUBJECT relatives (the subject of the verb in the relative clause), as in (3):

(3)   I saw the boy [who/*Ø likes you]

But a number of English dialects (e.g. AAVE, some Scottish, Irish and English varieties) do allow omission of subject relativizers, as in (4):

(4)   "...there were a boy in Ballyclare [Ø told me this]"
      (Tagliamonte et al., 2005, p. 76)

However, even in these vernacular varieties, subject relativizer omission is less common than object relativizer omission, and its constraint patterns (what favors or disfavors omission) are somewhat different.

Quantitative studies of relativizer variation and omission in English (revealing constraints that **non**-quantitative studies often missed) have been available since the 1980s (Romaine, 1982; Kikai et al., 1987). But' they've become more common since the 1990s, and in recent years, have attracted generativists as well as sociolinguists, scholars interested in purely syntactic and/or processing constraints on this variation (e.g. Lehmann, 2001; Wasow et al., 2004; Wiechmann, 2008).

3 Data and Methodology

The **Guyanese** data to be considered in this paper come primarily from informal spoken interviews made by myself (a native speaker) with cane-cutters, weeding-gang women, shop-owners and others from Cane Walk and elsewhere in Demerara and Berbice between 1975 and 1982,[3] supplemented by two recordings made for Don Winford by University of Guyana students in Mahaicony in 1991.[4]

The **Jamaican** data come from two sources: (a) Informal spoken recordings, made between 1991 and 2006. Some of these are sociolinguistic interviews (most conducted by native speakers, although a few were conducted by myself); others include arguments in public or on the air recorded by Kathryn Shields-Brodber of the University of West Indies, Mona, Jamaica, and her students.[5] (b) Extracts from *Lionheart Gal* (Sisteren with Ford-Smith 2005), a collection of oral narratives from Jamaican women first linguistically analyzed by Patrick,

---

[3]Cane Walk is a pseudonym for a rural village on the East Coast, Demerara, less than half an hour outside the capital city of Georgetown.

[4]I am grateful to Don Winford for sharing these materials with us, and to the following faculty members and students from the University of Guyana who helped with the transcription and coding of the Cane Walk and other Guyanese recordings: Andrea Ally, Kencil Banwarie, Alim Hosein, S. Hussein, and Daizal Samad, among others. Mackenzie Price, graduate student at UC Davis, also helped with the coding and variable rule analysis of the Guyanese data.

[5]I am grateful to Kathryn Shields-Brodber for making these recordings available to us. The following students and faculty members (most from the University of the West Indies, Mona), also helped to record, digitize, transcribe or code samples of Jamaican speech: Lisa Monique Barker, Annife Campbell, Dahlia Thompson, Tasheney Francis, Audene Henry, Trecel Messam, Velma Pollard, Angela E. Rickford, Jodian A. Scott, Andre Sherriah, Kadian Walters and Kedisha Williams.

Carranza, and Kendall (1993).[6] The relativizer omission patterns in these two subsets were similar.[7]

The **Appalachian** data come from two sources: (a) West Virginia recordings made in the 1970s by Walt Wolfram, Donna Christian and their associates; (b) recordings with older speakers in Beech Bottom, North Carolina, made by Christine Mallinson, Becky Childs, Daniel Schreier and others in 2001. We are grateful to these researchers and to Clare Dannenberg and Tyler Kendall for making these materials in the North Carolina Sociolinguistic Archive and Analysis (NCSLAAP) project available to us.[8]

The **AAVE** data are primarily from informal sociolinguistic interviews with working-class speakers in East Palo Alto, California, conducted by community insiders like Faye McNair-Knox and her daughter Rashida Knox (but some also by my students at Stanford and myself) between 1986 and 2008.[9]

Every occurrence of a restrictive relative clause we could find in these data sets was extracted,[10] and coded for relativizer variant (*that, who/which, what/wa/wi, Ø*), relativizer type (subject/non-subject), and the following additional constraints, most of which sociolinguists and syntacticians have found relevant to this variable:

---

[6]The following participants in the "Language Variation" course I taught at the 2008 Caribbean Linguistics and Language Institute (held at the University of the West Indies, Mona, Jamaica) helped to extract and code relativizers from the narratives in *Lionheart Gal*: Kencil Banwarie, Gregory Carter, Lars Hinrichs, Nicole Hohn, Sonia Marville-Carter, Anderlene Mohan-Ragbir, Andrea Moll, Marguerite Murray, Ferne Regis, Daidrah Smith, Jessica Spencer and Adrienne Washington. Laura Smith also played a critical role in the coding and analysis of the Jamaican data.

[7]This is reassuring, since the two Jamaican data sets are more different in genre than the other cases where I combined data sets (e.g. Appalachia, where I combined the transcripts from two different sociolinguistic projects). The *Lionheart Gal* texts differ from the usual transcripts of sociolinguistic interviews insofar as they are published records of "testimonies" collected and edited by Honor Ford-Smith, a member of the Sisteren collective whose story also appears in the volume. Ms. Ford-Smith has told me that the published texts are essentially faithful to what was originally said, but we don't have access to the original records.

[8]I am grateful to Michael Montgomery for sharing with me his transcripts of some of the West Virginia recordings, and to Patrick Callier, Pauline Cristy, Rebecca Greene, Cole Paulson, andDoug Kenter for helping to transcribe and code some of the Appalachian recordings.

[9]In transcribing and coding the AAVE data, I was ably assisted by Rachel Cristy, Catherine Howard, Lauren Hall-Lew, Monique King, Mackenzie Price and Lisa Young, among others.

[10]Excluded were adverbial relatives (*when, where*), incomplete relative clauses, and other tokens excluded by Tottie and Harvie (2000) and Tagliamonte et al. (2005).

- Structure of matrix sentence (existential, cleft, possessive, other)
- Adjacency of antecedent NP (adjacent, non-adjacent)
- Length of relative clause (3 words or fewer, more than 3 words)
- Definiteness of antecedent NP (definite, indefinite)
- Humanness of antecedent NP (human, non-human)
- Plurality of antecedent NP (singular, plural)

For example, the following [bracketed] subject relative clause from Raj, a Guyanese cane-cutter:

(5) Me ga' <u>wan brudda</u> [Ø live a' Enmore] "I have a brother who lives at Enmore"

was coded as follows:

- Zero (relativizer variant)
- Subject (relativizer type)
- Possessive (sentence structure)
- Adjacent (adjacency to antecedent NP)
- Short (length of relative clause)
- Indefinite (definiteness of antecedent NP)
- Human (humanness of antecedent NP)
- Singular (plurality of antecedent NP)

And the following [bracketed] non-subject relative clause from Jack, a Jamaican farmer:

(6) Dierz <u>nothing</u> a uman kyan du [wich a man kyaan du] "There's nothing a woman can do which a man can't do."

was coded as follows:

- *Which* (relativizer variant)
- Non-Subject (relativizer type)
- Existential (sentence structure)
- Non-Adjacent (adjacency to antecedent NP)
- Long (length of relative clause)
- Indefinite (definiteness of antecedent NP)
- Non-human (humanness of antecedent NP)
- Singular (plurality of antecedent NP)

The coded data were analyzed by Goldvarb, and the results compared to quantitative studies of other varieties (e.g. the spoken corpus analyzed by Kautzsch, 2002, including WPA, Hoodoo and other samples of Earlier African American English recorded between the 1930s and 1970s) and the "Northern" British (Irish, Scottish and English) varieties analyzed by Tagliamonte et al. (2005). Goldvarb is a widely used version of Varbrul, a computer program that uses logistic regression to calculate the significance or insignificance of factor groups (groups of constraints or conditioning factors) on the application of a variable rule, and which also estimates, within each factor group, the probability or weight of each factor towards rule application (see Sankoff, 1987; Bayley, 2002; Tagliamonte, 2007). Factor weights than greater than .5 favor rule application, those lower than .5 disfavor it and those at or around .5 have no effect in either direction.

4 Results

Let us begin the discussion of results by looking just at the Jamaican data, and considering how frequently the major relativizer variants occur in subject and object position. Although the relatively high frequency of the zero variant in subject position (25%) is striking, the Jamaican subject relativizers are pretty evenly divided among the four variants, with *who/which* (28%) slightly more common than the others. By contrast, among the non-subject relativizers, zero accounts for more than half of the tokens (56%), and the *wa/wi* creole variant for nearly a third (29%), with *that/dat* (13%) and English *who/which* (2%) trailing far behind.[11]

TABLE 1 Distribution of relativizers in Jamaican data by variant and type

Relativizer variant	Subject	Non-Subject
null/zero (Ø)	25% (61)	**56% (224)**
that/dat	22% (53)	13% (52)
who/which	**28% (70)**	2% (10)
wa/wi	25% (62)	29% (117)
TOTAL	100% (246)	100% (403)

Table 2[12] shows the distribution of subject variants more generally, both in our data and in data from Earlier African American English

---

[11]The creole *wa/wi* variant, unlike its historical source forms *what* and *which*, is not restricted to [-human] referents, and can be used with humans, non-human animates, and inanimates.

[12]Notes (Tables 2 & 3): Bold numbers = most common relativizer variant in each variety. *Source: Kautzsch, 2002, Table 144, p. 244, spoken corpus (Ex-Slave recordings and Hoodoo texts. **Source: Tagliamonte et al., 2005, Table 4, which excludes tokens of *which* (Scotland 9, England 7, Ireland 3) and *what* (Scotland 1, England 3, Ireland 3) reported in their Table 3 (subject + non-subject tokens combined).

[AAE] and northern British varieties (Lowland Scotland, Northwest England, Northern Ireland) examined by other researchers (Kautzsch, 2002 and Tagliamonte et al., 2005 respectively). Zero subject relatives are even more frequent in Guyanese (42%) than Jamaican, but by contrast with Standard or Mainstream English, where this is a minimal or non-existent option, the other varieties show relatively high percentages of zero too (from 11% in Modern AAVE to 30% in Appalachian). And for all varieties except Guyanese and Jamaican, *that*~*dat* is the primary subject variant, with relative frequencies ranging from 57% in Earlier AAE to 76% in modern AAVE).

Table 3 shows the distribution of non-subject relativizers in all the varieties. Zero is the majority variant (50% or more) in all varieties except Northwest England, Northern Ireland, and AAVE, where *that/dat* is the majority variant. In all the varieties in which zero is the main variant, *that/dat* is the secondary variant, and *who/which* a trivial or non-existent option. The striking exceptions to this are the creole varieties Jamaican and Guyanese, where *wa/wi* is the secondary option (29% and 26%). It is of potential interest for the creole hypothesis that the only other variety in which *wa/wi* is an option is Earlier AAE, where it accounts for 9% of the non-subject relativizers.

TABLE 2 Distribution of Subject relativizer variants, all varieties

Variety	Null (Ø)	*That dat*	*Who/Which*	*Wa wi* (no +/- human distinc- tion)	TOTAL
Jamaican	25% (61)	22% (53)	**28% (70)**	25% (62)	100% (246)
Guyanese	**42% (74)**	8.5% (15)	31% (55)	17.6% (31)	100% (175)
Earlier AAE*	18% (155)	**57% (493)**	14% (119)	11% (94)	100% (861)
AAVE (modern, Calif)	11% (43)	**76% (298)**	12.5% (49)	0% (0)	100% (390)
Appalachian	30% (66)	**68.6% (151)**	1% (3)	0%	100% (220)
Lowland Scotland**	15% (75)	**73% (353)**	10% (48)	n.d.	98% (484)**
Northwest England**	20% (96)	**64% (299)**	14% (65)	n.d.	98% (467)**
Northern Ireland**	20% (67)	**74% (242)**	5% (17)	n.d.	99% (328)**

TABLE 3 Distribution of Non-Subject relativizer variants, all varieties

Variety	Null (Ø)	*That dat*	*Who/Which*	*Wa wi (no +/- human distinc-tion)*	TOTAL
Jamaican	**56% (224)**	13% (52)	2% (10)	29% (117)	100% (403)
Guyanese	**62% (177)**	7% (21)	2% (7)	26% (74)	100% (285)
Earlier AAE*	**57% (578)**	32% (329)	2% (17)	9% (95)	100% (1019)
AAVE (modern, Calif)	41% (207)	**56% (281)**	2% (11)	0% (0)	100% (500)
Appalachian	**70.7% (181)**	47% (74)	3% (1)	0% (0)	100% (256)
Lowland Scotland**	**53% (139)**	45% (119)	0% (0)	n.d.	98% (262)
Northwest England**	47% (115)	**50% (124)**	0% (0)	n.d.	97% (247)
Northern Ireland**	27% (36)	**69% (93)**	0% (1)	n.d.	96% (134)

Let us turn now to the Goldvarb/Varbrul results, which reveal the factor groups that have a significant effect on relativizer omission, and the factors within those that favor or disfavor zero.[13] Table 4 shows the results for subject relativizers, and in relation to this we may make the following observations:

- With respect to **Sentence Structure**, we may be dealing with variety-independent processing constraints (cf. Wasow et al., 2004; Jaeger & Wasow, 2007), since existentials favor zero in all varieties, clefts and possessives in most, and "other" disfavors zero in all varieties.

- **Length** is significant in all the "White" varieties (British and Appalachian), but in none of the "Black" varieties (Guyana, Jamaican, AAVE) for which data are available.

- **Antecedent Type** is significant in two of the "Black" varieties, and non-significant in only one of the "White" varieties (Lowland Scotland). But while an indefinite NP favors zero in Lowland Scotland,

---

[13] In response to a concern expressed by Hal Tily (one of the reviewers of this paper) that Varbrul (Goldvarb) analysis does not provide for multilevel, mixed effects modelling (see Johnson, 2009), I submitted my non-subject relativizer omission data for AAVE to Daniel Ezra Johnson, who kindly ran it through a regular Goldvarb analysis and his new Rbul program that provides for mixed effects modelling. He reported that the results from both runs were nearly identical.

it disfavors zero both in Earlier AAE and Jamaican. We don't have data on superlative or unique NP subjects (e.g. *the best book, the only girl*) for the data from Kautzsch or Tagliamonte et al, but given the recent results from Jaeger and Wasow (2007) that prompted us to consider this factor in the first place, we would not be surprised if superlative and unique NP subjects turned out to significantly favor zero in all varieties.[14]

- **Adjacency of Antecedent** is non-significant in all varieties, except for Earlier AAE, where it is very significant (p =.007). However, it is important to remember that the Earlier AAE data have only been subject to relative frequency analysis, not to more reliable multi-variate variable rule analysis. This is indicated by the presence of percentages in the Earlier AAE column rather than probabilities (factor weights).

- **Humanness of Antecedent**: This is significant only in Earlier AAE, but note the qualification made in relation to Adjacency, and the absence of data for the British varieties.

Overall, apart from the shared effect of Sentence Structure, the differences between the Black and White varieties are striking, with regard to Length, Antecedent Type and Adjacency. Modern AAVE shows no significant constraints, and is in this respect different from both the Black and the White varieties, but Earlier AAE is definitely more Black than White, at least with respect to subject relativizer omission.

Table 5 shows the results for **non**-subject relativizers, in relation to which the following observations may be made:

- With respect to **Sentence Structure**, Jamaican looks most similar to Lowland Scots and Northwest England, with a shared favoring effect of clefts, although existentials also favor omission in the two British varieties but not in Jamaican. In all the other varieties except earlier AAE (for which we have no data), this factor group is non-significant.

- **Length** is significant in all the British varieties and none of the others (Jamaican, Guyanese, AAVE, Appalachian) for which we have data.

- **Antecedent Type** is **non**-significant for all the British Varieties, but significant for all the Black ones, and Appalachian English, with superlative NP most favorable for all four varieties with data on this factor.

---

[14]Sali Tagliamonte (p.c.) is planning to recode her Northern British data to check for the effect of this factor.

TABLE 4 Constraints on Subject Relativizer Omission, all varieties (Goldvarb/Varbrul results)

Factor groups		"BLACK" varieties — Guyanese	Jamaican	AAVE (E.Palo Alto, Calif.)	Earlier AAE* (% data only)	"WHITE" varieties — Appalachian	Lowland Scotland**	Northwest England**	Northern Ireland**
Input Prob		.362	.19	.113	18%	.262	.031	.058	.115
N		164	332	390	861	219	484	467	328
Sentence Structure	Existential	*.723*	*.737*	[.716]	n.d.	*.780*	*.99*	*.98*	*.95*
	Possessive	*.709*	*.260*	[.602]	n.d.	*.675*	*.83*	*.85*	*.50*
	Cleft	k*100%*	*.962*	[.522]	n.d.	*.260*	*.64*	*.65*	*.76*
	Other	*.388*	*.340*	[.459]	n.d.	*.317*	*.20*	*.16*	*.28*
Length of RC	Short, Simple	[.541]	[.494]	[.511]	n.d.	*.565*	*.73*	*.73*	*.72*
	Long, Simple	[.468]	[.498]	[.476]	n.d.	*.397*	*.37*	*.31*	*.37*
	Long, Complex	[.685]	[.926]	[.714]	n.d.	*.793*	*.48*	*.54*	*.54*
Type of Antecedent	Indef NP	[.552]	*.448*	[.435]	*22%*	[.565]	*.64*	[.56]	[.58]
	Def. NP	[.399]	*.425*	[.511]	*13%*	[.359]	*.33*	[.46]	[.48]
	Superl. NP	[.602]	*.673*	[.807]	n.d.	[.706]	n.d.	n.d.	n.d.
	Def. Pro.	[.563]	*.868*	[.423]	*16%*	[.533]	n.d.	n.d.	n.d.
	Indef. Pro.		*.587*	[.618]		[.375]	*.81*	[.39]	[.32]
Adjacency of antecedent	Adjacent	*.557*	[.492]	[.486]	*17%*	[.524]	n.s/d	n.s/d	n.s/d
	Non-Adj	*.162*	[.562]	[.558]	*29%*	[.404]	n.s/d	n.s/d	n.s/d
Humanness of antecedent	Human	[.480]	[.480]	[.499]	*50%*	[.475]	n.d.	n.d.	n.d.
	Non-hum.	[.575]	[.555]	[.505]	*58%*	[.557]	n.d.	n.d.	n.d.

[Cells with square brackets] = non-significant factor groups (numbers from first step-down Goldvarb run), groups that had no appreciable effect; *italicized* cells = significant factor groups; within those, **bold** numbers = factors that *favor* zero variant; regular (non-bold) numbers in significant factor groups represent factors that *disfavor* zero variant or are neutral; n.d.= no data; n.s/d = reported as non-significant from Goldvarb run, but no data provided. k100% in the Guyanese columns represents a 'knockout' factor that *always* favors zero and had to be removed for Varbrul to run; *Earlier AAE data source: Kautzsch, 2002, Table 144, p. 244, spoken corpus (Ex-Slave recordings and Hoodoo texts; **Scotland, England and Ireland data source: Tagliamonte et al., 2005, Table 4, which excludes tokens of *which* (Scotland 9, England 7, Ireland 3) and *what* (Scotland 1, England 3, Ireland 3) reported in their Table 3 (Subject + Nonsubject).

- **Adjacency of Antecedent** is non-significant for all the White varieties, but it's significant for two of the Black ones (Jamaican, AAVE).
- **Humanness** of Antecedent is significant only in the North American varieties (AAVE, Earlier AAE, and Appalachian).

Overall, apart from a shared sentence structure constraint (somewhat like what we saw for subject relativizers, but in a more limited way), the British varieties are off by themselves. When it comes to constraints on non-subject relativizer omission, both AAVE and Earlier AAE are quite different from them, and much more similar to each other and to Guyanese and Jamaican. This is particularly the case for Antecedent Type and Adjacency.

Let us return now to the three general questions posed at the beginning of this paper.

The answer to question 1, about how relativizer omission patterns in Guyanese, Jamaican, AAVE and Appalachian, lies in the details of Tables 1–5 and the discussion we have already provided about which relativizers occur most often in the different varieties, and which factor groups and factors significantly favor or disfavor zero.

The similarities and differences in these patterns, especially those between the "Black" and "White" varieties, do suggest some answers to question 2, about the history of AAVE. There is certainly no evidence for a British origin of AAVE here, and AAVE differs even from Appalachian, with which it shares continental space. There are tantalizing resemblances between AAVE and the other "Black" varieties, especially Jamaican. Together, these differences from the "White" varieties and similarities with the "Black" varieties provide more support for the creole origins of AAVE hypothesis, and less for the Anglicist or English dialects origins hypothesis, at least as far as relativizer omission is concerned. Of course the data from this variable would have to be balanced against the data from other variables and other kinds of evidence before any definitive conclusions on the Creole/Anglicist origins hypothesis could be reached.

What of question 3? Tagliamonte et al. (2005, p. 101–106) commendably raised the question of whether specific constraints on relativizer omission might be dialect specific, or might represent potentially "universal" cognitive processing constraints. But their preliminary answers, while entirely plausible, are not supported by our data. For instance, they felt (p. 105) that "length effects might be expected to be universal, as these are dependent on cognitive processing constraints, which are presumably shared by all speakers (Fodor, 1998)." However, length of

TABLE 5 Non-Subject Relativizer Omission Results

		"BLACK" varieties				"WHITE" varieties			
Factor groups	Factors	Guyanese	Jamaican	AAVE (E.Palo Alto, Calif.)	Earlier AAE* (% data only)	Appalachian	Lowland Scotland**	Northwest England**	Northern Ireland**
Input Prob		.618	.629	.408	57%	.739	.546	.462	.238
N		285	510	500	578	256	261	247	133
Sentence Structure	Existential	[.318]	*.431*	[.545]	n.d.	[.549]	**.55**	**.77**	[.66]
	Possessive	[.463]	*.330*	[.604]	n.d.	[.359]	*.11*	*.17*	[.44]
	Cleft	[.786]	**.909**	[.360]	n.d.	[.615]	**.69**	**.57**	[.41]
	Other	[.480]	*.432*	[.497]	n.d.	[.502]	*.45*	*.50*	[.50]
Length of RC	Short, Simple	[.485]	[.527]	[.531]	n.d.	[.537]	**.79**	**.80**	**.67**
	Long, Simple	[.517]	[.478]	[.490]	n.d.	[.463]	*.29*	*.38*	*.42*
	Long, Complex	[.540]	n.d.	[.340]	n.d.	[.296]	*.47*	*.39*	*.45*
Type of Antecedent	Indef NP	**.555**	*.294*	*.422*	47%	*.293*	[.57]	[.42]	[.35]
	Def. NP	*.282*	*.353*	*.468*	52%	*.286*	[.48]	[.54]	[.55]
	Superl. NP	**.919**	**.959**	**.873**	n.d.	**.745**	n.d.	n.d.	n.d.
	Def. Pro	**.597**	**.679**	*.452*	72%	*.262*	n.d.	n.d.	n.d.
	Indef. Pro.	*.379*	**.649**	**.508**		**.605**	[.46]	[.49]	[.67]
Adjacency of antecedent	Adjacent	[.508]	**.521**	**.534**	[57%]	[.510]	[n.s/d]	[n.s/d]	[n.s/d]
	Non-Adj	[.382]	*.238*	*.263*	[51%]	[.399]	[n.s/d]	[n.s/d]	[n.s/d]
Humanness of antecedent	Human	[.426]	*.419*	*.364*	50%	[.446]	n.d.	n.d.	n.d.
	Non-hum.	[.514]	*.518*	**.557**	58%	[.505]	n.d.	n.d.	n.d.

[Cells with square brackets] = non-significant factor groups (numbers from first step-down Goldvarb run), groups that had no appreciable effect; *italicized* cells = significant factor groups; within those, **bold** numbers = factors that *favor* zero variant; regular (non-bold) numbers in significant factor groups represent factors that *disfavor* zero variant or are neutral; n.d.= no data; n.s/d = reported as non-significant from Goldvarb run, but no data provided. *Earlier AAE data source: Kautzsch, 2002, Table 144, p. 244, spoken corpus (Ex-Slave recordings and Hoodoo texts; **Scotland, England and Ireland data source: Tagliamonte et al., 2005, Table 4, which excludes tokens of *which* (Scotland 9, England 7, Ireland 3) and *what* (Scotland 1, England 3, Ireland 3) reported in their Table 3 (Subject + Nonsubject).

the relative clause is irrelevant in all of the "Black" varieties in Tables 4 and 5 and in Appalachian as well in Table 5, so it's less likely to be a universal or even an Angloversal (cf. Mair, 2003; Szmrecsanyi & Kortmann, 2009). At the same time, Tagliamonte et al. (2005) suggested that "tendencies of *that* or zero for clefts and/or existentials might be dialect specific. If so, their ranking vis-à-vis other construcions for relative marker use may prove to be valuable diagnostics or origins and/or interdialectical relationships." However, our data show that existentials and clefts favor relativizer omission quite generally, especially with subject relatives. And the work of Wasow and his associates (with non-subject relativizers) suggests that the favoring effect of existentials on zero might be characteristic of English in general or, more broadly, attributable to a universal processing constraint. In the next section, I'll summarize Wasow et al's hypotheses and data, under the heading of the Predictability Hypothesis, and comment more specifically on how our findings support theirs.

5 The Predictability Hypothesis

Using a parsed Switchboard Corpus—650 telephone conversations between strangers in the US, yielding 3,701 Non-Subject Relative Clauses (NSRCs), 43% with *that*, and 57% with zero—Wasow et al. (2004) examined which factors "correlate with relativizer occurrence in NSRCs" and formulated the **Predictability Hypothesis:** "...determiners, adjectives and nouns that increase the likelihood of a following NSRC decrease the likelihood that the NSRCs following them will begin with relativizers." This has been restated more recently (Jaeger & Wasow, 2007) as: "The more predictable an NSRC is, the less likely it is to begin with *that*." The *more* likely it is that a noun phrase with certain characteristics is going to be followed by a relative clause, the *less* likely you are to need a relativizer like *that* (or for that matter, *who, which* or *wa*) to mark the onset of that relative clause.

Jaeger and Wasow (2007) report that they were led to their insight in part by Fox and Thompson (2007), who observed that the following sentence sounds incomplete without a relative clause, and also strongly disfavors *that* (i.e. it tends to favor zero, or relativizer omission).

(7) That was the ugliest pair of shoes (that) I ever saw.

Following up on this observation, Wasow et al. (2004) found that there was a strong correlation between the occurrence of certain kinds of adjectives in the head NP (e.g. superlative or unique adjectives like *best, only, first, last,* which commonly co-ocurred with relative clauses), and the likelihood that the relative clauses would occur with a zero relativizer. Note how strongly superlative NPs favor zero in our Table 5 (and to a lesser extent Table 4) in all the cells for which we have relevant data.

Interestingly enough, Wiechmann (2008) also reported that unique adjectives were one of three elements that constituted Type 1 relative clause constructions, the type that most commonly occurred with zero relativizers in his "Entrenchment model." Type 1 relative clause constructions like these become highly automized with zero, and are easier to process.

More recently, inspired by the evidence in Tagliamonte et al. (2005) that existentials in their Northern British varieties (see Tables 4 and 5 above) favor relativizer omission,[15] Jaeger and Wasow (2007) argued that there are good processing explanations for this and that their predictability hypothesis could account for it. They first noted that noun phrases in existential clauses and those that are objects of *have* tend to occur with NSRC relative clauses more often than than other noun phrases, as Table 6 shows:

TABLE 6 NPs in existentials and objects of *have* occur in NSRC RCs more often than others

% of Noun Phrases in existentials that occur with relative clauses	23.1% (461/1998)
% of Noun Phrases that are objects of *have* that occur with relative clauses	9.2% (583/6316)
% of all other Noun Phrases that occur with relative clauses	2.1% (6274/297,234)

By the predictability hypothesis, these higher frequency relative clauses (those modifying the noun phrases in existentials and the ones that are objects of *have*) should also occur more often without overt relativizers, which is exactly what Table 7 shows.

TABLE 7 Relative clauses modifying NPs in existentials and objects of *have* occur more often without *that*

% of relative clauses without *that* following Noun Phrases in existentials	85% (79/93)
% of relative clauses without *that* following Noun Phrase objects of *have*	87% (53/61)
% of relative clauses without *that* following all other Noun Phrases	55% (1968/3547)

[15]This point was also noted by Martin and Wolfram (1998) for AAVE and Henry (1995) for Belfast English.

Again, note the neat parallel with our Table 4, for subject relativizers, where existentials favor high rates of relativizer omission in
Jamaican and Guyanese as well as Appalachian and the British varieties.[16] This holds true for possessives too, except in Jamaican. Curi-
ously enough, for the non-subject relative clause data in Table 5, the
kind considered by Jaeger and Wasow, the parallels are not quite as
strong. They hold for existentials only in Lowland Scotland and Northern England, two of the four White varieties, and they do not hold for
possessives in any of the varieties. But the class of possessives in our
data is broader than "objects of *have*," and since we don't have syntactically tagged computer corpora for any of the data sets in Tables 4 or
5, we can't investigate the first half of the predictability hypothesis—
whether NPs in existentials or as objects of *have* indeed occur more
often with NPs than other NPs do. These are areas that await further
research.

6 Summary and Conclusion

Our quantitative study of relativizer omission in Appalachian, modern AAVE and two Caribbean English Creoles has yielded important
descriptive information we did not have before. For one thing, the relative frequency of *subject* relativizer omission in these newly studied
varieties (see Table 2) is relatively high (11%-25%), but comparable to
earlier reports for Early AAE and the Northern British Varieties (15%-
26%). Subject relativizer omission is highest of all (42%), however, in
Guyanese Creole, in part a reflection of its categorical operation in cleft
sentences. Non-subject relativizer omission (see Table 3) is higher than
subject relativizer omission in all varieties—ranging from 41% to 71%
in the newly studied varieties and from 27% to 57% in the previously
studied varieties. The White varieties show more variability with respect to non-subject relativizer omission than the Black ones do, with
the highest rate of omission overall (71%) coming from Appalachian.

If we ask not just how *often* relativizer omission occurs in these
newly studied varieties, but *how,* in terms of constraint effects, the answers are quite revealing. Like Tagliamonte et al. (2005), we do find
that some constraint effects seem to be specific to particular dialects or
dialect groups, while others reflect widespread, perhaps universal processing patterns. But the constraints that they found to be general (like
length), we found to be very specific (significant in the White or at least

---

[16]The favoring effect of existentials in the British varieties of Lowland Scotland,
Northwest England, and Northern Ireland, as analyzed by Tagliamonte et al (2005)
was, as noted, what led Jaeger and Wasow to consider this constraint in the first
place.

British varieties, but not in the creole or Black varieties). And the constraints they found to be dialect specific (like sentence structure), we found to be quite general (especially in relation to subject relativizers). With respect to *subject* relativizer omission, AAVE shows no significant constraint effects, and in this respect is neutral in relation to the Black and White patterns. In terms of *non-subject* relativizer omission, AAVE is quite dissimilar to the Northern British varieties, and shares a sensitivity to the Type of Antecedent with all of the other Black varieties. But Appalachian shares this feature too. However modern AAVE shares the effects of Antecedent Adjacency and Antecedent Humanness with at least one other Black variety and with none of the White varieties, and in this sense provides support for the creolist rather than Anglicist hypothesis of AAVE origins.

Perhaps what is more interesting about these newly studied varieties is what they contribute to the larger search for general processing constraints, like the Predictability Hypothesis on which Tom Wasow and his colleagues are focusing. Our data provide some intriguing support for the Predictability Hypothesis, from varieties of English much more non-standard than the American (Switchboard) data sets on which it was formulated. But the support, while very strong for some aspects of the Predictability Hypothesis (e.g. the effect of modification by superlative and unique adjectives) is more mixed with others (e.g. the effect of existentials and possessives), and varies depending on whether we consider subject or non-subject relativizers. (Recall that Wasow and his collaborators considered only non-subject relativizers.) We don't know yet the extent to which relativizer omission in the creoles, AAVE and Appalachian confirms to the Predictability Hypothesis and is affected by data size, and local constraints that don't surface in Switchboard and similar data. And there are alternative models (e.g. Wiechmann's Entrenchment model, just mentioned) that we will have to consider too. Fully testing either of these will require computerized corpora not readily available for creoles and many vernacular Englishes. Furthermore, such corpora would need to be regularized (to account for competing orthographies) and annotated for part of speech and constituency structure, a task which will be hampered by the fact that taggers and parsers developed for, e.g., Standard American English won't necessarily work directly with other varieties.

Overall, despite the challenges involved, the prospects for continued research along these lines is exciting, even if (or perhaps because) it takes us beyond our sectarian squabbles about the origins of AAVE and other varieties. While the findings of this study do support the creole origins hypothesis more than they do the English-origins hypothesis, they also reinforce the suggestion (cf. Schuchardt, 1979, Bickerton, 1984, Kihm, 2008, Siegel, 2008, p. 66-78) that creoles, sometimes ignored by linguists, often disparaged by non-linguists, can contribute to our understanding of language universals. The germ of this idea is more than a hundred years old,[17] but what is new here is the conception of universals in terms of language processing regularities rather than in terms of static/dynamic features assumed to be part of an innate 'faculté de langage', and the kinds of data furnishing the evidence: quantitative variable constraints rather than qualitative forms and structures. New data types, new analytical approaches, and new predictions from recent conferences and publications (like those of Tom Wasow and his colleagues) make the prospects of pursuing universals in this sense better than ever.

Acknowledgements

The research reported on in this paper is part of a larger project on Grammatical Variation and Change in Caribbean English Creoles, Appalachian English, and African American Vernacular English, supported by National Science Foundation Grant 9545424. I am grateful to the NSF for this support, and to my primary research assistant, Laura Smith (Stanford), for extensive data extraction, coding, analysis and discussion. I also wish to thank project consultants Robert Bayley (UC Davis) for advice and help with the variable rule analyses, and Tom Wasow (Stanford) for discussion of many aspects of the analysis, from classification of individual examples to details of the Predictability Hypothesis. Finally, I am grateful to Penny Eckert, Rebecca Greene, Lauren Hall-Lew, Kyuwon Moon, Rebecca Starr, and Laura Staum Casasanto for feedback on a talk presenting this research at Stanford, and to Angela E. Rickford of San Jose State University, for support and encouragement throughout this project.

References

Adamson, H. (1992). Social and processing constraints on relative clauses. *American Speech, 67*(2), 123–133.

Bailey, B. L. (1966). *Jamaican Creole syntax: A transformational approach.* Cambridge: Cambridge University Press.

Bayley, R. (2002). The quantitative paradigm. In J. Chambers, P. Trudgill, & N. Schilling-Estes (Eds.), *The handbook of language variation and change* (pp. 117–141). Oxford: Wiley-Blackwell.

---

[17]Schuchardt (1979) is a modern translation into English of works originally published in German in the 1880s and 1890s. (See Mühlhäusler, 1986, 114ff.)

Bickerton, D. (1984). The language bioprogram hypothesis. *The Behavioral and Brain Sciences*, *7*, 173–188.

Buchstaller, I., Rickford, J. R., Traugott, E., Wasow, T., & Zwicky, A. (to appear). The sociolinguistics of a short-lived innovation: Tracing the development of quotative all across spoken and usernet data. *Language Variation and Change*.

Fodor, J. D. (1998). Learning to parse? *Journal of Psycholinguistic Research*, *27*(2), 285–319.

Fox, B. A., & Thompson, S. A. (2007). Relative clauses in English conversation: Relativizers, frequency, and the notion of construction. *Studies in Language*, *31*(2), 293–326.

Guy, G. R., & Bayley, R. (1995). On the choice of relative pronouns in English. *American Speech*, *70*(2), 148–162.

Henry, A. (1995). *Belfast English and standard English: Dialect variation and parameter setting*. NY: Oxford University Press.

Huddleston, R. D., Pullum, G. K., & Bauer, L. (2002). *The Cambridge grammar of the English language*. Cambridge: Cambridge University Press.

Jaeger, T. F., & Wasow, T. (2007). *Probability-sensitive reduction and Uniform Information Density*. (Paper presented at the Interdisciplinary Workshop on Relative Clauses, Cambridge University)

Johnson, D. E. (2009). Getting off the GoldVarb standard: Introducing Rbrul for mixed-effects variable rule analysis. *Language and Linguistics Compass*, *3*(1), 359–383.

Kautzsch, A. (2002). *The historical evolution of earlier African American English: An empirical comparison of early sources*. Berlin: Walter de Gruyter.

Kihm, A. (2008). Creoles, markedness, and default settings: An appraisal. In S. Kouwenberg & J. Singler (Eds.), *The handbook of pidgin and creole languages* (pp. 411–439). Oxford: Wiley-Blackwell.

Kikai, A., Schleppegrell, M., & Tagliamonte, S. (1987). The influence of syntactic position on relativization strategies. In K. Denning, S. Inkelas, F. McNair-Knox, & J. R. Rickford (Eds.), (pp. 266–278). Stanford, CA.

Labov, W. (1980). Introduction. In W. Labov (Ed.), *Locating language in time and space*. New York: Academic Press.

Lehmann, H. M. (2001). Zero subject relative constructions in American and British English. *Language and Computers*, *36*(1), 163–177.

Mair, C. (2003). Keolismen und Verbales Identitätsmanagement im Geschriebenen Jamaikanischen Englisch. In E. Vogel (Ed.),

Zwischen Ausgrenzung und Hybridisierung: Zur Konstruktion von Identitäten aus Kulturwissenschaftlicher Perspektive. Identitäten und Alteritäten 14 (pp. 79–96). Würzburg: Ergon.

Martin, S., & Wolfram, W. (1998). The sentence in African American English. In S. Mufwene, J. R. Rickford, G. Bailey, & J. Baugh (Eds.), *African American English: Structure, History and Use* (pp. 11–36). London: Routledge.

Montgomery, M. (2001). Trans-Atlantic connections for variable grammatical features. *University of Pennsylvania Working Papers in Linguistics, 7*, 205–221.

Mühlhäusler, P. (1986). *Pidgin and creole linguistics*. Oxford: Blackwell.

Patrick, P. L., Carranza, I., & Kendall, S. (1993). *Number marking in the speech of Jamaican women.* (Paper presented at the 22nd Annual Conference on New Ways of Analyzing Variation (NWAV-XXII), University of Ottawa)

Poplack, S. (2000). *The English history of African American English.* Oxford: Blackwell.

Quirk, R., & Greenbaum, S. (1973). *A concise grammar of contemporary English.* NY: Harcourt, Brace, Jovanovich.

Rickford, J. R. (1997). Prior creolization of AAVE? Sociohistorical and textual evidence from the 17th and 18th centuries. *Journal of Sociolinguistics, 1*, 315–336.

Rickford, J. R. (2006). Down for the count? The creole origins hypothesis of AAVE at the hands of the Ottawa circle, and their supporters. *Journal of Pidgin and Creole Languages, 21*(1), 97–155.

Rickford, J. R., Wasow, T., Mendoza-Denton, N., & Espinoza, J. (1995). Syntactic variation and change in progress: Loss of the verbal coda in topic-restricting as far as constructions. *Language, 71*(1), 102–131.

Rickford, J. R., Wasow, T., Zwicky, A., & Buchstaller, I. (2007). Intensive and quotative ALL: Something old, something new. *American Speech, 82*(1), 3.

Romaine, S. (1982). *Socio-historical linguistics: Its status and methodology.* Cambridge: Cambridge University Press.

Sankoff, D. (1987). Variable rules. In U. Ammon, N. Dittmar, & K. J. Mattheier (Eds.), *Sociolinguistics: An international handbook of the science of language and society* (Vol. 2, pp. 984–997).

Schachter, P. (1985). Parts-of-speech systems. In T. Shopen (Ed.), *Language typology and syntactic description: Clause structure* (Vol. 1, pp. 3–61). Cambridge: Cambridge University Press.

Schuchardt, H. (1979). *The ethnography of variation: Selected writings on pidgins and creoles.* Karoma. (Translated by T. L. Markey)

Sells, P., Rickford, J., & Wasow, T. (1996). An optimality theoretic approach to variation in negative inversion in AAVE. *Natural Language & Linguistic Theory, 14*(3), 591–627.

Siegel, J. (2008). *The emergence of pidgin and creole languages.* Oxford: Oxford University Press.

Sisteren with Smith, H. F. (2005 [1986]). *Lionheart gal: Life stories of Jamaican women.* Mona: University of the West Indies Press.

Szmrecsanyi, B., & Kortmann, B. (2009). Vernacular universals and angloversals in a typological perspective. In M. Filppula, J. Klemola, & H. Paulasto (Eds.), *Vernacular universals and language contacts: Evidence from varieties of English and beyond* (p. 33-53). Routledge.

Tagliamonte, S. (2007). *Analysing sociolinguistic variation.* Cambridge: Cambridge University Press.

Tagliamonte, S., Smith, J., & Lawrence, H. (2005). No taming the vernacular! Insights from the relatives in northern Britain. *Language Variation and Change, 17*(01), 75–112.

Tottie, G., & Harvie, D. (2000). It's all relative: Relativization strategies in early African American English. In S. Poplack (Ed.), *The English history of African American English* (p. 199-230). Blackwell.

Tottie, G., & Rey, M. (1997). Relativization strategies in earlier African American Vernacular English. *Language Variation and Change, 9*(2), 219–47.

Wasow, T., Jaeger, T. F., & Orr, D. (2004). *Lexical variation in relativizer frequency.*

Wiechmann, D. (2008). *Towards an explanation of English relativizer omission: A quantitative corpus linguistic approach.* (Paper presented at the first conference of the International Society for the Linguistics of English (ISLE-1), University of Freiburg)

9

Corpus-based Research on Language Production: Information Density and Reducible Subject Relatives

T. Florian Jaeger

Preface

If it hadn't been for Tom, I probably would have had to leave academia. Justified or not, in my fourth year of graduate school, I had grown disillusioned with certain aspects of theoretical linguistics. One of Tom's classes stimulated my interest in psycholinguistics, and specifically what insights we can gain about the production system by studying the speakers' choices in alternations. Tom and I started to collaborate on a project that soon grew into my thesis and further projects, including the one presented here. Tom is a fantastic advisor. I received guidance and support when I needed it without feeling pressured into working within any particular framework. He read countless versions of my thesis, papers, and talks, giving excellent feedback that often made me rethink my arguments. Tom always stayed open to arguments and was supportive even in those rare cases when we disagreed on how to proceed. Now that I am an advisor myself, I know to admire his dedication even more. Most probably, my own students would love for me to be more like him—alas, luckily, Rochester is far away from Stanford so that they can't run away. Thank you, Tom, for your support and patience (e.g. when I was nowhere to be found until a few minutes

Language from a Cognitive Perspective.
Emily M. Bender and Jennifer Arnold, Editors
Copyright © 2011, CSLI Publications.

before our joint talk in Cambridge...). With your help, it felt easy to start over and dive into psycholinguistics and cognitive science!

1 Introduction

When speakers encode their thoughts into linguistic utterances, there are often several ways to encode the same message. For example, speakers can encode messages into one or several clauses (e.g. *Move the triangle to the left of the square* vs. *Take the triangle. Move it to the left of the square*, cf. Gómez Gallo, Jaeger, & Smyth, 2008); within a clause, speakers can choose between between different word orders (e.g. heavy NP shift, Arnold, Wasow, Losongco, & Ginstrom, 2000; Wasow, 1997; particle shift, Lohse, Hawkins, & Wasow, 2004; Wasow, 2002; the ditransitive alternation, Arnold et al., 2000; Bresnan, Cueni, Nikitina, & Baayen, 2007; Bock & Warren, 1985); speakers may morpho-syntactically contract certain words (e.g. *they are* vs. *they're*, Frank & Jaeger, 2008) and may choose phonologically reduced variants for others (e.g. *strawdiny* vs. *extraordinary*, Johnson, 2004; *t/d-* deletion, and vowel weakening in English, Bell et al., 2003). In other words, choice points are present at all levels of linguistic production—all the way down to articulation (cf. variations in speech rate and articulatory detail, Aylett & Turk, 2004; Bell et al., 2003; Bell, Brenier, Gregory, Girand, & Jurafsky, 2009; Pluymaekers, Ernestus, & Baayen, 2005; Son, Beinum, & Pols, 1998; Son & Santen, 2005).

Much of Tom's work has investigated choices during syntactic production, with a strong focus on word order variations (e.g. Wasow, 1997, 2002; summarized in Arnold, this volume). Here I present a study of a different type of syntactic choice, so-called syntactic reduction, where producers have a choice between omitting or producing optional function words. The study investigates syntactic reduction in passive subject-extracted relative clauses (henceforth SRCs), sometimes also called *whiz*-deletion. English SRCs can be produced in a full form with a relativizer and the auxiliary and a reduced form without these function words, as in (1b) and (1a), respectively.[1]

---

[1] I use the terms 'reduced' and 'reduction' without intending to imply a process where a full form undergoes change to become reduced. I merely refer to the fact that SRCs can be produced with or without the relativizer and auxiliary. Also, I use the term SRC reduction exclusively to refer to cases like (1). Some dialects of English also afford optional *that*-mentioning in SRCs. This type of alternation is not investigated here.

(1)   *The style of life ...*

    a. *... chosen by the beat generation ...*

    b. *... that was chosen by the beat generation ...*

    is designed to enhance sexual experience.

The work presented here derived from collaborations with Tom that were inspired by a class he taught on Hawkins'—as of then unpublished—book (Hawkins, 2004). Tom, Dave Orr (another student in Tom's class), and I first started to investigate the processing mechanisms driving optional relativizer *that*-mentioning in non-subject-extracted relative clauses (e.g. *Most typos (that) you will find in this paper are unintentional*, see Jaeger & Wasow, 2006; Wasow, Jaeger, & Orr, in press; see also Fox & Thompson, 2007; Race & MacDonald, 2003). Tom noticed an intriguing pattern: Some apparently idiosyncratic findings reported in previous work (e.g. Fox & Thompson, 2007) were compatible with the hypothesis that more predictable relative clauses are less likely to have a relativizer. Inspired also by work on probability-sensitive phonetic reduction by Dan Jurafsky (Jurafsky, Bell, Gregory, & Raymond, 2001) and work on expectation-based comprehension by Roger Levy (Levy, 2005, 2008), we set out to investigate to 'which extent'[2] speakers' preferences in syntactic reduction are driven by redundancy. We hypothesized that speakers should be more likely to omit redundant material. If this hypothesis is correct, speakers should show a higher preference for reduced syntactic constituents if the constituent is predictable (redundancy is negatively correlated with predictability; see below). In several corpus studies on the reduction of non-subject-extracted relative clauses in spoken and written American English, we found that this is indeed the case: The more predictable a relative clause is given preceding words, the less likely speakers are to produce a relativizer (Jaeger, Levy, Wasow, & Orr, 2005; Jaeger, 2006; Levy & Jaeger, 2007; Wasow et al., in press; see also Jaeger, 2006, Ch. 3 on *that*-mentioning in complement clauses).

This hypothesis about the link between redundancy and syntactic reduction has since evolved into a theory of efficient language production. The hypothesis of Uniform Information Density (UID, Jaeger, 2006, 2010; Levy & Jaeger, 2007) states that producers prefer to distribute *information* uniformly across the linguistic signal. The information carried by a linguistic unit is defined in information theory as the logarithm-transformed inverse of its probability (Shannon, 1948). So,

---

[2]This one is for you, Tom. Thank you, for getting me started in the psycholinguistics world and all the insightful and enjoyable collaborations!

$I(u) = \log \frac{1}{p(u)} = -\log p(u)$. That is, the less predictable something is, the more information it carries (and the less redundant it is). For the purpose of this paper, we can think of information density as the amount of information per word (but see Jaeger, 2010, for more detail).

Uniform information density can be shown to be a theoretically optimal solution for successful transmission of information across a noisy channel (cf. Aylett & Turk, 2004; Genzel & Charniak, 2002; based on Shannon, 1948). Thus, if there were no other constraints on language and language use, rational producers should distribute information absolutely uniformly across their linguistic signals. However, language *is* subject to many constraints and pressures, so this extreme case is unlikely to hold. For example, languages have to be learnable and their words and abstract structures need to be memorizable. But it is possible that a preference to distribute information uniformly is one of many pressures on language use. If such a preference affects syntactic production, we should observe that producers prefer syntactic variants that avoid peaks and troughs in information density. Choosing the full variant in syntactic reduction alternations, such as the SRC in (1) above, distributes the information that, for example, an SRC has started, $-\log p(\text{SRC} \mid context)$, over more words. Producers should then prefer the full variant (with *that was*) whenever the information at the SRC onset (e.g. on the verb *chosen* in (1) above) would otherwise be high.

This is the prediction of UID that I test in this paper using data from SRC reduction. Following much of Tom's work, I take a corpus-based approach. I follow recent work (e.g. Bresnan et al., 2007; Jaeger, 2006, 2010) in using multilevel logit models to simultaneously control for other processing mechanisms known to affect syntactic reduction. Despite a rich tradition of influential corpus-based work (e.g. Arnold et al., 2000; Clark & Fox Tree, 2002; Clark & Wasow, 1998; Fox Tree & Clark, 1997; Hawkins, 2001, 2004; Resnik, 1996; Roland, Elman, & Ferreira, 2005; Wasow, 1997, 2002), corpus studies are arguably still under-represented in psycholinguistics. Unfamiliarity with the decisions involved in this type of research understandably makes it difficult to assess the results. In this paper, I sacrifice conciseness for a more detailed discussion of methodological issues.

2 Processing Accounts of Production Preferences

Existing processing accounts of preferences in language production can be grouped into four major categories. I introduce and compare them with regard to their coverage across levels of linguistic production (see also Arnold, this volume; Hawkins, this volume).

Dependency processing accounts hypothesize that speakers prefer efficiently processable dependencies (Hawkins, 1994, 2001, 2004, 2007). Among other things, these accounts correctly predict that speakers prefer word orders that lead to shorter dependencies. For example, in word order variations following the verb (e.g. the ditransitive alternation), English speakers prefer to order long constituents after shorter constituents (Arnold et al., 2000; Arnold, Wasow, Asudeh, & Alrenga, 2004; Bresnan et al., 2007; Lohse et al., 2004; Wasow, 1997, 2002, inter alia). Crucially, speakers of verb-final languages show the opposite preference (for Japanese, see Yamashita & Chang, 2001; for Korean, Choi, 2007). Hence, across different languages, speakers seem to prefer word orders that order shorter constituents closer to the verb. Dependency processing accounts also receive support from syntactic reduction, such as *that*-mentioning (Elsness, 1984; Fox & Thompson, 2007; Hawkins, 2001; Jaeger, 2006; Race & MacDonald, 2003; Roland et al., 2005, inter alia). The prediction of dependency processing accounts for lower-level production choices, such as phoneme deletion and articulatory choices, are less clear. Hawkins discusses one such dependency processing account in more detail (Hawkins, 2004, this volume).

An alternative type of account holds that the relative 'accessibility' of referents is the primary driving force behind speakers' preferences. There are two types of accessibility-based accounts: Alignment accounts and availability accounts. **Alignment accounts** (Bock & Warren, 1985; F. Ferreira, 1994) hold that speakers prefer to align grammatical function assignment with the relative accessibility of referents. Here accessibility refers to the *conceptual* accessibility of referents. A referent's conceptual accessibility is affected by inherent properties (e.g. animacy, Bock, Loebell, & Morey, 1992; imageability, Bock & Warren, 1985), and by contextually conditioned properties (e.g. prior mention of the referent, Prat-Sala & Branigan, 2000).

Availability accounts (V. S. Ferreira, 1996; V. S. Ferreira & Dell, 2000; Levelt & Maassen, 1981; Prat-Sala & Branigan, 2000) also hold that the conceptual accessibility of referents affects speakers' preferences at choice points in production. However, availability accounts consider the effect of accessibility to be more direct: According to availability accounts, speakers prefer to order accessible material early since it is available earlier for pronunciation (cf. the Principle of Immediate Mention in V. S. Ferreira & Dell, 2000). Here 'accessibility' refers to ease of retrieval from memory. Note that accessibility is *not* the same as constituent length or weight. A heavier constituent may have a more accessible (and hence easier to retrieve) onset than a shorter constituent (cf. *a very nice idea* vs. *xylophones*). Since not all parts of a constituent have to be planned before speakers can initiate articulation (e.g. Griffin, 2003; Brown-Schmidt & Konopka, 2008), availability accounts do not necessarily predict that long constituents should be ordered after short constituents (contrary to Hawkins, 2007, 93-94). According to availability accounts, speakers choose between variants based on which one they can *start* pronouncing first (V. S. Ferreira & Dell, 2000, 289).

For word order variations in subject-initial languages, such as English, alignment and accessibility accounts make very similar predictions (for recent reviews, see Branigan, Pickering, & Tanaka, 2008; Jaeger & Norcliffe, 2009; see also Arnold, this volume). For syntactic reduction, such as the reduction of SRCs, the predictions of psycholinguistic alignment accounts are less clear. Availability accounts predict that speakers prefer to pronounce, rather than omit, optional words if the following material is not available for pronunciation. This prediction has received support from studies on *that*-mentioning in object-extracted relative clauses (Fox & Thompson, 2007; Jaeger & Wasow, 2006; Temperley, 2003) and complement clauses (Elsness, 1984; V. S. Ferreira & Dell, 2000; Roland et al., 2005), as well as from studies on SRC reduction (V. S. Ferreira & Dell, 2000, Experiment 3).

Availability accounts have been contrasted with **ambiguity avoidance accounts** (e.g. Bolinger, 1972; Hawkins, 2004; Temperley, 2003), which predict that speakers structure their utterances so as to avoid temporary ambiguities. Consider the SRC example in (2). Unlike in (1) above, the verb form *chased* is ambiguous out of context between the past tense and passive participle interpretation. In the reduced form (2a), this can cause comprehenders to be 'garden pathed' (Bever, 1970) into the unintended interpretation, where *chased* is temporarily interpreted as the past tense matrix verb to *three mail men*). Garden-pathing leads to comprehension difficulty at the disambiguation point (i.e. the word *by*). Speakers can avoid potential garden paths by producing a full SRC, as in (2b).

(2)   *Three mail men ...*

    a.   *... chased by dogs ...*

    b.   *... who are being chased by dogs ...*

    are indeed a hilarious sight.

There is evidence from corpus studies (Hawkins, 2004; Temperley, 2003) and experiments (Haywood, Pickering, & Branigan, 2005) that speakers sometimes avoid temporary syntactic ambiguities. However, many recent corpus studies (Roland et al., 2005; Roland, Dick, & El-man, 2007) and experiments (Arnold et al., 2004; V. S. Ferreira & Dell, 2000; Kraljic & Brennan, 2005) have failed to detect ambiguity avoidance effects (see in particular, Roland et al., 2007 vs. Temperley, 2003). Whether speakers avoid syntactic ambiguity is therefore still very much an open question.

3 The Production of Subject-Extracted Relative Clauses

Consider example (3). The information carried by the SRC onset, *left*, differs between the full and the reduced variant. In the reduced variant, (3a), *left* signals the beginning of an SRC constituent. This is in addition to its lexical information. In the full SRC variant, (3b), however, *left* carries less information, since the preceding words (*that was*) already signal the presence of an SRC constituent.[3]

(3)   *More work on government projects helped close the gap* ...

   a.   ... *left by cash-strapped home-owners.*

   b.   ... *that was left by cash-strapped home-owners.*

In information theoretic terms (Shannon, 1948), the information carried by *left* can be described as the the sum of two pieces of information: The information that there is an SRC, I(SRC | CTXT), and the information that the first word in that SRC is *left*, I(left | CTXT, SRC). Put more generally:

$$
\begin{aligned}
& \text{I(SRC ONSET | CTXT)} && && \text{(E-1)} \\
={}& \text{I(SRC | CTXT)} &&+\quad& \text{I(ONSET | CTXT, SRC)} \\
={}& -\log \text{p(SRC | CTXT)} &&+\quad& -\log \text{p(ONSET | CTXT, SRC)}
\end{aligned}
$$

If present, the optional function words spread the same information over two more words, thereby lowering information density. The function words reduced the information carried by the first content word in the SRC. To illustrate this, consider the extreme case where the function words signal an SRC with 100% certainty. In that case, the function words carry the information that there is an SRC (the left half of Equation 1), and the onset carries only its lexical information (the right half of Equation 1). If, as predicted by UID, producers avoid peaks and troughs in information density, they should prefer the full variant for SRC onsets that are high in information content. Given Equation 1,

---

[3]The two function words carry additional information, e.g. the tense of the SRC. Here I simplify and focus on the constituent boundary information.

producers should be more likely to use the full form, (a) the less probable an SRC is given the preceding context and (b) the less probable the words at the SRC onset are given the preceding discourse and given that there is an SRC. Here, I focus on the first prediction: The more predictable an SRC, the more likely producers should be to use the reduced form without the optional function words.

Like any methodology, the corpus-based approach involves judgment calls. While some of these are standardly part of the write-up, others are usually not mentioned for the sake of brevity. Here I am more explicit about the process that leads from the hypothesis formulation via a priori considerations (such as choice of model, choice of control predictors, etc.), corpus selection, data extraction, data exclusion, and variable preparation to the statistical analysis. I address general considerations and the specific decisions made for the current study (though the list of issues addressed below is by no means exhaustive).

3.1 A Priori Consideration: Envisioning the Analysis

Before embarking on a corpus-based project, it is a good idea to look ahead and to envision the type of analysis that will be necessary. While it is almost inevitable that inspection of extracted data will force revisions of initial assumptions, there are a few considerations that should guide decisions from corpus selection to statistical analysis. For example, what exactly is the outcome (dependent variable) of interest and what type of data should hence be collected? What predictors will be included in the analysis to avoid confounds and to model the predictions of alternative accounts? And approximately how many parameters will be required? Based on the anticipated number of parameters and the type of analysis required, how much data is necessary to have a *chance* to detect the hypothesized effects? I address these questions in the order mentioned.

Outcome of Interest

It is important to understand the outcome of interest. For example, for corpus-based studies on relativizer *that*-mentioning in Standard American English, only finite, restrictive, non-pied-piped, non-extraposed, non-subject-extracted relative clauses should be included in the analysis, because only those types of relative clauses allow both the full and the reduced form (cf. Jaeger, 2006, Appendix C). In other words, when we study producers' preferences in production, only cases where producers actually have a choice between at least two variants should be included. Failure to do so is likely to lead to spurious results. For the current study, only *passive* subject-extracted relative clauses are of interest, since active subject-extracted relative clauses do not afford the same type of choice (*whiz*-deletion, as in (1) above). Additional annotation (see below) excluded further cases that were incompatible with the alternation.

Likely Predictors

Whenever possible, predictor selection should be driven by *a priori* theoretical considerations (such as the need to account for theories of sentence production) as well as empirical considerations (such as what factors are known to affect the outcome).

Based on previous research on SRC reduction (V. S. Ferreira & Dell, 2000; Hare, Tanenhaus, & McRae, 2007; Trueswell, 1996) and other reduction phenomena (see references in Section 2), there are several controls that should be included in any serious test of a new hypothesis that makes predictions about SRC reduction. Since different corpora provide different annotations, it is worth considering what types of information will be needed for the model before choosing a corpus for the study. For the current purpose, I include the following controls (though additional controls may be necessary, as I discuss in Section Section 3.6):

- **length of SRC** to account for dependency length effects (cf. Elsness, 1984; Fox & Thompson, 2007; Hawkins, 2001; Jaeger, 2006, 2010; Lohse, 2000; Quirk, 1957; Race & MacDonald, 2003; Roland et al., 2005),
- **word form frequencies** of the word immediately preceding the SRC as well as the frequency of the first word in it to control for availability-based effects on sentence production (cf. V. S. Ferreira & Dell, 2000; Jaeger & Wasow, 2006; Race & MacDonald, 2003),
- whether the participle is **potentially ambiguous**, since producers may avoid ambiguity (cf. Bolinger, 1972; Temperley, 2003; Hawkins, 2004).

Assuming that the SRC length effect may require modeling of nonlinearities (as is the case for dependency length effects on complementizer-mentioning, Jaeger, 2006, 2010), a rule-of-thumb estimate of the number of required control parameters would be about 9 (one parameter for ambiguity, one each for the two frequency measures, 3 each for SRC length, plus 50% for predictors not considered a priori). Adding one parameter each for two estimates of the information density at the SRC onset (information density can be estimated given preceding material and given the words at the SRC onset, see Section 3.4 below), this comes to an estimate of 11 parameters. This lower bound estimate can be used for considerations regarding the avoidance of overfitting, which I describe next.

Avoiding Overfitting: How Much Data will be Necessary?

Once the approximate number of parameters for a model is known, it is possible to estimate how much data (i.e. how many observations) will be necessary to avoid overfitting. An overfitted model describes the sample rather than generalizing beyond the sample to the population. Exactly how many observations are necessary to avoid overfitting depends on the distribution of the dependent and independent variables and correlations between predictors that one wishes to distinguish between. Hence, there is no simple rule that is guaranteed to avoid overfitting. However, several rules of thumb have been suggested. Generally, 10-15 times as many observations as numbers of parameters in the model seems to be sufficient (for a very readable introduction to considerations about overfitting, see Babyak, 2004; for power simulations assuming effect sizes that are typical for behavioral research, see Green, 1991). Crucially, it is the *limiting* sampling size that matters. So, for binary outcomes like the choice of full over reduced passive SRC, it is the minimum number of observations of *the less frequent outcome* that should be 10-15 times higher than the number of parameters in the model (for simulations, see Peduzzi, Concato, Kemper, Holford, & Feinstein, 1996).

These rules of thumb for number of necessary observations have to be taken with caution. Especially for corpus-based work, they should be treated as a lower bound. It helps to consider a standard psycholinguistic production experiment. For example, V. S. Ferreira and Dell (2000, Experiment 3) present a recall experiment on passive SRCs with 48 subjects and 24 items for a 2 x 2 x 2 design (i.e. 8 parameters including the intercept). About 10% of the 1, 152 data points had to be excluded from the analysis for a variety of reasons. Participants produced full SRCs in about 30% of all trials. Hence, the less frequent outcome occurred a bit over 300 times, resulting in an approximately 4 times higher ratio of data to parameters than suggested above as the absolute lower bound ($8 * 10 = 80$; most recall experiments contain 4-6 items per condition and thus yield even more statistical power than the experiment described here).

Corpus data are usually highly unbalanced, which further reduces power since it leads to many cells in the overall design that contain little to no data. Hence, I recommend a more conservative criterion: For highly unbalanced data and complex analyses with many parameters, the less frequent outcome should be about 50-100 times more frequent than the number of parameters in the model. It is important to keep in mind though that these are rules of thumb. Several other factors determine whether an effect can be detected (e.g. effect size, distribution of the outcome with respect to the predictor, and the presence of collinear predictors that need to be accounted for).

A comparison of corpus analyses with experimental work on syntactic reduction suggests that experiments generally *over*estimate the relative frequency of full over reduced syntactic variants (cf. experiments in V. S. Ferreira & Dell, 2000; V. S. Ferreira, 2003 vs. corpus data in Roland et al., 2005; Jaeger, 2010). Hence, full SRCs are likely to be the less frequent outcome, possibly making up about 10-20% of all SRCs. Assuming this rate of full SRCs and assuming the number of parameters needed for the model (see previous section), a corpus with at least 550 to 1,100 or preferably closer to 5,500 to 11,000 SRCs is needed for the current study!

3.2 Selecting a Corpus

Now that we have an estimate of the lower bound for the number of observations needed for the current study, the next step is to find a suitable corpus. Several considerations affect what corpus is best suited for a research project. Corpora differ in terms of the type of language (e.g. in terms of modality, register, style, genre, monologue vs. dialogue data), available annotation (e.g. syntactic annotation vs. plain text), and the distribution of the event of interest. Available annotation affects how much time and money will have to be spent on additional annotations before it will be possible to extract all necessary information about the outcome and the predictors. Corpus size and distribution of the event of interest affect how much power the analysis will yield.

Speech corpora are arguably more appropriate for research on language production. However, passive SRCs are very infrequent in speech. For example, less than 500 passive SRCs are observed in the Switchboard corpus of American English telephone dialogues (Godfrey, Holliman, & McDaniel, 1992) of approximately 800,000 spoken words. Preliminary tests suggest that as few as 10-20% of these passive SRCs in these corpora are in the full form. Given the low-frequency of full SRCs, this suggests that even the 10 million spoken words of the British National Corpus would not provide enough data for the current study. When the most suited corpora do not contain the outcome of interest in sufficient numbers, researchers are faced with the decision of whether other corpora are appropriate approximations. Alternatively, the target structure can be elicited in controlled experiments.

Here, I take the former approach. The written portion of the British National Corpus (BNC) is used as a data source for the current study. This decision was made because there is some evidence that written language by and large exhibits the same processing pressures observed in speech (Jaeger & Wasow, 2005). More specifically, information density effects on *that*-mentioning have been observed in writing (Jaeger et al., 2005). The written parts of the BNC contain approximately 90 million words from various genres and styles (see Nation, 2004, 11). The corpus was automatically parsed by Benjamin Van Durme using the Charniak-Johnson parser (Charniak & Johnson, 2005). Additionally, all sentences were annotated with author and genre information using BNC meta data and scripts provided by Judith Degen.

3.3 Corpus, Data Extraction, Annotation, and Exclusion

After a corpus is selected, the relevant cases need to be extracted, along with the outcome and predictor values. Before the data can be entered into the analysis, erroneously included cases and outliers, as well as cases with missing or unreliable information, need to be excluded. Each of these steps includes decisions that can affect the final analysis and should therefore be handled with care. If a corpus is not already annotated for all variables of interest, additional manual annotation may be required, which requires the researcher to make further judgment calls.

Data Extraction

The syntactic search software TGrep2 (Rohde, 2005) was used to extract all passive SRCs of a certain type from the corpus. Whenever data is automatically extracted from corpora, there is a danger of introducing biases into the analysis by either erroneously in- or excluding cases. This danger is especially high when, as in the present case, the data are extracted by means of syntactic searches over an *automatically parsed corpus* that has not undergone manual correction by annotators. Blind reliance on the consistency of automatic syntactic annotation risks in- or excluding cases in a *non-random* and yet *uncontrolled* fashion. Statistical analysis of such data may simply reflect whatever features the parser is conditioned on and hence lead us to report spurious results as theoretically relevant. There are several strategies to reduce such confounds (see also Roland et al., 2007, Appendix A). If the outcome of interest is highly frequent, so that a small corpus can be used, the entire corpus can be manually annotated. If, as in the present case, a manual syntactic annotation of the entire corpus is not feasible, automatic syntactic searches have to be used in such a way that they do not introduce a bias.

To avoid biases, the first step is to become familiar with the annotation guidelines used for the corpus. For the current case, almost all full SRCs are marked as S̄ modifying an NP, where as almost all reduced SRCs are marked as VP modifying an NP, as in Figure 1a and Figure 1b, respectively.

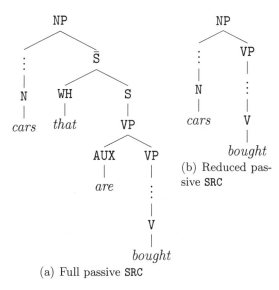

(b) Reduced passive SRC

(a) Full passive SRC

FIGURE 1 Example parses of the predominant syntactic annotation patterns used to encode (a) full and (b) reduced SRC in the corpus

Unfortunately, there is considerable variation in how exactly the S̄ or VP attaches to the NP it modifies and how the internal structure of the S̄ or VP was annotated. Additionally, exploratory searches revealed that the participle (*bought* in Figure 1) is not always marked as such (VBN in Penn Treebank annotation)—sometimes it is misparsed as past tense verb (VBD) or as adjective (JJ). All in all, SRC parses are relatively unreliable. For that reason, I employed search patterns that mostly rely on linear order information and only make reference to structural relations that are parsed reliably. Since false exclusions are harder to detect than false inclusions, I started with a very *inclusive* pattern based on *only* linear order constraints. For feasibility, only SRCs immediately following a noun are considered. This drastically reduces the number of false inclusions while not introducing a bias (UID predictions hold both for SRCs that are adjacent and SRCs that are non-adjacent to the noun). Hence, the first search looked for nouns that were either immediately adjacent to a word form compatible with a participle interpretation or only separated from it by a valid relativizer-auxiliary combination (e.g. *which had been, who are*, or *that will be*). Instead of relying on correct part-of-speech tagging for the participles, a regular expression matched any adjective ending in /-ed/ as well as all past tense and participle forms.

This pattern yields a very large number of hits ($> 100,000$), but contains many false inclusions (estimated by checking a small random sample). I then successively refined the pattern. At each step, I checked that only falsely *in*cluded cases were excluded by the refined pattern (using the same random sample). One criterion that considerably reduced the rate of false inclusions, while not leading to false exclusions, was the requirement for a *by*-PP immediately following the participle:

(4)   ...NOUN (REL AUX) PARTICIPLE *by*-PP ...
    ...*cars*   (*that are*)   *bought*   *by companies* ...

This excludes many false inclusions where a matrix verb is mistakenly parsed as a reduced passive SRC. While limiting matches to SRCs with *by*-PPs is non-random, it crucially does not introduce a bias into the analysis: UID's predictions are the same for SRCs with and SRCs without PPs. This decision is comparable to the decision of an experimenter to use only SRC stimuli with *by*-PPs.

Successive refinement led to the final TGrep2 search pattern, shown in Table 1. The syntactic tree of an example match is given in Figure 2. This pattern yielded 50,077 matches.

```
*=srcverb    , (/^NN/=nhead   ≫ (/^NP/ < (*=src   ≪ =srcverb
                                          !<< (*    ≪ =srcverb
                                                    ≪ =nhead)))
             . (by            > (* > /^PP/))
             [= /^VB(N|D)/
             |= /^JJ/         < /.+ed$/
                              !$ /^NP|NN\/)])
```

TABLE 1 TGrep2 search pattern for reduced SRCs

The result returned by the final pattern still contains a considerable number of erroneous inclusions. It would be possible to stop at this point and deem the error rate acceptable. This is an efficient approach as long as the remaining in- and exclusion errors are distributed non-randomly with regard to the outcome (for an example of such an approach, see Roland et al., 2005). Here, a different approach was taken. I first applied several automatic filters to exclude data that should definitely not be included. Just as subjects may skip a case or a device

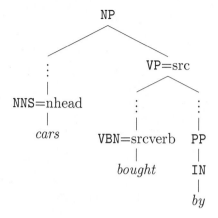

FIGURE 2 Tree representation of an example match for the SRC TGrep2
search pattern

may have a measurement error in experiments, data extracted from a
corpus may miss variable information. For example, many corpora contain annotation mistakes or inconsistencies that make it impossible to
extract all information about all cases. Especially when there is a lot of
data, it is easier to simply exclude those cases than to manually annotate the missing information (but caution is necessary, if there is any
reason to believe that missing information is not randomly distributed
over cases). This left over 48,000 cases (see Table 2 below for details).

Given the large number of remaining cases, I decided to further
exclude cases with infrequent idiosyncratic properties that may or may
not influence processing—a process I refer to as 'stratification'. At each
step, both full and reduced SRCs not meeting the inclusion criteria were
excluded. Cases for which variable information could not be estimated
with high reliability were also excluded.

After all automatic filters were applied, a manual annotation was
conducted on the remaining data. The purpose of the annotation was
to further reduce the rate of erroneous inclusions and to check how
accurately the values for the predictors were extracted. Next, I describe
the different data exclusion steps and the annotation.[4]

Data Exclusion: Stratification vs. Control

Data sampled from corpora are often highly unbalanced with regard
to infrequent effects. Unfortunately, infrequent effects can nevertheless

---

[4]The information density effect reported below was stable through all exclusion
criteria, as well as additional tests. The additional annotation did not change the
results either, although it was conceivable that it would.

be large. Consider adjacency effects on *that*-mentioning. Relative and complement clauses that are not adjacent to their head exhibit *substantially* higher rates of *that*-mentioning than adjacent clauses (Bolinger, 1972; Elsness, 1984; Fox & Thompson, 2007; Hawkins, 2001; Race & MacDonald, 2003). Since the effects are strong, it seems advisable to include corresponding controls in the model. However, non-adjacent complement or relative clauses are relatively rare (e.g., < 5% in spontaneous speech, Jaeger, 2006, 57 & 104). In such cases, it can be easier to exclude all of the infrequent cases (stratification) rather than to lose degrees of freedom in order to account for the effect. The main advantage of stratification is peace of mind: Not only is the potential effect held constant, but all of its potential interactions with other predictors in the model are held constant, too. By avoiding more control parameters, we also decrease the chance of overfitting. Fewer parameters also mean more power, although the decision to exclude data may also decrease power. So it's important to carefully consider the trade-off between fewer parameters and less data (e.g., by taking into consideration the rule-of-thumb mentioned above, according to which the minimum number of observations of the less frequent outcome should be 10-15 times higher than the number of parameters). Here, extremely long SRCs (> 23 words, which is 2.5 standard deviations above the mean) were excluded.

If applied appropriately, such stratification can be an effective way to reduce unaccounted-for variance in the data while keeping enough data for the final analysis.[5] Laboratory experiments can be thought of as employing extreme stratification. Most psycholinguistic experiments use small sets of stimuli types. Experiments either hold properties that are known to affect the outcome constant across conditions, or they hold the mean of those properties constant (the latter is more common, but can be insufficient, see Baayen, 2004).

Stratification can also be a good solution when values of predictors cannot be reliably estimated. For example, for the present study, it is necessary to estimate the information content of the SRC onset. These estimates are based on conditional probability estimates (see Section 3.4 below), and conditional estimates are unreliable if the value being conditioned on is infrequent. Consider an extreme case. If the word *snark* occurs exactly once in the BNC and that one time it is followed by an SRC, would we want to conclude that SRCs are entirely predictable

---

[5]Data exclusion has to be conducted on a priori defined criteria, such as power considerations described above. If multiple tests are conducted on different subsets of the data, the family-wise error rate will be inflated and appropriate corrections have to be applied.

after the word *snark?* Intuitively, the situation would be different if we had seen the word *snark* 100 times, each time followed by an SRC. Here cases were excluded if the head noun or the participle occurred less than 50 times in the corpus since the information density estimates introduced below are conditioned on the head noun and the participle. Note that this does not a priori exclude highly information dense SRC onsets from the data, since the conditional probability of an SRC is logically independent of the absolute frequency of the event conditioned on.

Cases with an SRC participle that was observed less than 5 times in the database were also excluded. This improves control for verb-specific effects in the rate of syntactic reduction (included in the analysis as random effect, see below). The effect of all automatic exclusions is summarized in Table 2.

Exclusion criterion	Cases	% of Total
Automatic Detection of Inclusion Errors	**1,905**	**4.0%**
Wrong parse (e.g. idioms)	25	0.1%
Missing variable information	1,407	2.9%
Match for participle not a verb	338	0.7%
Stratification	**8,931**	**17.8%**
SRC length in words > 23	3,392	6.8%
Frequency of preceding noun form in corpus < 50	1,606	3.2%
Frequency of participle form in corpus < 50	490	1.0%
Frequency of participle in database < 5	5,151	10.3%
Remaining cases	39,241	78.4%

TABLE 2 Summary of all automatic exclusion criteria and number of cases that did not meet criterion. Bold lines summarize the exclusions listed below them. The last column relates the exclusions to the number of hits returned by the search pattern in Table 1. The total number of exclusions is less than the sum of the exclusions since many cases failed to meet several conditions.

Data Annotation

Next, I discuss the manual annotation that was added in order to further exclude erroneously included cases and correct values of input variables. Three annotators (see acknowledgments) annotated 18,305 of the remaining cases in time for this article.

Annotators determined whether cases were actually passive SRCs and, if so, whether they were compatible with both the full and reduced form. Annotators also marked cases for which the entire sentence could not be understood (the BNC contains headlines and other sentence fragments). Those were later excluded from the analysis.

Additionally, annotators checked SRC length information since extraction of SRC length based on the automatic parses turned out to be unreliable. Automatically identifying the end of a relative clause is much harder than identifying where it starts. Even for human annotators, and sometimes even with additional context, it is hard or impossible to determine where an SRC ends for cases like (5), where the italicized material could modify the *the site*, in which case it is not part of the SRC, or it could modify the SRC's verb phrase. Such cases were marked and excluded from the analysis.

(5)   This was the site chosen by the jesuits *for their complex of college and churches* ....

To avoid degradation of the bigram estimates of information density used below, annotators also marked cases in which the modified NP was complex (e.g. conjoined NPs, partitive NPs), where the actual head noun was a multi-word compound, or where the actual head noun was not adjacent to the SRC.

The analysis was based on only SRCs that were (a) judged to be compatible with both the full and the reduced forms, (b) adjacent to the head noun of the modified NP, and for which (c) all variable information could be determined. The exclusions based on the manual annotation are summarized in Table 3.

Exclusion criterion	Cases	% of Total
Sentence incomprehensible	568	3.2%
SRC length could not be determined reliably	1,016	5.5%
Not an SRC	434	2.4%
SRC judged to be non-alternating	323	1.7%
Complex modified NP	1,767	9.7%
Multi-word head noun of modified NP	16	0.1%
Head noun of modified NPs non-adjacent to SRC	0	0.0%
Remaining cases	13,596	74.3%

TABLE 3 Summary of all exclusion criteria and number of cases that did not meet criterion. The last column relates the exclusions to the total number of *annotated* cases. The total number of exclusions is less than the sum of the exclusions since many cases failed to meet several conditions.

This left 13,596 SRCs, of which 899 (6.7%) were full SRCs. These SRCs contain 546 different participle forms, of which only 31 occur at least 100 times in the database. Figure 3 summarizes the distribution of participles types in the database and lists the 50 most frequent participles, which together account for over 61% of the data.

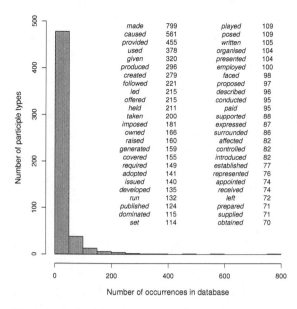

made	799		played	109
caused	561		posed	109
provided	455		written	105
used	378		organised	104
given	320		presented	104
produced	296		employed	100
created	279		faced	98
followed	221		proposed	97
led	215		described	96
offered	215		conducted	95
held	211		paid	95
taken	200		supported	88
imposed	181		expressed	87
owned	166		surrounded	86
raised	160		affected	82
generated	159		controlled	82
covered	155		introduced	82
required	149		established	77
adopted	141		represented	76
issued	140		appointed	74
developed	135		received	74
run	132		left	72
published	124		prepared	71
dominated	115		supplied	71
set	114		obtained	70

FIGURE 3   Histogram of participle types and sorted list of 50 most frequent
participles in the database

3.4   Variable Preparation and Analysis

Next, I describe the type of regression model used to analyze the data,
summarize the predictors in the model, and then describe the most
common issues with this type of analysis.

Type of Analysis: Mixed Logit Regression

A mixed logit model (Breslow & Clayton, 1993) was used to analyze
the effect of information density predicted by UID on producers' choice
of full over reduced SRCs, while controlling for effects predicted by alternative accounts. The model was fit using the function *lmer* from
the *lme4* library (Bates, Maechler, & Dai, 2008) within the statistics
software package R (R Development Core Team, 2008). A detailed introduction to mixed logit models is beyond the scope of this paper. I
briefly summarize their main properties (for a technical introduction,
see Agresti, 2002; Gelman & Hill, 2006; for introductions intended for
psycholinguistic audiences, see Baayen, 2008; Jaeger, 2008).

Mixed logit models can be thought of as an extension of logistic
regression. They are intended for the analysis of binomially distributed
categorical outcome variables. The outcome (a.k.a. dependent variable)
is regressed against the predictors (a.k.a. independent variables).

Logistic regression assumes that all observations were sampled randomly and hence are independent of each other. However, this assumption is typically violated in psycholinguistic research. The database for the present study, too, contains violations of independence. For example, many producers contribute more than one observation. Since producers may have different base rates of SRC reduction, this can make the analysis unreliable. Intuitively, we can learn more about how SRCs are distributed in English when we have 200 data points each from 20 speakers than when we have 4,000 data points from one single speaker. Analyses that fail to adequately account for violations of independence generally overestimate the amount of data and hence the confidence one can have in the results. Unlike ordinary logistic regression, mixed logit models can restore the assumption of (conditional) independence. Mixed logit models allow researchers to specify random effects that efficiently account for, e.g., random differences between producers (for an excellent introduction see Gelman & Hill, 2006). Here, two random effects were included: One to account for differences between writers and one to model idiosyncratic preferences of different participle forms.

Predictors in the Model

Table 4 summarizes all fixed effect predictors in the model along with the number of parameters used to model them. I first describe the control predictors and then the two information density measures.

The length of the SRC in words excluding the omissible function words (MIN= 3, MAX= 23, MEAN= 7.6, STDEV= 4.5) was included to control for effects of dependency processing (Hawkins, 1994, 2004). SRC length was modeled with restricted cubic splines (Harrell, 2001, 16-24) since previous work had found non-linear effect of constituent length on syntactic reduction (Jaeger, 2006, 2010).

The log-transformed frequency of the first word in the SRC (MIN= 4.2, MAX= 12.0, MEAN= 8.8, STDEV= 1.3), the participle, was included to control for effects of availability-based production (V. S. Ferreira & Dell, 2000; Levelt & Maassen, 1981; Jaeger & Wasow, 2006; Race & MacDonald, 2003). The log-transformed frequency of the head noun of the modified NP (MIN= 3.9, MAX= 15.5, MEAN= 8.7, STDEV= 2.0) was included to capture potential 'spill-over' effect due to high processing load immediately *preceding* the SRC onset.

To account for potential ambiguity avoidance effects, a predictor coding whether the participle was ambiguous was included in the model. This corresponds to what Section 3.3 Wasow and Arnold (2003) call 'syntactic ambiguity'. Under this coding, most SRCs in the database (93%) have a potentially ambiguous onset. However, many—if not

Predictor	Description	Type(βs)
INTERCEPT		(1)
Domain length		
LENGTH(SRC)	Length of SRC	cont(3)
Lexical retrieval at SRC onset		
FQ(PARTICIPLE)	Log frequency of participle	cont(1)
Lexical retrieval before SRC onset		
FQ(NOUN)	Log frequency of head noun	cont(1)
Potential ambiguity at SRC onset		
AMBIGUOUS SRC ONSET	SRC onset potentially ambiguous w/o optional function word	cat(1)
Information content of SRC onset		
I(SRC | NOUN)	SRC onset's information content given preceding word	cont(1)
I(SRC | PARTICIPLE)	SRC onset's information content given its first word	cont(1)
Total number of parameters in model		9

TABLE 4 The name and description of each input variable are listed; the last column describes the predictor type ('cat' = categorical, 'cont' = continuous) along with the number of parameters associated with the predictor.

most—syntactically ambiguous SRCs are not actually ambiguous *in context*. That is, many of the cases labeled as potentially ambiguous here are unlikely to cause garden path effects. In Wasow and Arnold's terms, they are not 'pragmatically ambiguous'. Unfortunately, only syntactic ambiguity annotation was available for the current study. I return to this issue below.

Finally, two measures of the information content of the SRC constituent boundary were included in the model. The information content given the preceding context was estimated using a simple bigram, I(SRC \| NOUN) $= -\log$ p(SRC \| NOUN) (MIN= 2.1, MAX= 11.8, MEAN= 5.7, STDEV= 1.2). Additionally, the information content of the SRC onset was also estimated given the participle, I(SRC \| PARTICIPLE) $= -\log$ p(SRC \| PARTICIPLE) (MIN= 1.2, MAX= 9.4, MEAN= 3.3, STDEV= 1.0). This can be understood as an approximation of how much information the presence of an SRC carries after the participle has been processed.

Preparing Variables for Analysis: Common Issues

As regression models allow us to assess the partial effects of multiple predictors, they allow the simultaneous test of multiple hypotheses in one model. Like for any statistical procedure, what specific hypothesis is being tested depends on the precise way the input variables were entered into the model. It is useful to distinguish between the input variables to a regression and the actual predictors in the model. Several decision steps lie between the choice of input variables and the final model. Unfortunately, a comprehensive description of the steps involved in regression analysis for corpus-based research is beyond the scope of this paper (for a tutorial, see Jaeger & Kuperman, 2009; for introductions to regression modeling, see Baayen, 2008; Gelman & Hill, 2006).

Figure 4 provides an overview of the process I followed in preparing and entering the predictors described above into the analysis.

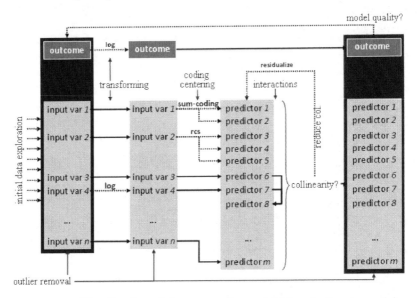

FIGURE 4 Visualization of the process from variable selection to model evaluation involved in regression analyses.

Initial data analysis leads to the input variables. It is a good idea to have at least an impression of the distributions of the predictor and outcome variables. The input variables are then transformed (dashed lines in Figure 4 indicate that the variable changes; the labels above the dashed lines give an example of what type of operation may be applied to the variable), as well as coded and/or centered and possibly standardized, before we create higher order terms based on any of the predictors (e.g. interactions or non-linear terms for continuous predictors, such as the restricted cubic splines for SRC length). At several steps during this process, we should check for outliers since they can be overly influential. During the initial data exploration, we may exclude cases that must clearly be measurement errors or that miss variable information. After the predictors have been transformed (cf. log-transformation of the frequency measures above), it is possible to exclude outliers based on distributional assumptions.

Collinearity must be assessed in the model to provide reliably interpretable coefficients. Collinearity can lead to biased standard error estimates. The good news is that collinearity increases standard error estimates (and hence Type II errors) for only those predictors in the model that are collinear. If there is collinearity in the model for the predictor of interest there are a variety of strategies to reduce it, such as centering, stratification, residualization, principal component analysis, and so on (see Baayen, 2008). Here all predictors were centered. Residuals were used to remove collinearity between the information density measures and the log-transformed frequency of the modified NP's head noun and the SRC participle. The log-transformed frequency of the head noun of the modified NP is highly correlated with the information density estimate based on that head noun ($r = 0.61$). The SRC onset's information content based on the head noun was regressed against the head noun's log-transformed frequency and the residuals were entered into the model instead of the original information density estimate. Although the correlation between the information density estimate based on the participle and the participle's log-transformed frequency was comparatively small ($r = 0.31$), the same residualization procedure was applied. The residualized information density estimates capture *the proportion of information density that is not explicable by the log-transformed frequencies of the participle or the modified NP's head noun.* No other predictors needed to be residualized.

3.5 Results

The final step before we can interpret the model is model evaluation. If model evaluation suggests that the model is flawed, some of the steps outlined above may need to be repeated.

Model Evaluation

The model with the information density predictors and all controls is significantly better than the baseline model (always guessing the more probable outcome given only random effects). A comparison between the model and the baseline model with only the random effects of writer and participle shows that the fixed effect parameters in the model are justified ($\chi^2_{\Delta(\Lambda)}(8) = 329.5$, $p \ll 0.0001$). However, the model also shows need for improvement. Plotting the predicted vs. actually observed proportions of full SRCs in Figure 5 shows a far from perfect fit. This is in part due to the low overall probability of full SRCs, which make it hard to accurately estimate effect sizes for bins for which almost no data is observed (i.e. anything above 0.15 on the x-axis of Figure 5). In the lower range of predicted probabilities, for which most data is observed, the model fits well.

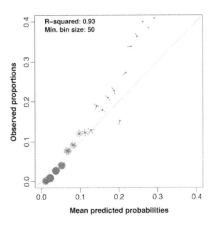

FIGURE 5 Mean predicted probabilities vs. observed proportions of full SRCs. The data is divided into bins based on 0.015 intervals of predicted values from 0 to 0.3 (there is not data with higher predicted or observed probabilities of full SRCs). The amount of observed data points in each bin is expressed as multiples of the minimum bin size. The top-most sunflower has 0 petals, so that the bin contains at least 50 data points. Each additional petal indicates 50 additional data points in that bin.

The only predictors that show signs of collinearity are the different components of the restricted cubic spline for SRC length. Since these components are only collinear with one another and since we are not interested here in their individual significances, these collinearities can safely be ignored (all other absolute fixed effect correlations < 0.2).

Effect Evaluation

As predicted by UID, both measures of the information density at the SRC onset have a highly significant positive effect on the log-odds of choosing the full form (I(SRC | NOUN): $\beta = 0.15$, $z = 3.7$, $p < 0.0002$; I(SRC | PARTICIPLE): $\beta = 0.77$, $z = 16.7$, $p \ll 0.0001$). The effects are visualized in Figure 6.

Most control parameters also had the expected effects. As predicted by availability-based production (V. S. Ferreira & Dell, 2000), the lower

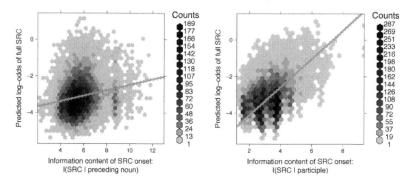

FIGURE 6 Effect of information density on log-odds of SRC reduction. (a)
shows SRC onset information content based on the preceding noun and (b)
shows SRC onset information content based on the participle. For ease of
presentation, visualizations are based on a model in which the information
density measures were not residualized against the frequency measures
(since residualization makes interpretation on the original scale difficult).
Hexagons visualize the distribution of SRC onset information content against
predicted log-odds of full SRCs considering *all* predictors in the model.

the log-transform frequency of the participle, the more likely producers
are to produce the optional function words of full SRCs ($\beta = -0.43$, $z =
-11.2$, $p \ll 0.0001$; all effects given in log-odds). For the least frequent
participle in the database (146 occurrences in the written BNC), the
odds of choosing a full SRC are 7.7 times higher than for the most
frequent participle (85,136 occurrences). In contrast to a recent study I
conducted on complementizer mentioning (Jaeger, 2010), there was no
sign of 'spill over' effects: the log-transformed frequency of the modified
NP's head noun has no significant effect ($p > 0.8$). The effects of the
two frequency predictors are illustrated in Figure 7.

There was no evidence for ambiguity avoidance accounts. Producers
do not seem to be more likely to use the full form if the participle is
ambiguous between a past tense and a passive participle interpretation
($p > 0.7$).

The effect of SRC length is also significant, as confirmed by comparison against a model without the restricted cubic spline of SRC length
($\chi^2_{\Delta(\Lambda)}(3) = 52.6$, $p \ll 0.0001$). The effect, which is illustrated in Figure 8, contains a significant non-linear component ($\chi^2_{\Delta(\Lambda)}(2) = 11.8$,
$p \ll 0.003$).

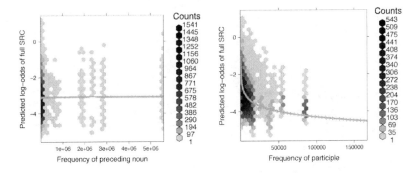

FIGURE 7 Effect of log-transformed frequencies on log-odds of SRC reduction. (a) shows the effect of the frequency of the modified NP's head noun and (b) shows the effect of the participle's frequency. Hexagons visualize the distribution of SRC onset information content against predicted log-odds of full SRCs considering *all* predictors in the model.

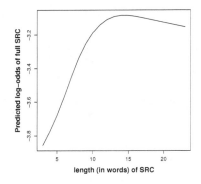

FIGURE 8 Effect of SRC length on log-odds of SRC reduction.

Finally, the two random effects confirmed that there is considerable variation in reduction rates between different writers ($\sigma_{writer} = 0.50$) and between different participles ($\sigma_{participle} = 0.34$).

3.6 General Discussion

Previous evidence for UID effects on syntactic reduction comes exclusively from *that*-mentioning (Jaeger, 2006, 2010; Levy & Jaeger, 2007; Wasow et al., in press). The current results extend this finding to another syntactic reduction environment, the reduction of passive subject-extracted relative clauses (SRCs). Unlike *that*-mentioning, SRC reduction involves a chain of optional words that have to be produced or omitted together, thereby further illustrating that SRC reduction is best thought of as a choice point during *syntactic* production. Hence the evidence obtained here further corroborates the claim that syntactic production is affected by Uniform Information Density (Jaeger, 2006, 2010; Levy & Jaeger, 2007).

Both estimates of the information density at the SRC onset have highly significant independent effects on producers' preferences. Information density is the single most important predictor of SRC reduction. Over 80% of the model improvement in terms of data likelihood compared to the base line model is due to information density (removal of information density measures from full model: $\chi^2_{\Delta(\Lambda)}(2) = 279.5$, $p \ll 0.0001$). A similarly strong effect of information density has been observed for complementizer *that*-mentioning (Jaeger, 2010), suggesting that a strong preference for uniform information density drives producers' choices during syntactic production.

These results are encouraging for UID as a theory of sentence production. There is, however, also reason for caution. First, the results are based on data from a *written* corpus. Written text is subject to editing, which involves both comprehension processes and conscious reasoning about comprehension. It remains to be seen whether SRC reduction in spontaneous speech also follows the predictions of UID— as observed for *that*-mentioning in relative clauses (Jaeger, 2006) and complement clauses (Jaeger, 2010). Second, the model presented above requires improvement. Model evaluation suggested that the effect of some predictors is over- and/or under-estimated and that other important predictors may be lacking from the model. For example, the model is lacking controls for syntactic priming and social variables, both of which have been argued to affect other syntactic reduction phenomena (for an overview, see Jaeger, 2010). Fortunately, there is no obvious reason to expect these predictors to confound the effect of information density.

The analysis also provided evidence for availability accounts (V. S. Ferreira, 1996; V. S. Ferreira & Dell, 2000; Levelt & Maassen, 1981; Prat-Sala & Branigan, 2000). It is worth mentioning that the evidence in support of availability accounts, the negative effect of log-transformed frequency, can alternatively be interpreted as additional evidence for UID. Recall that the information density of the SRC onset is determined by at least two pieces of information: The information that an SRC constituent has started and the lexical information of the SRC onset. In this paper, I have focused on the former component, but UID predicts that producers should prefer full SRCs if either of these two pieces of information is unexpected. Since a word's frequency can be seen as a very simple estimate of its probability (ignoring context), and since the Shannon information of a word is defined as the negative log-transformed inverse of its probability, the negative effect of log-transformed frequency is compatible with the predicted positive effect of lexical information content at the SRC onset. Future work is necessary to test whether this frequency effect is due to availability-based production or UID (or both).

In line with previous findings on different syntactic reduction phenomena (e.g. Hawkins, 2001; Jaeger, 2006, 2010; Race & MacDonald, 2003; Tagliamonte & Smith, 2005; Tagliamonte, Smith, & Lawrence, 2005), the effect of SRC length provides support for dependency processing accounts (Hawkins, 1994, 2004, this issue). The non-linear effect of SRC length seen in Figure 8 above resembles that observed in previous work on *that*-mentioning in relative and complement clauses (Jaeger, 2006, 2010).

There was no evidence of ambiguity avoidance (contrary to Hawkins, 2004; Haywood et al., 2005; Temperley, 2003, but in line with V. S. Ferreira & Dell, 2000; Jaeger, 2006; Roland et al., 2005). It is possible that producers only avoid ambiguities that comprehenders are likely to stumble over (cf. Wasow & Arnold, 2003, Section 3.3; see also Arnold, this issue; Jaeger, 2006, 2010). In every day language use, context usually provides cues towards the intended parse. It is well-known that comprehenders are highly efficient in taking contextual cues into consideration (Trueswell, Tanenhaus, & Kello, 1993; Trueswell, 1996; Garnsey, Pearlmutter, Meyers, & Lotocky, 1997; Hare, McRae, & Elman, 2003; Hare et al., 2007; Wilson & Garnsey, 2009). This suggests that many— if not most—syntactic ambiguities are unlikely to cause garden paths. In other words, the lack of strong replicable ambiguity avoidance effects in corpus studies may be due to the rare need for ambiguity avoidance in contextualized spontaneous speech.[6] Indeed, there is evidence from *that*-mentioning in complement clauses consistent with this hypothesis (Jaeger, 2010): where comprehenders would be likely to garden path *and* the ambiguity would be long lasting (i.e. when the disambiguation point occurs many words after the onset of the ambiguity), speakers *do* seem to be more likely to avoid syntactic ambiguity.

---

[6]This hypothesis would still leave a number of conflicting experimental results (cf. Haywood et al., 2005 vs. V. S. Ferreira & Dell, 2000; Kraljic & Brennan, 2005) unaccounted for. It is possible that the rare need for ambiguity avoidance may be the reason why ambiguity effects seem to depend a lot on the experimental items, task, and—potentially—individual differences between participants.

It is possible that the same holds for SRC reduction. Consider, for example, (6) where *released* is a potentially ambiguous verb form, but *smell* is a very unlikely agent to *released*. Comprehension experiments have shown that comprehenders are unlikely to be garden pathed in such environments (Trueswell, Tanenhaus, & Garnsey, 1994). Additional annotation will be necessary to determine whether producers avoid reduced SRCs if comprehenders are likely to be garden pathed otherwise.

(6)   *The smell released by a pig farm is indescribable.*

In the current study, the ambiguity also lasted only briefly: The point of disambiguation for the SRCs was always immediately adjacent to the point of ambiguity since the participle was immediately followed by a *by*-PP. In short, for the SRCs in the current study, there would have been very little *need* for ambiguity avoidance.

Finally, note that audience design can be construed more broadly than ambiguity avoidance (see, e.g. Brennan & Williams, 1995; Clark & Carlson, 1982; Clark & Murphy, 1982). The effect of information density, for example, could be attributable to audience design (for discussion, see Jaeger, 2010). In particular, the fact that the strongest predictor of producers' preference for a full SRC is the conditional (log) probability with which a participle occurs in a subject-extracted relative clause rather than in another syntactic environment (e.g. as a past tense matrix verb) is highly compatible with a more general audience design account. Consider that comprehension is a noisy process (e.g. because word recognition is not perfect), so that there are not just ambiguous vs. unambiguous cases, but rather more or less uncertainty about the parse. In that case, it is possible that producers aim to reduce uncertainty about the correct parse (rather than to avoid ambiguity). This interpretation of audience design would also predict the observed effect of information density. While this interpretation of the results is highly related to UID, it is not the same. I plan to explore this further in future work.

4   Conclusion

In conclusion, the corpus study presented above provides evidence that a preference for uniform information density drives producers' choices in the syntactic reduction of passive subject-extracted relative clauses. This lends further support to the hypothesis that language production at all levels of linguistic processing is affected by information density (Aylett & Turk, 2004; Frank & Jaeger, 2008; Jaeger, 2006, 2010; Levy & Jaeger, 2007).

I have discussed many of the steps involved in corpus-based research in an effort to make this methodology more transparent to researchers entering the field. While corpus-based research requires complex modeling in order to deal with highly heterogeneous unbalanced data, corpus-based studies complement psycholinguistic experiments. The trade-offs of the two approaches are discussed in more detail in Jaeger (2010).

Acknowledgements

I am grateful to Benjamin Van Durme and Judith Degen for creating a parsed version of the British National Corpus. Special thanks also go to M. Dizon and C. Hansen-Karr for doing a superb job in leading the annotation team consisting of them and J. Ferris. Thanks for feedback on earlier versions of this paper go to J. Arnold, A. Perfors, S. Riehemann, K. Housel, C. Hansen-Karr, M. Dizon, C. Hilliard, and K. Gruters. This work was partially supported by NSF grant BCS-0845059 and by the 2008 Provost's Multidisciplinary Award of the University of Rochester.

References

Agresti, A. (2002). *An introduction to categorical data analysis (2nd Edition)*. New York, NY: John Wiley and Sons Inc.

Arnold, J. E. (this volume). Ordering choices in production: For the speaker or for the listener? In E. M. Bender & J. E. Arnold (Eds.), *Language from a cognitive perspective: Grammar, usage, and processing*. Stanford: CSLI.

Arnold, J. E., Wasow, T., Asudeh, A., & Alrenga, P. (2004). Avoiding attachment ambiguities: The role of constituent ordering. *Journal of Memory and Language*, *55*(1), 55–70.

Arnold, J. E., Wasow, T., Losongco, T., & Ginstrom, R. (2000). Heaviness vs. newness: The effects of structural complexity and discourse status on constituent ordering. *Language*, *76*(1), 28–55.

Aylett, M. P., & Turk, A. (2004). The smooth signal redundancy hypothesis: A functional explanation for relationships between redundancy, prosodic prominence, and duration in spontaneous speech. *Language and Speech*, *47*(1), 31–56.

Baayen, R. H. (2004). Statistics in psycholinguistics: A critique of some current gold standards. *Mental Lexicon Working Papers*, *1*, 1–45.

Baayen, R. H. (2008). *Analyzing linguistic data: A practical introduction to statistics using R*. Cambridge, UK: Cambridge University Press.

Babyak, M. A. (2004). What you see may not be what you get: A brief, nontechnical introduction to overfitting in regression-type models. *Psychosomatic Medicine, 66*(3), 411–421.

Bates, D., Maechler, M., & Dai, B. (2008). lme4: Linear mixed-effects models using S4 classes [Computer software manual]. Available from http://lme4.r-forge.r-project.org/ (R package version 0.999375-28)

Bell, A., Brenier, J., Gregory, M., Girand, C., & Jurafsky, D. (2009). Predictability effects on durations of content and function words in conversational English. *Journal of Memory and Language, 60*(1), 92–111.

Bell, A., Jurafsky, D., Fosler-Lussier, E., Girand, C., Gregory, M., & Gildea, D. (2003). Effects of disfluencies, predictability, and utterance position on word form variation in English conversation. *Journal of the Acoustical Society of America, 113*(2), 1001-1024.

Bever, T. G. (1970). The cognitive basis for linguistic structures. In J. R. Hayes (Ed.), *Cognition and the development of language* (p. 279-362). John Wiley & Sons.

Bock, J. K., Loebell, H., & Morey, R. (1992). From conceptual roles to structural relations: Bridging the syntactic cleft. *Psychological Review, 99*(1), 150–171.

Bock, J. K., & Warren, R. K. (1985). Conceptual accessibility and syntactic structure in sentence formulation. *Cognition, 21*(1), 47-67.

Bolinger, D. (1972). *That's that* (Vol. 155; C. H. van Schooneveld, Ed.). The Hague and Paris: Mouton. (Studia Memoria Nicolai van Wijk Dedicata)

Branigan, H. P., Pickering, M. J., & Tanaka, M. (2008). Contributions of animacy to grammatical function assignment and word order during production. *Lingua, 118*(2), 172–189.

Brennan, S. E., & Williams, M. (1995). The feeling of another's knowing: Prosody and filled pauses as cues to listeners about the metacognitive states of speakers. *Journal of Memory and Language, 34*, 383–393.

Breslow, N. E., & Clayton, D. G. (1993). Approximate inference in generalized linear mixed models. *Journal of the American Statistical Association, 88*(421), 9–24.

Bresnan, J., Cueni, A., Nikitina, T., & Baayen, R. H. (2007). Predicting the dative alternation. In G. Bouma, I. Krämer, & J. Zwarts (Eds.), *Cognitive foundations of interpretation* (pp. 69–94). Amsterdam: Koninklijke Nederlandse Akademie van Wetenschapen.

Brown-Schmidt, S., & Konopka, A. E. (2008). Little houses and casas pequeñas: Message formulation and syntactic form in unscripted speech with speakers of English and Spanish. *Cognition*, *109*, 274-280.

Charniak, E., & Johnson, M. (2005). Coarse-to-fine n-best parsing and maxent discriminative reranking. In *Proceedings of the annual meeting of the Association of Computational Linguistics* (pp. 173–180). Ann Arbor, MI.

Choi, H. W. (2007). Length and order: A corpus study of Korean dative-accusative construction. *Discourse and Cognition*, *14*(3), 207–227.

Clark, H. H., & Carlson, T. B. (1982). Hearers and speech acts. *Language*, *58*, 332–373.

Clark, H. H., & Fox Tree, J. E. (2002). Using "uh" and "um" in spontaneous speech. *Cognition*, *84*, 73–111.

Clark, H. H., & Murphy, G. L. (1982). Audience design in meaning and reference. In J.-F. L. Ny & W. Kintsch (Eds.), *Language and comprehension* (pp. 287–299). Amsterdam: North-Holland.

Clark, H. H., & Wasow, T. (1998). Repeating words in spontaneous speech. *Cognitive Psychology*, *37*, 201–242.

Elsness, J. (1984). That or zero? A look at the choice of object clause connective in a corpus of American English. *English Studies*, *65*, 519–533.

Ferreira, F. (1994). Choice of passive voice is affected by verb type and animacy. *Journal of Memory and Language*, *33*, 715–715.

Ferreira, V. S. (1996). Is it better to give than to donate? Syntactic flexibility in language production. *Journal of Memory and Language*, *35*(5), 724–755.

Ferreira, V. S. (2003). The persistence of optional complementizer mention: Why saying a "that" is not saying "that" at all. *Journal of Memory and Language*, *48*, 379–398.

Ferreira, V. S., & Dell, G. S. (2000). The effect of ambiguity and lexical availability on syntactic and lexical production. *Cognitive Psychology*, *40*, 296–340.

Fox, B., & Thompson, S. A. (2007). Relative clauses in English conversation: Relativizers, frequency and the notion of construction. *Studies in Language*, *3*, 293-326.

Fox Tree, J. E., & Clark, H. H. (1997). Pronouncing "the" as "thee" to signal problems in speaking. *Cognition*, *62*, 151–167.

Frank, A., & Jaeger, T. F. (2008, July). Speaking rationally: Uniform information density as an optimal strategy for language production. In *The 30th annual meeting of the Cognitive Science Society (CogSci08)* (p. 939-944). Washington, DC.

Garnsey, S. M., Pearlmutter, N. J., Meyers, E., & Lotocky, M. A. (1997). The contributions of verb bias and plausibility to the comprehension of temporarily ambiguous sentences. *Journal of Memory and Language*, *37*, 58–93.

Gelman, A., & Hill, J. (2006). *Data analysis using regression and multilevel/hierarchical models*. Cambridge, UK: Cambridge University Press.

Genzel, D., & Charniak, E. (2002). Entropy rate constancy in text. In *Proceedings of the Association of Computational Linguistics* (pp. 199–206). Philadelphia, PA.

Godfrey, J., Holliman, E., & McDaniel, J. (1992). SWITCHBOARD: Telephone speech corpus for research and development. In *Proceedings of ICASSP-92* (Vol. 1, pp. 517–520). San Francisco, CA.

Gómez Gallo, C., Jaeger, T. F., & Smyth, R. (2008). Incremental syntactic planning across clauses. In *The 30th annual meeting of the Cognitive Science Society (CogSci08)* (p. 1294-1299). Washington, DC.

Green, S. B. (1991). How many subjects does it take to do a regression analysis? *Multivariate Behavioral Research*, *26*(3), 499–510.

Griffin, Z. M. (2003). A reversed word length effect in coordinating the preparation and articulation of words in speaking. *Psychonomic Bulletin & Review*, *10*(3), 603–609.

Hare, M., McRae, K., & Elman, J. L. (2003). Sense and structure: Meaning as a determinant of verb subcategorization preferences. *Journal of Memory and Language*, *48*(2), 281–303.

Hare, M., Tanenhaus, M. K., & McRae, K. (2007). Understanding and producing the reduced relative construction: Evidence from ratings, editing and corpora. *Journal of Memory and Language*, *56*, 410-435.

Harrell, F. E. J. (2001). *Regression modeling strategies*. Oxford: Springer-Verlag.

Hawkins, J. A. (1994). *A performance theory of order and constituency* (Vol. 73). Cambridge, UK: Cambridge University Press.

Hawkins, J. A. (2001). Why are categories adjacent? *Journal of Linguistics*, *37*, 1–34.

Hawkins, J. A. (2004). *Efficiency and complexity in grammars*. Oxford: Oxford University Press.

Hawkins, J. A. (2007). Processing typology and why psychologists need to know about it. *New Ideas in Psychology*, *25*(2), 124–144.

Hawkins, J. A. (this volume). Discontinuous dependencies in corpus selections: Particle verbs and their relevance for current issues in language processing. In E. M. Bender & J. E. Arnold (Eds.),

Language from a cognitive perspective: Grammar, usage, and processing. Stanford: CSLI.

Haywood, S. L., Pickering, M. J., & Branigan, H. P. (2005). Do speakers avoid ambiguities during dialogue? *Psychological Science, 16*(5), 362-366.

Jaeger, T. F. (2006). *Redundancy and syntactic reduction in spontaneous speech.* Unpublished doctoral dissertation, Stanford University, Stanford, CA.

Jaeger, T. F. (2008). Categorical data analysis: Away from ANOVAs (transformation or not) and towards logit mixed models. *Journal of Memory and Language, 59*(4), 434–446.

Jaeger, T. F. (2010). Redundancy and reduction: Speakers manage syntactic information density. *Cognitive Psychology, 61*, 23–62.

Jaeger, T. F., & Kuperman, V. (2009). *Standards in fitting, evaluating, and interpreting regression models.* UC Davis. Available from http://hlplab.wordpress.com (Presentation give at the Workshop on Ordinary and Multilevel Modeling)

Jaeger, T. F., Levy, R., Wasow, T., & Orr, D. (2005). The absence of "that" is predictable if a relative clause is predictable. In *Proceedings of Architectures and Mechanisms of Language Processing.* Ghent, Belgium.

Jaeger, T. F., & Norcliffe, E. (2009). The cross-linguistic study of sentence production. *Language and Linguistics Compass, 3*(4), 866-887.

Jaeger, T. F., & Wasow, T. (2005, March-April). Production-complexity driven variation: Relativizer omission in non-subject-extracted relative clauses. In *Proceedings of the 18th annual CUNY conference on sentence processing.* Tuscon, AZ.

Jaeger, T. F., & Wasow, T. (2006). Processing as a source of accessibility effects on variation. In R. T. Cover & Y. Kim (Eds.), *Proceedings of the 31st annual meeting of the Berkeley Linguistic Society* (p. 169-180). Ann Arbor, MN: Sheridan Books.

Johnson, K. (2004). Massive reduction in conversational American English. In *Spontaneous speech: Data and analysis, proceedings of the 1st session of the 10th international symposium (the national international institute for Japanese language)* (pp. 29–54). Tokyo, Japan.

Jurafsky, D., Bell, A., Gregory, M., & Raymond, W. D. (2001). Probabilistic relations between words: Evidence from reduction in lexical production. In J. L. Bybee & P. J. Hopper (Eds.), *Frequency and the emergence of linguistic structure* (pp. 229–254). Amsterdam: John Benjamins.

Kraljic, T., & Brennan, S. E. (2005). Prosodic disambiguation of syntactic structure: For the speaker or for the hearer? *Cognitive Psychology*, *50*, 194–231.

Levelt, W. J. M., & Maassen, B. (1981). Lexical search and order of mention in sentence production. In W. Klein & W. J. M. Levelt (Eds.), *Crossing the boundaries in linguistics* (p. 221-252). Dordrecht, The Netherlands: D. Reidel.

Levy, R. (2005). *Probabilistic models of word order and syntactic discontinuity.* Unpublished doctoral dissertation, Stanford University.

Levy, R. (2008). Expectation-based syntactic comprehension. *Cognition*, *106*(3), 1126–1177.

Levy, R., & Jaeger, T. F. (2007, December). Speakers optimize information density through syntactic reduction. In B. Schlökopf, J. Platt, & T. Hoffman (Eds.), *Advances in neural information processing systems (NIPS) 19* (p. 849-856). Cambridge, MA: MIT Press.

Lohse, B. (2000). *Zero versus explicit marking in relative clauses.* (Derpartment of Linguistics, University of Southern California)

Lohse, B., Hawkins, J. A., & Wasow, T. (2004). Domain minimization in English verb-particle constructions. *Language*, *80*(2), 238–261.

Nation, P. (2004). A study of the most frequent word families in the British National Corpus. In P. Boogards & B. Laufer (Eds.), *Vocabulary in a second language: Selection, acquisition, and testing* (pp. 3–14). John Benjamins.

Peduzzi, P., Concato, J., Kemper, E., Holford, T. R., & Feinstein, A. R. (1996). A simulation study of the number of events per variable in logistic regression analysis. *Journal of Clinical Epidemiology*, *49*(12), 1373–1379.

Pluymaekers, M., Ernestus, M., & Baayen, R. H. (2005). Articulatory planning is continuous and sensitive to informational redundancy. *Phonetica*, *62*, 146–159.

Prat-Sala, M., & Branigan, H. P. (2000). Discourse constraints on syntactic processing in language production: A cross-linguistic study in English and Spanish. *Journal of Memory and Language*, *42*(2), 168–182.

Quirk, R. (1957). Relative clauses in educated spoken English. *English Studies*, 97–109.

R Development Core Team. (2008). R: A language and environment for statistical computing [Computer software manual]. Vienna, Austria. Available from http://www.R-project.org (ISBN 3-900051-07-0)

Race, D. S., & MacDonald, M. C. (2003). The use of "that" in the production and comprehension of object relative clauses. In *Proceedings of the 26th annual meeting of the Cognitive Science Society* (pp. 946–951).

Resnik, P. (1996). Selectional constraints: An information-theoretic model and its computational realization. *Cognition*, *61*, 127–159.

Rohde, D. (2005). Tgrep2 manual [Computer software manual]. (http://tedlab.mit.edu/$\sim$dr/Tgrep2/tgrep2.pdf)

Roland, D., Dick, F., & Elman, J. L. (2007). Frequency of basic English grammatical structures: A corpus analysis. *Journal of Memory and Language*, *57*(3), 348–379.

Roland, D., Elman, J. L., & Ferreira, V. S. (2005). Why is that? Structural prediction and ambiguity resolution in a very large corpus of English sentences. *Cognition*, 1–28.

Shannon, C. E. (1948). A mathematical theory of communications. *Bell Systems Technical Journal*, *27*(4), 623–656.

Son, R. J. J. H. van, Beinum, F. J. Koopmans-van, & Pols, L. C. W. (1998). Efficiency as an organizing principle of natural speech. In *Fifth international conference on spoken language processing.* Sydney.

Son, R. J. J. H. van, & Santen, J. P. H. van. (2005). Duration and spectral balance of intervocalic consonants: A case for efficient communication. *Speech Communication*, *47*(1), 100–123.

Tagliamonte, S., & Smith, J. (2005). No momentary fancy! The zero in English dialects. *English Language and Linguistics*, *9*(2), 289–309.

Tagliamonte, S., Smith, J., & Lawrence, H. (2005). No taming the vernacular! Insights from the relatives in northern Britain. *Language Variation and Change*, *17*, 75–112.

Temperley, D. (2003). Ambiguity avoidance in English relative clauses. *Language*, *79*(3), 464–484.

Trueswell, J. C. (1996). The role of lexical frequency in syntactic ambiguity resolution. *Journal of Memory and Language*, *35*, 566–585.

Trueswell, J. C., Tanenhaus, M. K., & Garnsey, S. M. (1994). Semantic influences on parsing: Use of thematic role information in syntactic ambiguity resolution. *Journal of Memory and Language*, *33*, 285–318.

Trueswell, J. C., Tanenhaus, M. K., & Kello, C. (1993). Verb-specific constraints in sentence processing: Separating effects of lexical preference from garden-paths. *Journal of Experimental Psychology Learning, Memory, and Cognition*, *19*, 528–553.

Wasow, T. (1997). Remarks on grammatical weight. *Language Variation and Change, 9*(1), 81–105.

Wasow, T. (2002). *Postverbal behavior.* Stanford: CSLI Publications.

Wasow, T., & Arnold, J. E. (2003). Post-verbal constituent ordering in English. In G. Rohdenburg & B. Mondorf (Eds.), *Determinants of grammatical variation in English* (pp. 119–154). Berlin: Walter de Gruyter.

Wasow, T., Jaeger, T. F., & Orr, D. (in press). Lexical variation in relativizer frequency. In H. Wiese & H. Simon (Eds.), *Proceedings of the workshop on expecting the unexpected: Exceptions in grammar at the 27th annual meeting of the German Linguistic Association.* Berlin and New York: Mouton de Gruyter.

Wilson, M. P., & Garnsey, S. M. (2009). Making simple sentences hard: Verb bias effects in simple direct object sentences. *Journal of Memory and Language.*

Yamashita, H., & Chang, F. (2001). Long before short preference in the production of a head-final language. *Cognition, 81*(2), 45–55.

10

Ordering Choices in Production: For the Speaker or for the Listener?

JENNIFER E. ARNOLD

Preface

This paper reviews research on a question that motivates many of Tom Wasow's projects: why do speakers show variation in the syntactic structure that they use? In particular, what drives choices in constituent ordering, e.g. *Send the manuscript for Tom's book to me* vs. *Send me the manuscript for Tom's book.*? Tom introduced this question to me when I was studying with him in graduate school. Ordering phenomena are related to broader questions about how information structure and accessibility relate to the psychological processes of both language production and comprehension. These questions have infiltrated my attitude toward psycholinguistics and language research, and shaped my research in related areas. One theme that runs through Tom's work (and as a result, mine as well) is the focus of this paper: to what extent do speakers model the comprehension requirements of their addressee and use this to shape the details of their production, and to what extent are their production choices constrained by the nature of the production mechanism itself? Thus, this paper represents many of Tom's contributions to the field, both directly and as a result of his influence on my thinking.

1 Introduction

Whenever speakers decide to say something, they have to make many choices—for example, what words to say, what syntactic structure to

Language from a Cognitive Perspective.
Emily M. Bender and Jennifer Arnold, Editors
Copyright © 2011, CSLI Publications.

use, what order to put constituents in, and how to pronounce the utterance. These choices (even if they are not conscious) are complicated by the fact that the same meaning (more or less) might be communicated in a variety of ways. Among other things, speakers may have choices like those as in examples (1–4):

(1) a. Heavy-NP-shift: *That will bring to the plate Barry Bonds* (Wasow, 1997a)

   b. Unshifted: *That will bring Barry Bonds to the plate.*

(2) a. Double-object: *Chris gave the boy a book.*

   b. Prepositional: *Chris gave a book to the boy.* (Wasow, 2002)

(3) a. Verb-particle adjoined: *Write up your results.*

   b. Verb-particle split: *Write your results up.*

(4) a. Active: *Tom trained many students.*

   b. Passive: *Many students were trained by Tom.*

This kind of variation offers a testing ground for linguists and psycholinguists. By identifying the conditions under which speakers tend use one form or the other, we can learn something about the cognitive mechanisms underlying language use.

This paper provides an overview of research on how speakers choose to order phrases. Naturally, many of these choices are driven by the message—that is, the idea the speaker wants to convey (e.g., who did what to whom). For example, a description of the scene in Figure 1 would need to mention the participants in the event (woman, man, book), and the event of transferring the book from the woman to the man. The relative order of these elements is also highly constrained by the grammar of the language, especially one like English that uses word order to encode grammatical relations.

However, this paper is focused on choices that are not strictly driven by either the meaning or the grammar. Some of these choices are lexical—e.g., *the woman* vs. *she*, or *the book* vs. *the volume*. Once the words are chosen, should they receive an accented pronunciation or not? Should the utterance focus on the woman (*The woman gave...*) or the man (*The man was given...*)? Even if the utterance starts with the woman, dative verbs (like *give*) require a choice between the prepositional construction (*The woman gave the book to the man*) and the double object construction (*The woman gave the man the book*). Thus, ordering can be said to be influenced by both ordering concerns (e.g., whether *boy* or *book* comes first in example (2)), and the choice between

FIGURE 1 A event in which a book is given by a woman to a man.

syntactic constructions (e.g., between the double-object and prepositional form of the dative).

This paper reviews research on how speakers order constituents, with
a special focus on how it is influenced by two simultaneous pressures—
the speaker's desire to communicate a particular message, and the constraints inherent in the process of language production. For example,
speakers are more likely to use the "Heavy-NP-Shifted" structure when
the direct object NP is long or complex (*Put on the table the book that
I bought yesterday...*), but especially when the verb-PP form a conventionalized collocation, like *take into account* (Wasow, 1997b). On one
hand, these biases may reflect a desire to present the information in
such a way so as to maximize understanding. On the other hand, they
may stem from the pressures on the production system itself. Thus, the
examination of a particular choice, i.e. constituent ordering, is relevant
to the more general question of how language production is influenced
by both speaker-internal and addressee-oriented processes. This issue
has received a lot of attention recently (see also Arnold, 2008). As I will
show here, it is difficult to disentangle speaker- and addressee-oriented
processes. The mere fact that a particular choice influences either the
speed or outcome of language comprehension does not mean that the
choice was made with the addressee in mind. An example of this comes
from the domain of disfluency. Speakers often fail to meet their goal of
fluent speech, and instead produce disfluencies like *um, uh,* hesitations,
repetitions, or restarted utterances. Disfluency itself does not serve the
primary communicative goal of the speaker (even though it has been

argued to serve the communicative function of signaling an upcoming delay, (Clark & Fox Tree, 2002)). Nevertheless, listeners can use disfluency to make inferences about the speaker's intended meaning (see section 3.1).

Likewise, other production choices, including choices in word order, might be the result of procedural constraints on production, such as which constituents are more accessible (e.g., Arnold, Wasow, Losongco, & Ginstrom, 2000; V. S. Ferreira, 2003), yet simultaneously facilitate comprehension for the listener. I will examine this contrast between "speaker-oriented" and "addressee-oriented" production processes as they apply to the speaker's choices about constituent order, as illustrated in (1)-(4). This review focuses on data from experiments in English, although there is some evidence for cross-linguistic differences in ordering preferences (Hawkins, 1994; Yamashita & Chang, 2001).

2 Word Order and Syntactic Variation in English

When speakers decide how to construct an utterance, they have to decide both a) what order to put the elements of an utterance in, and b) which grammatical constructions to use to frame the utterance. These decisions are naturally connected, since the choice of (for example), an active structure necessarily restricts word order choices, and vice versa. So in principle either process could be the driving force behind ordering decisions. Bock, Irwin, and Davidson (2004) term the first approach the *elemental* view, and the second the *structural* view. There is evidence for both types of processes.

2.1 Ordering Syntactic Elements: What Comes First?

There is substantial evidence that speakers tend to organize their sentences so that they produce information early if it is more cognitively accessible (see Jaeger, this volume, for more on accessibility accounts of ordering). For now I will define accessibility simply as a property that makes a representation (linguistic or conceptual) easier to access during language processing, for whatever reason. In the next section of the paper we will turn to questions of why, how, and for whom the information is accessible. Words and concepts are claimed to be more accessible if they are more frequent, have been recently mentioned, or are predictable in the context. This is likely because frequency, predictability, and recency of mention involve activating both word and concept representations that are associated with a phrase, which facilitates their use. These features have been found to increase the use of pronouns, zeros, or acoustically reduced pronunciations for reference (see Arnold, 2008), in addition to increasing the chance that a word or phrase will be produced early in an utterance.

The accessible-early idea is supported by the most well-known fact about ordering, that grammatically "light" phrases tend to precede "heavy" ones (Behaghel, 1909; Quirk, Greenbaum, Leech, & Svartvik, 1972; Hawkins, 1994; Wasow, 1997a, 1997b, 2002). An exception to this is that head-final languages, like Japanese and Korean, put heavy phrases before light ones (Chang, 2009; Yamashita & Chang, 2001; Choi, 2007). Grammatical heaviness refers to the amount of linguistic material in a phrase, where heavy phrases are relatively long and syntactically complex, while light ones are short and simple. The lightest of all are pronouns, which are extremely short function words, with relatively little semantic content as well. Wasow (2002, chapter 2; see also Wasow 1997b) compared three definitions of grammatical weight: number of words, number of syntactic nodes, and number of major syntactic phrasal nodes. In corpus analyses he found that all three predicted ordering preferences for heavy-NP-shift, dative, and verb-particle constructions. Moreover, all definitions of weight were highly correlated. This makes it difficult to test the independent contributions of each, but strongly supports the light-before-heavy pattern in English and similar languages (for more detailed discussion see Wasow, 1997b, 2002; Wasow & Arnold, 2003).

Here I am presenting grammatical weight as one example of how accessible elements tend to precede less accessible ones. But note that this depends on the assumption that linguistically long and complex phrases are less cognitively accessible, or perhaps simply harder to produce, than short and simple ones. This assumption is quite plausible, since longer phrases are likely to be harder both linguistically and conceptually. However, longer phrases are not necessarily always harder. As pointed out by Jaeger (this volume), the critical property is the ease with which speakers can begin to utter the constituent, since speakers can continue to plan it as they speak.

Another finding that is consistent with the accessible-early proposal comes from the widespread tendency for speakers to produce given information before new (e.g., Behaghel, 1932; Gundel, 1988; Bock & Irwin, 1980; Chafe, 1994). That is, if I describe Figure 1 in a situation where I was already talking about the man (i.e., if the man is "given"), I would be far more likely to mention the man before the woman (Arnold et al., 2000; Bock & Irwin, 1980; Hawkins, 1994; Wasow, 2002). "Given" information is typically described as information which has already been evoked in the current situation, whereas "new" has not (e.g., Chafe, 1976; Haviland & Clark, 1974; Prince, 1981, 1992).

The contrast between given and new has been useful for a variety of linguistic phenomena, but there are two ways in which this distinction requires some refinement. First, information can be evoked in many ways, e.g. linguistically, or by being physically present (Clark & Marshall, 2002). "Given" could technically refer to either, but usually is used for information that has been given linguistically. Second, it appears that things can be considered either "more given", or "less given", in the sense that some given information is relatively more accessible. To the extent that we are talking about linguistic givenness, then perhaps a better measure would be termed "discourse status", or "accessibility" (Ariel, 1990). Accessibility can vary in a gradient way, where the most accessible things are those mentioned recently, in prominent syntactic and thematic positions, and those that are likely to continue to be important in the discourse (Arnold, 1998, 2008).

Both experiments and corpus analyses have demonstrated that speakers tend to start with the relatively more accessible entity. For example, Arnold et al. (2000) elicited utterances like "Give the scissors to the duck" in a production task, in a context where either the animal or object had been just mentioned in a question (either: *What about the pink duck... ?*, or *What about the scissors... ?*") Speakers tended to put the animal first, as in *Give the pink duck the scissors,* more often when the animal was given. By contrast, responses with the object first, like *Give the scissors to the duck*, were relatively more likely when the object was given. It is likely that ordering is sensitive to a wide variety of discourse features (cf. Jaeger & Wasow, 2006).

One complication for assessing the tendency for speakers to follow the light-before-heavy and given-before-new patterns is that the two are highly correlated. When an entity is mentioned for the first time in a discourse (i.e., when the referent is "new"), it often has to be referenced with a fairly long phrase, e.g. *Thomas Wasow*, or *The avid cyclist who also teaches linguistics*. Subsequently the referent is "given", and the speaker may use shorter expressions, like *Tom* or *he*. Nevertheless, there is evidence that both constraints matter. Arnold et al. (2000) used an experiment and a corpus analysis to examine the effects of both givenness and weight, and found that both influenced speaker's decisions. Moreover, the effect of each depended on the strength of the other. If two phrases differed a great deal in their weight, speakers were more likely to follow the pattern light-before-heavy, regardless of givenness. On the other hand, if one referent was substantially more accessible than the other in the discourse, "givenness" (aka accessibility) played a relatively stronger role on order preferences.

Further evidence for the role of cognitive accessibility on ordering comes from a host of conceptual features (see Bock et al., 2004). For example, references to animate entities tend to precede references to inanimate ones (Bock & Warren, 1985; Branigan, Pickering, & Tanaka, 2008; F. Ferreira, 1994; McDonald, Bock, & Kelly, 1993; Prat-Sala & Branigan, 2000; van Nice & Dietrich, 2003).

There is also some evidence that speakers put perceptually salient things before less salient things. However, this point is debated. On one hand, Bock et al. (2004) review a number of findings (e.g., Flores d'Arcais, 1975; Osgood, 1957, 1971) and conclude that the effects of perception on ordering are weak and task dependent. On their view, constituent order choices are made based on other factors, which then guide the speaker's attention as they formulate their utterance. This view is what Bock, Irwin, Davidson, and Levelt (2003) call "seeing for saying". They analyzed how speakers reported the time on a clock, e.g. *ten to two,* or *one-fifty.* They propose that speakers make a rapid decision about which structural frame to use for a given clock display. The speaker's visual attention toward the minute and hour hands is then driven by the order in which the clock features are formulated (see also Griffin & Bock, 2000, for evidence that order decisions drive visual fixations, and not the other way around).

On the other hand, Gleitman, January, Nappa, and Trueswell (2007) report striking evidence that the speaker's attention does guide ordering choices. They had people look at a picture and describe the event, e.g. *The man chases the dog* or *The dog runs away from the man.* Immediately before the picture appeared, a black square appeared very briefly (~80 msec) in the location of one character. This "visual capture cue" drew speakers' attention toward one of the characters in the event. Even though they were not aware of the flashing square, they still tended to begin their sentence with reference to the cued character. The same effect was also observed in an experiment with no flashing square, where they simply measured which character was fixated first after the picture appeared. This suggests that speakers' initial attention to a scene impacts their decisions about how to structure their utterance. This view is consistent with other accessibility-first effects, in that attention to a referent is likely to make all representations associated with it more accessible.

The evidence reviewed so far concentrates on questions of how linguistic phrases are ordered. But similar factors influence variation in constructions where speakers can decide whether or not to produce certain words at all. One such example is relative clauses. In some cases the use of the relativizer is optional—e.g., *This is the first president (that) nobody voted for* (Jaeger & Wasow, 2006; Rickford, this volume; for a related phenomenon see Jaeger, this volume). The relative clause here is the phrase *nobody voted for*, which modifies the NP *the first president*. Speakers are more likely to produce *that* if the relative clause is grammatically long and complex (Race & MacDonald, 2003), or when the relative clause is unpredictable (Wasow, Jaeger, & Orr, in press). Jaeger and Wasow (2006) also show that *that*-production is sensitive to discourse status in a gradient way. They analyzed the Switchboard corpus of spoken language, and categorized noun phrase types as an indirect (but robust) measure of their discourse status. For example, first-person pronouns (*I, we*) can be considered highly accessible, whereas definite NPs (*the cyclist*) are relatively less accessible, and indefinites (*a cyclist*) are even less accessible. Results revealed a steady increase in the use of *that* as the accessibility of the NP decreased. Similar effects of accessibility have been demonstrated for the variable production of *that* as a complementizer (e.g., *I know (that) Tom likes dogs;* V. S. Ferreira & Dell, 2000; V. S. Ferreira, 2003). Although variable-*that* production is not an ordering phenomenon, it is similar to ordering in that the presence of *that* postpones the production of the following segment.

Accessible-early is Good for the Speaker

The take-home message of the research reviewed so far is that speakers produce short, simple, predictable, and accessible phrases early, and they tend to postpone long, complex, unpredictable and less accessible ones. Why should this be? One plausible explanation focuses on the fact that the mechanisms of language production are facilitated when accessible information is produced early (Arnold et al., 2000; V. S. Ferreira, 2003; Jaeger & Wasow, 2006). It is simply easier to produce simple and accessible information before complex and inaccessible information.

The formulation of linguistic phrases is a cognitive task that takes time, however instantaneous it may seem. Speakers wish to produce language fluently, but they also wish to begin their contribution to the discourse without delay (Clark & Wasow, 1998). As speakers try to manage the conflict between these two pressures, they sometimes become disfluent, perhaps repeating words or hesitating, to provide themselves with more planning time (e.g., Clark & Wasow, 1998; Clark & Fox Tree, 2002). Phrase ordering and optional word production also provide speakers with mechanisms to postpone the relatively difficult segments.

A potential problem for the accessible-early generalization is that some languages (e.g. Japanese and Korean) appear to prefer long-before-short orders (Chang, 2009; Yamashita & Chang, 2001; Choi,

2007). However, the accessible-early constraint may still operate in these languages in other ways. For example, Choi (2007) observes that violations of Hawkins' EIC theory tend to occur when pronominal, definite, or discourse-given entities are ordered early. More work is need on the simultaneous constraints of information structure and syntactic complexity in these languages. Jaeger (this volume) also suggests that the early production of long phrases may occur when the phrase is easy to initiate, even if the entire phrase is complex.

If we think about accessible-early in terms of its facilitation on the production system, it offers a cohesive, single explanation for many word order phenomena. It accounts for why word order is modulated by conceptual properties like animacy, discourse properties like previous mention, and linguistic factors like grammatical weight. This view can also account for findings that speakers choose orders that allow semantically and associatively-related segments to be produced near each other (Lohse, Hawkins, & Wasow, 2004; Wasow, 1997b, 1997a; Wasow & Arnold, 2003). For example, speakers are more likely to produce conventionalized phrases as a unit, compared with other structurally similar but non-idiomatic phrases (Wasow, 1997b, 1997a). E.g., *Take into account. . .* is more likely to occur without an intervening direct object NP than *Take into summer. . . .* Multi-word collocations are like lexical items in that they are probably accessed as a unit. By contrast, the words in a semantically decomposable phrase like *Take the suitcases into the house* need to be accessed individually, and thus the later words are not necessarily facilitated by accessing the early words.

This facilitation view is also consistent with attentional effects on ordering (Gleitman et al., 2007). Attention to an entity might enhance the formulation of the nonlinguistic message, as well as the selection of appropriate lexical items. Such facilitation might promote orders that allow that constituent to be produced earlier. However, this does not necessarily mean that attentional effects are only speaker-oriented processes. It is often claimed that linguistic choices are made on the basis of *shared* attention, and not merely the speaker's egocentric attention. If so, the listener's attention may be monitored by the speaker for the purpose of linguistic processes like word order. On the other hand, shared attention includes speaker's attention, which means that attentional effects may be at least partially the result of speaker-internal facilitation (see Arnold & Lao, 2010 for discussion of a related issue).

Accessible-early is Good for the Listener

The previous section reviewed compelling evidence that accessible-early orders facilitate the process of language production. But we cannot conclude that this is the **reason** for ordering choices. That is because accessible-early orders also facilitate comprehension processes. Clark and Haviland (1977) argue that speakers anchor their utterances with reference to a previously-mentioned antecedent as a part of the Gricean maxim of cooperativeness, aiming to help listeners identify their meaning quickly. Similarly, it should be easier for listeners to interpret conceptually accessible, predictable, or attended information before less accessible, less predictable, or less attended information.

It has also been proposed that parsing in languages like English is easier when post-verbal constituents are ordered with shorter ones before longer ones. Hawkins (1994) argues that this arrangement allows listeners to identify the basic sentence structure more quickly (see also Jaeger, this volume, for more information on dependency processing accounts). For example, if the speaker says *The professor gave his class many sets of difficult problems,* the listener can identify the basic syntactic structure by the word *many*: Subject noun phrase (*the professor*) – Verb (*gave*) – Indirect Object (*his class*) – Direct Object (*many...*). In the alternate word order (*The professor gave many sets of difficult problems to his class*), the listener needs to maintain the phrase *many sets of difficult problems* in memory, while the immediate constituents of the verb cannot be fully identified until the word *to*. Hawkins calls this the principle of Early Immediate Constituents, and shows that it accounts for ordering choices in many languages (see also Hawkins, this volume).

In sum, there is substantial evidence that word order choices are sensitive to a variety of constraints, which together might suggest that speakers follow the pattern of accessible-before-inaccessible. It has been argued that these choices facilitates both the mechanisms of language production and the mechanisms of language comprehension. However, accessibility does not explain everything. In addition, speakers appear to have preferences for particular syntactic structures.

2.2 Structural Choices during Utterance Production

Speakers of English have relatively few production choices that are driven by ordering concerns alone. Word order is relatively fixed, which means that ordering choices often correspond to choices between different syntactic constructions. There is reason to believe that speakers can have preferences for particular structures, independently of the order of the elements themselves.

Clear evidence for structural preferences comes from syntactic priming (Bock, 1986; Bock & Loebell, 1990; Bock, Loebell, & Morey, 1992; Snider, this volume). In a classic production paradigm, subjects hear and repeat a sentence like *The boy gives the dog a bone,* (vs. *The boy gives a bone to the dog*), and then describe a picture of an event that can be described by a different dative verb, e.g. a woman handing a man a paintbrush. Speakers are more likely to repeat the previously-used syntactic structure when they describe the picture. Such priming is stronger when the verb is the same (Pickering & Branigan, 1998), but it even occurs across utterances with different verbs and verb types (Bock et al., 1992), and even from one speaker to another (Branigan, Pickering, & Cleland, 2000). Priming is highly robust, and shows up even when several other utterances have intervened (Bock & Griffin, 2000). Priming may be one explanation for why speakers tend to follow parallel structures throughout their own production, and repeat the structures produced by their interlocutors.

Another example of a structural preference is that active structures are chosen more often than passive structures, other things being equal (Bock et al., 2004). Active structures are more frequent, and therefore should be easier to access for the speaker. They also present the listener with the more frequent mapping between thematic roles and grammatical functions, which should facilitate comprehension.

Evidence for another structural preference has emerged in the behavior of participants in ordering experiments that I have done with Tom Wasow. We have found that it is much easier to get participants to produce the prepositional variant of dative verbs than the double-object variant. The double-object construction may be more frequent in actual usage, because the goal role is frequently human, frequently topical, and therefore frequently pronominalized (e.g., *gave him the book*). But in at least some experimental contexts, people are reluctant to use the double-object. For example, in an experiment reported by Arnold et al. (2000), speakers produced instructions to their partner to give physical objects to animals, which were represented by pictures on boxes. Pilot testing revealed that participants would not use the double object construction at all (even under supporting discourse conditions), unless we engaged them in a make-believe story about why they were instructing their partner to give the objects to the animals. Even so, 4 out of 24 participants were excluded for not producing anything but prepositional constructions (for a similar bias toward the prepositional construction, see Branigan, Pickering, McLean, & Cleland, 2007, and Pickering, Branigan, & McLean, 2002). This preference may stem from the fact that the prepositional form follows the canonical mapping between thematic roles and grammatical functions (Arnold, Wasow, Asudeh, & Alrenga, 2004).

Structural preferences also appear to attach to particular lexical items. Wasow (1997a, 1997b, 2002) reported that some verbs are more likely to occur in heavy-NP-shifted orders than others,. Similarly, some verbs (e.g., *offer*, *tell*, and *show*) are far more likely to occur in the double-object order than others (e.g., *assign*, *bring*, or *give*). Using a somewhat different category of verbs, Stallings, MacDonald, and O'Seaghdha (1998) also reported lexical preferences for heavy-NP-shift sentences.

Structural Preferences: for the Speaker or the Listener?

Just as cognitive accessibility preferences could benefit both production and comprehension mechanisms, so could structural preferences. For example, priming effects could be the result of simple facilitation within the production system. Alternatively, they could be a mechanism for coordinating common ground in dialogue (Branigan et al., 2000). People who copy the stylistic choices of their interlocutor help establish a common perspective on the things being discussed. Likewise, parallelism increases the predictability of references, and thus the ease of reference comprehension (Arnold, 1998).

Similarly, the verb biases reported by Wasow (1997a, 1997b, 2002) and (Stallings et al., 1998) could in principle facilitate either production or comprehension. Yet both studies describe these lexical preferences as constraints on production mechanisms. For example, Wasow (1997a) examined heavy-NP-shifting in obligatorily transitive verbs (e.g., *bring, carry, make, place*), compared with verbs that could be followed by either a direct object or something else, like a prepositional phrase (e.g., *add, build, call, draw*). He reasoned that production would be facilitated by using shifted structures more often for the optionally transitive verbs—by postponing the direct object NP, speakers are postponing their decision about whether to make the verb transitive (*wrote in the dark a letter*) or intransitive (*wrote in the dark quickly*). By contrast, comprehension is made more difficult by shifting optionally transitive verbs, because comprehenders have to wait to find out whether the speaker will produce the direct object NP at all. Wasow found that shifting was more common for optionally transitive verbs, supporting the idea that word order is constrained by production-internal constraints. He made a similar argument for lexical preferences for ordering with dative verbs. Stallings et al. (1998) also found lexical preferences for heavy-NP-shifting. They instead focused on the fact that some verbs are more likely than others to occur in constructions where the verb is not followed by an adjacent complement, as is more common with sentential complements (e.g., *Tom learned that the experiment was done*). In a sentence production experiment, they found that speakers used heavy-NP-shift structures more often for verbs that optionally occurred with sentential complements (e.g, *proposed*) than for verbs that obligatorily took noun phrase complements (e.g., *relinquished*). They suggested that nonadjacent verbs produce more competition between the shifted and nonshifted constructions during production.

3 Speaker- vs. Listener-oriented Processes

So far we have seen evidence that speakers prefer certain grammatical structures, especially those that enable them to produce accessible forms and information early, and postpone inaccessible forms and information. But we have not solved the question of why. We have considered two classes of explanation. The speaker-oriented view focuses on the architecture of the production system, which biases decisions in certain directions. A cartoon version of this position might paint a picture of a self-serving speaker, who makes choices just to make their own life easier.

The listener-oriented view instead focuses on the fact that language is used for the purpose of communicating. Presumably the speaker wants the listener to understand the message. It is therefore plausible that the speaker makes decisions that facilitate the listener's job. Such processes are said to be influenced by **audience design**.

Note that in some sense both views are speaker-oriented. Any account has to recognize the mental steps in the speaker's head that result in a spoken utterance. The difference is that the listener-oriented view assumes that the speaker has two goals: the primary goal is to put thoughts into words, and the secondary goal is to make the listener's understanding job as easy as possible. Evidence suggests that speakers can and do make contextual adjustments to their utterances so as to ensure successful communication (Clark & Krych, 2004). These adjustments may require keeping track of what is going on from the listener's perspective, and possibly making inferences about the listener's knowledge state. This can be relatively effortful, so it may influence some but not all aspects of language production.

The question of whether speakers design their utterances for listeners must therefore be asked with respect to specific processes. We need to understand both constraints that are production-internal (and blind to addressee needs), as well as constraints that are driven by addressee needs. The problem is that most situations are ambiguous as to whether the speaker makes a choice for production-internal reasons, or on the basis of audience design. This is because discourses are by definition public. Anything that has been uttered can be considered to be shared by the speaker and addressee. Therefore anything that helps the speaker could in principle help the listener (see Arnold, 2008 for a similar discussion about choices in reference form). Is there any way to distinguish speaker-oriented or listener-oriented influences on ordering?

3.1 Evidence for Speaker-oriented Processes

One phenomenon that has been argued to reflect production-internal processes is disfluency. Disfluent speech includes hesitation pauses, fillers like um and uh, repeated words, or even pronouncing *the* as "thee" (rhyming with tree) rather than "thuh" (Clark & Fox Tree, 2002; Clark & Wasow, 1998). Disfluency tends to occur when the speaker is having some difficulty with speech, perhaps planning the message, formulating the utterance, or retrieving a word. For example, disfluency increases during the production of syntactic structures that are not probable, compared to those that are more probable (Tily et al., 2009).

Whatever the cause, the difficulty that leads to disfluency reflects problems from within the production system. While social interactions may incur processing load, the load itself is not a shared commodity. Listeners do use disfluency to help them identify the speaker's meaning (e.g., Arnold, Hudson Kam, & Tanenhaus, 2007; Arnold, Tanenhaus, Altmann, & Fagnano, 2004; Barr & Seyfeddinipur, 2010; Corley, MacGregor, & Donaldson, 2007), but not because the speaker produced the disfluency for the purpose of communication. It has also been argued that speakers produce fillers like *um* and *uh* as a signal an upcoming delay to the listener (e.g., Clark & Fox Tree, 2002). But note that under this view, disfluency is a signal about the speaker's own fluency, and not about the message. The origin of the difficulty that resulted in disfluency is still within the production system. Therefore we can examine how disfluency correlates with production choices as a method of identifying effects that are related to production processes.

If disfluency correlates with particular ordering choices, it would suggest that word ordering is constrained by the same speaker-internal factors that result in disfluency. Arnold et al. (2000) reported just such an effect. We examined instructions like *Give the pink squirrel the strawberry*, identifying utterances that had a disfluency before or during the verb (which was always *give*). The onset of a clause is where speakers are likely to plan parts of the upcoming utterance; this is supported by the fact that disfluency and pausing at clause onset correlate with the complexity of the upcoming clause (Clark & Wasow, 1998; Watson & Gibson, 2004). We found that if a clause started out disfluently, it was relatively more likely to take the prepositional form than the double-object. This again reveals a general bias for the prepositional structure, which appears to be preferred under slightly "difficult" situations (see also Arnold, Wasow, et al., 2004, experiment 2).

In and of itself the correlation between disfluency and structural preferences is a small effect, but it merits mention because it is a fairly clean example of a speaker-oriented process. But the accessibility view of ordering is also highly consistent with a production-internal account of ordering: speakers produce accessible things early because it relieves memory load and facilitates fluent production. Moreover, both Wasow (1997a) and Stallings et al. (1998) have made compelling arguments that individual verbs are biased to appear in particular orders or constructions, and that these biases stem from constraints on the production system.

3.2 Tests for Listener-oriented Processes

On the flip side, is there any evidence that speakers' ordering choices are at least in part influenced by consideration for the needs of the listener? Speakers must certainly make many choices that reflect the needs of any generic addressee, as well as the specific addressee at that moment (Clark, 1996; Schober & Brennan, 2003). But do they specifically consider their listener when making ordering choices?

A strong test for listener-oriented processes can be found in the domain of ambiguity avoidance. It is often assumed that a helpful speaker (following Grice's maxims) should avoid ambiguity. For example, if a speaker was talking about *that letter you wrote to your mother*, it would be clearer to say *Please give your sister that letter you wrote to your mother,* rather than *Please give that letter you wrote to your mother to your sister.* The latter would temporarily garden-path the listener into thinking that the letter should be given to the mother, and not the sister. But to make the "helpful" word-order choice, the speaker must be able to generate the utterance, consider what possible interpretations the listener might get from it, and then revise if necessary. Can speakers do this?

Arnold, Wasow, et al. (2004) tested this idea in a production experiment. Speakers saw a sentence on a computer screen, e.g. *Everyone received my private message to you from the damn computer.* They were asked to read and remember the gist of the sentence. Their partner then asked them a leading question, like *What did the computer do?* They were asked to answer the question (e.g. *The computer sent...*), which required making a choice about how to phrase the sentence. Critically, the sentences were designed so that the prepositional order resulted in a temporary ambiguity (*The damn computer sent my private message to you to everyone*), whereas the same ambiguity could be avoided with the double-object construction (... *sent everyone my private message to you*). We predicted that speakers would be less likely to produce the prepositional order in sentences like this, compared with versions where we changed the preposition in the noun phrase (*my private message about you*) to avoid the potential temporary ambiguity. However, in two experiments we found no such avoidance of the ambiguous prepositional order—in fact, we found a slight preference for the prepositional order when it resulted in an ambiguity. This occurred despite the fact that temporary PP-attachment ambiguities of this kind are known to create comprehension delays (e.g., Altmann & Steedman, 1988; Boland & Boehm-Jernigan, 1998). We analyzed the location of prosodic breaks in speakers' utterances to find out if perhaps they were disambiguating the structure prosodically, but there was no strong evidence that this was the case.

Similar findings come from a study about whether speakers utilize optional *that* to avoid structural ambiguity. V. S. Ferreira and Dell (2000) had participants produce sentences like *The chiropracter observed (that) {you/I} couldn't stand up straight*. When the embedded sentence began with *you*, it was ambiguous between a direct object and a subordinate subject. Nevertheless, speakers were no more likely to use an overt *that* when the following word was *you* as when it was *I*.

By contrast, Haywood and colleague's study of optional *that*-production **did** find effects of disambiguation (Haywood, Pickering, & Branigan, 2005). Their participants gave instructions like *Put the pig {that's} on the block on the heart*, where the pig was on a block, and was supposed to be moved onto a heart. If there were two pigs in the scene, participants produced more *that*s than if there was only one pig in the scene. Note, however, that the syntactic ambiguity in this experiment also results in a **referential** ambiguity. With two pigs in the scene, and without a *that*, the listener would temporarily not know which pig to move. There is substantial evidence that speakers do regularly avoid referential ambiguities, at least if they notice them (see Arnold, 2008, for a review). It appears that non-referential syntactic ambiguities may be more difficult to avoid.

One possibility is that these situations do not compel speakers to go to any pains to avoid ambiguity, because the ambiguity is local and won't lead to any long-term misunderstanding. But in that case we should find that speakers use word order to avoid global ambiguities. Wasow (2002) describes a corpus analysis that tested this hypothesis. Prepositional phrase attachment ambiguities can occasionally be pragmatically felicitous with both interpretations, like *saw a man with a telescope*. An alternate ordering (*saw with a telescope a man*) would avoid this ambiguity. Wasow identified sentences with both NPs and PPs from the Brown corpus, regardless of which was ordered first. These pairs were coded for whether they were ambiguous (or, in the case of the PP-NP ordered tokens, they were coded for potential ambiguity in the unshifted order). However, the strongest determinant of ordering was syntactic weight, and there was little effect of ambiguity (see also Wasow & Arnold, 2003).

Perhaps it is not surprising that speakers do not use word order to avoid ambiguity. Most speech situations don't allow enough time to do the pre-planning that would be necessary to identify an ambiguity in time to change the basic structure of the utterance—you have to start speaking or lose the floor (or, look fairly foolish). Moreover, speakers do not typically plan out their entire utterance, and instead make many decisions incrementally as the utterance progresses (V. S. Ferreira, 1996; Griffin, 2003). Thus, the frame for the sentence may well be chosen before the specific noun phrases have been built, and thus before the ambiguity is discovered. Finally, it is plausible that most ambiguities, even global ones, may not result in severe long-term misunderstanding, given other contextual information. If so, speakers may not be motivated to avoid them.

4 Conclusion

The available evidence suggests that speakers are heavily influenced by production constraints when making word-order choices. The clearest evidence of an addressee-oriented strategy would be ambiguity avoidance, which does not play a strong role in ordering preferences. Other patterns in constituent ordering, like the tendency to start with salient information and short phrases, could result from speaker-internal processes, even though they benefit the listener as well.

Nevertheless, this is not to say that speakers are egocentric, asocial animals. Language is fundamentally used for communication, and the underlying psychological processes reflect this. Speakers take into account the listeners' knowledge state (to some extent) when they design referential expressions (see Arnold, 2008, for a review). They also seek evidence that they were understood (Clark & Krych, 2004). But they do not appear to be able to fine-tune constituent order to maximize the listener's ease of understanding.

It is important to point out that speakers' choices can still facilitate comprehension, even if they were not made for that purpose. As already noted, short-before-long and given-before-new are patterns that facilitate both comprehension and production. Listeners can even make use of information that was clearly not produced for their benefit at all, for example when the speaker is disfluent. Disfluency (e.g., saying *um*, *uh*, or repeating words) occurs when speakers have difficulty with production (e.g., Clark & Fox Tree, 2002; Clark & Wasow, 1998). Even though speakers do not use disfluency as a signal about the **kind** of thing they are saying, they are more likely to be disfluent when describing something difficult—either an object without a conventional name, or something that has not been mentioned recently. Listeners are sensitive to this, and find it easier to identify the referent for new or unfamiliar referents when they were preceded by a disfluent segment (*thee, um,....*) than a fluent one (Arnold, Tanenhaus, et al., 2004; Arnold et al., 2007).

Similarly, when speakers choose constructions like the Heavy-NP-shift, listeners can use the construction to anticipate the upcoming direct object noun phrase. Shifted constructions are rare, but when they occur, it is frequently the case that the direct object is very long, or refers to something discourse-new, or both. Therefore, a shifted fragment like *Put on the triangle the...* could signal that the upcoming referent has not been previously mentioned, and facilitate comprehension for new referents over given ones. This is exactly what Arnold and Lao (2008) found.

In sum, work by Tom Wasow and others has demonstrated that speakers make choices about constituent ordering based on a variety of factors, including the length of the constituent information status of the referent and individual verb biases. However, ambiguity avoidance does not seem to play a large role, plausibly because of the cognitive demands of utterance planning. Thus, the evidence reviewed here suggests that production-internal processes account for many of the observed preferences of constituent ordering.

Acknowledgements

Thanks to Neal Snider and Florian Jaeger for thoughtful comments on an earlier draft of this paper.

References

Altmann, G., & Steedman, M. (1988). Interaction with context during human sentence processing. *Cognition*, *30*(3), 191–238.

Ariel, M. (1990). *Accessing noun-phrase antecedents*. London: Routledge.

Arnold, J. E. (1998). *Reference form and discourse patterns.* Unpublished doctoral dissertation, Stanford University, Stanford, CA.

Arnold, J. E. (2008). Reference production: Production-internal and addressee-oriented processes. *Language and Cognitive Processes,* 23(4), 495–527.

Arnold, J. E., Hudson Kam, C. L., & Tanenhaus, M. K. (2007). If you say "thee uh-" you are describing something hard: The on-line attribution of disfluency during reference comprehension. *Journal of Experimental Psychology: Learning Memory and Cognition,* 33(5).

Arnold, J. E., & Lao, S. Y. C. (2008). Put in last position something previously unmentioned: Word order effects on referential expectancy and reference comprehension. *Language and Cognitive Processes,* 23(2), 282-295.

Arnold, J. E., & Lao, S. Y. C. (2010). *Effects of non-shared attention on pronoun comprehension.* (Unpublished ms, University of North Carolina at Chapel Hill)

Arnold, J. E., Tanenhaus, M. K., Altmann, R. J., & Fagnano, M. (2004). The old and thee, uh, new. *Psychological Science,* 15(9), 578–582.

Arnold, J. E., Wasow, T., Asudeh, A., & Alrenga, P. (2004). Avoiding attachment ambiguities: The role of constituent ordering. *Journal of Memory and Language,* 51(1), 55–70.

Arnold, J. E., Wasow, T., Losongco, A., & Ginstrom, R. (2000). Heaviness vs. newness: The effects of structural complexity and discourse status on constituent ordering. *Language,* 76(1), 28–55.

Barr, D. J., & Seyfeddinipur, M. (2010). The role of fillers in listener attributions for speaker disfluency. *Language and Cognitive Processes,* 25, 441–455.

Behaghel, O. (1909). Beziehungen zwischen Umfang und Reihenfolge von Satzgliedern [Relationships between size and ordering of constituents]. *Indogermanische Forschungen,* 25(110-142).

Behaghel, O. (1932). *Deutsche Syntax: eine geschichtliche Darstellung. Band IV. Wortstellung. Periodenbau.* Heidelberg: Carl Universitätsbuchhandlung.

Bock, J. K. (1986). Syntactic persistence in language production. *Cognitive Psychology,* 18, 355–387.

Bock, J. K., & Griffin, Z. M. (2000). The persistence of structural priming: Transient activation or implicit learning? *Journal of Experimental Psychology: General,* 129(2), 177–192.

Bock, J. K., & Irwin, D. E. (1980). Syntactic effects of information availability in sentence production. *Journal of Verbal Learning &*

Verbal Behavior, *19*(4), 467–484.

Bock, J. K., Irwin, D. E., & Davidson, D. J. (2004). Putting first things first. In J. M. Henderson & F. Ferreira (Eds.), *The integration of language, vision, and action: Eye movements and the visual world*. New York: Psychology Press.

Bock, J. K., Irwin, D. E., Davidson, D. J., & Levelt, W. J. M. (2003). Minding the clock. *Journal of Memory and Language*, *48*(4), 653–685.

Bock, J. K., & Loebell, H. (1990). Framing sentences. *Cognition*, *35*(1), 1–39.

Bock, J. K., Loebell, H., & Morey, R. (1992). From conceptual roles to structural relations: Bridging the syntactic cleft. *Psychological Review*, *99*(1), 150–171.

Bock, J. K., & Warren, R. K. (1985). Conceptual accessibility and syntactic structure in sentence formulation. *Cognition*, *21*(1), 47–67.

Boland, J. E., & Boehm-Jernigan, H. (1998). Lexical constraints and prepositional phrase attachment. *Journal of Memory and Language*, *39*(4), 684–719.

Branigan, H. P., Pickering, M. J., & Cleland, A. A. (2000). Syntactic co-ordination in dialogue. *Cognition*, *75*(2), 13–25.

Branigan, H. P., Pickering, M. J., McLean, J. F., & Cleland, A. A. (2007). Participant role and syntactic alignment in dialogue. *Cognition*, *104*, 163–197.

Branigan, H. P., Pickering, M. J., & Tanaka, M. (2008). Contributions of animacy to grammatical function assignment and word order during production. *Lingua*, *118*(2), 172–189.

Chafe, W. L. (1976). Givenness, contrastiveness, definiteness, subjects, topics, and point of view. In C. N. Li (Ed.), *Subject and topic* (pp. 25–56). New York: Academic Press.

Chafe, W. L. (1994). *Discourse, consciousness and time*. Chicago: University of Chicago Press.

Chang, F. (2009). Learning to order words: A connectionist model of word order and accessibility effects in Japanese and English. *Journal of Memory and Language*, *61*, 374–397.

Choi, H.-W. (2007). Length and order: A corpus study of Korean dative-accusative construction. *Discourse and Cognition*, *14*, 207–227.

Clark, H. H. (1996). *Using language*. Cambridge: Cambridge University Press.

Clark, H. H., & Fox Tree, J. E. (2002). Using uh and um in spontaneous speaking. *Cognition*, *84*(1), 73–111.

Clark, H. H., & Haviland, S. E. (1977). Comprehension and the given-new contract. In R. O. Freedle (Ed.), *Discourse production and comprehension, Volume 1 of Discourse processes: Advances in research and theory* (pp. 1–40). Hillsdale, NJ: Lawrence Erlbaum Associates.

Clark, H. H., & Krych, M. A. (2004). Speaking while monitoring addressees for understanding. *Journal of Memory and Language*, *50*(1), 62–81.

Clark, H. H., & Marshall, C. R. (2002). Definite reference and mutual knowledge. In A. K. Joshi, B. L. Webber, & I. A. Sag (Eds.), *Elements of discourse understanding* (pp. 10–63). Cambridge University Press.

Clark, H. H., & Wasow, T. (1998). Repeating words in spontaneous speech. *Cognitive Psychology*, *37*(3), 201–242.

Corley, M., MacGregor, L. J., & Donaldson, D. I. (2007). It's the way that you, er, say it: Hesitations in speech affect language comprehension. *Cognition*, *105*(3), 658–668.

Ferreira, F. (1994). Choice of passive voice is affected by verb type and animacy. *Journal of Memory and Language*, *33*(6), 715–736.

Ferreira, V. S. (1996). Is it better to give than to donate? Syntactic flexibility in language production. *Journal of Memory and Language*, *35*(5), 724–755.

Ferreira, V. S. (2003). The persistence of optional complementizer production: Why saying "that" is not saying "that" at all. *Journal of Memory and Language*, *48*(2), 379–398.

Ferreira, V. S., & Dell, G. S. (2000). Effect of ambiguity and lexical availability on syntactic and lexical production. *Cognitive Psychology*, *40*(4), 296–340.

Flores d'Arcais, G. B. (1975). Some perceptual determinants of sentence construction. In G. B. Flores d'Arcais (Ed.), *Studies in perception: Festschrift for Fabio Metelli* (pp. 344–373). Martello-Giunti.

Gleitman, L. R., January, D., Nappa, R., & Trueswell, J. C. (2007). On the *give* and *take* between event apprehension and utterance formulation. *Journal of Memory and Language*, *57*(4), 544–569.

Griffin, Z. M. (2003). A reversed word length effect in coordinating the preparation and articulation of words in speaking. *Psychonomic Bulletin and Review*, *10*(3), 603–609.

Griffin, Z. M., & Bock, J. K. (2000). What the eyes say about speaking. *Psychological Science*, *11*, 274–279.

Gundel, J. K. (1988). Universals of topic-comment structure. In M. Hammond, E. A. Moravcsik, & J. R. Wirth (Eds.), (pp. 209–

239). Amsterdam: John Benjamins.

Haviland, S. E., & Clark, H. H. (1974). What's new? Acquiring new information as a process in comprehension. *Journal of Verbal Learning and Verbal Behavior*, *13*(5), 512–521.

Hawkins, J. A. (1994). *A performance theory of order and constituency.* Cambridge: Cambridge University Press.

Hawkins, J. A. (this volume). Discontinuous dependencies in corpus selections: Particle verbs and their relevance for current issues in language processing. In E. M. Bender & J. E. Arnold (Eds.), *Language from a cognitive perspective: Grammar, usage, and processing.* Stanford: CSLI.

Haywood, S. L., Pickering, M. J., & Branigan, H. P. (2005). Do speakers avoid ambiguities during dialogue. *Psychological Science*, *16*(5), 362–366.

Jaeger, T. F. (this volume). Corpus-based research on language production: Information density and reducible subject relatives. In E. M. Bender & J. E. Arnold (Eds.), *Language from a cognitive perspective: Grammar, usage, and processing.* Stanford: CSLI.

Jaeger, T. F., & Wasow, T. (2006). Processing as a source of accessibility effects on variation. In *Proceedings of the 31st annual meeting of the Berkeley Linguistics Society* (pp. 169–180). Berkeley, CA.

Lohse, B., Hawkins, J., & Wasow, T. (2004). Processing domains in English verb-particle constructions. *Language*, *80*(2), 238–261.

McDonald, J. L., Bock, J. K., & Kelly, M. H. (1993). Word and world order: Semantic, phonological, and metrical determinants of serial position. *Cognitive Psychology*, *25*, 188–188.

Osgood, C. E. (1957). A behavioristic analysis of perception and language as cognitive phenomena. In J. Bruner (Ed.), *Contemporary approaches to cognition.* Cambridge, MA: Harvard University Press.

Osgood, C. E. (1971). Where do sentences come from. In D. D. Steinberg & L. A. Jakobovits (Eds.), *Semantics: An interdisciplinary reader in philosophy, linguistics and psychology* (pp. 497–529). London: Cambridge University Press.

Pickering, M. J., & Branigan, H. P. (1998). The representation of verbs: Evidence from syntactic priming in language production. *Journal of Memory and Language*, *39*(4), 633–651.

Pickering, M. J., Branigan, H. P., & McLean, J. F. (2002). Constituent structure is formulated in one stage. *Journal of Memory and Language*, *46*(3), 586–605.

Prat-Sala, M., & Branigan, H. P. (2000). Discourse constraints on syntactic processing in language production: A cross-linguistic study in English and Spanish. *Journal of Memory and Language*, *42*(2), 168–182.

Prince, E. F. (1981). Toward a taxonomy of given-new information. In P. Cole (Ed.), *Radical pragmatics* (pp. 223–255). New York, NY: Academic Press.

Prince, E. F. (1992). The ZPG letter: Subjects, definiteness, and information-status. In W. Mann & S. Thompson (Eds.), *Discourse description: Diverse linguistic analyses of a fund-raising text* (pp. 295–326). Amsterdam: Benjamins.

Quirk, R., Greenbaum, S., Leech, G., & Svartvik, J. (1972). *A grammar of contemporary English*. London: Longman.

Race, D. S., & MacDonald, M. C. (2003). The use of "that" in the production and comprehension of object relative clauses. In *26th annual meeting of the Cognitive Science Society*. Chicago, IL.

Rickford, J. R. (this volume). Relativizer omission in Anglophone Caribbean creoles, Appalachian, and African American Vernacular English [AAVE], and its theoretical implications. In E. M. Bender & J. E. Arnold (Eds.), *Language from a cognitive perspective: Grammar, usage, and processing*. Stanford: CSLI.

Schober, M. F., & Brennan, S. E. (2003). Processes of interactive spoken discourse: The role of the partner. In A. C. Graesser, M. A. Gernsbacher, & S. R. Goldman (Eds.), *Handbook of discourse processes* (pp. 123–164). Hillsdale, NJ: Lawrence Erlbaum Associates.

Snider, N. (this volume). Investigating syntactic persistence in corpora. In E. M. Bender & J. E. Arnold (Eds.), *Language from a cognitive perspective: Grammar, usage, and processing*. Stanford: CSLI.

Stallings, L. M., MacDonald, M. C., & O'Seaghdha, P. G. (1998). Phrasal ordering constraints in sentence production: Phrase length and verb disposition in heavy-NP shift. *Journal of Memory and Language*, *39*(3), 392–417.

Tily, H., Gahl, S., Arnon, I., Snider, N., Kothari, A., & Bresnan, J. (2009). Syntactic probabilities affect pronunciation variation in spontaneous speech. *Language and Cognition*, *1*(2), 147–165.

van Nice, K. Y., & Dietrich, R. (2003). Task sensitivity of animacy effects: Evidence from German picture descriptions. *Linguistics*, *41*(5), 825–849.

Wasow, T. (1997a). End-weight from the speaker's perspective. *Journal of Psycholinguistic Research*, *26*(3), 347–361.

Wasow, T. (1997b). Remarks on grammatical weight. *Language Variation and Change*, *9*(1), 81–105.

Wasow, T. (2002). *Postverbal behavior.* Stanford, CA: CSLI Publicatuions.

Wasow, T., & Arnold, J. E. (2003). Post-verbal constituent ordering in English. In G. Rohdenburg & B. Mondorf (Eds.), *Determinants of grammatical variation in English* (pp. 119–154). The Hague: Mouton: Mouton de Gruyter.

Wasow, T., Jaeger, T. F., & Orr, D. (in press). Lexical variation in relativizer frequency. In H. Simon & H. Wiese (Eds.), *Expecting the unexpected: Exceptions in grammar.* Berlin and New York: Mouton de Gruyter.

Watson, D., & Gibson, E. (2004). The relationship between intonational phrasing and syntactic structure in language production. *Language and Cognitive Processes, 19*(6), 713–755.

Yamashita, H., & Chang, F. (2001). "Long before short" preference in the production of a head-final language. *Cognition, 81*(2), 45–55.

11

Weight and Word Order in Historical English

HARRY J. TILY

Preface

This chapter reports part of a larger research project inspired by Tom Wasow's book *Postverbal Behavior* (2002). Tom's love of tackling problems by diving into empirical data is entirely evident from his work, and has been an inspiration throughout my discussions and meetings with him—ultimately, leading into this project.

1 Introduction

In his 2002 book, Tom investigates in detail the influence of "grammatical weight" on constituent ordering. Across a range of constructions in English, he finds a striking tendency for word order patterns to obey the "Principle of End Weight" (Behaghel, 1909; Quirk, Greenbaum, Leech, & Svartvik, 1972; Wasow, 1997): phrases are presented in order of increasing weight, where "weight" is understood as some measure of complexity or length. Although we often think of English as a "fixed word order" language, weight turns out to play a major role in determining speakers' choices. This is true in constructions where word order is relatively free, such as the order of object and particle in (1): speakers strongly prefer to place longer objects after the short particle, making (1c) more frequent than (1d).

(1)   a. the detective brought in [the suspect]

   b. the detective brought [the suspect] in

Language from a Cognitive Perspective.
Emily M. Bender and Jennifer Arnold, Editors
Copyright © 2011, CSLI Publications.

  c. the detective brought in [the man who was accused of having stolen the automobile]

  d. #the detective brought [the man who was accused of having stolen the automobile] in

It is also true in constructions where one order is much more common than the other: the canonical order (2a,b) is often flouted if doing so preserves end weight (2c) but rarely otherwise (2d).

(2) a. John took [his friends] [into account]

  b. John took [only his own personal acquaintances] [into account]

  c. John took [into account] [only his own personal acquaintances]

  d. #John took [into account] [his friends]

Wasow's (2002) investigations are limited to English, largely due to the availability of annotated data and the difficulties and dangers of working with other languages as a non-native speaker. But there is ample evidence that in other languages, grammatical weight has a qualitatively different effect (see Jaeger & Norcliffe, 2009; Hawkins, 2004). English is largely head-initial, and the phrases whose position Wasow studies appear uniformly after the verb. In head-final languages like Japanese, on the other hand, speakers seem to prefer to place heavier phrases close to the beginning of the sentence (e.g. Hawkins, 1994; Yamashita & Chang, 2001). Sentences like (3a) are therefore more frequent than (3b).

(3) a. [Tarou ga sono hon wo katta to] [Hanako ga] itta
   [Tarou.SBJ that book.OBJ bought.QUOTE] [Hanako.SBJ] said
   [Hanako] said [that Taro bought that book]

  b. [Hanako ga] [Tarou ga sono hon wo katta to] itta
   [Hanako.SBJ] [Tarou.SBJ that book.OBJ bought.QUOTE] said
   [Hanako] said [that Taro bought that book]

Hawkins (1994, 2004, this volume) accounts for the relationship between weight and word order with a psycholinguistic theory based on evidence from different constructions across multiple languages. He suggests that where they have the choice, speakers will order constituents to allow each of them to be recognized and processed as quickly as possible: in the case of the arguments of a verb, the hypothesis predicts that constituents should be ordered by length, with the shortest being the closest to the verb. The closely related *Dependency Locality Theory* (Gibson, 2000) makes the same predictions, by suggesting that processing difficulty is minimized when the total length of syntactic dependencies (the distance between words that are dependent on each other for syntactic interpretation, such as the head noun of an object noun phrase, and the verb) is minimized, as illustrated in (4).[1]

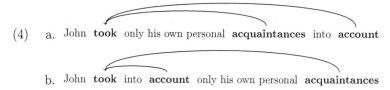

(4) a. John **took** only his own personal **acquaintances** into **account**

b. John **took** into **account** only his own personal **acquaintances**

The observation that weight effects in VO (verb-object order) languages like English seem to pattern in the opposite way to those in OV languages like Japanese raises an interesting question given the history of English. Old English, as spoken in the southern British Isles up until around 1100, allowed clauses to be produced in both VO and OV orders. Over the course of several hundred years, however, OV was gradually replaced with the VO order of the modern language.[2] The availability of large annotated corpora of Old and Middle English has opened the way for large-scale quantitative analyses of word order phenomena in the spirit of the studies in *Postverbal Behavior*. In this chapter, I use this data to explore weight effects in a language which allows both word orders in the main clause, but which is changing in that regard. Is the choice between VO and OV in historical English sensitive to weight effects, and do these effects pattern with those found in modern languages? Can these findings tell us anything about the relationship between language processing and language change?

---

[1]Strictly speaking, DLT is a theory about what is easy in comprehension, and it only follows that speakers should *produce* an the preferred order if we assume they are tailoring their sentences to be easy to comprehend. Hawkins' theory states that speakers are motivated to be *efficient* in production, though it isn't clear that there is a purely production-internal motivation for domain minimization being efficient. Further research is needed on the relationship between comprehension difficulty and production choice. Everything here is compatible with both Hawkins' and Gibson's theories.

[2]One broadly accepted view within historical syntax is that there was a relatively fast *parametric* change between two underlying orders, though the evidence for this has been called into question (see Allen, 2000). As I explain shortly I have nothing much to say here about syntactic analysis, and only consider the "surface" order of the phrases, which underwent gradual change.

2 Verb-object order in Old and Middle English

In accordance with the theories of Hawkins and Gibson, a difference in the dependency lengths of two alternants has been shown experimentally to be a good predictor of which of the two a speaker will choose in production. Stallings, MacDonald, & O'Seaghdha, 1998, showed that when asked to reproduce an NP-PP sentence similar to those in (2) that they had previously heard, speakers were more likely to shift the NP to the end of the sentence if it was long. J. Arnold, Wasow, Losongco, & Ginstrom, 2000 showed a similar effect for both heavy NP shift sentences and the ditransitive alternation in corpus data. In a lab experiment also reported in that article, participants interacted with each other in a cooperative task which entailed them producing large numbers of dative sentences like *"give it the small green crayon"*. The results show that again, participants prefer to place the shorter constituent closer to the verb (avoiding, for example, *"give the small green crayon to it"*).

Given that dependency length minimization apparently influences, or at least predicts the word orders in sentences that modern language users produce, it is not surprising that the same generalization could predict the choices of users of Old and Middle English (henceforth OE and ME). If this phenomenon represents a processing bias, then we would expect the human language users of just a few centuries ago to experience the same bias. In OE and ME, both VO and OV orders were available. As subjects were typically preverbal (and other preverbal dependents common), pressure to minimize dependency lengths might have led speakers to place the object after the verb more often if it was long, therefore avoiding long dependencies between the verb and subject or other preverbal material. The following two clauses of OE illustrate dependency lengths for the SVO (5a) and SOV (5b) structures respectively.

	subj		obj		
Unaberendlic	gyhþa	ofereode	ealne	þone	lichaman
unbearable	itching	overcame	all	the	body

(5) a. *'Unbearable itching spread over his entire body...'*

	subj			obj	
&	ungelyfendlic	toblawennys	his	innoþ	geswencte
and	unbelievable	bloating	his	innards	afflicted

'... and unbelievable bloating afflicted his stomach.'

b. (Herod's last days as described in Ælfric's Homilies, c1000)

Clearly, as the object becomes longer, the subject dependency in the OV sentence (5b) will become longer. On the other hand, neither the subject nor the object in the VO sentence (5a) spans the other, meaning that both are always close to the verb. Of course, pressure to place a longer object after the verb would equally well be explained by a simple "End Weight" explanation in which heavy material is placed later in the sentence.

Previous research on historical English has uncovered numerous correlations between constituent length and placement. Kohonen, 1978, for instance, shows that length played a role in the placement of several types of constituent in the relatively free word order of early ME. Seoane, 2006 additionally suggests that the passive construction, which exists in OE but increases drastically in frequency in late ME and Early Modern English, is used instead of an active construction more frequently in cases where the active would involve putting a long phrase before a short one. Traugott, 2007 finds that the majority of left-dislocation sentences in Old English involve a long and complicated object: as in the Present-Day English (henceforth PDE) sentences shown in (2), an infrequent word order is more common when it involves a particularly long constituent.

The most relevant finding is work by Pintzuk & Taylor, 2006, who provide a statistical analysis of OE and ME data, finding that length as well as certain other properties of the object influence its position: in clauses with auxiliary verbs, longer objects more often come after the main verb. They attribute the effect of length to processing factors: "length [...] may reflect a processing constraint against center-embedded material" (p. 252).

Below, I present a model that investigates many potential predictors of word order in OE and ME simultaneously, and using a broader class of sentences than Pintzuk and Taylor's study. I focus on the potential role of dependency length minimization as an influence on speakers' choices. I also test whether the influence of any of these variables on word order changes over time.

3 Analysis

3.1 Data preparation

The data analyzed here is taken from two corpora: the York-Toronto-Helsinki Parsed Corpus of Old Engish (YCOE; Taylor, Warner, Pintzuk, & Beths, 2003) and the Penn Parsed Corpus of Middle English 2 (PPCME2; Kroch & Taylor, 2000). The two corpora consist of texts from abutting time periods that have been parsed, yielding a collection of sentences annotated like the following one from late OE.

(6) [IP-MAT [ADVP-TMP [ADV-T ða]]   *there*
          [VBD *mæssede*]   *celebrated*
          [NP-NOM [MAN-N *man*]]   *one*
          [NP-DAT [D-D *ðam*]   *the*
                [N-D *cynge*]]   *king*
          [PP   [P *æt*]   *at*
                [NP [NP-GEN [NR *Sancte*]   *Saint*
                        [NR-G *Clementes*]]   *Clement's*
                [N *cyrcean*]]]]   *church*
     "There people celebrated the king, at St Clement's church"
     (*Vision of Leofric*, c1150)

The YCOE and PPCME2 were produced using similar annotation and coding standards, which minimizes the problems that can arise when combining data from multiple sources. Even so, the two corpora were tailored for two stages of English which had quite different grammatical properties, and so there are some differences in the annotations chosen. For instance, the YCOE annotates noun phrases for case (nominative, accusative, etc) while the PPCME2 instead includes grammatical function information (subject, direct object, indirect object, etc). This is motivated by the decay of case marking over the course of time: by the 13th century, the case paradigm had largely collapsed, and the grammatical function of a NP was indicated by an adposition or by word order, or was structurally ambiguous. See Allen, 1999, for discussion of changes in the English case system. Of course, case was lost gradually, and the sharp discontinuity between the two corpora therefore introduces artifacts into the data. For instance, NPs in the OE data which are morphologically ambiguous between two cases are annotated as such, even though their grammatical function may be evident and therefore included in the ME data. Equating the OE accusative/dative distinction with the ME direct/indirect object distinction is not ideal, but better than ignoring the difference between object types altogether.

All of the texts included in this data predate the use of Gutenberg's printing press, which was not invented until around 1440. Texts were copied manually, and this fact has a great influence on the amount and type of data we have today. First, it means that both the concept of *text* and *manuscript* are relevant: originals could be copied many times, and copies themselves copied, with no guarantee of accurate reproduction. Copied manuscripts may therefore reflect both the language of the original author and that of the copyist. Second, the overwhelming majority of writing was religious in nature: until the 13th century, almost all writing and copying was performed by Christian monks, and even after that, the secular scribes who increasingly replaced them as the major producers of books chiefly addressed the demand for religious texts. The time and labor involved in copying a text meant that only writing seen as very important was reproduced, so beside the bulk of religious texts there are some histories and handbooks, but very little early secular poetry or prose. Third, a great deal of the extant texts are translations from Latin, and so even the English "originals" may show an influence of the Latin word order. It isn't possible to exclude all these texts, since this would lead to the loss of a great deal of data, particularly in the earlier periods where there is already sparsity.

From a statistical point of view, it is important to model as accurately as possible the dependence and independence between the individual data points being analyzed, the clauses. For instance, clauses taken from a single text are not independent observations: they share properties such as the fact that they were written in the same year and by the same author, and therefore might be expected to behave more similarly than a set of clauses taken from different texts. We can model this nonindependence by including variables such as the year of composition, the author, and even the specific text. With large datasets like the one I describe here, it is good practice to include any available control variables that are theoretically justified: each of these may account for variation in the outcome variable (here word order) that might otherwise have been falsely attributed to the predictive variables of interest (here object weight). One serious problem for this particular dataset is the severe nonindependence introduced when there are several manuscripts corresponding to a single text. Ideally, we would model this dependency by including for each manuscript a per-clause control variable indicating the word-order in the original text. This would only leave deviations from the original word order introduced by later copyists to be accounted for by variables like manuscript date and object weight. Unfortunately, that solution is impractical for two reasons: first, an identifiable original manuscript often (typically) is not available; and second, the class of regression models I use here would not be able to account for *both* originals and copies with this control variable, as it would be undefined for originals. Instead, I take the expedient solution of identifying all sets of manuscripts with a single source text, and deleting all but one of them at random. This results in a substantial loss of data, but avoids the serious problem of "double counting" clauses that are copies of each other.

Manuscripts differ somewhat in the amount and accuracy of information we have about them. Later works tend to be easier to date accurately, although certain earlier works—such as a great number of laws, wills and charters—are explicitly dated. I used dates given in the Helsinki corpus (Kytö, 1996), in Ker's (1957) Catalogue, and in Sawyer's (1968) Anglo-Saxon Charters to establish dates for the composition of each text and copying of each manuscript. Although in some cases these dates are specific years, in many cases there is simply some interval of time within which the text or manuscript is believed to have been created, often as wide an interval as a century. In these cases, I took the midpoint of the range.[3]

For the purposes of this chapter, I restrict the object of study to word order in matrix clauses (rather than clauses embedded inside other clauses, such as "I think that [John lives here]") and non-co-ordinated verbs (as opposed to co-ordinations like "eat and drink"). I exclude clauses with an auxiliary (including (pre-) modals used with a second verb), since the dependency structure between subject and main verb is arguably different there. The variable of interest here is the order in which the verb and its dependents are placed, so I only include clauses with an overt subject and object. Both accusative/direct and dative/indirect objects are included but clauses with *both* a direct and indirect object are excluded.

The simple matrix clauses that are the object of study here often receive less attention by historical syntacticians than clauses which are embedded or have auxiliaries. The reason for this is that in a derivational theory of syntax, clauses are "base generated" with one underlying structure: typically this is understood to be VO for later texts, and before then either uniform OV (see Kemenade, 1987), or variable OV/VO (Pintzuk, 1991). Subsequent transformation or dislocation operations, however, can move words and yield a substantially different "surface" order. As the major question of theoretical interest is typically the underlying structure, more attention is paid to clause types that are assumed to more closely reflect that structure. In the case of historical English, two principal sources of word order dislocation are often discussed. The first is the V2 constraint: the tendency to place

---

[3]Pintzuk & Taylor, 2004 argue against this, saying that "assigning the midpoint of a 100-year period as the date of composition for a quantitive analysis seems meaningless." It is true and should be stressed that the less accurate the date estimate, the less useful and interpretable the resulting analysis. However, there is no good reason to throw away data for those texts that *can* be more accurately dated. The alternative approach of binning text dates—Pintzuk & Taylor in fact use 200 year periods for OE—reduces to fundamentally the same solution of assigning some value for an unknown date, and only differs in that the values chosen are arbitrary century boundaries rather than a best estimate, making it strictly *more* meaningless. More sophisticated techniques could preserve and model the different uncertainty associated with dating each text, but this I leave to later work.

the finite verb in second position in the main clause as in Modern German (see e.g. Kroch, Taylor, & Ringe, 2000), as in the sentence in (6). The second is extraposition of the object to the end of the clause (Kemenade, 1987; Pintzuk & Kroch, 1989). Most derivational analyses have the verb move to second position rather than being base generated there, and hence the order of verb and object cannot reveal the base VO/OV order unless the clause is embedded (in which case V2 movement is absent or at least infrequent) or there is also an auxiliary verb (in which case it is the auxiliary which moves to second position). Likewise, extraposition is posited to make underlying OV clauses appear superficially VO.

The English V2 constraint is not categorical: exceptions are common, with most but not all falling into three classes. First, verb-initial main clauses are common, particularly when new referents are being introduced, in sequences of related clauses, or at the beginning of a discourse episode (see Petrova, 2006; Petrova & Solf, 2008). Second, V2 order is variable after certain "scene setting" adverbs such as *þa* ("then"): there, the verb commonly appears in second or third position, and occasionally later, as in (7):

(7) þa   þy ylcan gere   onfaran winter   þa Deniscan   þe
     then   the same year   before winter   the Danes   that
     on Meresige   sæton   tugon   hira scipu   up on Temese
     on Merseyside sat   pulled   their ships   up on Thames
     (*Anglo-Saxon Chronicle: Parker MS*, c890, (Kroch et al., 2000))

Third, in OE, pronouns often appear before the verb even when there is another preverbal constituent, whether the pronoun is subject (8a) or object (8b). These sentences can still be analyzed as V2 if the pronoun is treated as a clitic that "does not count" as taking up the second position (Kemenade, 1987; Pintzuk, 1991). However, pronouns are not *always* preverbal, even in relatively early texts (9).

(8) a. þurh   his wisdom   he   geworhte   ealle þing
         through   his wisdom   he   worked   all things
         (*Ælfric's Homilies*, c1000, cited in Koopman, 1997)

     b. ah   twegen   culfran briddas   him   genihtsumedan
         but   two   pigeon birds   him   suffice
         &   twegen   turturan   gemæccan
         and   two   turtle-doves   a pair
         (*Blickling Homilies*, c900)

(9) ðonne ærnaþ hy ealle toweard ðæm feo
     then   gallop they all   toward   that treasure
     (*Orosius*, c925, cited in Traugott, 2007)

In summary, verbs do typically come second in both Old and Middle English, but not universally. Haeberli, 2002, estimates the rate of V2 in OE and early ME to be around 70%. Moreover, the exceptions are a diverse group: only the more frequent orders are mentioned above, but all of the logically possible orders of subject, verb, and object are used. (Hinterhölzl & Petrova, 2010) suggest that there is not really a V2 constraint, but that all backgrounded material appears preverbally, and this tends to include any pronouns and at most one full NP. It is unclear, of course, whether some of the more esoteric exceptional word orders are simply transliterations from Latin, which has extremely free word order. In any case, there is enough variation even in main clauses without auxiliaries to study the effect of phrase length on order.

The frequency of each possible word order over all clauses in the dataset is given in Table 1.

	SOV		OSV	OVS
OV	3576		1135	765
	(65%)		(21%)	(14%)
	SVO	VSO		VOS
VO	10292	2904		664
	(74%)	(21%)		(5%)

TABLE 1 Total number of clauses with each word order in dataset

These summaries show that all of the possible orders of the verb and two arguments occur in these corpora. The relatively high frequency of SOV and OSV suggest that V2 is not a categorical constraint, though of these 4,711 clauses, 3,986 have a pronominal subject or object (or both). This leaves at least 725 (15%) that cannot be explained by analyzing pronouns as clitics on the verb, even ignoring the possibility of preverbal adverbials or other constituents. Of the 3,568 VSO and VOS clauses, 3,194 begin with some adverbial or other constituent, leaving only 346 (10%) that are truly main verb-initial.

If we ignore the temporal dimension and just look at word order across the entire dataset, then, significant variation is evident. I focus here on the order in which the object and main verb appear: from Table 1 it is clear that most subjects are preverbal, so choosing OV over VO typically reduces the subject-verb dependency length. In the rest of this chapter I will limit the data to sentences where the subject precedes the verb. This excludes relatively few clauses, and limits the object of study to cases where the psycholinguistic theories discussed above make a clear prediction that longer objects should favor VO order.

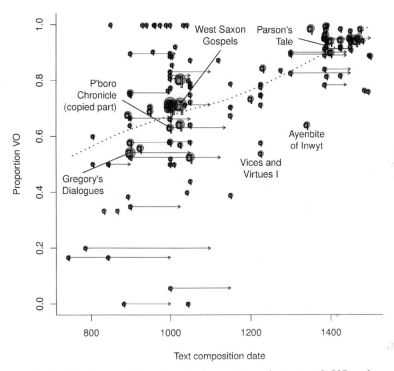

FIGURE 1 Proportion of main clauses in each text with VO order

The plot in Figure 1 gives an initial overview of the change in frequency of VO and OV orders. Points on this plot represent individual texts, and their relative size represents of the number of clauses in each that fit the criteria above. Some notable texts are labeled. The y-axis indicates the proportion of those clauses that are are VO, and the dotted line shows the trend of change in proportion over time.[4] Finally, for manuscripts which are believed to be copies, a horizontal arrow shows the period of time that elapsed between the approximate original text date and the approximate date of copying.

---

[4]This is a *loess smoother*, a statistical technique for approximating an arbitrary curve.

The figure shows that some periods contribute much less data than others. In particular, social changes resulting from the Norman invasion of 1066 led to a sharp decline in the output of written English, as scribes reverted to writing in Latin, or occasionally French. There are almost no newly composed English texts for a century after the invasion. It also appears that there is much more word order variation in OE than ME, though this should be taken with a grain of salt since there are many more short OE texts (mostly wills and charters) making per-text estimates less accurate.

3.2 Statistical analysis

To model the importance of object length and other factors on the choice of word order, I use a multilevel logistic regression (see Gelman & Hill, 2006; Jaeger, 2008) with VO order as the outcome variable.

Pintzuk & Taylor, 2006 used a VARBRUL style multivariate analysis to show that longer objects are more likely to be placed after the verb. In that analysis, both date and object length were binned and entered as discrete (and non-ordered) factors. Their results suggest that it would be possible to produce a single model of the effect of phrase length on word order choices for the entire period, including year and length as covariates. Multivariate analysis, which models multiple possible influences simultaneously is to be prefered over simple summaries for each influencing variable (see Jaeger, this volume). However, a multilevel logistic regression model is more suitable for this kind of analysis, and has many advantages over VARBUL. First, it is better to use continuous covariates for variables like date and length that are naturally continuous: binning reduces statistical power (see e.g. Cohen, 1983) and obfuscates smooth trends across time. In fact, treating each period separately prevents the direct investigation of possible differences in the influence of certain variables over the timecourse of the entire dataset. Second, multilevel regression allows sources of variation at different levels of analysis to be taken into account, which allows us to factor out variation due to observations coming from (e.g.) different texts and regions. For general arguments motivating multilevel analysis see Gelman & Hill, 2006 and Jaeger, 2008; for a specific comparison of traditional VARBRUL and multilevel analysis see Johnson, 2009.

Below I summarize the predictors to be entered into an initial model as fixed effects. The first are the variables investigated by Pintzuk & Taylor:

- **Text Date**, as a year.
- **Object length**, in words.

- **Object type/case**, either direct/accusative or indirect/dative.
- **Negated object**, a binary indicator of whether the object is negative: either inherently (e.g., PDE *none*) or by being negatively quantified (e.g. PDE *no*).
- **Quantified object**, a binary indicator of the presence of a non-negative quantifier such as *every* in the object.
- **RC modifying object**, a binary indicator of whether the object NP is modified by a relative clause.

The following fixed effects are added in this study:

- **Subject length**, in words.
- **RC modifying subject**, a binary indicator of whether the subject NP is modified by a relative clause.
- **Pronominal subject**, binary.
- **Pronominal object**, binary.
- **Manuscript lag**, the number of years between the date of the original text and the date of the manuscript.[5] It would not be a good idea to enter the raw manuscript date along with the text date in the model: the two are highly correlated, and for a majority of data the same value.
- **Latin original**, a binary indicator of whether the text is known to be a translation from a Latin original.
- **Verb POS**, the part of speech of the verb, from the set *base* (infinitive, imperative), *present tense* and *past tense*.

The following factors are entered as random effects; that is, they might be expected to capture individual deviations from the general population-wide trends, but I do not have enough interest in the specific nature of those deviations to invest degrees of freedom in modelling them (see explanations in Gelman & Hill, 2006).

- **Text**, the identity of the text (note that only one manuscript is included per text, so this could equivalently be considered as the identity of the manuscript).
- **Genre**, an indicator of text type from the set *science*, *law*, *religious*, and *other*.
- **Dialect**, an indicator of whether the text comes from the *West Saxon*, *Kentish*, or *Anglian* OE dialects or the *Southern*, *West Midlands*, *East Midlands* or *Northern* ME dialects (see below).

To investigate the possible changes in the importance of the variables over time, I also enter interactions between text Date and each of

---

[5] This intuitively interpretable measure is comparable to what would be obtained by the standard decorrelation technique of residualizing.

the following: Object Length, Subject Length, Object Pronominality, Subject Pronominality, Object Type/Case, and Dialect. Similarly, I included random slopes for Text Date to allow the potential for different levels of Genre and Dialect to display different rates of change.

The Dialect variable is problematic, and not just because of the intrinsic difficulty of determining where to impose dialect boundaries on the fluid space of regional variation. Although there is a reasonably good consensus on the division of extant OE texts into dialectic categories of West Saxon, Kentish, Mercian and Northumbrian, there is not a continuous record of text witnesses for each; rather, certain regions dominate in different years. All of the earliest extant manuscripts are West Saxon, and there are very few Kentish or Northumbrian documents at all. This means that the dialect variable is confounded with the date of the texts. The problem is compounded by the fact that dialect boundaries in the ME period—by which time there had been a great deal of levelling of the differences between regional varieties—are controversial, and do not map cleanly onto the OE dialects. See Görlach, 1997; Hogg, 2006 for details. In order to avoid this problem, I experimented by grouping the more northern and eastern dialects apart from the southern and western ones, yielding a binary variable which spans the entire dataset. However, this variable evidently conflates the differences between dialects, so I also tried a coding with different levels for the OE and ME texts based on the Helsinki corpus classifications. This includes the four ME dialects listed above, and for OE collapses together Mercian and Northumbrian texts as well as texts of unclear Mercian/West Saxon influence as the region "Anglian". In fact, neither coding improved model quality significantly, and whichever variable was used, it was removed during model comparison. The results reported below used the seven-way classification.

The Genre variable was designed to minimize similar problems of confounds with date: again, because different types of text were produced during different periods, a finer distinction would have made it impossible to tell differences between genres from differences due to change over time. I constructed four categories that have reasonable support across the entire dataset: *science*, texts which detail medicinal, astronomical and other technical knowledge; *law*, including charters, wills, and eclesiastic laws; *religious*, consisting of biblical text and apocrypha, sermons, homilies, and similar material; and *other*, a catchall category largely made up of philosophy, fiction, biographies, and history.

To a lesser extent, the Text variable is also conflated with date: in fact, it is nested within it, as each text has only one date. However, the large number of texts means that the model fitting procedure should be able to correctly partition variation into between-text and between-year effects, so this does not pose a problem.[6]

3.3 Results

A model was built by first entering all of the effects into a regression, and then deleting variables stepwise that do not significantly improve the fit to the data by chi-square model comparison. The "drop 1" procedure was used, removing predictors in turn in order of significance by model comparison until the $p = .1$ threshold was reached. The predictors removed are listed in order in Table (2). The final model had all VIFs < 1.5, indicating no obvious collinearity problem.

	df	χ^2	p_{χ^2}
Quantified object	1	<.001	0.98
RC modifying object	1	0.022	0.88
Manuscript lag	1	0.22	0.64
RC modifying subject	1	0.46	0.50
Subject length * Text date	1	0.84	0.36
Text date * Dialect	1	0.85	0.36
Dialect	1	0.74	0.39
Latin original	1	0.010	0.92
Text date * Pronoun subject	1	0.025	0.87
Text date * Object length	1	0.26	0.61

TABLE 2 Predictors removed during model comparison

Continuous variables were standardized by centering and divinding by two standard deviations, as suggested by Gelman, 2008. Centering means that the intercept represents the log odds of VO order for an "average" clause with mean object and subject length, from the middle of the time period, etc. Dividing makes the regression coefficients directly comparable as "effect sizes", revealing which predictors have a greater effect on the word order outcome.

In Table (3), I present the coefficients (β) for all fixed effects in the final model, and plot them with error bars indicating the standard error of those estimates. Intuitively, variables with effects further from the zero value have a larger influence on the outcome, with variables favoring VO having a positive effect size and those favoring OV negative.

---

[6] Accordingly, later inspection of the model's per-text random intercept estimates (Gelman & Hill's 2006:251–278) α_j, sometimes called BLUPs) show no correlation with date, and no differences in distribution across time.

	β	p_z	-1.5	0.0	1.5
Intercept	1.9	<.001			
Dative/indirect	0.031	0.58			
Negated object	-0.33	0.011			
Pronoun object	-1.2	<.001			
Object length	0.92	<.001			
Subject length	-0.087	0.0012			
Text date	1.5	<.001			
Text date * Dative/indirect	1.4	<.001			
Text date * Pronoun object	0.43	<.001			
Pronoun subject	-0.089	0.0033			
Verb POS=base	0.72	<.001			
Verb POS=past	0.16	<.001			
	sd				
Intercept | Text	0.84				

TABLE 3 Final model for VO/OV order (positive outcome is VO)

The standard deviation of the significant random effect is also listed and plotted on the same scale.

The variable of most interest is of course the length of the object, and its effect patterns in the expected direction: longer objects have a higher probability of being placed postverbally, controlling for all the other variables in the model. This is in accordance with the predictions of the Principle of End Weight as well as with domain minimization principles. This can be seen more clearly in Figure 2, which shows the model's predictions for objects of different lengths over time: throughout the data, longer objects have a higher probability of being realized postverbally, though by the ME period VO order has almost reached ceiling. This figure also illustrates the effect of the object case/type interaction with text date: in early texts, indirect objects are more likely to be preverbal, while in later texts the reverse is true. Unexpectedly, the model also suggests that shorter and pronominal subjects lead to more VO sentences. However, these effects are extremely small, and may be spurious.

The significant effect of object pronominality shows that pronouns display exceptional placement even controlling for their short length. In OE, pronominal subjects and objects were both usually preverbal, and the tendency to keep pronouns before the verb survived well into the ME period. Remnants of this tendency exist even today in fossilized language, such as standard Christian wedding vows, which include phrases like "I *thee wed*", and "until death do *us part*". The distributional be-

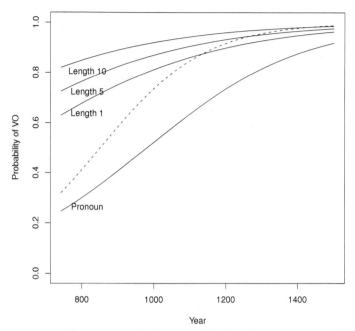

FIGURE 2 The estimated influence of the length and pronominality of accusative/direct objects on order over time (solid lines); predictions for a 2 word dative/indirect object over time (dashed line). Other predictors are at baseline level.

havior of OE pronouns has led some syntacticians to analyze them as bound morphemes: clitics, or "weak" pronouns (Kemenade, 1987). However, there is no evidence for any period in English when pronouns unambiguously patterned like clitics (see Koopman, 1997). As expected, the model shows that pronominal objects tend to be placed preverbally.

The fact that the Dialect variable does not improve the model probably reflects the inadequacy of this measure rather than being evidence that there were not dialect differences in word order. As described above, the dialect coding I chose avoids confounds with date and genre at the cost of conflating together potentially real differences between speakers of different dialects, perhaps leading to non-significance. The non-significant genre variable can be explained similarly. Coding for Latin originals also fails to improve the model. This is not surprising: as Latin has free word order, there is no particular reason why translating from Latin should systematically bias the scribe in one direction or the other; rather, we might simply expect "more noise" due to influence from the original word order, which may be OV or VO in each clause. More advanced modelling techniques could investigate this possibility.

As found by Pintzuk & Taylor, negated objects tend to appear pre-verbally. Unlike their findings, however, neither quantification nor the presence of a relative clause are found to be significant predictors of word order. In the case of the RC, this is probably due to a different coding system: Pintzuk & Taylor binned together long objects with objects of any length having relative clauses. This analysis controls for both seperately, suggesting that relative clauses do not influence word order above the additional length they add. This supports the idea that weight effects are well captured by simple phrase length rather than any more nuanced metric of syntactic complexity (Wasow, 1997, 2002; Szmrecsányi, 2004). There isn't an obvious explanation for quantification not being significant here, except to say that it is possible that this effect only manifests itself when there is an auxiliary verb, or that whatever influence object negativity had in the earlier analysis may have in fact been due to one of the other variables controlled for simultaneously here. Finally, the type of verb has a significant effect: although there is little difference between present and past tense inflected forms, base forms (imperatives and infinitives) favor VO.

4 Discussion

The fact that object length influences word order choice in historical English matches the observations made by Wasow and colleagues in support of Behaghel's (1909) Principle of End Weight, as well as the dependency minimization principles of Hawkins, 1994, 2004/Gibson, 2000. Nothing in the corpus study here distinguishes between the dependency minimization theory and the simpler principle of putting longer constituents later. However, previous work by Traugott, 2007 may bear on the issue. Traugott investigated OE left dislocation structures like the following, where rather than using a full object noun phrase within the clause, the writer has placed the object at the beginning of the sentence, and refers back to it with a pronoun afterwards:

(10) **ealle þa Romaniscan men** þe   Hannibal on Crece
all those Roman men   whom Hannibal into Greece
  geseald hæfde, **him** bebead   se consul   þæt
  sold   had   them commanded the consul that
  hie eal hiera heafod bescearen.
  they all their heads   shaved
  'The consul commanded all the Roman men whom Hannibal had

sold as slaves in Greece to shave their heads.'
(*Orosius*, c925, quoted in Traugott, 2007)

Traugott notes that the majority of these sentences occur with a long and complicated NP: in 49 (94%) of the 52 object left dislocations she finds, the object is followed by an adverbial or relative clause. The tendency for a particularly long object to be followed by a short pronoun bears some similarity to the long-before-short preference reported for modern OV languages like Japanese (Hawkins, 1994; Yamashita & Chang, 2001). This pattern follows from the dependency minimization hypothesis: in (10), the object pronoun is adjacent to the verb, and so there is a short object-verb dependency. If the dislocation construction had not been used, that dependency would extend over the entire relative clause *(þe Hannibal ... hæfde)*. Of course, if the only pressure was to place heavier material later in the sentence, then there would be no reason to dislocate long objects more than short ones.

Unfortunately, object left dislocation structures are quite rare, so it is difficult to investigate the role of weight in the limited OE data in any more detail. However, in a quantitative analysis of left dislocation in spoken Present Day English, Snider & Zaenen, 2006, found a significant effect of the length of the object: longer NPs are more likely to be left dislocated than short ones. In ongoing work, I am investigating the role of weight in OE object topicalization: preliminary results suggest that a long object is in fact more likely to appear in topic position, and therefore before the subject, than a short object is.

While the regression model presented here is a production model in the sense that it predicts the probability with which a speaker should produce a VO or OV ordered clause, it is unlikely to be a good model of the actual syntactic choices that a language user would go through when producing Old or Middle English. In particular, the model collapses over all possible constructions that result in a surface VO order, and all that result in a surface OV order. For the purposes of the psycholinguistic theories of interest here, this is legitimate: dependency lengths are calculated based on the linear distance between words. Earlier attempts to predict processing difficulty as a function of the syntactic operations thought to be used in deriving a sentence made little progress and were abandoned (see Fodor, Bever, & Garrett, 1974).

However, equating all structures with the same order of object and verb obscures potential differences that prove to be relevant both in the choice of word orders and in the change towards VO. Regardless of which syntactic theory is chosen to describe the data, it is likely that the frequency of V2 sentences influenced the change from OV to VO.

In OE, OVS sentences were more common when the object was given, but the reanalysis of the preverbal position as a marker of syntactic rather than information structural status led to the loss of this order, and perhaps to the introduction of alternative constructions to express a nonsubject topic (see Los, 2009). Of course, this is not the whole picture: all Germanic languages seem to have had V2 at some point, and as many of these have remained stable as have switched. The V2 construction may therefore be an "enabling" cause for change in that it provides an SVO structure, but cannot be a "sufficient" cause.

Unfortunately, information structure is not annotated in this data. It is likely that object length is related to givenness, if old or more accessible material can be expressed with shorter referring expressions. Thus, shorter objects might be predicted to appear preverbally in OE. Including pronominality in the model should control for this possibility to a large extent, as given referents are typically pronominal. Even so, without explicitly controlling for accessibility or givenness, it's not clear how much of the residual effect is "purely" due to object length, and how much due to something else with which it is correlated. Hawkins' (1994) original theory suggested that weight is the primary determinant of word order, and that other putative influences like information status in fact only affect order choices through their correlation with phrase complexity or length. However, there is more recent evidence for both weight and accessibility/givenness having independent roles: given two NPs of similar weight, speakers of present-day English are more likely to choose a word order that puts given information first; but when both NPs are given, they are also more likely to put the heavier one last. For more discussion of these issues, see J. Arnold et al., 2000; Wasow, 2002; J. E. Arnold, this volume; Jaeger, this volume. Unfortunately, the annotation needed to tackle the problem in this historical data is currently lacking.

In summary, the results here confirm that relationships between weight and word order like those discussed by Wasow, 2002, can be identified even in the textual record of a long dead language. It seems likely that universal processing preferences underlie these trends; perhaps a preference for syntactic structures with shorter total dependency lengths. The data here do not disentangle this hypothesis from the simpler principle that heavy material should be placed last, but there is limited evidence from other work that the dependency hypothesis may prove a better explanation.

Acknowledgments

In addition to Tom's guidance and encouragement, this work has benefited enormously from generous advice and ideas from Florian Jaeger, and from ongoing conversations with Elizabeth Traugott. I'm also grateful for input from the organizers and participants of the 2007 Interdisciplinary Approaches to Relative Clauses Workshop, the 2008 Complex Systems & Language Workshop, and the 2009 LSA Symposium on Individual Differences in Language, as well as the reviewers and editors of this volume. Any errors are my own.

References

Allen, C. (1999). *Case marking and reanalysis: Grammatical relations from Old to Early Modern English.* Oxford, UK: Oxford University Press.

Allen, C. (2000). Obsolescence and sudden death in syntax: The decline of verb-final order in Early Middle English. In R. Bermudez-Ortero, D. Denison, R. M. Hogg, & C. B. McCully (Eds.), *Generative theory and corpus studies: A dialogue from 10 ICEHL* (pp. 3–25). Berlin: Mouton de Gruyter.

Arnold, J., Wasow, T., Losongco, A., & Ginstrom, R. (2000). Heaviness vs. newness: The effects of structural complexity and discourse status on constituent ordering. *Language, 76*, 28–55.

Arnold, J. E. (this volume). Ordering choices in production: For the speaker or for the listener? In E. M. Bender & J. E. Arnold (Eds.), *Language from a cognitive perspective: Grammar, usage, and processing.* Stanford: CSLI.

Behaghel, O. (1909). Beziehungen zwischen Umfang und Reihenfolge von Satzgliedern. *Indogermanische Forschungen, 25.*

Cohen, J. (1983). The cost of dichotomization. *Applied Psychological Measurement, 7*, 249–253.

Fodor, J., Bever, G., & Garrett, M. (1974). *The psychology of language.* New York, NY: McGraw-Hill.

Gelman, A. (2008). Scaling regression inputs by dividing by two standard deviations. *Statistics in Medicine, 27*, 2865–2873.

Gelman, A., & Hill, J. (2006). *Data analysis using regression and multilevel/hierarchical models.* Cambridge, UK: Cambridge University Press.

Gibson, E. (2000). The dependency locality theory: A distance-based theory of linguistic complexity. In A. Marantz, Y. Miyashita, & W. O'Neil (Eds.), *Image, language, brain: Papers from the first mind articulation project symposium*. Cambridge, MA: MIT Press.

Görlach, M. (1997). *The linguistic history of English: An introduction*. Basingstoke, UK: Macmillan.

Haeberli, E. (2002). Inflectional morphology and the loss of verb-second in english. In D. Lightfoot (Ed.), *Syntactic effects of morphological change*. Oxford, UK: Oxford University Press.

Hawkins, J. A. (1994). *A performance theory of order and constituency*. Cambridge, UK: Cambridge University Press.

Hawkins, J. A. (2004). *Efficiency and complexity in grammars*. Oxford, UK: Oxford University Press.

Hawkins, J. A. (this volume). Discontinuous dependencies in corpus selections: Particle verbs and their relevance for current issues in language processing. In E. M. Bender & J. E. Arnold (Eds.), *Language from a cognitive perspective: Grammar, usage, and processing*. Stanford: CSLI.

Hinterhölzl, R., & Petrova, S. (2010). From V1 to V2 in West Germanic. *Lingua, 120*, 315–328.

Hogg, R. (2006). Old English dialectology. In A. van Kemenade & B. Los (Eds.), *The handbook of the history of English* (pp. 395–416). Oxford, UK: Oxford University Press.

Jaeger, T. F. (2008). Categorical data analysis: Away from ANOVAs (transformation or not) and towards logit mixed models. *Journal of Memory and Language, 59*(4), 434–446.

Jaeger, T. F. (this volume). Corpus-based research on language production: Information density and reducible subject relatives. In E. M. Bender & J. E. Arnold (Eds.), *Language from a cognitive perspective: Grammar, usage, and processing*. Stanford: CSLI.

Jaeger, T. F., & Norcliffe, E. (2009). The cross-linguistic study of sentence production. *Language and Linguistics Compass, 3*, 866–887.

Johnson, D. E. (2009). Getting off the GoldVarb standard: Introducing Rbrul for mixed-effects variable rule analysis. *Language and Linguistics Compass, 3*, 359–383.

Kemenade, A. van. (1987). *Syntactic case and morphological case in the history of English*. Dordrecht, The Netherlands: Foris.

Ker, N. (1957). *Catalogue of texts containing Anglo-Saxon*. Oxford, UK: Oxford University Press.

Kohonen, V. (1978). *On the development of English word order in religious prose around 1000 AD*. Turku, Finland: Research Institute of the Abo Akademi Foundation.

Koopman, W. (1997). Another look at clitics in Old English. *Transactions of the Philological Society, 95*, 73–93.

Kroch, A., & Taylor, A. (2000). Penn-Helsinki parsed corpus of Middle English (2nd ed.) [Computer software manual].

Kroch, A., Taylor, A., & Ringe, D. (2000). The Middle English verb-second constraint: A case study in language contact and language change. In S. Herring, L. Schoesler, & P. van Reenen (Eds.), *Textual parameters in older language* (pp. 353–391). Philadelphia: John Benjamins.

Kytö, M. (1996). *Manual to the diachronic part of the Helsinki corpus of English texts: Coding conventions and lists of source texts.* (Helsinki: Department of English, University of Helsinki)

Los, B. (2009). The consequences of the loss of verb-second in English: Information structure and syntax in interaction. *English Language and Linguistics, 13*, 97–125.

Petrova, S. (2006). A discourse-based approach to verb placement in early West Germanic. *Interdisciplinary Studies on Information Structure, 5*, 153–185.

Petrova, S., & Solf, M. (2008). Rhetorical relations and verb placement in early Germanic. a cross linguistic study. In C. Fabricius-Hansen & W. Ramm (Eds.), *'Subordination' vs. 'coordination' in sentence and text: A cross-linguistic perspective* (pp. 333–351). Amsterdam, The Netherlands: John Benjamins.

Pintzuk, S. (1991). *Phrase structures in competition: Variation and change in Old English word order.* Unpublished doctoral dissertation, University of Pennsylvania.

Pintzuk, S., & Kroch, A. (1989). The rightward movement of complements and adjuncts in the Old English of Beowulf. *Language Variation and Change, 1*, 115–143.

Pintzuk, S., & Taylor, A. (2004). Objects in Old English: Why and how early English isn't Icelandic. *York Papers in Linguistics*, 137–150.

Pintzuk, S., & Taylor, A. (2006). The loss of OV order in the history of English. In A. van Kemenade & B. Los (Eds.), *The handbook of the history of English* (pp. 249–278). Oxford, UK: Oxford University Press.

Quirk, R., Greenbaum, S., Leech, G., & Svartvik, J. (1972). *A grammar of contemporary English.* New York, NY: Seminar Press.

Sawyer, P. H. (1968). *Anglo-Saxon charters, an annotated list and bibliography.* London: Royal Historical Society.

Seoane, E. (2006). Information structure and word order change: The passive as an information-rearranging strategy in the history of

English. In A. van Kemenade & B. Los (Eds.), *The handbook of the history of English* (pp. 360–391). Oxford, UK: Oxford University Press.

Snider, N., & Zaenen, A. (2006). Animacy and syntactic structure: Fronted NPs in English. In M. Butt, M. Dalrymple, & T. H. King (Eds.), *Intelligent linguistic architectures: Variations on themes by Ron Kaplan.* Stanford, CA: CSLI Publications.

Stallings, L., MacDonald, M., & O'Seaghdha, P. (1998). Phrasal ordering constraints in sentence production: Phrase length and verb disposition in heavy-NP shift. *Journal of Memory and Language*, *39*, 392–417.

Szmrecsányi, B. M. (2004). On operationalizing syntactic complexity. In G. Purnelle, C. Fairon, & A. Dister (Eds.), *Le poids des mots: Proceedings of the 7th international conference on textual data statistical analysis* (Vol. 2, p. 1032-1039). Louvain-la-Neuve, Belgium: Presses universitaires de Louvain.

Taylor, A., Warner, A., Pintzuk, S., & Beths, F. (2003). The York-Toronto-Helsinki parsed corpus of Old English prose [Computer software manual].

Traugott, E. (2007). Old English left-dislocations: Their structure and information status. *Folia Linguistica*, *41*, 405–441.

Wasow, T. (1997). Remarks on grammatical weight. *Language Variation and Change*, *9*, 81-105.

Wasow, T. (2002). *Postverbal behavior.* Stanford, CA: CSLI Publications. (Distributed by University of Chicago Press)

Yamashita, H., & Chang, F. (2001). "Long before short" preference in the production of a head-final language. *Cognition*, *81*, B45–B55.

12

Investigating Syntactic Persistence in Corpora

NEAL SNIDER

Preface

I was first inspired to the work reported in this paper when I read *Postverbal Behavior* (Wasow, 2002), and my subsequent conversations with Tom. Tom's work makes a strong case for the importance of corpus work, and certainly inspired me to use corpora as a primary source of data in my research. More importantly, to me, Tom's work provides a convincing argument that linguistic theorists should pay attention to empirical results from the psycholinguistic literature, and those who perform empirical studies using experiments or corpora should take linguistic theories seriously as hypotheses to be tested by their studies. This paper falls into the former category: I review the relevant literature on syntactic persistence and argue why it is relevant to syntactic theory, and then provide two case studies exemplifying how it can be examined in natural language corpora.

1 Introduction

Syntactic persistence is a phenomenon in which syntactic structures are re-used in conversation, monologue, or other language use. For example, in the dialogue below from the Switchboard corpus (Godfrey, Holliman, & McDaniel, 1992):

Language from a Cognitive Perspective.
Emily M. Bender and Jennifer Arnold, Editors
Copyright © 2011, CSLI Publications.

(1) I don't feel we should *loan them money* ... I wish our leaders were really seeking the Lord on these things, and if we feel led to *give a country money* to help them, fine...

The speaker first chooses the double object (DO) dative construction *loan them money*, even though the prepositional object (PO) construction is possible (*loan money to them*). Later, when the speaker chooses to produce another dative, they again choose the DO alternate. This is an instance of persistence. Of course it is possible that the speaker chose the DO both times for independent reasons, thus persistence cannot be detected with certainty on one token, and many tokens are necessary along with statistical tests and controls (statistical or via experimental design) to determine whether persistence has occurred. In this paper, I argue that syntactic persistence is relevant to syntactic theory, using data from the literature. Determining what types of structures persist in natural language use is an important way to probe the structure of syntactic representations employed in language use. I also present two case studies of persistence using corpus data, and discuss the empirical techniques that are particular to this phenomenon.

1.1 Importance of Persistence in the Study of Language

Persistence is an extremely important phenomenon in the study of the representations involved in language processing and dialogue. It was first discovered by corpus- and socio-linguists (Sankoff & Laberge, 1978; Poplack, 1980; Weiner & Labov, 1983; Estival, 1985), but experimental psychologists (Bock, 1986; Pickering & Branigan, 1998) have argued most strongly for its role in illuminating the representations involved in language processing. In the psychological literature, persistence is often called "priming", as part of a more general process (i.e. occurring in both production and comprehension) where the processing of a stimulus (the 'target') is facilitated if a similar stimulus (the 'prime') has been processed previously. This facilitation is greater the more similar the prime and the target, and in fact only occurs if they are similar along some cognitive dimension. As Branigan, Pickering, Liversedge, Stewart, and Urbach (1995) argue, this is why priming can illuminate the mental representation of linguistic knowledge, because if people's behavior is sensitive to this similarity, then that similarity must arise from the two structures having the same cognitive representation of that dimension. Thus, by experimentally finding the dimensions of similarity between stimuli that cause priming, one can determine the nature of the mental representations of those stimuli.

As an example, priming has played a key role in the study of the mental lexicon and how mental representations of words are structured. Lexical priming is studied as the facilitation in comprehending or producing a word when that word or a similar word has recently been processed. The mental lexicon has been argued to be a structured network on the basis of frequency (Scarborough, Cortese, & Scarborough, 1977; Forster & Davis, 1984; Norris, 1984; Perea & Rosa, 2000), similarity (Ratcliff & McKoon, 1981), and neighborhood density (Perea & Rosa, 2000; Anaki & Henik, 2003) effects (among others) on priming.

Syntactic persistence and priming have also been used as evidence to decide between different theories of syntactic representation and grammar, although it has not yet made much impact on linguistic theories. For example, Bock (1989) found that benefactives with a PP ("the secretary was baking a cake for her boss") primed the dative PO alternant just as well as a dative PO prime did ("the secretary was taking a cake to her boss"). These results argue that the benefactive and dative constructions share a level of abstract syntactic representation that is independent of their lexical semantics and argument structure, and also that there is an abstract PP representation independent of its lexical head (*for* or *to*). Bock and Loebell (1990) weighed in on the debate whether the passives and actives were related by a lexical rule or by a syntactic one (see Bresnan, 1978, for discussion of the debate about the lexical status of the passive). They found that sentences with locative *by*-phrases ("the 747 was landing by the airport's control tower") primed passives just as well as actual passive constructions ("the 747 was alerted by the airport's control tower"), or perhaps only slightly less, (Potter & Lombardi, 1998). This indicates that there is an abstract level of phrase structure that is shared by the locative and passive constructions, and argues against theories that analyze one structure as involving a passive transformation.

More recently, Griffin and Weinstein-Tull (2003) performed a series of priming experiments relevant to the debate over the representation of subject-to-object raising and control constructions (as discussed in Runner, 2006). Both subject-to-object raising ("A teaching assistant reported the exam to be too difficult") and control ("Rover begged his owner to be more generous with food,") constructions have a verb followed by an object NP and an infinitival VP, but only control verbs assign a semantic role to their object NPs. Some syntactic theories hold that the two constructions involve radically different syntax, with raising, but not control, involving a transformation via Exceptional Case Marking (Chomsky, 1981). Other theories hold that they have the same syntactic analysis in that both involve a transformation (Boeckx &

Hornstein, 2004), or that neither involves a transformation (Pollard & Sag, 1994). Griffin and Weinstein-Tull performed a production priming experiment that tested whether raising and control structures have the same representation. Their experiment utilized priming of the choice between the subject-to-object raising structure ("A teaching assistant reported the exam to be too difficult") and the sentential complement structure ("A teaching assistant reported that the exam was too difficult,"). They found that both subject-to-object raising and control structures prime the choice of a subject-to-object raising structure versus a baseline prime, although raising structures prime raising a bit more than control structures do. These results indicate that raising and control constructions share a similar representation at some level because both prime raising to an extent, but the fact that there is slightly less priming of raising by control shows that semantic roles are also part of the representation because priming is sensitive to the extra semantic role that control structures have but raising does not.

In summary, these studies show that studies of syntactic persistence can provide interesting evidence that tests the predictions of syntactic theories. See Pickering and Ferreira (2008) for an overview of the various constructions that have been shown to prime.

Persistence effects are also very important in the study of coordination of reference in dialogue. Clark and Wilkes-Gibbs (1990) showed that interlocutors using dialogue to successfully complete a task coordinate their referring expressions through whole or partial repetition, as they come to use the same referring expression for an object. In this tradition, the repetition and persistence is evidence of coordination in dialogue (Clark & Brennan, 1991), in contrast to the mechanistic theories of dialogue that involve persistence and priming (Pickering & Garrod, 2004). If priming is an epiphenomenon of the mechanism by which we maintain common ground in dialogue, then it will be very important to understand how persistence effects relate to successful communication, and there is some evidence that interlocutors that reuse each others' syntactic structures more have greater success in a dialogue task (Reitter, Moore, & Keller, 2006).

Persistence effects are extremely useful in probing the representations involved in language processing. In the next sections, I will present two case studies discuss the practical issues that arise in measuring persistence effects.

1.2 How Persistence is Measured

Most structural persistence experiments measure the effect of persistence on production (but see Traxler & Foss, 2000, for persistence in comprehension). A typical structural persistence study relies on syntactic variables, pairs (or sets of constructions) that are different in structure, but with respect to meaning, are essentially paraphrases of one another. Classic examples are the dative alternation and the voice alternation. The dative alternation is exemplified as follows (the first is drawn from the Switchboard corpus):

(2)　a.　"we ... give [a country] [money]" (DO)

　　　b.　we give [money] [to a country] (PO)

These two sentences are basically paraphrases of one another, but have different word orders, so the dative may be called a syntactic variable. The voice alternation is as follows (again the first is from Switchboard):

(3)　a.　she was charged with murder (Passive)

　　　b.　they charged her with murder (Active)

These sentences have the same basic meaning, where an unnamed entity charges a woman with murder, but the first uses passive syntax and the second uses active syntax with a generic subject. Persistence occurs when one of these constructions (say PO) is more likely to be produced when it is preceded by another token of that construction (PO). This persistence effect can be measured experimentally, or through a statistical analysis of a corpus of language.

Persistence for the voice alternation in a corpus of natural speech was shown by Weiner and Labov (1983). Persistence for the dative alternation in a corpus was shown by Gries (2005) and Bresnan, Cueni, Nikitina, and Baayen (2007). Szmrecsányi (2005) showed persistence for several other constructions using corpus. These researchers showed that studying persistence in a corpus requires that the one take more care with controls in analyzing the data because there are many reasons that a speaker or writer might choose to use the same construction on two given instances besides the fact one instance occurred right after the other. For example, choice of word order is often driven by the relative givenness of one argument, so two utterances might involve the same structure because their arguments have the same information structural relation. The earliest studies did not always carefully control for such factors, although more recent ones have applied such controls either by including them in a statistical model (Bresnan et al., 2007; Szmrecsányi, 2005) or by selecting a more controlled data set (Gries, 2005). These studies show that one must control for many other factors that influence the choice of construction in a given instance. There are also particular techniques that one needs to use in extracting and measuring persistence in a corpus, and these techniques differ slightly depending on whether the corpus is of spoken or written language. In the next two sections, I will present detailed case studies of how to examine persistence in corpora. The first section deals with studying persistence in a corpus of spoken dialogue, the second with a corpus of written texts.

2 Persistence in a Spoken Corpus

Studying persistence in spoken dialogue is of particular interest because of the naturalness of the task over experimental methods that do not involve dialogue or an interlocutor, and because it presents a way to measure coordination in dialogue. Most studies of persistence in spoken dialogue have used corpora (Gries, 2005; Szmrecsányi, 2005; Bresnan et al., 2007), although some experiments have used controlled dialogue tasks (Branigan, Pickering, & Cleland, 2000).

In this section, I present a study of persistence of the voice alternation in a spoken corpus. Usually when production of the voice alternation is studied (e.g. Bock, 1986), the two structures involved are the active transitive (4a) and the "full" passive (4b):

(4) a. The police invaded their privacy.

b. Their privacy was invaded by the police.

However, full passives are extremely rare in spoken conversation, and they account for only 149 of the 2661 passives in Switchboard. This is too small a number to conduct a fully controlled study. Therefore, following Weiner and Labov (1983), I consider the true syntactic variable in the voice alternation to involve the agentless passive (5a) and the impersonal active (5b). Agentless passives do not include a *by*-phrase containing an agent NP, and impersonal actives are actives with a generic subject such as "you" or "they".

(5) a. ...you don't feel *your privacy has been invaded* any time recently... (Switchboard conversation 4834)

b. ...if I deviate from social norms of behavior, if I run up and down the street yelling or something, *someone's going to invade my privacy* very quickly... (Switchboard conversation 2012)

2.1 Data and Methods

The Structure of the Corpus

The Switchboard corpus (Godfrey et al., 1992) is a corpus of spoken English that was compiled from telephone conversations. It is particularly useful for the current study because it is a large collection of natural-istic language data. This corpus has also been annotated to make it more useful for syntactic studies. The Penn Treebank Project (Marcus, Santorini, & Marcinkiewicz, 1994) of the Linguistic Data Consortium released a version of Switchboard annotated for part of speech and hierarchical syntactic structure. This annotation was essential for the extraction of passives from the corpus. Also, some of the NPs in the Switchboard Treebank were also annotated for animacy and informa-tion status by the Edinburgh-Stanford LINK project, as in the following example:

(6) (NP-N405271_MARKABLE_human_new (DT the) (NN electri-cian))

The annotation indicates that *the electrician* referred to with this NP has *human* animacy and *new* information status, which means it has not been referred to before. This annotation is essential for extracting one of the voice alternations, the impersonal active because there was a separate annotation category for NPs with generic referents like some instances of *you* and *they*. In addition, this annotation allows one to extract animacy- and givenness-related control factors for the patient argument in each token of the voice alternation.

Voice Alternation Data

For the passive study, I extracted passives and actives from the animacy- and information-status-annotated Switchboard Treebank. A passive is annotated in the Treebank as a past participle verb (VPN) that is either a sister of an NP dominating a trace, or a sister of an S that dominates an NP-SBJ that dominates a trace. This disjunction in the passive verb's argument allows the pattern to capture both transitives and subject-to-object raising and control verbs (which are analyzed in the Treebank as taking sentential complements with a subject trace). I ignored 'pseudopassives', where the object of a preposition is passivized (there are only 57 in the Treebank Switchboard). The passive participle is also the sister of a verb that is a form of *be* or *get*[1]. Certain partici-ples were excluded because they were not considered to be passivizable (*been, had,* and *supposed*). A schematic tree representing this pattern is shown in Figure (1).

This pattern finds 2661 passives in the Treebank Switchboard. In order to extract features of the passivized patient argument, I made use

---

[1] Of course there are reduced passives such as *the price attached to it*, but the passive participles are inconsistently coded as verbs or adjectives, so I excluded them

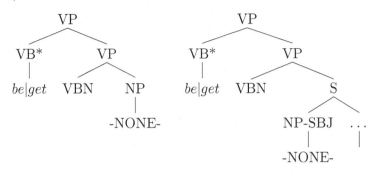

FIGURE 1 Basic Treebank trees for a VP containing a passive participle

of the fact that the passive participle's argument's trace is coindexed with the verb's subject. A pattern that implements this simple heuristic extracts 1604 passive patients. However, I want to extract all of the passive patients, so several *tgrep2* patterns are actually required to implement the relatively simple heuristic for finding passives because, although the passive argument trace is coindexed with the subject, the subject might also be in a long-distance dependency or raising/control structure and therefore may also contain a trace. I developed these passive patient patterns one class of syntactic structure at a time, until I had identified 16 different configurational relations between the passive verb and its subject. There are some passive verbs (151) that do not have a patient argument that matches one of these patterns, but these are all fragments where the patient is not mentioned, purpose clauses and gerunds where the subject of the passive cannot be determined, or parsing mistakes in the Treebank. All the passive *tgrep2* patterns may be found in Snider (2008).

In order to extract the actives in the voice alternation, I extracted all verbs that did not match the patterns in Figure (1) but still were a monotransitive (where the verb has one object argument, *e.g. hit* in *The boy hit the ball*) or subject-to-obect raising/control verb (exemplified in section 1.1), a total of 40585 verbs. Next, I extracted the object NPs of these verbs, or, if the object was in a long-distance dependency, the NPs that were coreferential with the verb's object NP. The patterns used to extract the objects were the same as those used to extract passive objects, which extracts all objects that contain traces because they are in a long-distance dependency, plus two patterns to extract transitive and raising/control objects that appeared *in situ* (this was the vast majority of the object NPs, 34374). Extracting the subjects of the actives is extremely important because the information status of the subject determines whether the active is impersonal and therefore an alternant for the passive in the syntactic variable of the voice alternation (Weiner & Labov, 1983). Such subjects could be identified from the information status coding: NP subjects marked as "generic". Subjects are more difficult to capture in the Treebank because, even though they are coded with the tag NP-SBJ, there is no coding to link a subject with its verb, and of course, the subject can also be in a long-distance or raising/control dependency. They can also be embedded very deeply below several modal and auxiliary verbs or in conjunctions. Most of the subjects were not in long distance dependencies, but were embedded within 1 to 5 auxiliary verb phrases (27989 of 43273). However, I wanted to extract all subjects, so I carefully developed patterns that extract all of the subjects of actives, including those in long-distance dependencies, except subjects and verbs that are in trees that are parsed incorrectly, and as such have patterns that do not generalize or will lead to the extraction of spurious subject-verb relations. There are a total of 17 patterns to extract verbs. I extracted all the active and passive verbs, as well as their associated patient and agent NPs (if available), and added them to the database.

2.2 Statistical model of control factors in passive choice

When studying persistence in a corpus, a control model is extremely important because there are many reasons besides persistence that might cause a speaker to repeat a construction. For example, both instances might be in the same information-structural environment, so the same alternation is used because the same referents are being discussed in the same way. Therefore, one must control for these factors to maximize the chance that the observed repetitions are due to persistence. However, as mentioned in the last section, many of the control factors in the database are highly correlated, so their trends, when examined monofactorially, may not reflect the actual effect of the factor on the choice of passive. Therefore, in this section I statistically model the choice of passive using mixed logit models (Breslow & Clayton, 1993; Bates & Sarkar, 2006) using the statistical package R.

Mixed logit models can be thought of as an extension of logistic regression that includes modeling of random effects. Inclusion of random effects is necessary to generalize beyond the speakers in the current data (Clark, 1973). In this study, the random intercept accounts for the fact that speakers may have different rates of passive use. Here and in all following studies, I report the coefficient for each independent variable and its levels of significance. Coefficients in logistic regression models are given in log-odds (the space in which logistic models are fitted to the data). For categorical factors, significant positive coefficients mean that a correct answer is more likely in the tested level of the variable than in the other level. For example, if the coefficient of PRONOMI-NALITY is positive, then having a patient that is a pronoun makes the passive more likely. Negative coefficients mean the opposite, so if the coefficient of SPEAKER SEX=*female* is negative, then a passive is less likely when the speaker is female. For continuous factors, significant positive coefficients indicate how much more likely a passive is for each 1 unit increase in the level of the variable. For example if the coefficient for LOG LENGTH is -0.08, then the passive is $e^{-0.08} = .92$ times more likely, or actually $e^{0.08} = 1.08$ times less likely, for each $e = 2.72$ times longer the patient. I also report the difference in odds between conditions (odds are simply $e^{log-odds}$). Odds range from 0 (for probabilities of 0) to positive infinity (for probabilities of 1), with probabilities of 0.5 corresponding to odds of 1. Odds are a multiplicative scale, so I will talk about an x-fold increase or decrease in odds between conditions. The dependent variable was structure choice, active or passive.

I also report statistical tests on the model. The Wald's Z tests whether the log-odds coefficient of the factor is significantly different from zero, and therefore tests the directionality of the coefficient, whether it is positive, and biases towards the passive, or negative, and biases against the passive. In order to determine whether the factor is significantly predictive in the model (regardless of direction), one performs a likelihood ratio test $(\Delta_x(\Lambda))$. To perform this test, one runs a model with all the factors included in order to determine the log-likelihood of the data according to the full model, where the likelihood is the probability of exactly the observed data being generated by this model. Then, to test for the significance of a factor x, one removes that factor and notes how much the data's log-likelihood changed according to the model. This change in log-likelihood (more precisely 2 times the difference in log-likelihood) is distributed according to the χ^2, so one is able to determine the probability that that factor did not contribute significantly to the model. Further, the χ^2 value literally corresponds to the difference in likelihood of the data assigned by a model with the predictor versus a model without the predictor, so it can be seen as a measure of the predictor's importance in the model. The $\Delta_x(\Lambda)$ test is also robust against collinearity in the model (Agresti, 2002), so even though the factors are highly correlated, one can determine which are actually driving the effects on passive choice.

The coefficients in log-odds and standard errors associated with the control factors are given in the second and third column of Table 1. The corresponding odds coefficients are given the fourth column. The fifth and sixth columns summarize the Wald's Z statistic, which tests whether the coefficients are significantly different from zero. Finally, the last two columns give the χ^2 over the change in data likelihood $(\Delta_x(\Lambda))$ associated with the removal of the predictor (x) from the final model.

TABLE 1 Summary of statistical analysis of passive control factors

Predictor (independent variable)	Parameter estimates			Wald's test		$\Delta_x(\Lambda)$-test	
	Log-odds	S.E.	Odds	Z	P	χ^2	P
Givenness=*old*	0.73	0.19	2.1	3.9	≪ 0.001	8.2	< 0.003
Animacy	0.66	0.14	1.9	4.6	≪ 0.001	11.6	< 0.001
Definiteness	0.25	0.16	1.3	1.5	< .15	1.2	< 0.15
Pronominality	0.05	0.19	1.05	0.26	< 0.8	0	< 1
Person=*local*	0.25	0.21	1.3	1.24	< 0.3	1.1	< 0.25
log(Length)	-0.08	0.11	0.92	-0.7	< 0.5	0.4	< 0.6
Speaker Age	0.01	0.01	1.01	1.1	< 0.3	0.1	< 1
Speaker Sex=*female*	-0.1	0.15	0.99	0.7	< 0.5	0	< 1
Speaker Dialect=*NYC*	0.6	0.3	1.8	1.9	< 0.05	3.3	< 0.05
Verb bias	3.9	0.33	49	12	≪ 0.001	30.7	≪ 0.001

Random effect: Speaker

This model achieves a classification accuracy of 0.834, while a baseline model that only takes into account the overall frequency of agentless passives has an accuracy of 0.795. The model has a Somers' D_{xy} of 0.542. There is clearly much more variance to be captured in the voice alternation, but this model does improve over the baseline.

2.3 Persistence in the Voice Alternation

My investigation of persistence of the voice alternation in the Treebank Switchboard corpus begins with adding a factor to the database that indicates which of the two constructions was used in the previous opportunity for passive choice by either speaker in the dialogue. In addition to making the persistence effect measurable, this also has the effect of reducing the size of the database slightly, because the first opportunity for the voice alternation in the dialogue has no measurable previous construction. I consider a construction a prime if it is passive or any type of active, not just impersonal actives. The "no-prime" cases could also be studied as a baseline comparison in a model of persistence, but there were only 47 tokens without a prime (due to the overall high frequency of transitives regardless of alternant). Therefore only tokens with a prime were included in the analysis. Reducing the database to only those tokens that have a measurable prime reduces it to 2044 (1609 actives and 435 passives). Figure 2 illustrates a spine plot of the proportions of passives and actives by prime construction. The vertical size of each box represents the proportion of target structures produced, and the horizontal size represents the proportion of prime structures produced. The effect of priming is evident in that more passives are produced following a passive than following an active (the upper right box represents a larger proportion on the y-axis than the upper left box), and more actives are produced following an active (the lower left box represents a larger proportion on the y-axis than the lower right). The x-axis shows that active primes still represent the majority of the data. There is an apparent trend of persistence of each construction,

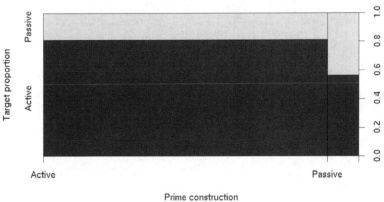

Proportions of prime construction and passive choice

FIGURE 2 Spine plot illustrating the the effect of prime construction on passive choice.

because when the previous construction is passive, 43.9% (90 of 205) tokens are passive, while if the previous construction is active, only 18.8% (345 of 1839) tokens are passive. Thus, the odds $(p/1 - p)$ of of a passive target after a passive prime is 0.78 (roughly 3:4), and the odds of a passive target after a passive prime is 0.23 (roughly 1:4), so a passive is 3.39 times more likely after a passive than after an active, if no other factors are controlled. However, as I argued previously, some of this tendency to repeat structures could be due to other reasons besides persistence, so to show that this effect is statistically significant controlling for all the other factors, I add this persistence factor to the model. I also include the significant control factors from above in order to control as much as possible for persistence effects that are due to the prime and target being in similar linguistic environments, as opposed to the persistence effect purely due the repetition of the construction.

In this analysis, I only include the control factors that were at least of near-marginal significance in order to avoid over-fitting effects in the model. A summary of the statistical analysis of the effect of the prime construction is in Table 2.

TABLE 2 Summary of statistical analysis of the effect of the prime construction on passive choice

Predictor (independent variable)	Parameter estimates			Wald's test		$\Delta_x(\Lambda)$-test	
	Log-odds	S.E.	Odds	Z	P	χ^2	P
Givenness=*old*	0.86	0.15	2.4	7.4	≪ 0.001	17	≪ 0.001
Animacy	0.73	0.13	2.1	5.7	≪ 0.001	15.2	≪ 0.001
Definiteness	0.26	0.16	1.3	1.6	< .15	1.3	< 0.15
Speaker Dialect=*NYC*	0.4	0.3	1.5	1.2	< 0.25	0.7	< 0.3
Verb bias	4.1	0.34	60	12	≪ 0.001	83.5	≪ 0.001
Prime=*passive*	1.26	0.18	3.5	6.9	≪ 0.001	29	≪ 0.001

Random effect: Speaker

The effect of persistence in this data set is highly significant: a passive is 3.5 times as likely in the target if the prime construction is passive than if the prime construction is active. Also, collinearity between the persistence factor and the controls was minimal: all correlations with persistence were less that 0.1. The Somers' D_{xy} of the model is 0.531, so there is a small improvement in fit when persistence is accounted for.

The effect of priming in the fully controlled model (3.5) was approximately the same as that calculated without including any controls (3.39), so the tendency to repeat structures in this data set is not strongly driven by confounding information structural factors and is likely driven by the priming mechanism itself. This study provides a detailed demonstration of how persistence can be measured in a corpus of spoken dialogue, and how one can account for other factors in construction choice besides persistence. I have also described the particular techniques necessary to extract persistence information in a spoken corpus. In the next section, I describe a case study of persistence in a written corpus.

3 Persistence in a Written Corpus

Syntactic persistence can also be found in a written corpus. The Gries (2005) and Szmrecsányi (2005) studies used corpora that contained data from written sources, and found syntactic persistence in the written modality. In this section, I will present a study of syntactic persistence in a corpus of written language, in order to practically illustrate the peculiarities of extracting and analyzing persistence effects in the written modality.

I present a study of persistence of the dative construction in the written portions of the Penn Treebank (Marcus et al., 1994), which consists of portions of the Wall Street Journal and Brown (Kucera & Francis, 1964) corpora. As in the previous study of passive persistence, it is of primary concern to include control factors relating to other predictors of the alternation in the statistical analysis. The dative alternation has been studied in a subset of this corpus before (Bresnan et al., 2007), but the Bresnan et al. study C only used the WSJ portion of the treebank and did not examine persistence effects. Gries (2005) examined persistence in the dative, but did not include the control factors associated with the alternation in the study. Therefore, I present a another conservative study of persistence in written dative use, utilizing a larger corpus and appropriate control factors.

3.1 Data and Methods

The Structure of the Corpus

The data for this study of persistence in a corpus of written language comes from the Wall Street Journal and Brown corpus portions of the Penn Treebank. Just as in the previous study, the corpus is annotated for part of speech and hierarchical syntactic structure. However, unlike the data in the previous study, there exists no version of the corpus that contains annotation of the NPs for animacy and givenness features of their referent. Therefore, features that can be automatically extracted from the form of the dative NP arguments will be used as approximate controls. These controls performed fairly well compared to previous work, as will be explained in the next section.

Dative alternation data

The first step in the extraction of dative data is to extract the two dative alternants and their recipient and theme arguments. Recall the two alternants are as follows:

(7) a. "we ... give [a country] [money]" (DO)

  b. we give [money] [to a country] (PO)

The Double Object alternant has a VP that dominates the dative verb, followed by the recipient NP ("a country" in the example above), followed by the theme NP ("money"). The Prepositional Object (PO) alternant has a VP that dominates the dative verb, followed by the theme NP ("money"), followed by a PP headed by *to* whose object is the recipient NP ("to a country"). These patterns can be implemented in the following *tgrep2* patterns:

(8)   a. @ OBJ /^NP[^-]/|/^NP$/;
         (a "macro" defining the object of a verb)

      b. DO:
         /^VB/=verb $ (@OBJ=rec $.. @OBJ=th)

      c. PO:
         /^VB/=verb $ (@OBJ=th $.. (/^PP-DTV/ < @OBJ=rec))

Using these patterns, I extracted each token in the corpus of both alternants, along with their verbs and arguments. I also used some slightly more complicated patterns, like those described in the passive study, to extract arguments that were in long-distance dependencies or passives. I only included tokens of verbs that participate in the dative alternation, defined as the set of verbs used in the Bresnan *et al* study.

I also extracted various features of the verb and arguments to use as control factors in the analysis. I extracted the DEFINITENESS of both the recipient and theme, which was defined using Gundel's definiteness hierarchy (Gundel, Hedberg, & Zacharski, 1993); an NP was definite if it contained a definite determiner, a possessor NP, or was a proper name or pronoun. I also added factors indicating whether the theme and recipient were pronominal. I also added the LENGTH in words of the argument NPs, PRONOMINALITY, and PERSON (local or non-local). I also lemmatized the verbs to their base forms, so that verb bias could be modeled. Again, these factors were defined just as for the passive study above. The final data set, which includes only those tokens for which a value for each control factor could be determined, contains 1156 tokens of the DO, and 437 tokens of the PO.

3.2   Statistical Model of Control Factors in Dative Choice

Just as in the passive study, the control factors in dative choice in written language were modeled using mixed logit models. All the factors mentioned above were added to a model as fixed effects, except for verb, which was modeled as a random effect (to facilitate comparison with the Bresnan et al. study C, which used a subset of this data set). Model comparison and 40-fold validation was used to determine which factors made the data more likely according to a model that contained them. The interactions of all factors with corpus (WSJ or Brown) were tested, and only one approached marginal significance, so it was included. Also, PERSON of the theme contained only 4 instances of local person, so this factor was excluded. Table 3 gives the results of the control model. The positive response is PO. The model fits the data

TABLE 3 Summary of statistical analysis of dative control factors

Predictor (independent variable)	Parameter estimates			Wald's test		$\Delta_x(\Lambda)$-test	
	Log-odds	S.E.	Odds	Z	P	χ^2	P
Recipient definite	-0.56	0.19	0.57	-2.8	< 0.005	6.2	< 0.05
Theme definite	0.86	0.23	2.4	3.6	< 0.001	10	< 0.005
log(Rec length)	1.98	0.29	1.3	7.2	≪ 0.001	47	≪ 0.001
log(Th length)	-4.91	0.92	0.007	-5.3	≪ 0.001	214	≪ 0.001
Rec pronominal	-3.42	0.59	0.03	-5.7	≪ 0.001	82	≪ 0.001
Th pronominal	1.43	0.55	4.1	2.5	< 0.01	16	≪ 0.001
Rec local person	0.92	0.88	2.5	1.0	> 0.25	1.8	> 0.15
Corpus = WSJ	0.38	0.48	1.5	0.7	> 0.4	1.5	> 0.4
Corpus*log(ThLen)	1.41	0.95	4.1	1.4	> 0.1	1.8	> 0.1

Random effect: Verb

fairly well, with a Somers' D_{xy} of 0.891, and a classification accuracy of 0.890, on unseen data (using 40-fold validation). A baseline model that only takes into account the frequency of each construction has an accuracy of 0.726. Compare this model to the classification accuracy of 0.92 reported in the Bresnan et al. (2007) study C on the WSJ Treebank, which had hand-annotated animacy and givenness factors. The controls used here clearly capture a lot of variance, despite the fact that they were automatically extracted, and their effects are all comparable to those in Bresnan et al. study C.

This analysis indicates that this is a reasonable control model to use as a starting point in a study of persistence of the dative alternation in written language. In the next section, I describe how the persistence was extracted and analyzed.

3.3 Persistence in the Dative Alternation

Studying persistence effects in written language has some particular problems. There is no dialogue in the written materials of the Brown and WSJ corpora, but each article can be viewed as a sort of mono-logue, in which the writer's previous use of a construction may make that construction more likely later in the document. As in the previous study, persistence was defined as a previous use of a dative alternant in the document. However, determining if two tokens occurred in the same document required some pre-processing of the corpus to indicate which dialogue that each token occurred in. Prime-target pairs were defined as those tokens that had no intervening datives in the text of the same document. 753 tokens had no available prime, so unlike in the passive study above, persistence could be modeled as a three-level factor with a baseline "no-prime" case. Figure 3 shows the distribution of primes and targets in the data, there is a clear tendency for DOs to follow DOs and POs to follow POs, because more POs are produced following a PO than following an DO (the upper right box represents a larger proportion on the y-axis than the upper left box), and more DOs are produced following an DO (the lower left box represents a larger proportion on the y-axis than the lower right). There is a apparent trend of persistence of each construction, because when the previous construction is PO, 44.8% (91 of 203) tokens are PO, while if the previous construction is DO, only 15.9% (101 of 637) tokens are PO, and if there is no prime, 32.5% (245 of 753) are PO. Thus, the odds $(p/1 - p)$ of a PO target after a PO prime is 0.81 (roughly 9:11), the odds of a PO target after a DO prime is 0.19 (roughly 1:5), and the odds of a PO with no prime is 0.48 (roughly 12:25). Thus a PO is 1.7 times more likely after a PO than with no prime, if no other factors are controlled.

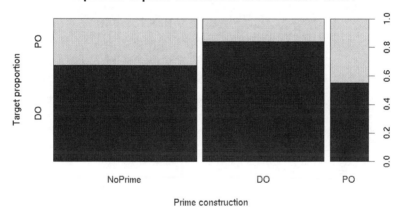

FIGURE 3 Spine plot illustrating the the effect of prime construction on dative choice.

To determine if the trend of persistence shown in the figure above is significant controlling for other factors, a factor representing the presence of a prime construction was added to the model of the previous section. The results of the model are summarized in Table 4. There is a clear effect of persistence in this data set, the presence of a previous PO construction makes the PO 1.9 times more likely than if there was no prime, and the effect is highly significant. There is also a marginal effect

Predictor	Parameter estimates			Wald's test		$\Delta_x(\Lambda)$-test	
(independent variable)	Log-odds	S.E.	Odds	Z	P	χ^2	P
Recipient definite	-0.56	0.19	0.57	-2.8	< 0.005	6.1	< 0.05
Theme definite	0.9	0.23	2.4	3.8	< 0.001	10	< 0.005
log(Rec length)	1.92	0.28	1.3	6.6	≪ 0.001	47	≪ 0.001
log(Th length)	-5.11	0.93	0.007	-5.4	≪ 0.001	214	≪ 0.001
Rec pronominal	-3.41	0.59	0.03	-5.7	≪ 0.001	82	≪ 0.001
Th pronominal	1.42	0.54	4.1	2.5	< 0.01	16	≪ 0.001
Rec local person	0.87	0.88	2.5	0.99	> 0.25	1.8	> 0.15
Corpus = WSJ	0.12	0.49	1.5	0.3	> 0.4	1.4	> 0.4
Corpus*log(ThLen)	1.58	0.96	4.1	1.6	> 0.1	1.7	> 0.1
Prime=PO	0.69	0.24	1.9	2.7	< 0.01	15	≪ 0.001
Prime=DO	-0.39	0.21	0.67	-1.8	< 0.1		

Random effect: Verb

TABLE 4 Summary of statistical analysis of the effect of the prime construction on dative choice

such that a DO prime makes the DO more likely in the target. Also, collinearity between the persistence factors and the controls was minimal: all correlations with persistence were less that 0.15. The model still provides a good fit to the variation in the data, with a Somers' D_{xy} of 0.893, and a classification accuracy of 0.890, on unseen data (using 40-fold validation). Recall that the baseline model that only takes into account the frequency of each construction has an accuracy of 0.726. A possible confound with this study is that the tendency to repeat these constructions may be merely due to each author's individual bias towards one construction or another. This was controlled in the passive study with a random effect of speaker. In this data set, there is too little data from each author, but the cross-validation would reveal such data clustering effects, therefore one can safely conclude that there is a robust persistence effect in written language.

The importance of controlling for other factors when analyzing persistence in corpora can be illustrated very clearly if the data is analyzed in a slightly different way, by excluding tokens without primes, as is sometimes done (Gries, 2005). I also did this in the previous study, but only because there were too few non-primed tokens. If one models the dative data just like the passive data set above by only including the tokens with primes (which reduces the data set to 192 PO and 648 DO), the priming effect calculated without controls is much higher than the effect with controls. Recall that the odds of a PO target after a PO prime is 0.81, and the odds of a PO target after a DO prime is 0.19, making a PO 4.26 times more likely after a PO prime than after a DO prime. In a fully controlled model of this smaller data set with all the factors listed above, the odds are only 2.88 ($p \ll 0.001$). The uncontrolled model vastly overestimates the effect of persistence.

4 Conclusion

The two case studies presented here show how persistence can be measured in corpora of natural language, and demonstrate some of the particular details of conducting a corpus study of persistence in two types of corpora. Study 1 demonstrates how persistence can be measured in natural dialogue, using the example of the the agentless passive alternation. Study 2 demonstrates how to study persistence in written dialogue using the dative alternation. Also, this study demonstrates that persistence effects can be overestimated if other factors are not controlled.

As I argued in the Introduction, the study of structural persistence or priming can provide useful evidence to test theories of linguistic representation and processing. The processing of a target is facilitated by a prime only when the two linguistic structures are related along some representational dimension. Different theories will make different predictions about what structures are similar, and priming studies can test these predictions. In the spirit of Wasow (2002), linguistic theorists should pay attention to the empirical results on language processing, in this case persistence/priming, and those who perform empirical studies using experiments or corpora should take linguistic theories seriously as hypotheses to be tested by their studies.

This paper has also shown in detail how to conduct corpus studies of syntactic persistence. It is my hope that corpus studies of persistence will be increasingly pursued and regarded as complementary to lab-based experimental studies of syntactic persistence. These results further demonstrate how corpus studies can be well-controlled like laboratory studies.

References

Agresti, A. (2002). *Categorical data analysis*. New York: Wiley.

Anaki, D., & Henik, A. (2003). Is there a "Strength Effect" in Automatic Semantic Priming? *Memory and Cognition*, *31*(2), 262–72.

Bates, D., & Sarkar, D. (2006). lme4: Linear mixed-effects models using S4 classes [Computer software manual]. (R package version 0.995-2)

Bock, J. K. (1986). Syntactic persistence in language production. *Cognitive Psychology*, *18*(3), 355-387.

Bock, J. K. (1989). Closed-class immanence in sentence production. *Cognition*, *31*(2), 163-86.

Bock, J. K., & Loebell, H. (1990). Framing sentences. *Cognition*, *35*(1), 1–39.

Boeckx, C., & Hornstein, N. (2004). Movement under Control. *Linguistic Inquiry*, *35*(3), 431–452.

Branigan, H. P., Pickering, M. J., & Cleland, A. A. (2000). Syntactic co-ordination in dialogue. *Cognition*, *75*(2), 13–25.

Branigan, H. P., Pickering, M. J., Liversedge, S. P., Stewart, A. J., & Urbach, T. P. (1995). Syntactic priming: Investigating the mental representation of language. *Journal of Psycholinguistic Research*, *24*(6), 489–506.

Breslow, N. E., & Clayton, D. G. (1993). Approximate inference in generalized linear mixed models. *Journal of the American Statistical Association*, *88*(421), 9–24.

Bresnan, J. (1978). A realistic transformational grammar. In M. Halle, J. Bresnan, & G. Miller (Eds.), *Linguistic theory and psychological reality* (pp. 1–59). MIT Press.

Bresnan, J., Cueni, A., Nikitina, T., & Baayen, H. (2007). Predicting the dative alternation. In G. Bouma, I. Krämer, & Z. J (Eds.), *Cognitive foundations of interpretation* (pp. 69–94). Amsterdam: Royal Netherlands Academy of Science.

Chomsky, N. (1981). *Lectures on government and binding*. Foris, Dordrecht.

Clark, H. H. (1973). The language-as-fixed-effect fallacy: A critique of language statistics in psychological research. *Journal of Verbal Learning and Verbal Behavior*, *12*(4), 335–359.

Clark, H. H., & Brennan, S. E. (1991). Grounding in communication. In J. Levine, L. B. Resnick, & S. D. Teasley (Eds.), *Perspectives on socially shared cognition*. APA, Reading, MA.

Clark, H. H., & Wilkes-Gibbs, D. (1990). Referring as a collaborative process. *Intentions in Communication*, 463–493.

Estival, D. (1985). Syntactic priming of the passive in English. *Text*, *5*, 7–21.

Forster, K. I., & Davis, C. (1984). Repetition priming and frequency attenuation in lexical access. *Journal of Experimental Psychology: Learning, Memory, and Cognition*, *10*(4), 680–698.

Godfrey, J. J., Holliman, E. C., & McDaniel, J. (1992). SWITCHBOARD: Telephone speech corpus for research and development. In *IEEE ICASSP* (pp. 517–520). San Francisco, CA.

Gries, S. T. (2005). Syntactic priming: A corpus-based approach. *Journal of Psycholinguistic Research*, *34*(4), 365–399.

Griffin, Z. M., & Weinstein-Tull, J. (2003). Conceptual structure modulates structural priming in the production of complex sentences. *Journal of Memory and Language*, *49*(4), 537–555.

Gundel, J. K., Hedberg, N., & Zacharski, R. (1993). Cognitive status and the form of referring expressions in discourse. *Language*, *69*(2), 274-307.

Kucera, H., & Francis, W. N. (1964). *A standard sample of present-day edited American English for use with digital computers*. Providence, RI: Linguistics Department, Brown University.

Marcus, M. P., Santorini, B., & Marcinkiewicz, M. A. (1994). Building a large annotated corpus of English: The Penn Treebank. *Computational Linguistics*, *19*(2), 313–330.

Norris, D. (1984). The effects of frequency, repetition and stimulus quality in visual word recognition. *The Quarterly Journal of Experimental Psychology Section A*, *36*(3), 507–518.

Perea, M., & Rosa, E. (2000). Repetition and form priming interact with neighborhood density at a brief stimulus onset asynchrony. *Psychonomic Bulletin and Review*, *7*(4), 668–77.

Pickering, M. J., & Branigan, H. P. (1998). The representation of verbs: Evidence from syntactic priming in language production. *Journal of Memory and Language*, *39*(4), 633-651.

Pickering, M. J., & Ferreira, V. S. (2008). Structural priming: A critical review. *Psychological Bulletin*, *134*(3), 427.

Pickering, M. J., & Garrod, S. (2004). Toward a mechanistic psychology of dialogue. *Behavioral and Brain Sciences*, *27*(02), 169–190.

Pollard, C. J., & Sag, I. A. (1994). *Head-driven phrase structure grammar*. University of Chicago Press.

Poplack, S. (1980). The notion of the plural in Puerto Rican Spanish: Competing constraints on /s/ deletion. In W. Labov (Ed.), *Locating language in time and space* (pp. 55–86). New York: Academic Press.

Potter, M. C., & Lombardi, L. (1998). Syntactic priming in immediate recall of sentences. *Journal of Memory and Language*, *38*, 265–282.

Ratcliff, R., & McKoon, G. (1981). Does activation really spread? *Psychological Review*, *88*(5), 454–462.

Reitter, D., Moore, J. D., & Keller, F. (2006). Priming of syntactic rules in task-oriented dialogue and spontaneous conversation. In *Proceedings of the 28th annual conference of the Cognitive Science Society*.

Runner, J. T. (2006). Lingering challenges to the raising-to-object and object-control constructions. *Syntax*, *9*, 193–213.

Sankoff, D., & Laberge, S. (1978). Statistical dependence among successive occurrences of a variable in discourse. *Linguistic Variation: Methods and Models*, 119–126.

Scarborough, D. L., Cortese, C., & Scarborough, H. S. (1977). Frequency and repetition effects in lexical memory. *Journal of Experimental Psychology: Human Perception and Performance*, *3*, 1–17.

Snider, N. (2008). *An exemplar model of syntactic priming*. Unpublished doctoral dissertation, Stanford University, Stanford, CA.

Szmrecsányi, B. M. (2005). Language users as creatures of habit: A corpus-based analysis of persistence in spoken English. *Corpus Linguistics and Linguistic Theory*, *1*, 113–149.

Traxler, M., & Foss, D. (2000). Effects of sentence on priming in natural language comprehension. *Journal of Experiment Psychology: Learning, Memory & Cognition*, *26*(5), 556–560.

Wasow, T. (2002). *Postverbal behavior*. CSLI Publications, Stanford.

Weiner, E. J., & Labov, W. (1983). Constraints on the agentless passive. *Journal of Linguistics*, *19*, 29–58.

13

Discontinuous Dependencies in Corpus Selections: Particle Verbs and Their Relevance for Current Issues in Language Processing

JOHN A. HAWKINS

Preface

I have been in contact with Tom Wasow and learning from him for well over a dozen years, and he has been a wonderful guide. When he emerged as a psycholinguist from his formal grammar background and after a period of university administration, we discovered we had numerous interests in common, in syntactic weight and complexity, word order, Heavy NP Shift, verb-particle constructions, relative clauses and relativizers, and complement clauses and complementizers. We started talking and I found his approach and his openness so refreshing and his feedback and support invaluable. We exchanged manuscripts, and I was flattered when he devoted a seminar at Stanford to my forthcoming OUP book *Efficiency and Complexity in Grammars*, which then put me in contact with several of his students and with their work. Meanwhile he was a wonderful mentor to my USC student Barbare Lohse (now Barbara Jansing). Without him she and I could not have brought our work on verb particle constructions to a successful conclusion, a publication in *Language* in 2004. He and his students figured prominently at the relative clause conference that I organized at Cambridge in the summer of 2007, and my dialogue with them continues to this day.

Language from a Cognitive Perspective.
Emily M. Bender and Jennifer Arnold, Editors
Copyright © 2011, CSLI Publications.

The collaboration with Barbara Lohse examined the alternation between split (*look the number up*) and joined (*look up the number*) particle verbs in English. The former constitutes a discontinuous dependency and as such provides data of relevance to a number of issues that are currently being fought over in the field of language processing. Many of Tom's current and former Stanford students and collaborators are at the forefront of these debates.

1 Introduction

In this paper I begin by defining some of these general issues in language processing, as I see them. The first issue (section 2.1) involves different kinds of data that are currently being used in psycholinguistics, on-line experimental methodologies, acceptability judgements and corpus data, and the different patterns of results that are emerging and their different consequences for theories of language processing. The second issue (section 2.2) involves conflicting preferences for "locality" versus "antilocality" in syntactic dependencies that are visible within and across these different methodologies. A third issue (section 2.3) concerns the long tradition of constrained capacity models of working memory in psycholinguistics. I question whether the kinds of data to which these models have been applied are adequately explained in terms of the upper limits proposed, suggesting instead that we need to think in terms of different types of efficiency or principles of least effort operating well within whatever upper limits there are. The fourth issue (section 2.4) involves the relationship between production and comprehension, where they are similar and where they are different. An important consideration in any discussion of competing word orders involves the processing of head-final languages like Japanese, which pose real challenges on the surface to the view that production and comprehension mechanisms can be closely aligned.

In section 3 I summarize some of the key predictions and results from my joint work with Tom and Barbara on particle verbs that are relevant to these issues. In section 4 I conclude with remarks about their relevance.

2 Some Current Issues in Language Processing

2.1 On-line versus Acceptability versus Corpus Data

Different kinds of data in psycholinguistics can reveal very different patterns of results, which can then lead to very different theories of processing, of ease versus difficulty, of structural simplicity and complexity, and so on. Discontinuous dependencies in syntax provide striking examples of these different patterns. One of the first sets of studies to draw systematic attention to the differences was conducted on extraposed and unextraposed relative clauses in German by Lars Koniezny and his colleagues (cf. Uszkoreit et al., 1998, and Konieczny, 2000). The data were examined in corpora, in an off-line acceptability judgement task, and in an on-line self-paced reading experiment. The relevant structures are illustrated in (1a) and (1b). In the former the relative clause is adjacent to its nominal head, in the latter it is extraposed:

(1) a. Er hat die Rose [die wunderschön war] hingelegt ...
         (Rel clause adjacent)
         'He has the rose [that beautiful was] laid-down.'

     b. Er hat die Rose hingelegt [die wunderschön war] ...
         (Rel clause extraposed)
         'He has the rose laid-down [that beautiful was] ...'
         He has laid down the rose that was beautiful.

Different patterns of preference in the different kinds of data raise general questions about locality versus anti-locality preferences, about capacity constraints in working memory, and about the production-comprehension relationship. Let us first establish what the different patterns are.

The corpus study by Uszkoreit et al. (1998) set out to test some predictions that were made for this alternation by the Early Immediate Constituents (EIC) principle that I proposed in Hawkins, 1994. EIC and its more recent version, Minimize Domains (MiD, Hawkins, 2004), predict that the adjacent (1a) will be preferred over (1b) in proportion to the *in*creasing potential distance between head noun (*Rose*) and relative, and also in proportion to the *de*creasing weight and complexity of the relative clause itself; the extraposed (1b) will be preferred in proportion to the *de*creasing distance between the two and the *in*creasing weight and complexity of the relative (see Hawkins, 1994, p.69–83, Hawkins, 2004, p.31 for definitions of EIC and MiD, also section 3.1 below, and Hawkins, 1994, p.198–210 and Hawkins, 2004, p.142–146 for precise predictions).

This pattern of preferences was confirmed in Uszkoreit et al.'s data. Figure 1 shows their results for the potential distance prediction. It reproduces the corpus selections for extraposed versus adjacent relatives, expressed as a percentage (as given in their Abbildung 2) and reveals a preference for the extraposed version over short distances (1-3 words) but a strong preference for adjacency over middle (4-6) and long distances (7-9) (the percentage of relatives extraposed over a distance of 1 word was 95.2%, over a distance of 2 words 77.1%, and over a distance of 3 words 34.7%). The corpus consisted of written journalistic German from the Frankfurter Rundschau which was subjected to both automatic and manual parsing techniques. The various subcorpora analysed by Uszkoreit et al. (see their Tabelle 1 as well as Abbildung 2) yielded very similar results. The predicted increase in the frequency of extraposition as a function of the increasing weight of the relative was also supported (see Hawkins, 2004, p.146 ex. (5.32) for a summary of Uszkoreit et al.'s figures). Figure 1 shows a clear crossing and complementary pattern of preferences that follows the predictions of EIC/MiD closely and supports the kind of "locality" principle that underlies EIC/MiD and much related work reported in Gibson (1998, 2000).

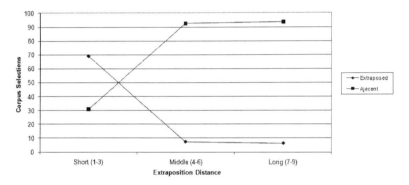

FIGURE 1 Mean corpus selection percentages for extraposed vs. adjacent relatives a different distances

Uszkoreit et al. (1998) and Konieczny (2000) also give data from off-line psycholinguistic studies measuring the relative acceptability of adjacent and extraposed relative clauses and using the magnitude estimation technique of Bard, Robertson, and Sorace (1996). Participants provided a score indicating how much better or worse the current sentence was compared to a given reference sentence (for example if the reference sentence was assigned 100 and the target sentence was judged five times better it received 500). Figure 2 shows the mean acceptability scores for the two relative clause possibilities over a short distance (1 word), a middle distance (3-4 words), and a long distance (5-6 words) (following Abbildung 5 in Uszkoreit et al., 1998, and Table IV and Figure 3 in Konieczny, 2000). As in the pattern of Figure 1, extraposition is judged worse in Figure 2 when there are increasing distances between head and relative. Adjacency is also less preferred in their acceptability data for relative clauses of increasing weight and complexity (see again

Abbildung 5 in Uszkoreit et al., 1998 and Table IV and Figure 3 in Konieczny, 2000). But in contrast to the corpus data, the acceptability data show a strong preference for adjacency over extraposition overall, as seen in Figure 2. Only in the case of the longest possible relative clause of 9-11 words separated by its head from 1 word was extraposition actually preferred in the acceptability task (this is not visible in Figure 2 since this extreme was averaged out with relative clauses of shorter weights in the one-word condition). Whereas the patterns of Figure 1 are predicted by EIC/MiD, therefore, the overall result of Figure 2 is not, though similar tendencies are evident in both.

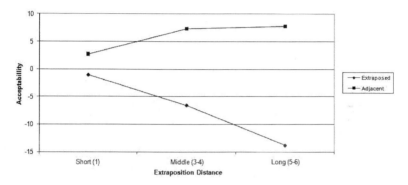

FIGURE 2   Mean acceptabillity scores for extraposed vs. adjacent relatives at different distances

In addition to the off-line data of Figure 2, Konieczny (op cit) conducted an on-line self-paced reading experiment using the same materials as in the off-line acceptability task and measuring reading times at the clause-final matrix verb (*hingelegt*). The experiment revealed that the verb was read systematically faster when the relative clause preceded it, i.e. when the relative clause was adjacent to the head noun, as shown in Figure 3 (which reproduces Konieczny's Table V and Figure 5). There was also a main effect of distance between head noun and relative in the on-line experiment, but not of relative clause weight and complexity.

Konieczny concludes that on-line reading times do not support locality-based predictions. I shall return to this in the next section, but notice first an important general point. Different types of data, and different methodologies, give different patterns of results. Corpus selections show strong EIC/MiD effects in these German structures, with preferences for the extraposed or the adjacent relative depending on the potential distance between head and relative (see Figure 1) and

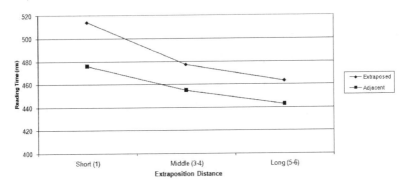

FIGURE 3 Mean reading times at the clause-final verb for extraposed vs.
adjacent relatives at different distances

also on the size and complexity of the relative clause. On-line data show
a consistent preference for the adjacent relative clause (see Figure 3),
with a subsidiary distance effect and no relative clause weight effect.
Off-line acceptability data are inbetween the two, with an overall adjacency preference (see Figure 2) but with both distance and weight
effects evident in the data.

A similar set of differences has been established for the corresponding Extraposition from NP alternation in English (involving pre-verbal
subject NPs) by Francis (2010) exemplified in (2):

(2)   a. New sets [that were able to receive all the TV channels]
          soon appeared.

      b. New sets soon appeared [that were able to receive all the
          TV channels].

Her corpus findings fully support EIC and MiD predictions in terms
of relative clause weight and complexity and in terms of the potential
size of the distance between nominal head and relative. But a self-
paced reading study provided only partial support (extraposed sentences showed an advantage when the relative clause was heavy), while
an acceptability judgement task showed the same preference for adjacency of the relative clause as in German, leading Francis to speculate
that a prescriptive rule banning misplaced modifiers might be impact-
ing native speakers' judgements here.

We have to ask where these different patterns come from and how
we can account for them. EIC/MiD is a principle that assigns a quantified and gradient preference to one structure over another among
alternative, truth-conditionally equivalent sentences. Corpus data that

involve a structural discontinuity with competing demands on language processing provide a challenging test for it and have shown strong support. This suggests, at the very least, that this is a principle that guides structural *selections* in language production, supporting Wasow (1997, 2002)'s point that we need to look at weight effects from the speaker's perspective. On-line self-paced reading data like those of Konieczny (2000), on the other hand, reflect processing ease and speed at certain temporal points in competing structures. These data do not implicate a principle that is relevant for structural selection, since if they did the adjacent structures would be selected almost all the time. Faster processing at the matrix verb does not mean that the relevant structure is necessarily easier to process as a whole, therefore. In fact, the corpus selections suggest that overall structural complexity can be quite independent of ease of processing measured at the verb (compare Figures 1 and 3). (I am grateful to Florian Jaeger for discussion of this point.) Whether the relevant processing facilitations that these on-line data do implicate at the verb are unique to comprehension, or compatible with both production and comprehension models, seems less clear (see section 2.4 below). Language producers could experience points of high and low processing load at different points in their on-line structure generation just like comprehenders do, while still selecting one structure over an alternative based on a global measure of processing ease and minimality for the whole sentence, which is what EIC/MiD is. There is nothing contradictory about this and both the on-line and the corpus data are presumably tapping into different and real aspects of processing. The acceptability ratings, on the other hand, suggest a possible confound resulting from normative bias.

2.2 Locality versus Anti-locality Effects

Gibson's (1998, 2000) Syntactic Prediction Locality Theory (SPLT) is similar in spirit to EIC/MiD and defines many similar preferences, but differs from it in certain ways. It is an on-line measure of processing complexity, whereas EIC/MiD calculates the complexity of each processing domain of a sentence globally in terms of its overall size and in terms of the quantity of syntactic, semantic and other properties that are assigned within it, without regard for the moment-by-moment measurements of processing ease. The ultimate units of processing cost for SPLT are measured in terms of new discourse referents within processing domains, whereas the ultimate units for EIC/MiD are word quantities, though this may just be a convenient and readily measurable shorthand for the full set of syntactic, semantic and other properties that are assigned within each processing domain, with which word quantity totals are claimed to correlate (see Wasow, 2002 and also Szmrecsanyi, 2004 for a demonstration of the correlations between word quantities and other syntactic complexity measures). This difference between SPLT and EIC/MiD may not be an essential one, therefore (Ted Gibson, personal communication).

Konieczny (2000) contrasted the "anti-locality" effects in his study with the predictions of both SPLT and EIC/MiD and this has since led to a number of other experimental findings supporting "anti-locality". The result is a major current debate in the field involving when exactly locality effects will be found, and when not. For example, Vasishth and Lewis (2006) report that clause-final verbs are read faster in Hindi when processing domains are increased through the addition of relative clause modifiers, PPs and adverbs. At the same time they recognize the existence of locality effects. They propose an activation-based model of sentence processing using the ACT-R architecture that combines activation decay and interference (accounting for locality) with the possibility of re-activating dependents, which is argued to account for anti-locality effects. Konieczny (2000) and a number of other studies have appealed instead to the facilitating role that longer processing domains can have in predicting the upcoming matrix verb, making it faster to recognize and read. See, for example, Levy (2008) and Jaeger, Fedorenko, and Gibson (2005) for particularly sophisticated recent developments of this prediction- or "expectation-"based approach to processing, controlling for numerous factors and alternative explanatory possibilities.

What is interesting about the current locality versus anti-locality debate, and about the different data summarized in section 2.1, is that corpora seem to strongly and consistently support locality, when there are alternating pairs of structures to choose from. Anti-locality is supported by a subset of on-line experimental measures.

2.3 Memory Strain versus Efficiency and Least Effort

Gibson's (1998, 2000) SPLT is the latest version in a tradition of working memory models in psychology that build on the idea of "constrained capacity" (cf. e.g. Frazier & Fodor, 1978; Just & Carpenter, 1992). The ceiling effects within this capacity are claimed to make certain sentence types unprocessable beyond the complexity limit. Lewis and Vasishth (2005) and Vasishth and Lewis (2006) have developed their alternative working memory model in terms of activation, using primitives taken from cognitive psychology and from mechanisms of neural activation (cf. e.g. Anderson, 1993).

My own EIC/MiD theory has been widely linked to the constrained capacity tradition, but I have often stated (most recently in Hawkins, 2004, p.268–269) that I make no commitment as to what this capacity may ultimately be, stressing only that processing complexity and difficulty increase as the size and complexity of the different processing domains increase (the constituent recognition domains of Hawkins, 1994, filler-gap domains in Hawkins, 1999, etc). Moreover, all current claims of working memory capacity are derived ultimately from psycholinguistic studies on English and a handful of related languages. They are quite premature at this point and risk defining as unprocessable certain structures that are productive in other language types (see Hawkins, 1994, p.266–7 for illustration of this point, and Hawkins, 2007 and Jaeger & Norcliffe, 2009 for discussion of the urgent need for more cross-linguistic work in sentence processing).

More generally, I believe that many phenomena that have been attributed to working memory capacity are really just the product of Zipfian "least effort" processing and of efficiency (see e.g. Zipf, 1949). Speed in communicating the intended message from speaker to hearer and minimal processing effort in doing so are the two driving forces of efficiency proposed in Hawkins (2004, 2009). The former is captured in the principle of Maximize On-line Processing which defines a preference for selecting and arranging linguistic forms so as to provide the earliest access to as much of the ultimate syntactic and semantic representation as possible. The latter is captured in MiD and in a second minimization principle, Minimize Forms (MiF). MiD explains, for example, why corpora reveal such clean, gradient weight effects, whereby the selection of short before long phrases in English-type languages is in direct proportion to the degree of weight difference between them, reflecting the increasing inefficiency of long before short orders when there are larger weight differentials. These efficiency preferences are visible well within the capacity constraints of working memory theories and are not explained by them. Nor do they appear to be explainable by activation-based models of memory, which predict numerous anti-local preferences at variance with EIC/MiD's efficiencies (Vasishth & Lewis, 2006).

Minimize Forms (MiF) defines a preference for minimizing the formal complexity of linguistic forms (phonemes, morphemes, etc) and the number of forms with unique conventionalized property assignments, in proportion to the ease with which grammatical and lexical properties can be assigned to these forms. MiF explains why many structural alternations in English between, say, explicit relativizer and zero, or explicit complementizer and zero, show a pattern whereby the zero alternate is preferred in environments where a relative clause is more expected, and hence where the assignment of relative clause status to a clause is easier. Wasow, Jaeger, and Orr (2009), Jaeger and Wasow (2006) and Jaeger (2006) show that in environments where a restrictive relative is more predictable, relativizers are less frequent. This suggests that corpus selections between zero and explicit alternatives can be structured by fine-tuned efficiencies resulting from predictability. Such efficiencies as well as those that result from minimizing domains ultimately involve a minimization of the amount of neural activity that takes place within relevant processing domains.

2.4 Production versus Comprehension

I have traditionally defined EIC and MiD and the processing domains to which they apply primarily from the hearer's, rather than the speaker's perspective. Wasow (1997, 2002) has stressed that the data that motivate them include significant amounts of corpus data, i.e. data from language production, and he has stressed the speaker's perspective when accounting for "end weight" in English. I agree with him with respect to English. It needs to be pointed out, however, that my focus on parsing has been largely for practical reasons, not theoretical ones. More work has traditionally been done on the parsing of syntax than on its production, and more is known about parsing. The precise relationship between production and comprehension models is also currently a matter of intense debate (cf. e.g. Kempen, 2003 for an attempted synthesis). In Hawkins (1998, p.762–764) I advocated a position in which the domain minimization benefits of EIC/MiD apply to both production and comprehension. See also MacDonald (1999) for discussion of numerous production-comprehension parallels, including weight effects.

One challenge for a unification of production and comprehension models comes from head-final languages and from head-final structures generally (like subordinate clauses with final complementizers, or prenominal relative clauses before a head noun) whether they occur in consistently head-final languages (Japanese and Korean) or not (Chinese). For example, de Smedt (1994)'s Incremental Parallel Formulator builds on Levelt's (1989) Production Model and has a ready explanation for the postposing of heavy constituents as in section 2 and Heavy NP Shift. Syntactic constituents are assembled incrementally, following message generation within a Conceptualizer. The relative ordering of constituents in his model can reflect both the original order of conceptualization and the processing time that is required by the Formulator for more complex constituents. The late occurrence of heavy constituents is explained in terms of the greater speed with which short constituents can be formulated in the race between parallel processes in sentence generation.

For head-final structures, however, there is growing evidence for the prediction made back in Hawkins (1994) for a heavy-first *pre*posing preference, i.e. for the mirror-image of English *post*posing rules, see Yamashita and Chang (2001, 2006) for Japanese, Choi (2007) for Korean, and Matthews and Yeung (2001) for Cantonese (a comprehension study). Preposing appears to be in direct conflict with the predictions of the Incremental Parallel Formulator. An alternative way of capturing domain minimization benefits in a production model is outlined in Hawkins (1998, p.763–764), where it is assumed that Constituent Recognition Domains and Constituent Production Domains are closely aligned. The interesting consequence of this alignment for head-final languages is that the Conceptualizer could be cognitively aware that a clause currently being processed is a subordinate one within a matrix S, at the same time that its syntactic status as a preposed subordinate clause within a matrix will not yet have been constructed by the Formulator until the right-peripheral complementizer is reached. The efficiency of head-final languages derives from their adjacent positioning of heads of phrases on the right periphery of their respective phrases. It is this consistent right adjacency that minimizes phrasal processing domains, corresponding to the consistently left peripheral positioning of heads in head-initial languages. It also results in frequent bottom-up processing effects, including certain late syntactic property assignments like those just mentioned, compared with head-initial languages. This result does not necessarily argue against the alignment of production and comprehension benefits, however, and hence it does not argue against a possible production theory of mirror-image weight effects in head-initial and head-final languages.

3 Verb Particle Constructions in English Corpora

The verb-particle construction in English, and the corpus data reported in Lohse, Hawkins, and Wasow (2004) documenting the alternation between split and joined variants, are relevant to the general issues raised in the last section. They show, first, that actual usage is highly sensitive to efficiency *differences* between competing truth-conditionally equivalent structures and that selections are fine-tuned to these differences. Second, they provide evidence for a number of subtle locality effects, defined in terms of both syntactic and semantic processing domains. Third, the domain minimizations in question operate well within any proposed capacity constraints, and show no clear evidence

for non-locality of the type that activation-based models of memory
and prediction/expectation models predict. And fourth these production data implicate an efficiency-based theory of language production,
that is plausibly aligned with comparable benefits for comprehension.
I present these data in this section and discuss their relevance to the
general issues in the next.

The data used to test EIC's and MiD's predictions in Lohse et al.
were taken from the (spoken) Switchboard corpus, and from three written corpora: the Brown corpus, the Lancaster-Oslo/Bergen corpus, and
the Wall Street Journal corpus. Some of the predictions made for them
are briefly summarized and illustrated here.

3.1 The Weight of the Object NP

Lohse et al. (2004) begin by defining a VP Phrasal Combination Domain, as follows:

(3) *VP Phrasal Combination Domain* (VP PCD)
The PCD for a VP containing a transitive verb-particle phrase
consists of the smallest contiguous substring containing the
verb, the particle, and the first constructing word in the object NP.

The basic idea behind establishing syntactic processing domains like
PCDs is that orderings can differ with regard to the amount of material
that needs to be processed in order to construct a mother node like VP
and the immediate constituents (ICs) of this mother: the less material
in the domain, the faster and more efficient phrase-structure processing
can be. This is illustrated in (4), using "IC-to-word" ratios. The fewer
words in a domain that need to be accessed for the construction of
all ICs (indicated by the underlinings), the higher is the IC-to-word
ratio, as shown in the comparison of (4a) and (4b) (see Hawkins, 2004,
p.105–108 for detailed discussion).

(4) a. Joe VP[looked up NP[the number of the ticket]]
$$\quad \underline{1 \qquad 2 \qquad 3}$$
VP PCD: IC-to-word ratio of $3/3 = 100\%$

b. Joe VP[looked NP[the number of the ticket] up]
$$\quad \underline{1 \qquad\quad 2 \quad 3 \quad\;\; 4 \;\; 5 \quad 6 \qquad 7}$$
VP PCD: IC-to-word ratio of $3/7 = 43\%$

The same constituency information (constructing three ICs) can be
accomplished in the three-word domain of (4a) as in the seven-word

domain of (4b). As a result, phrase-structure recognition and production can be accomplished sooner in (4a) and there is less additional (phonological, morphological, syntactic, and semantic) processing that needs to occur simultaneously with phrase-structure processing. The optimal IC-to-word ratio of (4a) holds regardless of the length of the NP, on account of its left-peripheral construction by the definite article *the* (Hawkins, 2004).

The general predictors, EIC and MiD, are defined in (5) and (6) respectively:

(5) *Early immediate constituents* (EIC) (Hawkins, 1994, p.69–83)
The human processor prefers linear orders that minimize PCDs (by maximizing their IC-to-word ratios) in proportion to the minimization difference between competing orders.

(6) *Minimize Domains* (MiD) (Hawkins, 2004, p.31)
The human processor prefers to minimize the connected sequences of linguistic forms and their conventionally associated syntactic and semantic properties in which relations of combination and/or dependency are processed. The degree of this preference is proportional to the number of relations whose domains can be minimized in competing sequences or structures, and to the extent of the minimization difference in each domain.

Their predictions for VP PCDs amount to a prediction for the joined verb-particle construction in proportion to the length or weight of the object NP:

(7) *Prediction 1* (VP PCDs)
The length of the object NP will be a significant factor for performance preferences regarding the adjacency of verb and particle. With increasing length of the object NP there will be an increasing preference for adjacency of the verb and particle.

Figure 4 shows this to be the case. An initial steep decline in the split ratio can be seen as the NP length reaches three words, with a second one for five-plus words (where the preference for the joined construction reaches 97%). There were no split orders for NPs greater than eight words in length.

3.2 The Dependency of the Particle

For semantic processing Lohse et al. propose a classification of verb particle constructions based on the dependency of either the particle or the verb. Building on the definition of dependency for prepositional

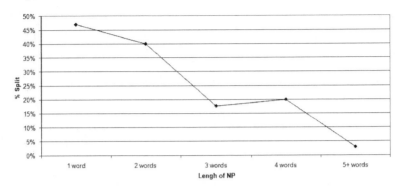

FIGURE 4 Split vs. joined by NP length

phrase complements and adjuncts given in Hawkins (2000) and on Wasow's (1997, 2002) classification of V-PP collocations as transparent or opaque, they propose the following entailment tests for dependency:

(8) *Verb entailment test*
     If [X V NP Pt] entails [X V NP], then assign V_i. If not, assign V_d.

(9) *Particle entailment test*
     If [X V NP Pt] entails [NP PredV Pt], then assign Pt_i. If not, assign Pt_d.
     PredV = predication verb (BE, BECOME, COME, GO, STAY)

These entailment tests lead to four possible combinations of verbs and particles. The first, V_i Pt_i, has a fully compositional meaning in which both elements are processable independently. For example, *they lifted the child up* entails *they lifted the child*, cf. (8). The entailment of (9) also holds for the particle here: *the child GOES up.* The other end of the compositionality spectrum is found in the combination of V_d Pt_d, where both verb and particle depend on each other for their interpretation. *They looked the number up* does not entail *they looked the number* (cf. (8)) nor *the number IS/BECOMES/COMES/GOES* or *STAYS up* (cf. (9)). For the remaining two combinations, only one of the two elements can be processed independently. An example of V_i Pt_d is *they washed the dishes up* (the entailment of (8) goes through, but that of (9) does not), and an example of V_d Pt_i is *they turned the light on* (the entailment of (8) does not go through, that of (9) does).

For the processing of dependent particles the following lexical dependency domain is defined:

(10) *Pt$_d$-V lexical dependency domain* (Pt$_d$-V LDD)
The LDD for a dependent particle (Pt$_d$) consists of the smallest contiguous substring that contains the Pt$_d$ and the verb on which it depends for semantic and/or syntactic property assignments.

In the split construction, the size of a Pt$_d$-V LDD is determined by the length of the object NP. As with VP PCDs, increasing length of the NP results in increasing differentials in the Pt$_d$-V LDD between the two orderings, as shown in (11). We expect that particle dependency will result in a strong preference for the joined construction, therefore, cf. (12)):

(11) a.   look NP[the number] up$_d$
          Pt$_d$-V LDD: 1   2   3   4

      b.   look up$_d$ NP[the number]
          Pt$_d$-V LDD: 1   2

(12) *Prediction 2* (Pt$_d$-V LDD)
Dependency of the particle within a verb-particle phrase will be a significant factor for performance preferences regarding the adjacency of verb and particle. There will be a preference for adjacency if the verb-particle contains a dependent particle.

The overall split ratio for dependent particles (16%) is significantly lower than it is for independent particles (42%). As Figure 5 shows, the stronger adjacency preference for dependent particles is independent of NP length and is consistently stronger than that for independent particles.

3.3 The Dependency of the Verb

Interestingly, whereas the dependency of a particle is predicted to result in a preference for the joined construction, the dependency of a verb on a particle (as in *they looked the number up* (V$_d$ Pt$_d$) and *they turned the light on* (V$_d$ Pt$_i$)) is not predicted to have such an effect. The basic reason that is hypothesized for this asymmetry is that a particle that is dependent on a verb for assignment of its lexical status as a phrasal verb and for its meaning needs to access the verb for this purpose; a verb, on the other hand, whether it is dependent on, or independent of, a particle must also access the direct object for crucial aspects of its interpretation. Compare the different senses of *wrap up* in *wrap up the parcel* on the one hand with *wrap up the meeting* on the other. When lexical domains are defined precisely on this assumption and

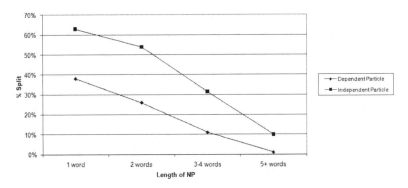

FIGURE 5 Split vs. joined by NP length and particle type

compared across the split and joined orders, verb dependency turns out not to predict a significant preference for the joined construction, independently of the other factors. Relevant lexical dependency domain definitions are given in (13) and (14):

(13) V_d-*(N; Pt) lexical dependency domain* (V_d-*(N; Pt) LDD*)
The LDD for a dependent verb (V_d) consists of the smallest contiguous substring that contains the V_d, the particle, and the head noun of the object NP on which the V_d and Pt depend for semantic and/or syntactic property assignments.

(14) V_i-*N lexical dependency domain* (V_i-*N LDD*)
The LDD for an independent verb (V_i) consists of the smallest contiguous substring that contains the V_i and the head noun of the object NP on which the V_i depends for semantic and/or syntactic property assignments.

The placement of the particle does not usually affect the size of a V_d-(N; Pt) LDD. Both orderings (15a) and (15b) result in identical domain sizes, independently of NP length, as long as the head noun occurs at the right periphery of the object NP, which is the case in over 85% of our corpus data.

(15) a.   pick$_d$ NP[the heavy boxes] up
       V_d-(N; Pt) LDD   1   2   3   4   5

       b.   pick$_d$ up NP[the heavy boxes]
       V_d-(N; Pt) LDD   1   2   3   4   5

For independent verbs, there is a slight processing advantage for the split construction (16a), in which the particle occurs outside the V_i-N LDD.

(16) a.   lift$_i$ NP[the heavy boxes] up
          VP PCD   1   2   3   4   5
          V$_i$-N LDD   1   2   3   4

     b.   lift$_i$ up NP[the heavy boxes]
          VP PCD   1   2   3
          V$_i$-N LDD   1   2   3   4   5

In the joined construction (16b), the particle increases the size of the
V$_i$-N LDD. The added cost of this one (short) word remains constant,
independently of the length of the NP. A one-word differential is not
likely to result in an ordering preference, however. The LDD difference
between (16a) and (16b) is small, and in addition the minimization
benefit of (16a) for the V$_i$-N LDD is counteracted by the VP PCD
minimization effect in (16b) which increases as the NP becomes longer.
(16a) results in a V$_i$-N LDD that is shorter by one word, (16b) results
in a VP PCD shorter by two words. There should not be a significant
preference for one particle ordering over the other with independent
verbs, therefore; nor will there generally be one with dependent verbs.
The corpus data support this, as shown in Figure 6.

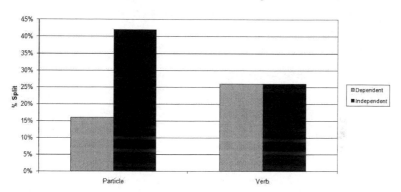

FIGURE 6 Split vs. joined by particle and verb dependency

Some further domain minimization predictions are formulated on
various subsets of the data in Lohse et al. (2004) and found to be
supported. For example, the equivalence between (15a) and (15b) no
longer holds when there is postnominal material following the head
noun (e.g. *boxes that are heavy to lift*). The joined order is significantly
preferred in these cases, since verb, particle and head noun are now in a
smaller processing domain, cf. Lohse et al., 2004, p.253–254. Conversely
a preference is defined for the split ordering with independent particles

(16a) when the object NP is pre-modified rather than post-modified since the meaning of a particle such as *on* can then be assigned within a smaller domain linking head noun and independent particle (*put the uncomfortable hat on* versus *put the hat that was uncomfortable on*). This prediction is also supported (Lohse et al., 2004, p.250–2).

4   Conclusions

The selection of a split or joined particle verb by English speakers and writers in these corpora appears to reflect the processing ease and efficiency of one variant over another. When we examine the factors that lead to these selection preferences, a very general one involves the minimization of the structural and lexical domains required for the processing of syntactic and lexical-semantic relations holding between the verb, the particle and the direct object NP. These domains can be measured globally and selections appear to be made in corpora on the basis of their overall size (fewer items in each domain preferred over more) and their number (more domains favoring the adjacency of verb and particle result in a stronger preference for the joined structure) (see section 2.1). The selections show strong minimization or locality effects (see section 2.2). They support a general efficiency explanation, ultimately a principle of least effort that is calibrated to the overall minimization benefit associated with one or the other order. These gradient efficiencies operate well within any constrained capacity for working memory and are not explained by it (see section 2.3). Finally, these data point to the reality of a systematic selection process in language production whereby alternative structures for expressing the same meaning are compared and assessed and from which one is chosen (see section 2.4). Exactly how this selection process works within a Levelt-type production model (Levelt, 1989) remains to be specified, but without it the systematic nature of the corpus selections is unexplained. These selections then determine the frequency patterns that influence on-line processing in ambiguity resolution (MacDonald, Pearlmutter, & Seidenberg, 1994), in parsing attachments (MacDonald, 1999), and so on.

Some recent experimental work has been conducted on particle verbs in English and Dutch by Kuperman, Piai, and Schreuder (2008). They found support for both locality and anti-locality effects (measured at the particle) in on-line studies of English. They also found anti-locality effects in Dutch verb-particles constructions and they unify the findings from both languages in terms of the kind of expectation-based and surprisal model of comprehension proposed by Hale (2001) and Levy (2008). But as I pointed out in section 2.1 above, the fact that processing is faster or slower at a certain temporal point, like a particle or a verb, is not necessarily indicative of the overall simplicity or complexity of the structure that contains it. Corpus selection data, as summarized in section 3, are arguably a more accurate reflection of this overall preference for one syntactic variant over another that has been made by the speaker or writer on each occasion of use. These data regularly show tighter adjacency between words when there are more combinatorial and dependency relations linking them, as seen for example in Figure 6 (in which dependent particles are closer to their verbs than independent particles), or when the overall degree of minimization is greater for the processing of all phrases in one variant of a sentence rather than another, as seen in Figure 1 (involving extraposed versus adjacent relative clauses). Further examples of these two types of interactions, involving multiple factors and multiple phrases, are given in Hawkins (2004). The results suggest that corpus selections are a good indicator of overall sentence complexity, and that apparent anti-locality effects linked to the probabilities of certain items appearing at certain temporal points in a structure should not necessarily be taken as evidence for or against the overall complexity of a sentence.

Let us return to the extraposition structures with which I began this paper. If, as in Konieczny's (2000) and Francis's (2010) studies, on-line data involving self-paced reading times are at partial variance with principles made on the basis of more global structural measures that successfully predict the selections made by native speakers, then, I submit, it is not the corpus selections whose ultimate significance we should be questioning, but the on-line data. It does not follow from these data that there are anti-locality preferences for whole structures, beyond the advantages for the subregions with high probability and low surprisal. Nor does it follow that domain minimization is not relevant for comprehension in addition to production (contrary to what Konieczny, 2000 argues). On-line measures are not currently being subjected to critical scrutiny regarding their significance for theories of ease or difficulty in language processing. They can certainly not be taken as indicative of overall structural simplicity or complexity in production and comprehension.

A challenge for all processing theories at the moment is how to integrate the multiple factors that determine efficiency and complexity into an integrated whole. In the approach of Hawkins (2004) a number of interacting general principles are proposed, MiD, Minimize Forms (MiF) and Maximize On-line Processing (MaOP), see also Hawkins, 2009. Vasishth and Lewis (2006) capture both locality and anti-locality effects using their activation-based architecture, ACT-R. Jaeger (2006) proposes a theory of Uniform Information Density that accounts for the relative weighting of different factors, while Levy (2008) develops the expectation-based theory into a general model. The purpose of the current paper is to remind readers of a range of subtle predictions that were formulated, tested and supported with Tom Wasow's help in Lohse et al. (2004), and to affirm the value of corpus frequencies as reflections of overall efficiency and complexity, arguably in both language production and comprehension. The principle of MiD goes a long way to explaining these corpus data. It remains to be seen how well other models do in accounting for them.

References

Anderson, J. R. (1993). *The architecture of cognition.* Cambridge, MA: Harvard University Press.

Bard, E. G., Robertson, D., & Sorace, A. (1996). Magnitude estimation of linguistic acceptability. *Language, 72*(1), 32–68.

Choi, H. W. (2007). Length and order: A corpus study of Korean dative-accusative construction. *Discourse and Cognition, 14*(3), 207–227.

de Smedt, K. (1994). Parallelism in incremental sentence generation. In G. Adriaens & U. Hahn (Eds.), *Parallel natural language processing* (pp. 421–447). Norwood, NJ: Ablex.

Francis, E. J. (2010). Grammatical weight and relative clause extraposition in English. *Cognitive Linguistics, 21*, 35–74.

Frazier, L., & Fodor, J. D. (1978). The sausage machine: A new two-stage parsing model. *Cognition, 6*(4), 291–325.

Gibson, E. (1998). Linguistic complexity: Locality of syntactic dependencies. *Cognition, 68*(1), 1–76.

Gibson, E. (2000). The dependency locality theory: A distance-based theory of linguistic complexity. In Y. Miyashita, P. Marantz, & O. W. (Eds.), *Image, language, brain* (pp. 95–112). Vancouver, B. C., Canada: MIT Press.

Hale, J. (2001). A probabilistic Earley parser as a psycholinguistic model. In *Proceedings of NAACL* (Vol. 2, pp. 159–166). Pittsburgh, PA.

Hawkins, J. A. (1994). *A performance theory of order and constituency.* Cambridge: Cambridge University Press.

Hawkins, J. A. (1998). Some issues in a performance theory of word order. In A. Siewierska (Ed.), *Constituent order in the languages of Europe* (pp. 729–781). Berlin: Mouton de Gruyter.

Hawkins, J. A. (1999). Processing complexity and filler-gap dependencies across grammars. *Language*, *75*, 244–285.

Hawkins, J. A. (2000). The relative ordering of prepositional phrases in English: Going beyond Manner-Place-Time. *Language Variation and Change*, *11*, 231–266.

Hawkins, J. A. (2004). *Efficiency and complexity in grammars*. Oxford: Oxford University Press.

Hawkins, J. A. (2007). Processing typology and why psychologists need to know about it. *New Ideas in Psychology*, *25*(2), 124–144.

Hawkins, J. A. (2009). An efficiency theory of complexity and related phenomena. In D. Gil, G. Sampson, & T. P. (Eds.), *Complexity as an evolving variable*. Oxford: Oxford University Press.

Jaeger, T. F. (2006). *Redundancy and syntactic reduction in spontaneous speech*. Unpublished doctoral dissertation, Stanford University, Stanford, CA.

Jaeger, T. F., Fedorenko, E., & Gibson, E. (2005). Dissociation between production and comprehension complexity. In *Poster presentation at the 18th CUNY sentence processing conference*. University of Arizona, Tucson.

Jaeger, T. F., & Norcliffe, E. (2009). The cross-linguistic study of sentence production: State of the art and a call for action. *Language and Linguistics Compass*, *3*(4), 866–887.

Jaeger, T. F., & Wasow, T. (2006). Processing as a source of accessibility effects on variation. In R. T. Cover & Y. Kim (Eds.), *Proceedings of the 31st annual meeting of the Berkeley Linguistic Society* (pp. 169–180). Ann Arbor, MN: Sheridan Books.

Just, M. A., & Carpenter, P. A. (1992). A capacity theory of comprehension: Individual differences in working memory. *Psychological Review*, *99*(1), 122–149.

Kempen, G. (2003). *Cognitive architectures for human grammatical encoding and decoding*. (Max Planck Institute for Psycholinguistics, Nijmegen)

Konieczny, L. (2000). Locality and parsing complexity. *Journal of Psycholinguistic Research*, *29*(6), 627–645.

Kuperman, V., Piai, V., & Schreuder, R. (2008). *Bridging locality and anti-locality effects in the processing of long-distance dependencies*. (Paper presented at AmLap 2008.)

Levelt, W. J. M. (1989). *Speaking: From intention to articulation*. Cambridge, MA: MIT Press.

Levy, R. (2008). Expectation-based syntactic comprehension. *Cognition*, *106*(3), 1126–1177.

Lewis, R. L., & Vasishth, S. (2005). An activation-based model of sentence processing as skilled memory retrieval. *Cognitive Science*, *29*(3), 375–419.

Lohse, B., Hawkins, J. A., & Wasow, T. (2004). Domain minimization in English verb-particle constructions. *Language*, *80*, 238–261.

MacDonald, M. C. (1999). Distributional information in language comprehension, production, and acquisition. In B. MacWhinney (Ed.), *The emergence of language* (pp. 177–196). Mahwah, NJ: Lawrence Erlbaum.

MacDonald, M. C., Pearlmutter, N. J., & Seidenberg, M. K. (1994). The lexical nature of syntactic ambiguity resolution. *Psychological Review*, *101*(4), 676–703.

Matthews, S., & Yeung, L. Y. Y. (2001). Processing motivations for topicalization in Cantonese. In K. Horie & S. Sato (Eds.), *Cognitive-functional linguistics in an East Asian context* (pp. 81–102). Tokyo: Kurosio Publishers.

Szmrecsanyi, B. (2004). On operationalizing syntactic complexity. *JADT-04*, *2*, 1032–1039.

Uszkoreit, H., Brants, T., Duchier, D., Krenn, B., Konieczny, L., Oepen, S., et al. (1998). Studien zur Performanzorientierten Linguistik: Aspekts der Relativsatzextraposition im Deutschen. *Kognitionswissenschaft*, *7*(3), 129–133.

Vasishth, S., & Lewis, R. L. (2006). Argument-head distance and processing complexity: Explaining both locality and antilocality effects. *Language*, *82*(4), 767.

Wasow, T. (1997). End-weight from the speaker's perspective. *Journal of Psycholinguistic Research*, *26*(3), 347–361.

Wasow, T. (2002). *Postverbal behavior*. Stanford, CA: CSLI Publications.

Wasow, T., Jaeger, T. F., & Orr, D. M. (2009). Lexical variation in relativizer frequency. In H. Simon & H. Wiese (Eds.), *Proceedings of the 2005 DGfS workshop: Expecting the unexpected, exceptions in grammar*. Cologne, Germany.

Yamashita, H., & Chang, F. (2001). Long before short preference in the production of a head-final language. *Cognition*, *81*(2), 45–55.

Yamashita, H., & Chang, F. (2006). Sentence production in Japanese. In M. Nakayama, R. Mazuka, & Y. Shirai (Eds.), *Handbook of East Asian psycholinguistics* (Vol. 2). Cambridge: Cambridge University Press.

Zipf, G. K. (1949). *Human behavior and the principle of least effort*. New York: Hafner.

14

Information in Virtual Spaces

Susanne Riehemann

Preface

This paper describes a potential new interdisciplinary research field that could emerge as a result of developments in immersive interactive virtual 3D spaces, geographic information systems, information visualization, pattern recognition, linguistics, knowledge representation and sharing, and other related areas. Remembering Tom Wasow's open-mindedness about new methodologies and interdisciplinary ideas encouraged me in pursuing this unusual topic and attempting to combine aspects of my current and previous fields.

1 Introduction

The research field described in the preface has many dimensions and is therefore difficult to describe in a paper that is mostly linear. The space under discussion is briefly described and visualized on a map in the first section. The next section discusses some of the key 3D concepts that are referred to throughout the rest of the paper. Then, the paper discusses the representation and communication of concrete spatiotemporal information, such as trips, life events, and sporting events, which make it clear that neither a virtual reproduction nor a natural language description alone are sufficiently complete for all purposes, and suggests ways of integrating them. Finally, applications of this type of approach to the visualization of language and abstract information are discussed.

Language from a Cognitive Perspective.
Emily M. Bender and Jennifer Arnold, Editors
Copyright © 2011, CSLI Publications.

The journey through this space will show how visualizations differ from and complement natural language. The journey has two main goals. One aim is to argue that significant linguistic insight can be gained by researching how to best integrate language elements with these visualizations and by studying automatic verbalization of virtual events and automatic creation of virtual events from natural language descriptions.

A more general goal is to show where these new technologies have the potential to aid with communication and the sharing of knowledge, lead to deeper understanding and novel insight, and enable people to deal with a larger amount of complex abstract information.

2   Putting the paper on a map

To orient the reader, the information representation space is depicted as a 'map' based on the two most important dimensions, with the range of concrete to abstract information from bottom to top, and symbolic to analog representation left to right, as in Figure 1.

Written language can be placed in the center of that map, covering the area from bottom to top, with more formally structured texts to the left of the center, and more evocative narratives to the right.[1]

Children start out with concrete experiential data in the bottom right corner and move via language acquisition and formal education towards the top left corner, where abstract relationships are represented in symbolic ways, such as mathematical and logical formalisms. This paper starts in the same place, at the bottom right, with concrete spatiotemporal information, but instead of moving diagonally across the map, it moves up towards the top right corner, where abstract patterns are represented visually, as in the field of information visualization.[2]

Note that this map only depicts the two dimensions that are the most central to the paper. Other relevant dimensions are 'static/dynamic', 'passive/interactive', 'distant/immersive', 'individual/collaborative', etc. In this paper these dimensions are mostly discussed in conjunction with the visual representations on the right side of the map. In this context, 'dynamic' is the ability to show changes over time, which can be conceived as a fourth dimension, and 'interactive' means that the

---

[1]The map is not intended to be complete – items like 'Google Earth' and 'Semantic Web' are merely examples of information representation in particular parts of the space.

[2]The term 'information visualization' is conventionally used only for abstract information that is not inherently visual in nature. However, it is useful to consider in what ways 'visualization' techniques can help clarify and communicate information that has a visual aspect to begin with, and explore the space between these two extremes.

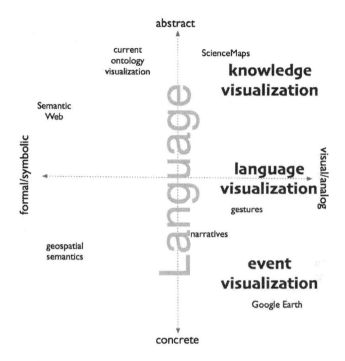

FIGURE 1 The space of concrete to abstract information, and symbolic to analog representation

user has control over viewpoints and can manipulate data or affect events. The range of 'immersive' starts with 3D spaces displayed on regular 2D computer screens that appear three-dimensional because of the ability to move through the space and change viewing angles (also called 2.5D), and goes via 3D screens and projectors to IMAX domes and stereoscopic head-mounted displays (HMDs).

The reason for journeying through this space is to convince the reader that natural language is not always sufficient for a complete understanding of a complex event or system, and that visualization technologies have various advantages for understanding and communicating such information.

Linguists already know about language, but may not have thought about some of its limitations when compared to visualization. Language excels at summarizing information, focusing on particular aspects, framing an event from a particular point of view, and expressing abstract information like emotions, intentions, properties, and relationships. Stories help listeners make sense of information and provide a structure that is easy to remember and integrate into a visual model. However, natural language descriptions are by nature sequential, and when the information is very complex and detailed, listeners may have forgotten some of the earlier information by the time they hear about all the aspects of the picture. It is also impossible to control what exactly each listener will 'see'. Section 5 discusses these properties of language in more detail.

In contrast, virtual representations are more analog and can map directly onto the spatio-temporal domain, or project abstract data into that domain, taking advantage of the human abilities to integrate complex visual information, systematically explore a space and use spatial inference, and detect temporal changes. They overcome the limitation of sequential language and make it possible to include more detail than one can hold in memory, and to examine the space from different perspectives to gain a better understanding and see new connections.

The advantages and disadvantages of natural language and virtual representations are such that they complement each other very well. Visualizations of abstract information usually need to be explained verbally, and even spatio-temporal data has important abstract properties that need to be communicated. Imagine taking a book about fictional events, including characters' thoughts and narrator's explanations, and combining it with a complete interactive 3D movie version of the book in which one can explore the events from different perspectives, see movements on a map, and see highlights condensed in space and time. This would lead to a more complete understanding than either the book or the 3D movie alone could accomplish. The remainder of this paper tries to show how virtual representations can provide valuable information, including insights into language.

3 Background: 3D concepts

This section discusses some of the key concepts in 3D technology that are presupposed by the rest of the paper and that may be unfamiliar to the reader: levels of detail (LODs), overlays, perspective, and devices for 'flying' in virtual spaces and for creating an immersive experience.[3]

One important concept in the area of 3D virtual reality is that of levels of detail (LODs). This technique was developed so as to stay within the limitations of current computer hardware. It takes advantage of the

---

[3]This paper was written in late 2009, and technology in this area is likely to change quickly. However, these general concepts should remain important, and changing technology will only make the research outlined in this paper more feasible.

fact that objects at a distance can be approximated by simpler shapes requiring far less geometry, without the difference being noticeable.

For example, from a distance a tree can be represented by two 'billboards' intersecting at right angles, and still look like a tree because the textures on those billboards are photographs of a tree with enough resolution to look good from that distance. This tree looks unrealistic when viewed from nearby, especially from above, so more complexity is required at that level of detail. Similarly, when looking at the entire planet in Google Earth[4], one cannot perceive elevation differences or see an individual car, so this information does not need to be represented at that level. There are several intermediate levels between the 'whole planet' level and the highest fidelity level. Similarly, one can specify that from nearby, a certain avatar is a full-fledged model of a particular unique individual or a male of a certain height wearing a particular type of uniform, at a medium distance he is made up of two billboards, and from afar simply represented as a colored dot, or not at all, depending on the purpose of the visualization.

The concept of LODs can be useful when applied to more abstract domains, e.g. one can think of 1) paper, 2) excerpts, 3) summary, 4) topic as four levels of detail of a research paper.

The second important concept is that of overlays and layers of overlays. Hillshaded or shadow hachured (Imhof, 2007) topographic maps use shading to indicate the steepness of slopes and to simulate light sources. Overlaying such a map on the 3D terrain view in Google Earth provides information that is not as easily extracted from either source alone. In particular, aerial imagery does not look very three-dimensional when viewed from straight above, and it is not always possible to see where the highest or lowest points are. When moving through the terrain and viewing it at an angle, the elevation information can be perceived even without an overlay, but at those angles features obscure each other, and not all significant features like ridge lines and creeks are highlighted.

In contrast, a map alone does provide good overview information, but users who are not experienced with such maps can confuse ridges with valleys, may have a poor sense of the steepness of the terrain, and are often unable to form a mental picture of the actual 3D terrain.

The combined 3D-and-overlay representation minimizes these problems, making the spatial features of a larger area clear at first glance,

---

[4]http://earth.google.com/. All URLs were current in late 2009.

while also being viewable from a ground level or from an oblique perspective.[5]

It is possible to make semi-transparent overlays, or only overlay hiking trails and creeks, so that the satellite imagery remains visible at the same time. The route of an actual hiking trip tracked with GPS can be overlaid on top of that. In this way, many different types of information can be combined and visualized, for example erosion, population movements, etc.

Another important aspect is the interface for navigating these 3D environments. It is possible to automatically follow a particular 'tour' as it unfolds over time. For example, in Google Earth it is possible to follow a GPS-tracked hiking trip at an accelerated pace, 'looking' in the direction of the tracked movement. The pace could be slowed down for important sub-events. This 'time lapse' method also makes the passage of time more perceptible, could be used to visualize daily and seasonal cycles, and clarifies temporal relationships. When there are simulated or tracked people in the environment, it is possible to see the events as if through their eyes.

More interestingly, the user can interact with the environment, see places and events from different perspectives, and have an experience as close as possible to 'being there'. For this purpose, computer games typically use keyboard-and-mouse approaches, special game controllers, or UI elements for zooming in, panning, rotating, and pitching the view. But these methods can be challenging to learn for older novices, especially when fine-grained control over movement in a 3D space is required.[6] There is no intuitive way to control the relative speeds of translation versus rotation.

However, there are now affordable USB-based six degrees of freedom (6DoF) controllers, e.g. the SpaceNavigator, that are fairly intuitive to learn and create the feeling of being able to 'fly' anywhere one wants to go. To navigate, one pushes, pulls, and twists the device in the desired directions – and these actions can be combined into one smooth complex motion. For example, with these devices it is easy to move forward quickly, while gently pitching downward, and slightly curving to the left, like flying an airplane on a landing approach.

---

[5]The value of an oblique perspective will be clear to anyone who has seen Pictometry's Bird's Eye imagery at http://maps.bing.com/

[6]It can be particularly confusing to mentally translate the effects of a particular control element when looking at an area from above, compared to the effects of that same control element when standing at ground level, i.e. with a viewing angle that differs by 90 degrees. Different applications also vary in using 'object pull/push' vs. 'eyepoint movement' metaphors.

HMDs or 'VR goggles' make the virtual environment even more immersive. But for most of the purposes described in this paper, a flat screen actually has the advantage of more readily allowing for inset/side windows to display related information. When 3D screens and projectors become available, they are likely to be a good compromise.

4 Visualizing concrete information

For some concrete information it is very easy to see how the various types of visual representations help with understanding and communicating information. This section starts at the bottom right corner of the map in Figure 1, and later sections build on the concrete examples to move towards the more abstract ones.

4.1 A spectrum from map to virtual reality

This section covers the space from simple 2D representations to virtual reality – that is, along the dimensions that are not directly depicted on the map, such as dynamics, immersiveness, and interactivity.

Starting with geographical maps, whether paper or digital ones, it is clear that they have advantages over natural language descriptions for many purposes. For example, showing the locations of multiple travel destinations on a map can be very helpful in identifying a sensible route, especially if the addressee is not familiar with the landmarks in the area. The map can contain more locations than one can easily keep in memory, including all the spatial relationships between them. There are already existing tools for this purpose, e.g. we can share such information using pins and descriptions on a customized Google map.[7] In this example one can also see that additional linguistic information is valuable and can help clarify the semantic relationships between the locations: *I included the bus stops near your hotel and near the department because it is very hard to find parking on campus.*

Combined with GPS, 2D maps are also valuable for the purpose of seeing where one is located on a map while actually moving through real space, e.g. driving on a highway in an unfamiliar city. This makes it possible to establish a much more direct and detailed link between places in the real world and the location of one's current position on a map, including information about what exactly one is seeing from those places, especially if a compass heading is also provided.

Moving from 2D to 3D, a Google Earth KML (Keyhole Markup Language) file with custom locations can show elevation and building models, and it is possible to define 'levels of detail' such that from a

---

[7]http://bit.ly/5FjjeL

distance, only the most important locations are displayed, and further detail is added when getting closer.

Spatiotemporal data like pictures of life events and their locations can be visualized by 'touring': automatically zooming into and out of the locations in sequence. The pictures can be oriented so that the viewpoint matches, where that adds value. To add more of a 'story' element, one could control the timing, and integrate verbal narration and video elements. While the animation is 'playing' one could show the current location for each event on a small inset map, and the current date on a time line inset for easy orientation and context. This is already possible with the Google Earth plugin API, as used e.g. by the driving simulator.[8]

Ideally one could define levels of detail and topic tags for each element, so that for example only a few of the most important events in a person's life ones are shown for a very brief version, and more detail could be added for viewers with various backgrounds, interests, and goals.

Immersive 3D environments are closer to an actual 'experience' and provide the additional benefit of the users being able to see an environment or an event from multiple perspectives, and to be able to use pointing and deictic language to refer to things. For example, when trying to understand a historical battle outflanking maneuver in hilly terrain, it is important to have a bird's eye view of the scene and who is located where, and it is also necessary to understand what is visible from where, and what areas are within range of the available types of weapons. We can visit the location of the battle in Google Earth, see the elevation and get an idea of the vegetation from the satellite imagery and images taken in the area. Vegetation and rocky outcroppings can be automatically modeled based on photogrammetry and lidar scanning, and modified manually if necessary. The ranges of various weapons can be visualized as semitransparent overlays.

Currently, Google Earth is not set up for the purpose of displaying simulated or tracked movement with many human avatars, but its engine is in principle capable of doing so, and other software, e.g. MetaVR's VRSG, is available for that purpose. At a distance the avatars for the opposing forces could be represented by symbols in different colors, and when they are closer, their height could be taken into account for the purpose of judging line of sight. Speeding up the playback of the event can clarify the temporal relationships.

---

[8]http://earth-api-samples.googlecode.com/svn/trunk/demos/drive-simulator/index.html

If we are dealing with a current event in which this technology is used for training purposes, the individual participants in the event can be equipped with GPS devices and compasses, allowing the playback of the event and viewing from any perspective. (See for example SRI's JTEP[9] project.) Video footage can be integrated, either by showing the locations of the cameras in the 3D environment, and allowing users to 'fly into' the live video camera feeds, or by automatically projecting the video images as textures onto the 3D models (see e.g. Sentinal AVE[10]). A 3D model can also be used to identify from which location videos and photographs were taken, and integrate that information into one spatiotemporally coherent picture, which can be important for example in the case of a crime that happened in a crowd.

In the case of movement by car around populated areas, the tracking does not need to be very accurate to provide meaningful data. The accuracy of the GPS in current cell phones is usually sufficient to know what street someone is on. Most routes can be simplified and described as discrete segments between turns at known intersections, which in turn can be grouped into segments between landmarks or other salient features. These partially abstract routes can be represented visually as in Mapblast's LineDrive[11] option, which are based on the types of simplifications found in human-generated route sketches (Agrawala & Stolte, 2001). These higher level abstractions from the analog data correspond well to natural language route descriptions (Dale, Geldof, & Prost, 2005).

These tools can be used to visualize and communicate a wide variety of information that is spatiotemporal in nature, for example weather patterns, urban sprawl, the history of the Tour de France, or rent patterns changing over time in different neighborhoods. Note that presenting information in a geospatial context can add value even for some relatively abstract information like e.g. properties of fictional characters. For some examples, see the Google Earth gallery.[12] Changes over time, such as building activity or deforestation, can also be visualized using historical aerial imagery.[13]

A particularly good example of concrete information that is useful to visualize is space. A good 3D show, like in the Planetarium at the California Academy of Sciences, allows one to virtually leave the planet,

---

[9]http://www.jtepforguard.com/

[10]http://www.sentinelave.com/ave.html

[11]http://www.mapblast.com/directionsfind.aspx

[12]http://earth.google.com/gallery

[13]At the time of writing, the Stanford Campus is a good example in Google Earth, with imagery going back to 1949.

see how thin the atmosphere really is, and explore space, traveling faster than the speed of light. In this example, that experience is as close as the human mind can get to being there. It is possible to incorporate multiple scales and allow users to fly straight from outer space into subatomic levels.

4.2 Sporting events

We will examine sporting events as a good potential testbed for natural language technology because they provide a rich and relatively complete set of information to work with, and show that neither analog reproduction nor natural language description alone are sufficient to fully understand what is happening and why.

Current game technology (e.g. Madden NFL[14]) can produce very realistic looking football game simulations. Because real life sporting events such as football happen on playing fields surrounded by cameras, they can be recorded in such a way that they can be re-visited in 3D and viewed from any angle. By extrapolating the players' fields of view from their head and eye positions it is possible to see the game through their eyes.

Coaches can use this as a tool to understand why their players behaved in certain ways, to show what a particular play will look like from their point of view, and to visualize the automatically detected weaknesses of opposing players. When available in real time, it can benefit referees trying to decide what a player was actually looking at, and whether an action was intentional.

However, even the most perfect analog reproduction of a football game is meaningless if not accompanied by an understanding of the goals of the game, and the particular situation of the teams and players. If a foreigner has never seen a football game and does not know the rules, they can learn more from a verbal description than from watching a game without any commentary. Even people who do know the game still benefit from listening to an expert, because the commentators' knowledge of the teams and leagues and the full complexity of the rules can add valuable information.

Analog reproduction and natural language description need to be combined to be able to understand the patterns of activity and the motivations behind the actions at all levels. An interactive virtual representation is better at clarifying the spatiotemporal properties and exact details of the event, and letting people form an impression of it,

---

[14]http://www.ea.com/games/madden-nfl-09

while language is required to clarify the more abstract relations, and add information about intentions, thoughts, and emotions.

At the most general level of detail, a football game can be distilled down to the question of which team won. At the next level, information might include the final score, whether or not the outcome was a surprise given the recent records of the teams, and what implications the outcome has on the teams' chances to advance. Language is both necessary and sufficient at these levels.

But at a more detailed level, it becomes helpful to be able to see the actual event rather than just descriptions of it. In spite of dividing up the playing field into various zones, language is not ideally suited to describing the positions and trajectories of multiple players. On the other hand, those positions and trajectories form patterns that can be usefully characterized as a certain type of play, adding information beyond what is directly observable to an untrained eye. A skilled human commentator will also be able to verbalize the dynamics of the events.

The Madden NFL game already provides game analysis, summarization, and automatically generated commentary, but it is assembled from relatively 'robotic' pre-recorded phrases such as *got the completion*, *got just past the first down marker*, and *that'll keep this drive alive*. Both the computer game and the virtual version of the real event make a very good domain for natural language generation software, because so much knowledge of the events is available for reference, including what the intended actions were. The domain is restricted enough to be tractable, and the rules of the game provide relatively clear categories and labels for each role, action, and location.

In addition to generating natural language descriptions, a natural language interface is valuable for the purpose of revisiting parts of the events. People are not likely to remember the exact time at which each event happened, but a unique verbal description is easy to produce, e.g. *go back to the moment when our quarterback made a handoff after dodging three tackles*. Similarly, natural language could be used to ask for a visualization of possible alternative scenarios: *what could have happened if the wide receiver had run at his personal best during that play?*

However, not all of the relevant higher level patterns are best communicated verbally. For example the 'flow' of the game can be visualized by showing a time lapse version with a sequence of scoring points along with a visualization of the score – making it clear which team is ahead, and by how much, at what point. If various relevant properties of the players are indicated visually, that information forms a spatial pattern that shifts with their movements on the field and makes the combined information easily accessible.

4.3 Virtual lives

Virtual lives are another illuminating example. Automatically narrating real life events in addition to visualizing them would help identify the important abstract concepts and relations in the raw data and provide a summary for easy reference, facilitating learning from the past for the benefit of the future. This is currently not feasible even as a research project because of a lack of input data. People's lives are not being tracked with GPS and recorded on video. However, Bell and Gemmell (2009) argue that this will become common very soon. It is possible to start working on the technology now and seeing what its benefits and limitations are by doing this for 'life events' in virtual worlds like Second Life or World of Warcraft (WoW).

Because these environments are 'multiplayer', all the data about the movements and actions of each player are being transmitted in a compact symbolic form, and could be recorded. This would allow for a perfect playback of each event, viewable from any perspective desired, including the actual viewpoints each player had during the event. Several hours of playing could be summarized by showing the most significant events in detail (e.g. leveling or achievements in the case of WoW), and including snapshots of the somewhat smaller events if desired (finishing quests, entering significant areas, meeting people, etc.), while condensing a relatively long period of time into a statement like like 'after freeing the hostage, he took the boat from place A to place B'. Visualization of the track on a map could be one major aid not only to summarization but also to the future retrieval of these events.

Even though many events in WoW are 'discrete' – for example it is never unclear whether or not a player laughed – there is also much activity that is relatively analog, most notably in the movement of the characters around the landscape. With some natural restrictions (walls or steep slopes) the players can walk or ride or swim (and later fly) anywhere. Spoken languages are not good at describing complex spatial trajectories, and maps with tracks overlaid can communicate this information much better. But language is useful for describing the higher level patterns. In this domain there are many clues as to the intended destinations – what 'quests' a player has available or looked at before setting out, what the significant locations are, where the player ultimately ends up, and what they wrote in chats with fellow players. Goals can be described at various temporal horizons and levels of concreteness, e.g. *I am on my way to the store – I am going to do some engineering and will stop by the store to pick up supplies – I am making the explosives that I need for the dungeon later today – I am working on improving my contribution to group quests*, that are successively harder to identify automatically.

The typed and spoken communications among players would be a good corpus of natural language expressions with known referents and full contexts, and a good environment for tuning intention detection and other behavior analytics methods, and learning how to identify and summarize an otherwise random seeming pattern of movement, e.g. *he was trying to take a shortcut to location X but couldn't find a way through the hills*, or *while looking for person X in area Y, she got attacked by a wolf*, or *she needed to make space in her bags and made a detour via the trading post to sell some items*. For complex events like a battle between many players, some of the mistakes and other factors that explain the outcome could be automatically identified.

This artificial environment makes it more tractable to study various aspects of life events and how to represent them: concrete geospatial 'who, when, where' information, fairly complex activities and relationships, and internal states like health (visualized in the game as a bar), emotions and goals. If automatically generated natural language summaries of each day's events and achievements were provided in a textual and/or audio-visual form, the researchers could probably get feedback on the quality of the summaries, or even corrections, from large numbers of players.

5   Visualizing linguistic information

This section discusses visualizing the information conveyed in natural language utterances, and how this can lead to a deeper understanding of the effects of natural language. On the map in Figure 1, language is positioned between concrete and abstract information. It can be about both, but is somewhere in the middle most of the time. Natural language descriptions of abstract objects are often based on analogies with more concrete ones. Conversely, natural language descriptions of very concrete events are usually abstractions that generalize, simplify and leave out much specific information.

The simplifying effect of language is particularly true for spatial expressions, at least for languages other than sign languages.[15] We do not usually specify exact distances, elevations, and dimensions. Worse, we do not have a conventional way of talking about orientation angles,

---

[15]Sign languages make it possible to express many more categories and elements at the same time and in more flexible combinations (Talmy, 2001).

at least in English and most other spoken languages. The most precise it seems to get is the 30° increments one gets from descriptions like *the bird is at 11 o'clock*, and even those are being used less frequently in the age of digital clocks. Phrases like *the bird is at 30 degrees* do not have a standard interpretation specifying from what axis and in which direction to rotate, and are not frequently used, even in increments that could be distinguished.

It gets worse when the third dimension is added, with no conventional way to describe pitch or roll angles, distinguishing between them, distinguishing them from yaw angles, describing combinations of them, or verbalizing any type of motion through 3D space. Some of this information can be communicated through gestures, but this is not helpful for written language.

In addition, the interpretation of prepositions is often dependent not only on the geometry of the objects that are being related but also their function in the context. For example, there are two interpretations for *The girl was in front of the car*: in front of the front of the car in the direction it is normally traveling, or in front of the car from the point of view of the speaker, i.e. not visually obscured by the car - see Figure 2. So for most natural language utterances it is not the case that there is exactly one correct visualization.

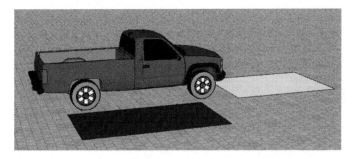

FIGURE 2 Two interpretations for *in front of* the pickup truck

However, it can be highly instructive to depict the range of possible visualizations and clarify what the area of uncertainty is for each type of expression and to show the source of some misunderstandings.[16] And

---

[16]Some of the same methods can also be used for memories of past events and thoughts about future events, which are incomplete in many of the same ways that natural language descriptions are, and often consist of separate threads or stories that are not combined into a coherent picture.

it can provide insight for linguists studying spatial language who do not always seem to consider how language maps onto the real world.[17]

There is already some related work in linguistics. Pustejovsky and Moszkowicz (2008) try to derive spatiotemporal data automatically from textual information. To that end, SpatialML markup was developed and used to annotate corpora. Bergen, Lindsay, Matlock, and Narayanan (2007) give evidence for the role of mental imagery and simulation in language comprehension. WordsEye[18] is an interesting attempt to automate the creation of 3D scenes from natural language descriptions about the sizes, locations, and orientations of objects (Coyne & Sproat, 2001). It analyzes the natural language inputs into sets of semantic elements and combines them graphically. The 3D scenes it generates are static, but do use 'poses' to depict actions. This work contrasts with formal linguistics, which has been mostly concerned with bridging the gap from language, in the middle of my map, to precise formal representations that computers can make use of, on the left. WordsEye instead tries to bridge the gap between language and what it is about in the real world, towards the right.

A WordsEye type of approach could be augmented to show the range of possible objects, properties, locations, and poses that are consistent with the language input. It could be used to visualize differences in individuals' mapping between language and the world, and when applied cross-linguistically, lexical gaps for categories at different levels of generality. It could also visualize the notion of 'focus', by highlighting the focused elements visually, e.g. with a halo of light.

Other aspects of language, such as generalized quantifiers, tenses, modals, negation, and embedded clauses of various types, are harder to visualize. One might think that it is not worth trying, because language seems clearly superior. It may well be the case that for practical applications it is best to use verbal elements for these purposes, but it is still instructive to think about how one would go about trying to visualize them. This could lead to novel linguistic insights and an appreciation for why they can be hard to learn. It might also become clearer when the state of the virtual model of the world in a listener's mind is such that a particular utterance is harder to process. For example, some aspects of natural language expressions require more than one virtual world, fast-forwarding through the changing state of one world over time, or even running simulations of various possibilities.

---

[17]At a recent conference discussion at CSLI, several semanticists were surprised about the fact that a road that *narrows* in one direction can be described as *widening* from the other perspective.

[18]http://www.wordseye.com/

Negations like *I did not do laundry this weekend* are particularly interesting. While it might be possible to come up with a convention to mark negated content visually, it is also interesting to consider what happens if someone's representation is the assumed state of affairs given that the action did not take place, such as a pile of dirty laundry in the example above. In most contexts there is probably an implicature that this state of affairs is true, assuming that the speaker was cooperative. But it is not necessarily true, and might result in a false belief that this information was actually directly communicated.

A language visualization system, when combined with user feedback, could also be used to investigate what viewpoints, i.e. camera angles, are the most natural to distinguish active and passive, or describe the perspective differences between *he loaded hay onto the wagon* and *he loaded the wagon with hay*, and how these influence what is communicated. Conversely, this would lead to more insight into how language can 'frame' an event such that the listener 'sees' it from a certain perspective. One could study how a 3D movie can tell a different story when the same events are shown from different angles, or how certain perspectives result in a cognitive mismatch because they do not fit the story. One could also visualize how someone's knowledge and goals highlight certain elements in their environment and focus their attention, and how language can refocus them on other properties, objects, or patterns. And such a system makes it clearer what elements are not being communicated directly and need to be supplied by the listener's imagination unless the language is made more vivid. Combining WordsEye with Google Earth or Second Life would open up another large set of research opportunities.

Comparing a virtual reproduction of a real event with a visualization of the aspects that are being communicated verbally would yield insights into what exactly is gained and lost in the process. The details that are lost can be visualized as the uncertainty inherent to the underspecification in various aspects of the natural language description, and what is gained can be visualized as the focusing effect that language has to direct our attention to the important aspects of the event or its context, as well as the categorizing effect it has on seeing a variety of actual events as 'the same' at that level of abstraction.

6 Visualizing abstract information

This section gradually moves into the upper right quadrant of the map in Figure 1 and suggests how the same methods described above can be used for more abstract information. As a starting point, it is relatively straightforward to visualize some properties of concrete objects, relationships between them, and abstract information that is spatial in nature, like coordinate systems or geometry.

For example, one could make an overlay of latitude and longitude lines in Google Earth, and an animation that shows what effect projecting the 3D globe down onto a 2D computer screen has on, for example, a round lake that is far from the equator, or on the size of the landmass of Greenland, and compare the various distortions of commonly used map projections.

The octants in a three-dimensional Cartesian coordinate system, and vectors in that space, can also be represented much more clearly and unambiguously than in any graphical representation projected onto a two-dimensional page.

6.1 Metaphors

Many types of abstract information have structural similarities with more concrete knowledge. Metaphors exploit these analogies (Lakoff & Johnson, 1980), and make it possible to visualize aspects of the abstract concepts. For example, it is possible to visualize many aspects of relationships using the 'love is a journey' metaphor. For the purpose of this paper it is not important whether this metaphor is seen as directly influencing the 'love' concept, or whether it merely shows enough structural similarity with that concept for the mapping to be meaningful (Murphy, 1996; Nunberg, Sag, & Wasow, 1994).

The high-dimensional similarity space of various life goals (learning, contributing, meaning, happiness, health, relationships, children, respect, honor, attention, legacy, pleasure, leisure, comfort, wealth, power, independence, security, peace of mind, ...) could be mapped down to 2D using information visualization methods. For example, when looking at a large corpus of data one might find that power overlaps with wealth but is more distant from peace of mind. Elevation in the terrain could be used to show the relative difficulty of getting to certain places, i.e. the amount of effort it usually takes to e.g. become a doctor.

For the purpose of elucidating relationship issues, it is helpful to be able to see the metaphorical locations of the life goals of the partners with respect to each other. For example, if one partner has exploration and learning from other cultures and *expanding their horizons* as one of their goals, then they might feel like things *aren't going anywhere* if the other partner prefers to maximize their comfort and relaxation and stay at home. If one partner values their career above all else, and to the other partner family relationships are the most important, then they may well reach a *crossroads* where they have to *go their separate ways*. Some roads, for example the one towards having children, cannot be traveled successfully by one partner alone, resulting in a *dead end* if the other partner does not share that common goal and does not wish to travel in that direction. Some regions can be visited without any effect on which other regions are reachable later, while other roads are *one-way streets* that cause other options to become inaccessible and make it impossible to *turn back*. Life's vicissitudes like diseases and accidents can be visualized as obstacles along the road.

If such a metaphorical life space were available to visit virtually, one could visit various possible future locations, see what some of the properties of that area are, and look at the journey to see how much energy it will take to get there. This might help people place more emphasis on how and where the bulk of their time is spent instead of only chasing new destinations to get to. It would also make it clearer which goals are incompatible or hard to combine with each other. Comparing how different people visualize themselves and their goals in such a metaphorical space might also help elucidate the causes for misunderstandings, for example when a linguistic expression is being is being wrongly interpreted as an act of aggression when in fact the collision was accidental and due to crossed paths and lack of attention to where the other person was coming from and where they were trying to go.

6.2 Information Visualization

For other abstract information, it is somewhat less obvious that visualization, especially visualization in 3D, is beneficial. Visualizations that are trying to depict complex information and relationships require guidance to interpret the visualization. Many 'visualization' attempts on the web are more confusing than helpful because labels, captions, and accompanying explanatory text are absent or insufficient. Information visualization in 3D also faces the challenge that information can be obscured by other items, and text can be hard to handle.

One reason to believe that visualizations are helpful even on the most abstract end of the scale is the mounting evidence for the perceptual basis of reasoning (Levinson, 2003; Casasanto, 2005; Landy, Allen, & Zednik, 2009), and the fact that mathematical and logical concepts can benefit from visualization, cf. Tarski's World (Barwise & Etchemendy, 1993), Mathematica (Wolfram, 2003), Venn diagrams, and visual proofs, e.g. of Pythagoras' theorem (Nelsen, 1997). In some cases the visualizations for more abstract properties can be combined with representations of the concrete data they are describing.

The field of information visualization focuses on visualizing the most complex scientific and other phenomena we deal with today, highlighting the salient features and allowing researchers to detect patterns in very large data sets much faster than they otherwise could (Johnson et al., 2006). This is achieved with very sophisticated methods compared with the other 'visualization' methods discussed in this paper. Google Earth has made geospatial data visualization accessible to more than just geographic information systems (GIS) experts, but other tools are not as easily available or combinable. Connecting all the way to the top right corner of the map in Figure 1 would require interdisciplinary collaboration with visualization researchers. It is necessary to study what types of information are best communicated verbally, which are better suited to visualization, and how to combine the two modalities the most effectively.

As one example, the Science Map project (Boyack, Klavans, & Börner, 2005) used statistical similarity measures to map the space of academic publications. This resulted in a high-dimensional space which was simplified down to a 3D version and also projected on to 2D. This makes it possible to locate interdisciplinary topics on a map.

Using these maps in a manner analogous to Google Earth, it becomes possible to represent the areas of knowledge of individuals, and of locating the knowledge that someone is trying to share in a communication attempt. Then the directions to this communicative goal can be read off the map and explained with respect to known landmarks. By looking at the space from different perspectives, new and previously unexplored connections become apparent. Missing connections can be filled in by people with expertise in both subject areas. Someone's intellectual history can be visualized in a manner analogous to the life events described above. When people collaborate online, their background and their stated goals can be taken into account to make sure their contributions are seen from the right perspective.

6.3 Knowledge Models

For any complex knowledge to be acquired and fully mastered, it is necessary to combine the individual pieces of information into a coherent structure. Consider for example a relatively complex piece of software such as Photoshop. If one simply teaches someone how to perform a few fixed procedures, they may not get enough information to build a reasonably good working model of the software, and may not be able to solve new problems. The connections between some of the individual pieces of knowledge will be obscure to them, and new knowledge harder to remember because it is not integrated with anything else. They can also spend a lot of time looking at irrelevant parts of the screen and may not be able to quickly scan the menus and toolbars to find what they need.

One way to build a good model of such a new domain of knowledge is to figure it out on one's own, which can result in a relatively deep understanding, good connections to other knowledge, and a decent likelihood of remembering the information. However, this can be a lengthy process which time and other factors can make infeasible, so that it becomes necessary to try to learn from someone who already knows it.

However, because the structure of the model is multidimensional, it is hard to share via documentation written in natural language. In addition, people who have complete knowledge of the domain have often forgotten what it was like not to have that knowledge, and have trouble identifying even basic sources of problems. They may not know which technical terms are confusing, and which pieces of information someone may be missing, especially if these are the most fundamental ones. In this example, that could be the concepts of pixels and resolution, information about the range of functionality to be expected from the software, or familiarity with certain types of UI elements, which might not even be identifiable from verbal descriptions.

This problem gets worse as the knowledge to be acquired becomes more complex and abstract. Even in the case of this type of software, 3D development or GIS software is far more complex than Photoshop. In a more abstract case, for example while doing research for a paper, the amount of information that needs to be integrated can be extremely complex, there is no documentation to consult, and there are no good tools to help with this process. The best available one appears to be Tinderbox,[19] which allows for notes to be organized visually. It is useful to be able to spatially arrange, group, color-code, and link ideas and concepts, especially in the brainstorming phase of a project. Tinderbox also allows for symbolic properties and parallel structured views of the same data. However, it requires a major time investment to master, does not include 3D visualization, and is not suitable for collaboration.

A good knowledge model tool needs an intuitive 3D UI allowing for the dynamic rearranging of items, saving multiple arrangements from multiple viewpoints for easy revisiting, and sharing these with others, perhaps even automatically comparing perspectives and identifying mismatches. Techniques from the information visualization field are required to solve the problems of representing textual information in 3D and avoiding issues with occlusion, i.e. information being obscured by

---

[19]http://www.eastgate.com/Tinderbox/

other information. The system also needs LODs for abstractions, e.g. the ability to zoom or 'fly' with a 6DoF controller or another effortless method into a note that is a three-word description of an idea to see a more detailed summary, with each sentence of the summary in turn linking to a relevant section, down to the ability to fly to the location in a source document in which the information originated. These tools would help make sure that the most significant information is not lost when 'squinting' to see things at lower levels of detail, and accelerate the process of integrating diverse bits of symbolic information into a complex picture that is a closer model of the analog reality. This is analogous to speeding up the process of building a complete mental map of a complex new neighborhood by sketching a map during the exploration process, or having someone else's sketch available to start from. Such a virtual knowledge model is beneficial even to people who have internalized one already for a particular subject area. The computerized version can contain far more detail than one can hold in memory, allows for viewing from multiple perspectives, enables a more systematic exploration of the space, and utilizes the human capacity for spatial inference. It can also be shared with others and saved for the future without degrading.

But it also needs to be possible to see structured views of the same information, which should be linked to formal ontologies and the semantic web[20]. Someone who has a complex model of a domain in their head may be able to 'see' solutions to problems intuitively without being able to justify them to others verbally, because the symbolic complexities are hidden in a more analog representation and the solution was not derived by logical reasoning. An integrated visual and structural representation of the problem space can help explain the solution, and build a bridge between an analog state to a more symbolic one that can be shared more easily in words.

Sharing knowledge between two individuals is easier if their virtual mental models are similar. This is facilitated if both use the external world as the basis for their virtual model, and have integrated a sufficiently similar range of experiences into that model, or managed to communicate the missing aspects. However, for most people there are too many differences between their internal virtual world and the real world, and consequently between two individuals' internal worlds. Jacobson (1991) argues that this is partly due to the fact that so much of our information is indirect and supplied by the media. Visualizing

---

[20]http://semanticweb.org/

the most common 'TV tropes'[21] might help make it clear in what ways our perceptions of reality are skewed.

Technological tools can help bridge the gap between individuals' models by visualizing the differences, transforming the information so that it lines up, and helping people make better virtual models. They can help put new pieces of information in the right place in the virtual model analogous to the way a GPS enabled phone shows your location on a map. If information from many individuals needs to be combined, such as for online collaboration projects, it becomes essential that there is a shared reference model, so that the contributions from various different perspectives can be integrated appropriately.

Better virtual models and natural language interfaces to them will also become indispensable in the context of the 'e-memory revolution'. The more information an individual can store, the more important it will become to have intuitive ways of accessing that information, finding the relevant parts, and organizing it in such a way that one can derive insight from it. If the information is not integrated into an existing mental model, one is less likely to remember it and make use of it.

7   Conclusions

This paper has attempted to summarize currently available 3D virtual world and visualization technology and its benefits for gaining insight and sharing knowledge. The analysis of the strengths and weaknesses of these tools compared to language suggested that they complement each other well if the visual representations are supplemented with integrated natural language descriptions of the more abstract levels of the information. Two domains, virtual game environments and sporting events, were discussed in terms of their value as a testbed for natural language technology, because they include detailed information about events as they unfold over time. It was argued that much can be learned about spatial and other aspects of language by constructing 3D representations of natural language descriptions and visualizing what is gained and lost in the process.

This has been but one thread woven through the complex multidimensional space of information visualization and virtual reality, trying to use language to evoke the depth of that space in your imaginations. Once this interdisciplinary research field is more established and the tools are available, expect to be able to visit a model of this space directly, see it both from this author's perspective and many others, and hopefully contribute to it.

---

[21]http://www.tvtropes.org/

Acknowledgements

Thanks to Edward Zalta and John Pacheco for patiently listening to me talking about this subject for far too long. Thanks to Mike Beebe, Brett Heliker, James Steele, and Daniel Gruver for sharing their 3D and GIS wisdom with me, and a special thanks to Jesse Alama for exploring the virtual world with me. In addition to the above-mentioned people, Emily Bender and Chris Culy provided helpful comments on an earlier draft.

References

Agrawala, M., & Stolte, C. (2001). Rendering effective route maps: Improving usability through generalization. In *ACM SIGGRAPH proceedings* (p. 241-249). Addison Wesley.

Barwise, J., & Etchemendy, J. (1993). *Tarski's world.* CSLI Publications, Stanford, CA.

Bell, G., & Gemmell, J. (2009). *Total recall: How the e-memory revolution will change everything.* Dutton, New York.

Bergen, B., Lindsay, S., Matlock, T., & Narayanan, S. (2007). Spatial and linguistic aspects of visual imagery in sentence comprehension. *Cognitive Science, 31,* 733-764.

Boyack, K., Klavans, R., & Börner, K. (2005). Mapping the backbone of science. *Scientometrics, 64,* 351-374.

Casasanto, D. (2005). *Perceptual foundations of abstract thought.* Unpublished doctoral dissertation, MIT.

Coyne, B., & Sproat, R. (2001). WordsEye: An automatic text-to-scene conversion system. In *ACM SIGGRAPH proceedings* (pp. 487–496). Addison Wesley.

Dale, R., Geldof, S., & Prost, J.-P. (2005). Using natural language generation in automatic route description. *Journal of Research and Practice in Information Technology, 37,* 89-105.

Imhof, E. (2007). *Cartographic relief presentation.* ESRI Press, Redlands, CA.

Jacobson, R. (1991). Virtual worlds, inside and out. In D. Mark & A. Frank (Eds.), *Cognitive and linguistic aspects of geographic space: An introduction* (p. 507-514). Kluwer Academic.

Johnson, C., Moorhead, R., Munzner, T., Pfister, H., Rheingans, P., & Yoo, T. (2006). NIH/NSF visualization research challenges report summary. In *IEEE computer graphics and applications* (Vol. 26(2), p. 20-24).

Lakoff, G., & Johnson, M. (1980). *Metaphors we live by.* University of Chicago Press.

Landy, D., Allen, C., & Zednik, C. (2009). *A perceptual account of symbolic reasoning.* (ms, University of Richmond)

Levinson, S. (2003). *Space in Language and Cognition: Explorations in Cognitive Diversity.* Cambridge University Press, New York.

Murphy, G. (1996). On metaphoric representation. *Cognition, 60,* 173-204.

Nelsen, R. (1997). *Proofs without words: Exercises in visual thinking.* The Mathematical Association of America.

Nunberg, G., Sag, I., & Wasow, T. (1994). Idioms. *Language, 70,* 491-538.

Pustejovsky, J., & Moszkowicz, J. (2008). Integrating Motion Predicate Classes with Spatial and Temporal Annotations. In *COLING 2008 Companion Volume - Posters and Demonstrations* (p. 95-98).

Talmy, L. (2001). How spoken language and signed language structure space differently. In D. R. Montello (Ed.), *Spatial information theory: Proceedings of COSIT 2001* (p. 247-262). Springer, Berlin.

Wolfram, S. (2003). *The Mathematica book.* Wolfram Media.